Contention in Times of Crisis

This is the first comprehensive overview of the waves of protest mobilization that spread across Europe in the wake of the Great Recession. Documenting the extent of these protests in a study covering thirty countries, including the issues they addressed and the degree to which they replicated each other, this book maps the prevalence and nature of protest across Europe, and explains the interactions between economic and political grievances that lead to protest mobilization. The authors assess a range of claims in the literature on political protest, arguing that they tend both to overstate the importance of anti-austerity sentiments and underestimate the relevance of political grievances in driving the protest. They also integrate a study of the electoral and protest arenas, revealing that electoral mass politics has been heavily influenced in protest mobilization, which amplified the electoral punishment at the polls.

Hanspeter Kriesi holds the Stein Rokkan Chair in comparative politics at the European University Institute, Florence.

Jasmine Lorenzini is a research fellow at the Institute of Citizenship Studies, University of Geneva.

Bruno Wüest works at the research center Sotomo in Zurich. He was postdoctoral research fellow at the Institute for Political Science of the University Zurich.

Silja Häusermann is professor of Swiss politics and comparative political economy at the Institute for Political Science of the University Zurich.

Contention in Times of Crisis

Recession and Political Protest in Thirty European Countries

Edited by

Hanspeter Kriesi
European University Institute

Jasmine Lorenzini
University of Geneva

Bruno Wüest
University of Zurich

Silja Häusermann
University of Zurich

CAMBRIDGE
UNIVERSITY PRESS

CAMBRIDGE
UNIVERSITY PRESS

University Printing House, Cambridge CB2 8BS, United Kingdom

One Liberty Plaza, 20th Floor, New York, NY 10006, USA

477 Williamstown Road, Port Melbourne, VIC 3207, Australia

314–321, 3rd Floor, Plot 3, Splendor Forum, Jasola District Centre, New Delhi – 110025, India

79 Anson Road, #06-04/06, Singapore 079906

Cambridge University Press is part of the University of Cambridge.

It furthers the University's mission by disseminating knowledge in the pursuit of education, learning, and research at the highest international levels of excellence.

www.cambridge.org
Information on this title: www.cambridge.org/9781108835114
DOI: 10.1017/9781108891660

First published 2020

A catalogue record for this publication is available from the British Library.

Library of Congress Cataloging-in-Publication Data
Names: Kriesi, Hanspeter, 1949- editor. | Lorenzini, Jasmine, 1981- editor. | Wüest, Bruno, 1976- editor. | Häusermann, Silja, 1977- editor.
Title: Contention in times of crisis : recession and political protest in thirty European countries / edited by Hanspeter Kriesi, European University Institute, Jasmine Lorenzini, University of Geneva, Bruno Wüest, University of Zurich, Silja Häusermann, University of Zurich.
Description: Cambridge, United Kingdom ; New York, NY : Cambridge University Press, 2020. | Includes bibliographical references and index.
Identifiers: LCCN 2020024886 | ISBN 9781108835114 (hardback) | ISBN 9781108799706 (ebook)
Subjects: LCSH: Recessions--Europe--History--21st century. | Europe--Economic conditions--21st century.
Classification: LCC HB3782 .C665 2020 | DDC 322.4/4094090511--dc23
LC record available at https://lccn.loc.gov/2020024886

ISBN 978-1-108-83511-4 Hardback

Contents

Figures

Tables

Contributors

ARGYRIOS ALTIPARMAKIS is a research fellow at the European University Institute in Florence, studying political conflict and contentious politics.

ENDRE BORBÁTH is a postdoctoral researcher at the Chair for Political Sociology at the Free University of Berlin and at the Center for Civil Society Research at the WZB Berlin Social Science Center.

BJÖRN BREMER is senior researcher in Comparative and International Political Economy at the Max Planck Institute for the Study of Societies in Cologne.

MATTHIAS ENGGIST is a PhD researcher at the Department of Political Science at the University of Zurich.

THERESA GESSLER is a postdoctoral at the Digital Democracy Lab and the Institute for Political Science of the University of Zurich.

SILJA HÄUSERMANN is professor of Swiss Politics and Comparative Political Economy at the Institute for Political Science of the University of Zurich.

SOPHIA HUNGER is a PhD researcher at the European University Institute in Florence and a research fellow of the Center for Civil Society Research at the WZB Berlin Social Science Center.

SWEN HUTTER is Lichtenberg professor in Political Sociology at the Free University of Berlin and vice director of the Center for Civil Society Research, a joint initiative of Free University and the WZB Social Science Center.

HANSPETER KRIESI holds the Stein Rokkan Chair in Comparative Politics at the European University Institute in Florence. He is also affiliated with the Laboratory for Comparative Social Science Research, National Research University Higher School of Economics, the Russian Federation.

THOMAS KURER is a Weatherhead postdoctoral fellow at Harvard University.

JASMINE LORENZINI is a research fellow at the Institute of Citizenship Studies, University of Geneva. She leads a four-year research project on food activism.

PETER MAKAROV is a PhD researcher at the Institute of Computational Linguistics, the University of Zurich.

JULIA SCHULTE-CLOOS is a post-doctoral assistant at the Geschwister Scholl Institute of Political Science, LMU Munich.

CHENDI WANG is a PhD researcher at the European University Institute in Florence.

BRUNO WÜEST is a researcher at Sotomo in Zurich. He was postdoctoral research fellow at the Institute for Political Science of the University of Zurich.

Preface and Acknowledgements

Contention in Times of Crisis presents key findings from a joint effort of the project 'Political Conflict in Europe in the Shadow of the Great Recession' (POLCON), funded by the European Research Council, and the project 'Years of Turmoil: The Political Consequences of the Financial and Economic Crisis in Europe', funded by the Swiss National Science Foundation.[1] Our joint effort focuses on the development of European democracies and political conflict in the context of the Great Recession. Since the world entered the Great Recession with the breakdown of Lehman Brothers in autumn 2008, commentators have been worrying about the political repercussions of the economic crisis. The spectre of the 1930s has been haunting many observers of European politics, and the most pessimistic among them have been wondering whether democracy is going to survive in the face of the grave economic consequences of the crisis.

To tackle this question empirically, POLCON has studied the structuration of political conflict in Europe by analysing contestation in the electoral arena, in the protest arena, and in policy-specific contentious episodes. The main research question has been whether the Great Recession and its consequences have changed the long-term trends in the development of political conflict in Europe as they were previously assessed in *West European Politics in the Age of Globalisation* (Cambridge University Press, 2008) and *Political Conflict in Western Europe* (Cambridge University Press, 2012). These long-term trends include, above all, an increasing importance of the cultural dimension in the two-dimensional political space in western Europe and its reinterpretation as a deepening divide between those who embrace further integration and those who favour demarcation and nationalism. The 'Years of Turmoil' project has also studied the repercussions of the

[1] The project was supported by ERC grant Nr. 338875 and by SNF grant Nr. 100017_146104.

economic crisis on democracy, but with a focus on linking aggregate patterns of conflict and competition with democratic engagement, participation, and choice at the level of individual citizens.

The present volume follows up on POLCON's first major book publication, *European Party Politics in Times of Crisis* (Cambridge University Press, 2019). While the previous volume lays out our answers to the questions of whether and to what extent party competition has been restructured in Europe since the onset of the Great Recession, the present volume studies the impact of the Great Recession on the mobilization of protest across Europe.

The present volume has been long in coming. We have had more than the usual difficulties in getting it completed, but are all the happier to be finally able to present our key findings to the public. It was unusually risky to embark on a study of protest across no fewer than thirty European countries for a sixteen-year period in the first place. To limit the risks involved in collecting such an ambitious set of data, we relied on a well-established tool – protest event analysis – but also made an attempt to innovate by applying new methods from the toolbox of automated content analysis to this type of research. As it turned out, our initial hopes regarding the versatility and capacity of these new kinds of tools were too high. These tools are constantly improving, but, at the time when we applied them, they fell short of our expectations: While we were able to quite reliably identify texts with a high probability of containing a protest event, we were not able to develop an automated scheme for coding them as we had originally hoped. As a matter of fact, we ended up coding the texts – which we had classified using automated procedures – in the old way, i.e. manually. As one can easily imagine, it was a time-consuming and costly experience to manually code the more than 30,000 protest events that we identified for the period covered. The database on which this study builds proves to be all the more valuable. It is unique in its kind and so is the story we are able to tell based on it.

Social science today is teamwork. All the members of the two project teams have contributed to the construction of the database, but we have also relied on external support. Most notably, we benefited from the support provided by Michi Amsler, Klaus Rothenhäusler, and Gerold Schneider from the Institute of Computational Linguistics at the University of Zurich; Patrice Wangen from the European University Institute; Ondrej Cisar and his team from the Charles University in Prague; and a large number of coders at both the European University Institute (where the POLCON project was located) and at the University of Zurich (where the Years of Turmoil project was located).

At the European University Institute the team of coders included Gulzat Baialieva, Ieva Bloma, Reto Bürgisser, Alves De Almeida, Feike Fliervoet, Nisida Gjoksi, Ieva Grumbinaite, Inkeri Haavisto, Nodira Kholmatova, Grzegorz Krzyżanowski, Joldon Kutmanaliev, Hugo Leal, Michal Matlak, Radek Michalski, Chiara Milan, Trajche Panov, Svetlana Poleschuk, Javier Ruiz Soler, Sanna Salo, Daniel Schulz, Lev Shilov, Lisa Volpi, Andrea Warnecke, and Agata Wiącek. At the University of Zurich, it included Özge Akyol, Alessandra Biagioni, Lino Bruggmann, Camilla Frei, Lena Hochuli, Ahmet Köken, Blertan Kurtisi, Sandro Lüscher, Kim Mendelin, Yannick Schiess, Lucian Seebacher, Anna Staubli, Raffael von Arx, and Jenny Yi.

We also received support from two members of our external advisory board, Edgar Grande (Ludwig Maximilian University, Munich) and Zsolt Enyedi (Central European University, Budapest), and from our administrative staff, above all from Maureen Lechleitner, without whose daily effort to keep the project running this study would never have been completed. Finally, we have benefited from the feedback of a large number of colleagues who commented on previous versions of this text at various occasions. In particular, the constructive critique of the anonymous reviewers of Cambridge University Press helped to improve our manuscript considerably. We would like to thank them all for their invaluable support.

Part I

A Study of Protest in Thirty European Countries

1 Introduction

Hanspeter Kriesi, Silja Häusermann, and Jasmine Lorenzini

In September 2008, Lehman Brothers collapsed and the global money markets seized up. This was the beginning of a financial crisis that started in the United States and soon spilled over to Europe. In Europe, the shock period of the financial crisis was followed by the eurozone crisis, which started in early 2010 with the sovereign debt crisis in Greece. While the worst of the crisis seemed to be over by fall 2012, after the head of the European Central Bank (ECB) had declared that he would do 'whatever it takes' to save the euro, the fallout of the crisis continued to haunt Europe at least until the conclusion of the third Greek bailout in summer 2015. It is hard to overstate the sheer magnitude of the impact the economic crisis has had on the lives of people in Europe. Between 2007 and 2013, the number of unemployed people in the European Union (EU) rose from 17 to 26 million. Dramatic losses of income for large social groups combined with a severely tightened and restricted labour market, especially for the younger generation in the countries hardest hit by intensified structural decline. As Adam Tooze (2018: 5) observed in the introduction to his account of 'the first crisis of a global age', the combination of these crises and the economic and political responses to them are essential to understanding the changing face of the world today. As Tooze also noted, politics loomed large during the economic crisis. This period saw not limited but big government and massive executive action, as well as economic and political interventionism of an unprecedented kind, with massive distributive implications both across and within countries. For this reason, the Great Recession became tremendously politicized throughout Europe, both in the surplus and the deficit countries (Beramendi et al. 2015a; Walter 2016).

Hence, the Great Recession was not an instance of depoliticization, but – quite to the contrary – a context that spotlighted the importance of political decision-making for both national and international macroeconomic (in)stability and societal consequences. Therefore, the economic upheaval of the financial and eurozone crises has left deep traces in electoral mobilization across Europe (Hutter and Kriesi 2019). However, electoral politicization is only one aspect of democratic contestation of the crises. This book sheds light on protest mobilization, together with its prevalence, its drivers, and its links to crises of representation. Under circumstances of extreme economic disruption, the protest arena can become important for democratic contestation, and some observers have indeed hailed it as the key locus of transnational 'voice' and democratic innovation (della Porta and Mattoni 2014).

The present volume documents, for the first time, the extent to which protest spread across Europe, the degree to which the protest action repertoire was regenerated, and the kinds of issues that were addressed. The intent of the book is twofold. On the one hand, the book maps the prevalence, thrust, and actors of protest across Europe; on the other hand, it explains protest mobilization as a result of economic grievances interacting with political grievances. The book not only assesses a range of claims in protest literature, which tend both to overstate the importance of anti-austerity protests and to underestimate the relevance of economic grievances in driving protests; it also integrates the study of the electoral and the protest arena to show that electoral mass politics has become largely dissociated from protest mobilization, with potentially impairing consequences for democratic performance.

1.1 Mapping Protest: Who Protests, How, and What For?

The first research question we pursue in this book asks how Europeans reacted to the financial and eurozone crises in the protest arena. In answering this broad and important – more descriptive than explanatory – question, we address three claims about protest that have been made in the literature on protest mobilization during the Great Recession: the existence of an internationally interconnected protest wave, the transformation of action repertoires and the radicalization of crisis protest, and the 'return of the economy' in the demands of protesters.

Some observers have suggested that an enormous and interconnected wave of protest mobilization against austerity swept not only across the European continent but across the entire globe. These observers situate the origin of this global wave at the beginning of 2011 in the Arab Spring, after which it is said to have spread to Europe, particularly to southern Europe (SE) – to Portugal first, followed by Spain and Greece. It then moved on to New York, where the first Occupy Wall Street camp was established before spreading all over the United States and beyond (della Porta and Mattoni 2014: 3). Later on, starting in spring 2013, these movements against austerity were said to have been followed by another protest wave, which covered a diversity of countries in western and eastern Europe, as well as certain countries of Latin America and Africa (della Porta 2017). Even if these observers are attentive to some country-specific differences, they end up characterizing the development of protest during the Great Recession in rather loose terms as interconnected protest waves that diffused across Europe as part of a global wave. Thus, Flesher-Fominaya (2017) writes of 'a wave of European anti-austerity mobilization' that was part of a global wave of protest following the global financial crisis. Other authors just take such a wave for granted and discuss their own empirical cases (e.g. Peterson et al. 2015; Sabucedo et al. 2017) or theoretical considerations (e.g. Nulman and Schlembach 2018) against the background of such a wave.

However, such a global wave of protest may be too loose of an empirical concept. As a matter of fact, a closer look at the different elements of these alleged waves has revealed important differences. As Navrátil and Cisar (2014: 227) point out, the Occupy Wall Street movement in the United States and the Indignados in Spain had a strong national or even local dimension and their claims focused on national and local rather than transnational and global publics and authorities. Similarly, Genovese et al. (2016) contest the sweeping, interconnected character of protest mobilization on the basis of a comparative study of select European countries. Our book is the first study that allows testing these claims for all European countries over a longer time span. We shall amply demonstrate that Europe did not experience one big wave of political mobilization and protest after 2008 and that diffusion processes remained very limited indeed. Despite intense protest mobilization in some countries and periods, protest remained confined geographically and temporally, indicating that the national political arena has remained predominant in explaining protest.

The second claim we want to address in mapping protest relates to the action repertoire that has been mobilized, as well as the intensity and radicalization of protest. Kerbo (1982), who introduced the distinction between 'movements of crisis' and 'movements of affluence', suggested that 'movements of crisis' are relatively unorganized and develop more spontaneously, and that they are more likely to be characterized by hostile outbursts and collective violence. If this were to hold, we would expect a change in the action repertoire of protestors in the course of the crisis, away from 'business as usual', i.e. from an action repertoire of protest dominated by demonstrations and strikes towards a more confrontational and more violent repertoire. Previous protest waves have been observed to result in either the institutionalization or the radicalization of protest (Tarrow 1989). It has also been observed that in periods of crisis, new or innovative modes of action are 'tested' (Fillieule 2010) and that during protest waves the repertoire of contention is often transformed, with an emergence of new forms of action that end up characterizing a specific protest wave (Taylor and van Dyke 2004). Therefore, we ask whether, during the Great Recession, ordinary forms of protest, such as demonstrations, were supplemented by innovative protest actions such as occupations or protest camps. The Indignados and Occupy Wall Street movements and their practices of occupying and organizing deliberative assemblies in public squares attracted a great deal of media attention and they have been considered to have introduced true innovations (Maeckelbergh 2012). Hence, we consider the extent to which protest mobilization during the great economic crises led to the spread of such innovations. We shall show that in spite of some innovations and the predominance of 'movements of crisis' in some parts of Europe, 'business as usual' predominated. Protestors mostly enacted the established patterns of action, although there were creative moments that assumed great significance. Most importantly, we shall show that protest remained largely non-violent, even in the most contentious countries.

Third, our book explores the claims that protesters have made, i.e. the demands they have voiced towards authorities. Given the massive economic decline that large social groups of lower- and middle-class citizens experienced in the wake of the Great Recession, much of the political economy literature expected 'a return of the economy' (due to protest mobilization) as compared to pre-crisis periods, i.e. a return of economic grievance-driven mobilization of socio-economic claims (Bernburg 2015; Genovese et al. 2016; Rüdig and Karyiotis 2014; Solt 2015; Walter 2016). Such a return of economic protest would imply a massive transformation of political protest in Europe. Indeed, while the traditional conflicts – those between classes and regions – had been the most mobilizing ones in a country like Spain in the not too distant past (Koopmans 1996), it is well known that since the rise of new social movements in the 1970s, protests in north-western Europe have been driven predominantly by new cultural conflicts (Hutter 2014: 82f.; Kriesi et al. 1995). The middle-class 'movements of affluence', which mobilized political demands on behalf of others, neglected economic issues and mobilized primarily on issues such as women's rights, human rights, ecology, peace, and global social justice. In times of economic crisis, and in line with the political economy literature, we may thus expect the proactive 'movements of affluence' to be replaced by 'movements of crisis', i.e. by social movements that emerge as direct reactions to the life-disrupting situations of sudden deteriorations in economic conditions, and which articulate socio-economic demands to alleviate these grievances.

The 'return of the economy' – scenario is, however, only one hypothesis and by no means self-evident. The experience of economic grievances may – just as in the electoral arena – be mobilized politically in socio-cultural terms, e.g. against immigrants or in favour of authoritarian limitations of pluralism (Inglehart and Norris 2016). Hence, we should not take the return of predominantly economic claims in the protest arena as a foregone conclusion, especially in those countries where political protest has been mainly culturally framed over the past decades. Indeed, our data show that while there has been a rise in economically framed protest in the wake of the crisis, the issue–orientation of protest has remained regionally specific. In addition, it has also remained partial in the sense that it targets the economic crisis management of the government but not that of private corporations. Because of the lack of sustained and radicalized protest mobilization, even in the heavily affected political economies of Europe, we can hardly speak of a 'return' to economic-distributive politics in the protest arena.

1.2 Explaining Protest: How Economic Grievances Relate to Protest Mobilization

The second aim of this book is to study the drivers of protest mobilization. In theorizing these drivers in the context of the Great Recession, we rely on three key concepts of social movement studies: grievances, resources, and political opportunity structures (McAdam 1982). More specifically, we assess three sets of questions. First, we ask about the role of economic and political grievances in driving protest: Do economic grievances mobilize or demobilize protest? Do economic and political grievances cumulate or interact? And are political grievances a result of economic grievances? Second, regarding resources, we analyse the role of political parties in organizing protest in times of crisis and we ask which parties take to the streets in times of crisis. Lastly, we consider the role of political opportunity structures in moderating the link between economic grievances and protest. Here, we ask whether and how fiscal and administrative state capacities condition the effect of grievances. How does supranational intervention in national politics affect protest? Are transnational or intraregional diffusion processes at play? And how do protest politics and electoral politics interact?

For the analyses of the drivers of protest, *grievances* constitute our starting point. The social movement literature has sidelined the study of economic grievances, arguing that resources and mobilization, not grievances, drive protest. For a long time, grievances have had a bad name in this literature as a result of the legacy of collective behaviour models, also known as strain or breakdown theories (Buechler 2004; McAdam 1982: 5–19). These theories conceived of collective behaviour as a largely spontaneous, unregulated, and unstructured group activity, and even went as far as considering it as irrational, disruptive, dangerous, or excessive. As a result of the discredited legacy of collective behaviour theories, economic deprivation has largely been neglected as a driving force in the study of protest mobilization. However, there is ample reason to re-examine the role of economic grievances in explaining protest, as the Great Recession led to much more massive economic deprivation than we saw in the preceding decades. And, indeed, the Great Recession brought the concept back to the centre in the study of protest, both at the macro- (Beissinger and Sasse 2014; Brancati 2014; Quaranta 2016) and the micro-level (Galais and Lorenzini 2017; Grasso and Giugni 2016; Rüdig and Karyotis 2014).

While exogenous shocks such as the financial and eurozone crises create a tremendous amount of popular discontent, it is unlikely that they create mobilization potentials from scratch. They rather contribute to pre-existing latent mobilization potentials that are linked to structural conflicts, which predate the crisis and which pre-structure the way the crisis mobilization will play out. The mobilization potentials newly created by the crisis add to the existing stock of grievances. In addition, a crisis is likely to serve as a catalyst for the mobilization of these latent potentials. It may reshape, redirect, or reinvigorate an ongoing mobilization process, or it may trigger the articulation of the latent potentials that had already been accumulating before the occurrence of the crisis and have been reinforced by the crisis.

People with grievances seek to express them, and they do so by raising their voices or by exiting (Hirschman 1970). Exit has been an important reaction to the great economic crisis in many countries in southern and eastern Europe. We do not deal with this type of reaction to the crisis here, but rather with people raising their voices collectively. In democratic societies, citizens have the right to vote and they have the opportunity to express their grievances as voters. As Piven and Cloward (1977: 15) noted several decades ago, 'ordinarily, defiance is first expressed in the voting booth simply because, whether defiant or not, people have been socialized within a political culture that defines voting as the mechanism through which political change can and should properly occur'. Accordingly, one of the first signs of popular discontent is a sharp shift in voting patterns. More generally, in democratic societies, the action repertoire of protests is likely to make use of the available institutionalized channels of access, which means that the privileged institutional space, i.e. the privileged arenas to voice grievances, are the electoral, and, where available, the direct democratic arena. But the next elections might still be far away, and the grievances suddenly imposed by the economic crisis may call for immediate reaction. The protest arena provides an alternative channel that is available for the expression of grievances to the extent that there are organizations that are ready and have the resources to mobilize them.

Given the importance of politics during these economic crises, there is reason to expect that *economic* grievances are linked in different ways to *political* grievances. In the course of our study we shall thus distinguish between economic and political crises as two potentially interrelated sources of grievances that help explain the emergence of protest. Indeed, political crises intensified across Europe during the Great Recession (Armingeon and Guthmann 2014; Cordero and Simón 2016; Magalhães 2014). Let us clarify our understanding of *'political crisis'*. A political crisis may be expressed in attitudinal and behavioural terms (Mainwaring et al. 2006). Political grievances correspond to the attitudinal indicators of a political crisis, among which we can count lack of trust in political institutions and lack of satisfaction with the way democracy works. Among behavioural indicators, we can include lower turnout, electoral volatility, the rise of new challengers in the electoral channel, or even the collapse of party systems, and the rise of protest events in the protest arena. The attitudinal component refers to the latent mobilization potentials, which constitute a more or less fertile ground for the political crisis. The political crisis, however, breaks out in the open, only once these latent potentials are mobilized and manifest themselves in behavioural terms. This is to say that political crises do not develop as a matter of course but are the result of political mobilization – in electoral terms or in terms of protest, or both (Kriesi 2015: 21). Focusing on the interaction of these economic and political crises, we ask how the management of the crisis by the government and international actors contributed to the mobilization of protest and, inversely, how the mobilization of protest contributed to the demise of incumbents and the transformation of party systems. Most generally, our study shows that sustained and intense protest follows when and where economic grievances raise expectations among citizens with respect to their national governments and these expectations are not met.

For political mobilization, *resources* are crucial. Both the intensity and action repertoire of protest, as well as the claims made, depend not least on the types of actors mobilizing and organizing protest. We are particularly interested in the role of political parties and organized interests (such as unions) as drivers of protest. In line with the notion of protest depending on the presence of organizational resources for mobilization (McCarthy and Zald 1977: 1215), and given the increasingly constrained electoral arena (Hutter and Kriesi 2019), one may expect traditional political organizations such as parties and unions to have played a key role in the mobilization of protest across Europe during the entire period covered, especially in countries with an otherwise weak civil society.

In western Europe, protest over the past decades was sponsored mainly by parties on the left (e.g. della Porta and Rucht 1991; Kriesi et al. 1995; Maguire 1995). Moreover, government participation of these parties was identified as a crucial condition for the facilitation of movement activities. In opposition, the left-wing parties were more likely to act as allies of ideologically close movements, such as the new social movements in the 1970s and early 1980s. By contrast, in central and eastern Europe (CEE), parties with little influence in the electoral arena in general, irrespective of their political orientation, were more likely to sponsor protest (Cisar and Navratil 2015; Cisar and Vrablíkova 2016). We shall show that the influence of party sponsorship of protest still varies from one European region to another.

More recently, the assumption of necessary organizational resources for mobilizing protest has been questioned with reference to social media. It is argued that social media have lowered organizational costs to a great extent, such that large-scale protest events can be organized in a rather spontaneous fashion without established organizational resources (Anduiza et al. 2014). Thus, the largest demonstration in Portugal during the peak years of the crisis, 2010–2013, was organized by a Facebook group and a blog (Accornero and Ramos-Pinto 2015: 3). These are, however, single instances of protest mobilization and our data allow tracing the prevalence of traditional organized actors in organizing protest even today.

The relevance of the political context goes beyond the role of parties and other established organizations and also includes political processes such as policy-making and the way government and the system of representation function more generally. Earlier versions of the political process approach have been criticized for 'surveying the terrain of collective action from so high an altitude that crucial processes and internal variations cannot be seen' (Tarrow 1988: 436). Here we pay attention to four aspects of political context: political management of the economic crisis, supranational interventions, cross-national influence, and elections.

Political management of the economic crisis captures government actions to handle the crisis in its different phases. Political dissatisfaction which is expressed in political protest may be the *direct* consequence of a government's poor management of the economic crisis. After the initial 'shock period', when governments countered the economic impact of the crisis by relying on some version of 'liberal' (Pontusson and Raess 2012) or 'emergency Keynesianism' (Hall 2013), they turned to austerity policies with the beginning of the eurozone crisis, which were the key sources of economic hardship in the most hard-hit countries. While the welfare states buffered the negative consequences of the crisis initially (Bermeo and Bartels 2014b), especially in the countries of north-western Europe (NWE), which had strong automatic stabilizers, the turn to austerity impeded the redistributive functions of the state and crucially contributed to the hardship of the populations. This is likely to have focused the minds of the protestors on government policy on the one hand and on supranational interventions that contributed to both economic and political grievances on the other. Indeed, in globalized economies and in countries belonging to the EU, *supranational interventions* constrain available choices for the management of the economic crisis. This was clearly the case when bailout agreements were signed between specific countries and supranational institutions. Furthermore, processes of cross-national emulation could have been at play as well. When austerity prevails as the solution to economic problems, it is more difficult for a government to defend an alternative approach (Alonso 2014).

Hence, a political crisis may *directly* result from the reactions to a government's management of the economy. However, it may also have other, non-economic, origins. Political grievances may result from corruption and partiality, disregard for the rule of law, large-scale scandals, and general ineffectiveness of government. Importantly, political grievances may also result from a representation crisis that is not directly linked to an economic crisis, to economic grievances, or to poor governance. In the case of a representation crisis, political discontent arises from the tension between new societal demands and their inadequate representation in the political system in general, and in the party system in particular. Specifically, this tension between the political representatives ('the elites') and the voters ('the people') results from the inability/unwillingness of the established parties to represent the new demands. For some time, party scholars in Europe have been pointing out the weakening of the representative function of established parties – their increasing remoteness from their constituencies, their programmatic convergence, and the decline of their mobilizing capacity (e.g. Mair 2013). Arguably, this kind of crisis set in long before the Great Recession hit Europe and has become important in NWE countries, as we shall argue in the next section. More generally, we shall argue that the type of political crisis varied significantly from one European region to another, with important implications for the mobilization of protest.

Finally, let us clarify our approach to the relationship between *elections* and protest. This relationship has multiple dimensions, as has been pointed out by McAdam and Tarrow (2010, 2013). Political parties organizing protest is one of them. Beyond that, the mobilization of protest in the streets may contribute to the agenda-setting in the electoral channel (e.g. Vliegenthart et al. 2016), and it may influence the electoral outcomes in different ways (McAdam and Tarrow 2013). Movements may also exert a direct influence over established parties, like the Tea Party did on the Republican Party (McAdam and Kloos 2014), or they may even mobilize in the form of parties in the first place, like the radical populist right or the Italian 'Movimento 5 Stelle'. We shall analyse the interaction between the electoral and the protest arenas and show that protests can amplify the impact of economic conditions on electoral punishment. We shall argue that the impact of protest on electoral outcomes and on the shape of the party systems is probably the most important political consequence of the mobilization of protest during the Great Recession.

1.3 The Empirical Approach in This Study

In this study, we adopt a macro-approach that attempts to cover all of Europe. This design is well suited for the evaluation of both the descriptive and the explanatory theoretical expectations developed in Section 1.2. We study the development of protest across no less than thirty European countries – the twenty-seven EU member states at the time when we started this study in 2014 plus three additional western European countries (Iceland, Norway, and Switzerland). More specifically, we study *protest events*, which we broadly define as all politically motivated unconventional actions performed by one or more individuals (Kriesi et al. 1995: 263). Protest events cover multiple forms of contentious political action, such as demonstrations, strikes, and riots, and we rely on an extensive list of protest actions that allows us to identify protest in its various forms. Protest events can be distinct or they can be part of a protest wave, an instance when multiple events are tied together by the issues they address, their organizers, or the time and place in which they happen (Dyke and Soule 2002; Gurr 1970; Opp 1988; Snow et al. 1998).

In our attempt to cover protest systematically across such a large number of countries, we rely on a well-established methodological approach – *protest event analysis* (Hutter 2014). This approach is based on media data – we use English-speaking news wires as our source. As has been amply discussed in the literature (e.g. reviews by Earl et al. 2004 and Ortiz et al. 2005), this kind of data is subject to biases. However, these biases are quite well known and can thus be considered in the analysis. The great advantage of this method is that, in spite of its drawbacks, it allows us to trace systematically the development of protest over time. We are not aware of any other approach that would allow us to do this on the scale we are aiming at. Our study covers the development of protest from 2000 to 2015; i.e. we cover the pre-crisis period up to the collapse of Lehman Brothers in fall 2008; the shock period of the financial crisis that went up to the first Greek bailout programme in spring 2010; and the period of the eurozone crisis that, in our interpretation, lasted until the summer 2015, as well as the last five months of 2015 that was influenced by the rising refugee crisis.

Even if this methodology is well known and widely used, the application of protest event analysis at the scale we are undertaking in this study is unprecedented, and we had to develop new, original semi-automated procedures for data collection to be able to implement this approach for our purposes. As our answers to the questions guiding our research depend to a large extent on these procedures, we shall present and evaluate them extensively in the next two chapters of the book. Our data are far from perfect, but they enable us to present the general trends which will allow us to provide answers to the key factual questions about changes with respect to protest mobilization in the course of the financial and eurozone crises across Europe (our descriptive research questions) and to our explanatory inquiries. The answer to our explanatory questions will above all make use of longitudinal variation.

1.4 Our Analytical Perspective: The Three Regions of Europe

In this study, we shall repeatedly distinguish between three regions of Europe – northwestern Europe (NWE), southern Europe (SE), and central-eastern Europe (CEE) – when presenting the findings and discussing their interpretation. This cross-regional analysis allows us to point to the large differences that exist between the different European regions with respect to the development of protest during the Great Recession. As we shall show, it is above all SE that experienced the emergence of a tremendous amount of protest during the Great Recession, while the development of protest in the other two regions was much more subdued. For lack of data, few studies systematically compare protest scenes across European regions. We contribute to getting a clear idea of similarities and differences on a grand scale, even if we shall also point out the considerable country-specific variation within each region. Hence, while focusing on the 'grand' regional story, we are well aware of intraregional cross-national variations, and we openly discuss and highlight typical countries in a region, as well as outliers that stand out from the identified regional pattern, to offer cross-regional analyses that avoid the trap of oversimplification or generalization.

As the distinction between the macro-regions is so important for our presentation of the results, we shall provide three sets of arguments why this distinction makes sense as a general grid in the analysis of the data. These three sets of arguments are linked to our three sets of explanatory factors which we take from social movement theory: grievances, resources, and political opportunity structures.

1.4.1 Economic and Political Grievances

The first set of arguments concerns the crisis experience, which has varied greatly from one region to another. Figure 1.1 provides a schematic overview of the development of *economic and political grievances* in the three regions during the period covered by our study. We use unemployment rates as a rough indicator of economic grievances and satisfaction with democracy as an equally rough indicator of political grievances. The left-hand subgraph for economic grievances shows that unemployment rates increased sharply in the immediate aftermath of the onset of the financial crisis in both southern and eastern Europe, while they remained comparatively weakly affected in the export-led and tertiarized economies of continental and northern Europe (Baccaro and Pontusson 2016). The unequal development of the regional unemployment rates demonstrates that the eurozone crisis accelerated and exacerbated structural economic imbalances that had accumulated for decades (Boix 2015). The countries of southern and eastern Europe had experienced severely lagging job growth in productive service employment for a long time, and these structural weaknesses acted as a catalyst when the financial crisis hit their economies, leading to rampant decline in economic demand and occupational performance.

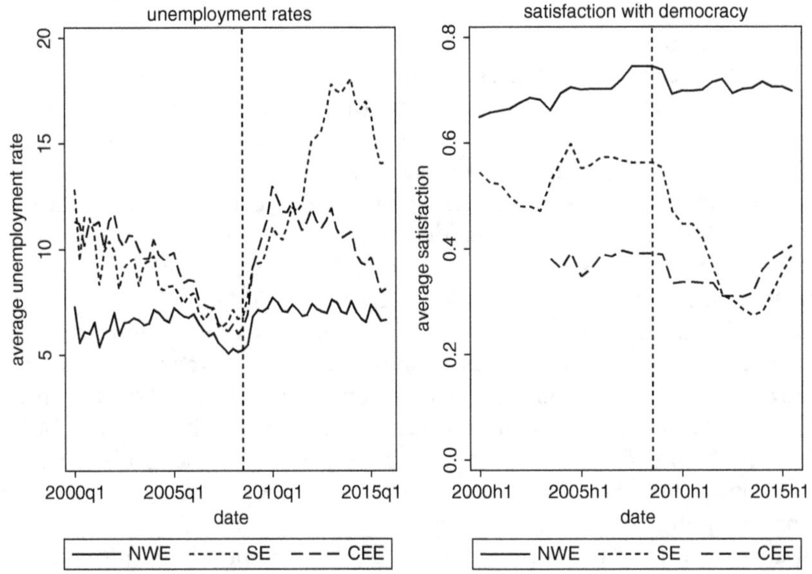

Figure 1.1 Economic and political grievances: average unemployment rates (quarterly) and average satisfaction with democracy (half-yearly) per region, 2000–2015.

But while both eastern and SE countries were on average heavily hit by the crisis, we nevertheless observe two important differences. First, the eastern European pattern blends into a more long-term picture of volatile employment performance, even before the crisis (Bohle 2016), whereas in SE the crisis represented a sudden discontinuity after an extended period of macroeconomic stability, expansionary fiscal policies, and easy access to financing for deficits and debt (Hassel 2014). Hence the actual *decline* in economic performance was much more strongly and sharply felt in the south than in the east. Second, the countries of eastern Europe show a relatively quick recovery, with declining unemployment rates from 2011 onwards, as a reaction to painful measures of external (Poland and Czech Republic) and internal devaluation (Lithuania, Latvia, Estonia, and Romania) implemented by national governments (Walter 2016). The same does not hold for the countries of the European south, where unemployment not only rose to much higher levels but also remained at these levels for a longer time. Here, external adjustment was ruled out because of eurozone membership, and internal adjustment policies were either impeded or – via conditional bailout packages – externally forced upon these countries. We expect that it is the strong and lasting increase in economic grievances that accounts for the emergence of widespread protest in SE.

The second part of Figure 1.1 shows that satisfaction with democracy experienced a tremendous decline in SE in the aftermath of the initial shock in fall 2008, falling from close to 60 per cent to below 30 per cent of respondents satisfied with democracy, which contrasts with a steady high level of democratic satisfaction in NWE and the continuously low level of democratic satisfaction in CEE. The massive collapse of satisfaction with democracy in the south represents an actual watershed in political legitimacy that may not be explained by the absolute levels of economic grievances alone. The economic difficulties may have reduced citizens' tolerance of poor governance in general. As Royo (2014) argues for the case of Spain, we cannot understand the Spanish real estate bubble, the country's loss of competitiveness, or its financial crisis without taking into account what he calls the 'extractive behaviour' of the Spanish political elite and the general 'institutional degeneration' in Spanish politics. However, as he also argues, the problem in Spain has been both the extractive behaviour of the elite and the fact that civil society tolerated this behaviour. It was only when the economic crisis exposed the economic model as unsustainable that the public became outraged with the actions of its political elite. SE countries suffered from a *double crisis* during the Great Recession – an economic *and* a political crisis (Hutter et al. 2018) – with important consequences for the mobilization of protest, as we shall show in our study. As with the economic grievances, we expect that the strong *increase* in political grievances accounts for the emergence of protest in SE. Where citizens had been dissatisfied for a long time, as in CEE, dissatisfaction is expected to have triggered less protest, even when combined with economic grievances.

The individual countries vary of course with respect to the extent that they follow the overall regional pattern, and we do take this intraregional variation into account in the individual analytical chapters of this book. Figure 1.2 shows the relevant intraregional variation, by highlighting those countries that deviate from the regional trend (such as Ireland among the north-western countries) and extreme cases (such as Greece in SE), as well as other countries which exemplify the regional trends. More specifically, in NWE, Ireland had clearly been more heavily hit by the economic crises than the rest of the countries, while Germany's unemployment rate continued its decline that had started in 2005 throughout the economic crises, as illustrated by the first two subgraphs in Figure 1.2. On the whole, however, the experience of the countries in this part of Europe was rather similar.

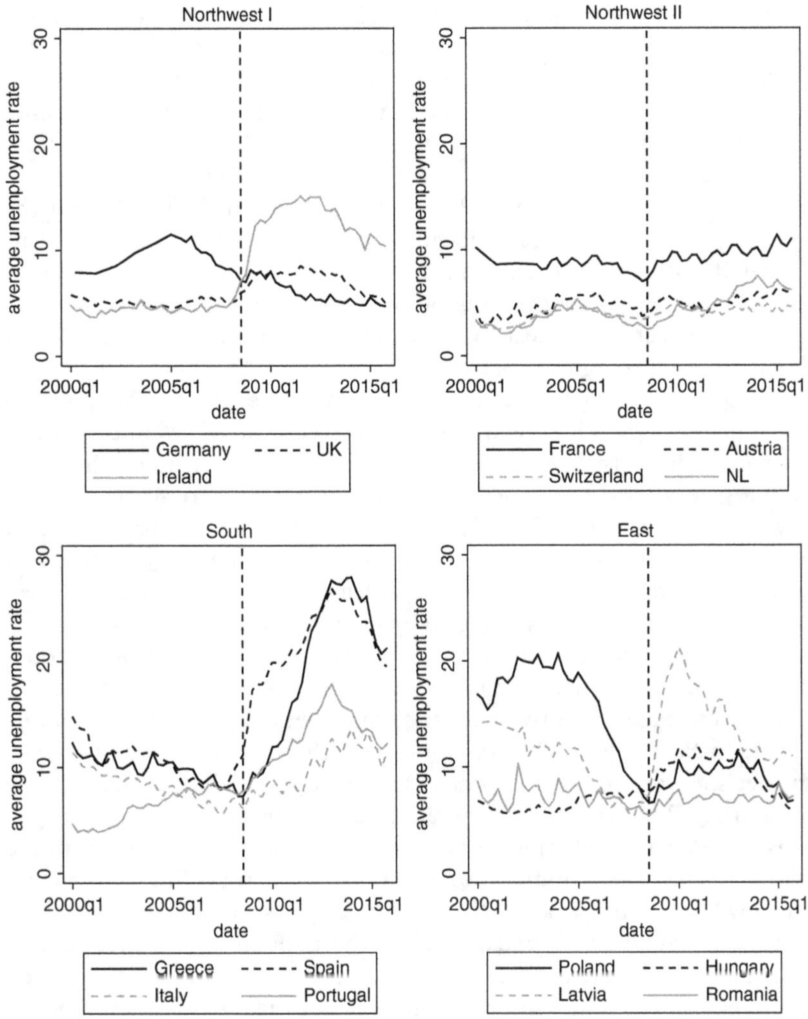

Figure 1.2 Economic grievances: average unemployment rates (quarterly) per country, 2000–2015.

The third subgraph shows that Greece and Spain are the two SE countries that have been hit most heavily. By contrast, the unemployment rate in Italy did not increase much in the course of the crises. In Portugal the rise in unemployment accelerated as a result of the crises, but it had already started to rise before the shock period and it never reached the extreme levels of Greece and Spain. In eastern

Europe, the Baltic republics were most heavily hit, with unemployment at least tripling between 2007 and 2009 (Kattel and Raudla 2013). This is illustrated by the case of Latvia in the fourth subgraph of Figure 1.2. Compared to the Baltic states, however, unemployment increased much less in the other countries in this region. The greatest contrast is with the case of Poland, because in Poland unemployment had reached very high levels in the early 2000s, from which it declined until the beginning of the crisis, and hardly increased at all during the crisis. We shall deal with this country and other country-specific variations in grievances within a given region by showing how the development of different aspects of protest in some countries may deviate accordingly from the general regional pattern.

There is also intraregional variation with regard to the political grievances. In NWE, Ireland is again a case apart: While political grievances increased to some extent, in line with the increasing economic grievances, the level of political satisfaction remained generally high in this part of Europe. This is shown in the first subgraph of Figure 1.3. In some NWE countries, such as Germany or Sweden, political satisfaction even increased, at least up to 2015, when the Great Recession ended and was followed by the refugee crisis. By contrast, all SE countries experienced a strong decline in political satisfaction during the economic crises. This decline was particularly pronounced in Greece and Spain, the two countries most heavily hit by the economic crises. In Portugal, by contrast, just as with the state of the economy, the decline was more continuous, as it already set in before the collapse of Lehman Brothers. In CEE, Poland again constitutes a case apart, as satisfaction with democracy follows an increasing trend throughout the crises. In the other countries, political satisfaction declines somewhat, but nowhere as much as in SE, and it recovers rather rapidly to pre-crisis levels. Against the background of these rough crisis indicators, we would expect the greatest amount of protest in some SE countries such as Greece and Spain, while we would expect the most limited amount of protest in NWE countries such as Germany or Sweden, and Poland as the CEE European outlier.

1.4.2 Resources: The Strength of Civil Society and Political Legacies

In addition to these short-term factors linked to the crisis, the political legacies vary systematically between the three regions. For the study of protest, it is very important that the countries of SE – with the exception of Italy – were governed by authoritarian regimes until the mid-1970s, while the countries of CEE were governed by

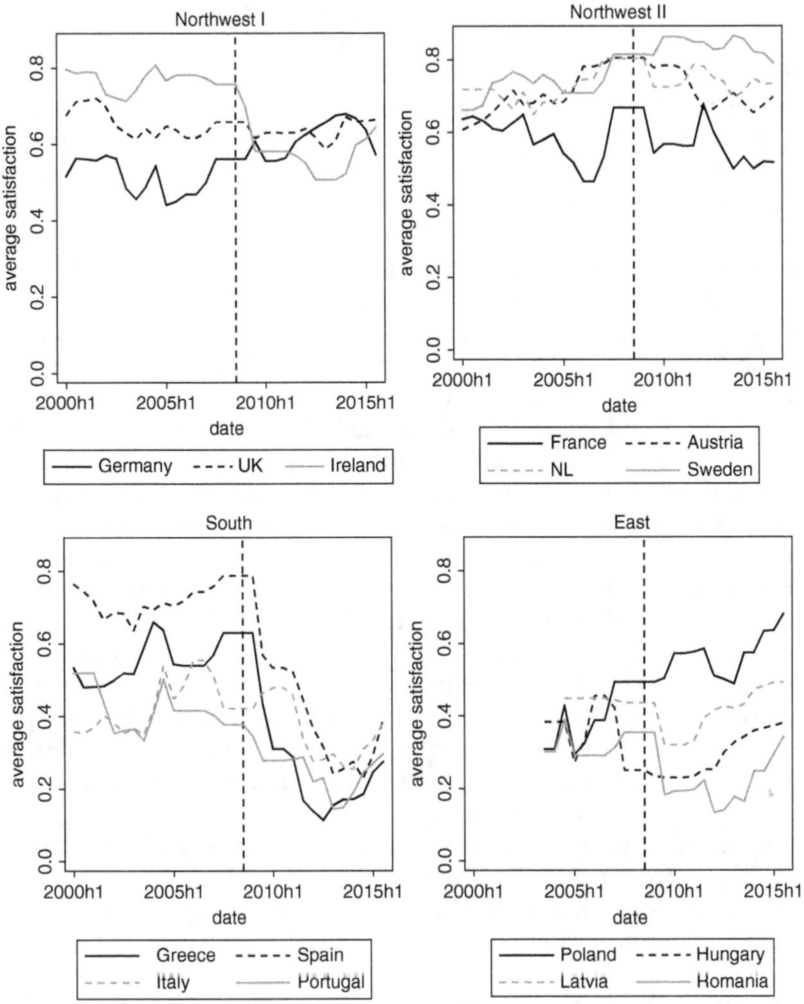

Figure 1.3 Political grievances: Average satisfaction with democracy (half-yearly) per country, 2000–2015.

Communist regimes until 1990. As a result of their belated democratization, these countries missed the wave of mobilization of the new social movements and were hardly affected by the wave of the radical populist right, which had strongly influenced protest mobilization in NWE. The first wave (the wave of the new social movements or the New Left) is an expression of the 'silent revolution' and was driven by the socio-cultural segment of the new middle class. This wave gave rise to the 'new politics': The new social movements stood at the origin of the rise of the Green parties and of the transformation of the NWE social-democratic parties which, in the process, have become middle-class parties (e.g. Gingrich and Häusermann 2015; Häusermann 2015). The second wave (the wave of the radical populist right or the New Right) is an expression of the social conflicts arising from 'globalization' and was driven by a heterogeneous set of 'losers of globalization' (Kriesi et al. 2008). In this process, the parties of the populist radical right have become the parties of the working class in NWE countries (Afonso and Rennwald 2018; Oesch 2008, 2013). These two waves of mobilization have in common that they concerned above all *cultural issues*. The rise of the parties of the New Left and the New Right is an expression of a crisis of representation that reflects the increasing distance of mainstream parties from their constituencies and their increasing convergence on the economic dimension. In the process, the two waves increased the importance of the cultural dimension of the partisan space and transformed its meaning, which, in the European context, had traditionally been dominated by issues related to religion. We expect the legacy of these two waves of mobilization to have left its imprint on the pattern of protest mobilization in NWE during the Great Recession. Against the background of this legacy and given the limited impact of the Great Recession in NWEg, we expect the 'return of the economy' and transformations on the protest scene to have been particularly weak in this part of Europe.

In the authoritarian countries of SE, the new social movements hardly got a foot on the ground until recently. Even in Italy they did not develop as much as in NWE because of the strong presence of the Communist left, which explains the continued salience of the class cleavage, the mobilization on economic issues, and the corresponding weakness of the new social movements. In our earlier comparative study of new social movements in western Europe we argued this point for the case of France (Kriesi et al. 1995: 14–19), but the same applies to an even greater extent to Italy and, by extension, to the other countries of the European south: A strong Communist Party restricted the independent development of new social movements in these countries (della Porta and Rucht 1991: 38). Moreover, the authoritarian legacy largely discredited the radical right and has limited the rise of these parties until the unfolding of the refugee crisis after 2015. Only in Italy did the fascist right survive the fall of the regime and was able to organize itself openly. But, paradoxically, the Italian neo-fascists started to decline at the very moment when the radical right began its rise in NWE, precisely because of their solid neo-fascist lineage (Ignazi 2003: 52). Only by distancing themselves from this legacy could they make a fresh start. Against this background, we would expect cultural issues to have been much less influential in the protest arena in SE already before the crisis. Moreover, given this legacy and the strong impact of the economic crisis we expect a particularly strong 'return of the economy' in this part of Europe. In the formerly Communist countries of CEE, by contrast, it is the Communist legacy that left its imprint on the protest arena. Neither new social movements nor the radical right had been a significant presence in these countries prior to the Great Recession. Civil society has traditionally been weak (Bernhard 1996; Bernhard and Karakoç 2007; Howard 2003; Pop-Eleches and Tucker 2013), and party systems in particular have remained weakly institutionalized (Casal Bértoa 2014 Casal Bértoa and Enyedi 2016). The very high level of volatility in these systems since the democratic transition is the most important empirical evidence for their lack of institutionalization (Powell and Tucker 2014). In the absence of other strong intermediary organizations, parties are likely to play a comparatively important role in the mobilization of protest in this region.

In terms of the issues structuring political conflict in CEE, it is important to keep in mind that, in order to distance itself from the Communist legacy, the post-Communist left has pursued rightist policies of fiscal responsibility and economic reform (Tavits and Letki 2009). This led to the convergence of the major parties on economic issues, which means that cultural issues have become more prominent in structuring the CEE party systems. But these cultural issues are of a different kind than the ones mobilizing in NWE (Kriesi 2016: 38): Their common denominator seems to be a 'defensive nationalism' asserting itself against internal enemies (such as ethnic minorities: Russians, Roma, and Jews) and external ones (such as foreign corporations colonizing the national economy). Given the importance of cultural issues in the party system, we expect them to be rather prominent for the mobilization of protest in this part of Europe, too, even in the course of the crisis.

The relative weakness of the civil society in CEE is visible in Figure 1.4. This figure presents the development of civil society from the time of the transition to democracy in 1990 up to 2017. As this figure shows, CEE has hardly caught up with NWE during this period.

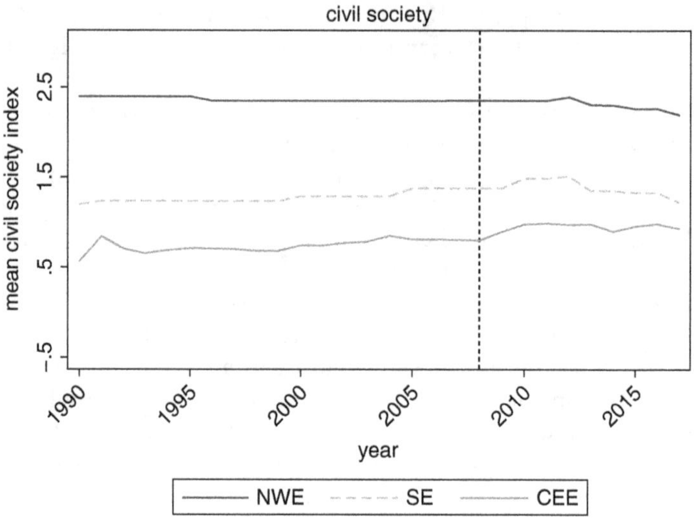

Figure 1.4 Strength of civil society by region, 1990–2015. *Source:* V-Dem indicator for CSO participatory environment (Bernhard et al. 2015, *V-Dem Working Paper Series* 2015: 13).

In terms of social movement theory, this suggests that the *resources* for mobilization in the protest arena are generally rather limited in this region, which, in turn, means that, ceteris paribus, we would expect a comparatively low level of mobilization in the corresponding countries. Figure 1.5 documents the variation of the strength of civil society within each region in 1990 and in 2015. Countries above the diagonal experienced a strengthening of their civil society during the twenty-five years that separate these two snapshots, while countries below the diagonal experienced a weakening of their civil society. The figure shows that, with the exception of Slovenia, civil society seems to be generally weak in CEE when compared to NWE. On average, SE lies between the other two regions in this respect (Figure 1.4), but the average hides large differences between, on the one hand, Greece and Italy with rather strong civil societies (at the top of the graph) and, on the other hand, Spain and Portugal with rather weak civil societies. The two SE countries with the largest grievances – Greece and Spain – turn out to be distinct in this respect. In other words, the combination of severe grievances with a rather strong civil society sets Greece apart from the other SE countries and leads us to expect a particularly strong mobilization of protest in Greece during the crises.

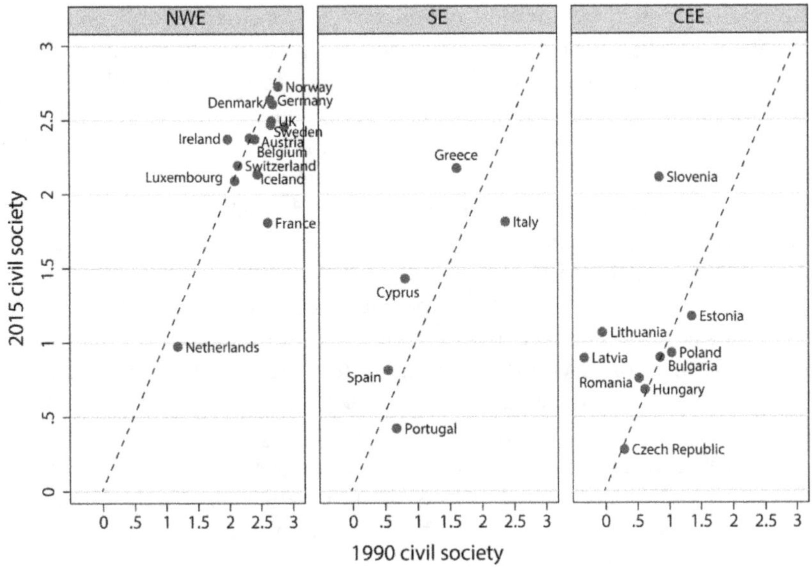

Figure 1.5 Strength of civil society by region and country, 1990 versus 2015. *Source:* Economic grievances: average unemployment rates (quarterly) per country, 2000–2015.

1.4.3 *Political Opportunity Structures: Government Capacity and International Interventions*

Finally, the distinction among the three regions is also related to two aspects of the *political opportunity structure* that play an important role in the quality of the management of the economy and governance more generally: the institutional structures and international interventions. Both may seriously constrain a government's capacity to respond to citizens' grievances. Institutional structures entail both *administrative* and *fiscal state capacities*, with the first referring to the strength, stability, and reliability of the administrative–political apparatus governments rely on when implementing policies, and the latter referring to the actual control political authority exerts over economic interactions in a particular country. These institutional structures also relate directly to the varieties of capitalism and different stages of structural development (Beramendi et al. 2015a; Bohle 2016; Hassel 2014), and they correlate with a range of institutional policy legacies that were relevant in shaping the countries' experiences during the Great Recession. Thus, the post-industrial export-led economies of continental and northern Europe proved to be very resilient in the crisis, not least because of their effective macroeconomic stabilizers, which in turn are causally related to strong administrative and fiscal state capacities. On the other hand, the (neo-) liberal economies of CEE felt the impact of the crisis directly and very strongly, because of their weak stabilizers and high international interdependence. Moreover, the CEE democracies were plagued with corruption, defined as 'the misuse of public office for private gain' (Klašnja et al. 2014: 69).

However, it was in the southern political economies, with their overall higher levels of particularism and (economic and social) clientelism that the governing capacity of the political elites turned out to be most constrained (Beramendi et al. 2015a). Figure 1.6 presents the development of two indices for state capacity in the three regions from 1990–2000 to 2015. Administrative state capacity is operationalized by clientelism, corruption, and rule of law, and fiscal state capacity is operationalized by the size of the shadow economy (hence, higher levels here mean

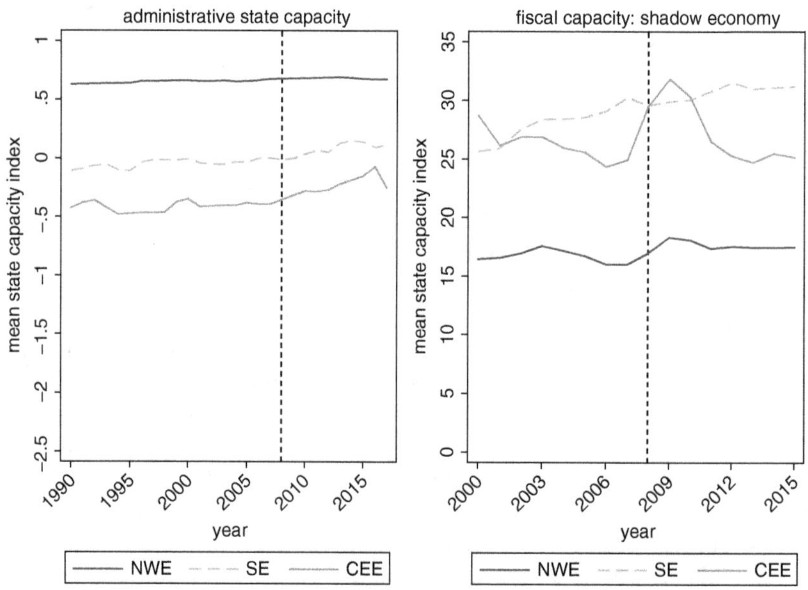

Figure 1.6 Administrative and fiscal state capacity by region, 1990–2015. *Source:* Administrative state capacity: factor based on V-Dem clientelism index, regime corruption index (Sigman and Lindberg 2017, *V-Dem Working Paper Series* 2017: 56) and rule of law index.

lower state capacity). As the graph suggests, with respect to state capacity, on average both SE and CEE fall short of NWE throughout the period covered. While the NWE countries are relatively homogeneous in this respect, the countries of the other two regions vary considerably. This variation is documented in Figure 1.7, which follows the format of Figure 1.5. In CEE, Poland, the Baltic states, and Slovenia, with rather strong administrative state capacities, appear to be clearly distinct from the Czech Republic, Hungary, and especially Bulgaria and Romania, with much weaker administrative state capacity. In SE, administrative state capacity is considerably higher in Portugal and Spain than in Greece. The level of administrative state capacity remained relatively stable across our period of observation, and even increased slightly in Greece in particular (even though remaining at an overall much lower level than in the rest of the SE countries, let alone the north-western countries). This confirms the findings of Afonso et al. (2015), who showed that parties in Greece rely much more on clientelistic linkages than their Portuguese counterparts in particular.

The pattern in terms of fiscal state capacity, i.e. the size of the shadow economy, is similar to some extent. However, more strikingly so than for administrative state capacity, between 2000 and 2015 fiscal state capacity deteriorated in all countries of SE except Malta, most pronouncedly in Greece. In eastern Europe, by contrast, the shadow economy contracted rather than expanded over time. We see that SE is the context in which state capacity has deteriorated most over the crisis, which is yet another justification for an analytical focus by region and accounts for the expected unfolding of a protest wave in this region. Greece is an extreme case in this respect. Assuming that a lack of administrative and fiscal state capacity to deal with the economic crises effectively contributes to the political grievances and enhances the effect of economic grievances on the mobilization of protest, Greece meets yet another condition for the strong mobilization of protest in the economic crises.

In addition to domestic institutional constraints, governments are also constrained by the *interventions of inter- and supranational actors*. Two institutions were particularly central to the understanding of supranational constraints on economic policy-making: the eurozone (Sanchez-Cuenca 2017) and international bailouts supervised by the International Monetary Fund (IMF), the ECB, and the European Commission (Armingeon and Guthmann 2014; Mair 2013). Governments belonging to the EU – and even more so to the eurozone – have faced a tension between responding to their national constituencies (responsiveness) and respecting Europe-level agreements (responsibility). In light of these double constraints, some observers speak of 'democracy without

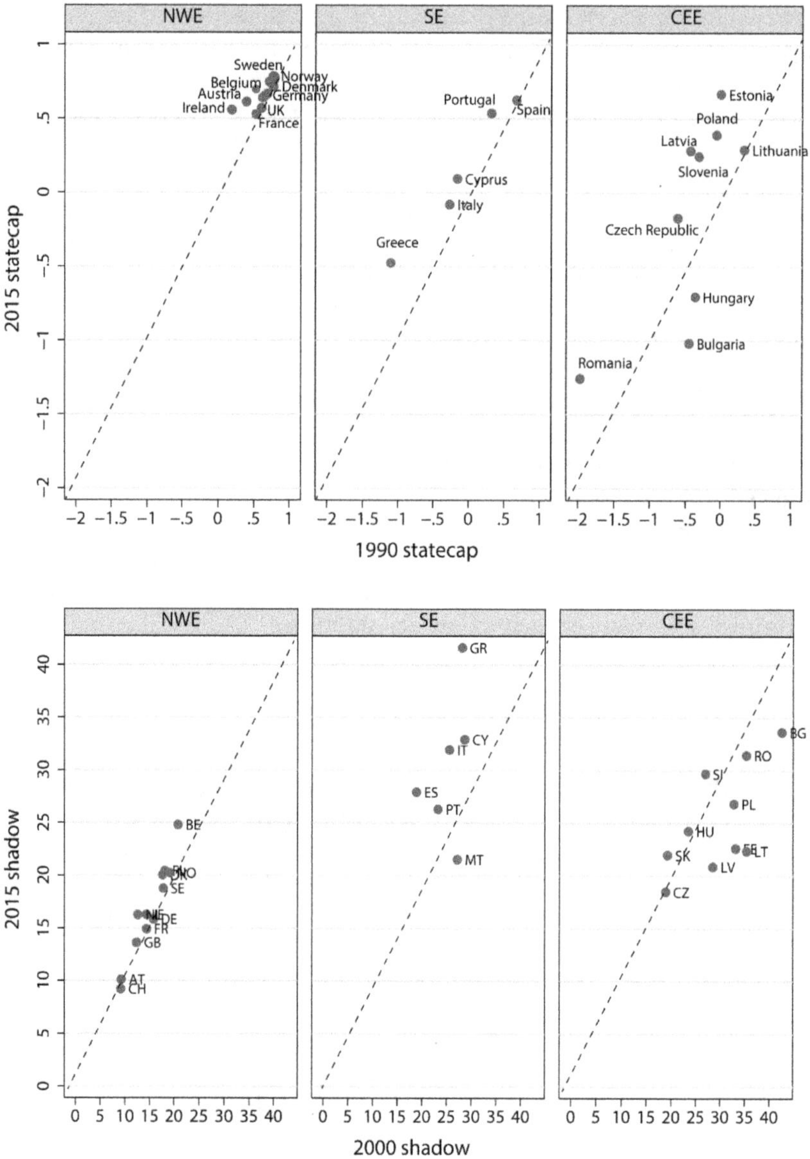

Figure 1.7 Administrative and fiscal by region and country, 1990–2015. (a) Administrative capacity and (b) fiscal capacity: shadow economy, 2000–2015. *Source:* Administrative and fiscal state capacity by region, 1990–2015.

choices', arguing that the eurozone agreements resulted in both a lack of alternatives regarding the socio-economic policies available to deal with the crisis (Alonso 2014; Mair 2013) and a growing power of technocrats (Sanchez-Cuenca 2017). These constraints weakened domestic responsiveness and blurred the chain of responsibility. Previous studies came to contrasting conclusions with regard to the impact of these constraints on protest. While Beissinger and Sasse (2014) found that IMF interventions increased protest in eastern Europe, other studies found that the imposition of supranational constraints on choices reinforced support for national democracy (Cordero and Simón 2016), and a study of six western and SE countries showed that ECB decision-making reduced protest (Genovese et al. 2016). The paradigmatic case of foreign interventions is, of course, Greece, which has been the object of no fewer than three bailouts, with very severe conditionality attached. In other words, Greece really ticks all the boxes that enhance the structural potential for protest mobilization. In Greece, the preconditions for a 'perfect storm' were reunited (Altiparmakis 2019b). It is, therefore, not surprising that Greece did experience an exceptional wave of protest during the Great Recession, as we shall document throughout this study.

1.5 Outline of the Book

The book starts with a data section presenting and assessing our strategy for the semi-automated coding of protest events. In Chapter 2, we introduce the tools used, explain the rationale behind the choice of tools and the data collection procedure, and evaluate their performance. Chapter 3 assesses the quality of our data by comparing them with a variety of other existing datasets.

Part II focuses on the dependent variable: Three chapters discuss the trends and characteristics of protest, notably general trends in frequency and intensity (Chapter 4), action repertoires (Chapter 5), and protest issues (Chapter 6). These chapters show the development of and variation in protest over time across Europe. Chapter 4 maps the intensity of protest and protest waves over time in different regions and countries. It investigates whether we observe sweeping cross-national protest waves or instead more contained national waves of protest. Chapter 5 studies the forms protest took in this period. It addresses the question of whether and to what extent we see novel innovative forms of protest spread across Europe or just 'business as usual'. Chapter 6 investigates the issues of protest and responds to the question about the 'return of the economy'.

Part III moves our analysis to the explanatory side. Chapter 7 conceptualizes economic and political grievances and analyses the direct and conditional impacts of economic deprivation and political dissatisfaction on protest. In studying the extent to which economic and political grievances trigger protest, Chapter 7 studies not only the direct link between economic deprivation and protest mobilization but also how this direct link is conditioned by the government's capacity to respond to these grievances. In addition, it investigates whether political grievances act as a mediating mechanism linking economic grievances and protest. Chapter 8 complements this focus on the relationship between economic hardship and protest with an analysis of the austerity policies which had to be implemented either as a consequence of supranational bailout agreements or for domestic reasons. Again, we are mainly interested in the interaction between economic grievances (austerity measures) and political grievances (the international constraints on government capacity imposed by bailout agreements) and investigate whether the latter reinforce the effect of the former on protest. Chapter 9 looks into the linkages between different national dynamics of protest mobilization by investigating the diffusion of protest across national arenas. It assesses the idea of a Europeanization of protest by testing for diffusion effects of sharing common borders or belonging to the same European region.

In Part IV of this study, we add a focus on the interaction of protest with wider national and international political dynamics. Chapters 10 and 11 study the relationship between protest and electoral politics. Chapter 10 compares the dynamics of opposition in the two arenas by asking whether the punishment of elites in the electoral arena is reinforced by economic protest, or whether the two dynamics are distinct. Chapter 11 then focuses on political parties as actors and initiators of protest. Chapter 12 summarizes the main results and concludes the book.

2 Design and Methods of Semi-automated Protest Event Analysis

Jasmine Lorenzini, Peter Makarov, and Bruno Wüest

This chapter presents our approach to the large-scale collection of protest event data from news text. We move away from purely manual coding, which has traditionally dominated protest event analysis (Hutter 2014; Koopmans and Rucht 2002), and join a recent trend towards the automation of much of the event data collection. Through the extensive application of natural language processing (NLP; Jurafsky and Martin 2009; Grimmer and Stewart 2013) and machine learning, we scaled up the coding of protest events beyond what would be possible with just the traditional method. We constructed a multisource dataset (Jenkins and Maher 2016) of 30,000 unique protest events, having analyzed in a semi-automated fashion more than 5 million English-language newswire reports published by ten international and local news agencies. Our dataset covers thirty European democracies over a period of sixteen years, from 2000 through 2015. In our semi-automated approach to coding (Nardulli et al. 2015), we employed NLP tools to detect protest-related news reports and then had domain experts manually code events and event properties, such as their action forms or issues addressed by event participants. Thus, we capitalized on the power of automated tools to process large amounts of text efficiently and effectively solve basic document classification tasks, and leveraged the unrivaled capacity of humans to cope with complex, cross-document information and draw reliable inferences from text.

In the following, we first discuss previous approaches to collect event data automatically from text and then present the steps of our semi-automated approach. For every stage of our data processing pipeline, we describe the tools that we developed, explain the technological and methodological choices that we made, and provide some evaluation. Finally, we introduce our weighting procedure and construct our measures of protest frequency, intensity, and radicalness that lay the foundations for the cross-national analyses of protest activity in the rest of the book.

2.1 Automated Approaches to Protest Event Analysis

Protest event analysis (PEA), a form of content analysis used to systematically collect and quantify textual information[1] on political protest, has for decades remained a core method of the study of contentious politics. Although it has traditionally been conducted manually, attempts to machine code political event data go back as far as the early 1990s and were first applied to the study of international relations and conflicts. In the simple and efficient automated approach pioneered by the highly influential Kansas Event Data System project (Gerner et al. 1994; Schrodt and Gerner 1994), the software program codes events by attempting to match manually constructed word patterns, such as 'take to streets', to the text. Some prominent examples of protest event datasets collected with machine assistance are the 'European Protest and Coercion Data' (Francisco 1996; Nam 2006, 2007; Reising 1998, 1999), the Imig and Tarrow (2001) data on European protest, and the Jenkins et al. (2012) project for a new edition of the *Handbook of Political and Social Indicators.*

Aside from the limitations in data quantity, one weakness of these earlier works was the lack of sufficient detail of coding (Imig and Tarrow 2001: 256). A typical coding program uses a predefined event ontology, such as CAMEO (Gerner et al. 2002; Schrodt 2012): Event types are thus fixed and might not be fine grained enough for some specific research questions. Extending the coding program so that it codes additional event properties (the number of participants, issues considered, etc.) becomes a research problem of its own.

There are also questions related to the fullness of event data. Pattern-based information-extraction systems are known to miss a large number of events, as it is difficult to build sufficiently exhaustive sets of word patterns for every type of event. Statistical NLP methods, which have been growing increasingly popular over the past years, generalize much better to unseen data, as their predictions are based on a multitude of weak textual cues. Statistical NLP has been successfully used in the machine coding of political event data (Beieler 2016; Boschee et al. 2013; Croicu and Weidmann 2015) and, specifically, protest (Hanna 2017; Nardulli et al. 2015). Virtually all these solutions are supervised.

[1] Protest event data collection usually relies on newspaper coverage as data source, but is sometimes also performed on police records, social movement documents, or other written material documenting contentious political actions (e.g. McCarthy et al. 1996; Oliver and Maney 2000).

One typically fits a statistical model to (the mathematical representations of) manually coded documents. The rationale is that the model learns useful generalizations to then be able to identify events in previously unseen documents.

2.2 Semi-automated Coding of Protest Events

Given the tight schedule of our data collection effort and the sheer difficulty of developing a fully automated event coding procedure, we settled on a hybrid approach, very similar to the one advocated by Nardulli et al. (2015). While it might not be hard to retrieve potentially relevant documents by simply searching a database with keywords such as 'protest' or 'demonstration', a challenge lies in identifying the small subset of these documents that would actually report on protests from countries of interest and fall into the right time period. Thus, just as Nardulli et al. (2015), who emphasize the effectiveness of automated detection of simple factual content, we focused on developing an NLP solution for the identification of relevant news reports. Human coders then performed the actual coding of events and event properties on automatically preselected reports.

Table 2.1 provides an overview of our multistep approach. The first six steps involve the sequential application of fully automated techniques. At the end, we obtain a document collection from which we draw a sample for manual coding. The table highlights the dramatic decrease in the number of documents when moving from all the news reports identified through keyword searches in multiple sources to the collection of documents most likely to report on protest events, as indicated by our NLP tools.

2.2.1 Retrieval of Relevant News Reports

We obtained news reports from the LexisNexis data service.[2] We used ten English-language newswire agencies[3] and retrieved news reports published in the sixteen-year period from 2000 through 2015. We aimed to include as many news agencies as possible to cover as precisely

[2] www.lexisnexis.com/.

[3] We included the following news agencies: AFP, AP, APA, BBC, BNS, CTK, DPA, MTI, PA, and PAP. Our goal was to include not only the major news agencies (AFP, DPA, PA) but also some regional ones covering eastern and southern Europe more specifically.

Table 2.1. *NLP pipeline for selection of documents and sampling for manual coding of protest events*

	Keyword search	Unique LexisNexis identifier	Location-based filter	Document classifier (doc > 61%)	Near-duplicate removal	Protest mention classifier (doc > 85%)	Sampling for manual coding	Documents with events
Number of documents	5,251,894	4,211,759	1,116,337	157,572	147,846	101,877	45,680	21,173
Per cent documents removed		19.8	73.5	85.9	6.2	31.1	—[a]	—[b]

[a] In this step, we did not remove any documents but we sampled them according to the size and news coverage of the country in the international news agencies. We applied three sampling rates, 0.25, 0.50, and 1, depending on these criteria.

[b] In this step, the relevant information is the share of documents without protest events (not the removed documents). We found 53.6 per cent of documents without events.

as possible the different regions and countries included in our study. In this way, we followed the multisource approach to PEA (Jenkins and Maher 2016). The search query comprises about forty keywords that describe different protest actions.[4] We opted for a query that is little constrained: It retrieves as many relevant documents as possible, even at the expense of obtaining a large share of non-relevant documents that need to be filtered out in the later stages. The query returned an initial set of 5.2 million news reports.

Among these 5.2 million documents, only about 5 per cent reported on protest events. The vast number of irrelevant documents is one of the biggest challenges for both automated and manual coding of protest events. For automated coding, the imbalance in the number of events compared to the number of non-events makes it difficult to identify recurrent patterns of how protest events are reported. As for manual coding, this imbalance forces coders to read many documents containing no events in order to identify the few reported events. To go from such a large number of documents to a subset of documents that can be coded manually with a reasonable deployment of resources, we performed the following steps: (1) We removed duplicate documents; (2) we built a location filter to discard documents not associated with any of our countries of interest; and (3) we implemented a supervised document classifier and a supervised protest mention classifier to distinguish relevant documents from non-relevant ones.

2.2.2 *Duplicate Removal Using LexisNexis Document Identifiers*

New agencies often release multiple versions of the same news report, to which LexisNexis assigns the same document identifier. To code each document only once, for each LexisNexis document identifier we picked only the document with the latest publication time. This step already reduced the number of documents by a million, to 4.2 million unique documents.

[4] Our query string is 'initiative OR referendum OR petition! OR signature! OR campaign! OR protest! OR demonstrat! OR manifest! OR marche! OR marchi! OR parade OR rall! OR picket! OR (human chain) OR riot! OR affray OR festival OR ceremony OR (street theatre) OR (road show) OR vigil OR strike! OR boycott! OR block! OR sit-in OR squat! OR mutin! OR bomb! OR firebomb! OR molotov OR graffiti OR assault OR attack OR arson OR incendiar! OR (fire I/1 raising) OR (set AND ablaze) OR landmine OR sabot! OR hostage! OR assassinat! OR shot OR murdered OR killed'.

2.2.3 Location-Based Filtering

As the search query included only protest action words, it naturally returned a vast number of documents reporting on protests outside our countries of interest. To remove them, we built a simple location filter that relies on the document metadata provided by LexisNexis. Among other things, the metadata includes a ranked list of countries associated with the document. We filtered out the documents whose metadata did not mention any relevant country. We also excluded about 3.5 per cent of documents featuring large countries for which we already had many news reports (e.g. France, Germany, or the United Kingdom) but where this country was ranked low according to the metadata. With this step, we achieved a drastic reduction of 73.5 per cent in the number of documents: from 4.2 million to 1.1 million.

2.2.4 Document Classification

We built a supervised statistical model whose function was to decide whether or not a newswire document mentions any relevant protest events. We modeled document contents with a classic bag-of-words document model. Under this model, a document is represented with a set of independent variables – one for each word or short phrase – whose values are the (weighted) relative frequencies of these words and phrases in that document (Manning et al. 2008). Thus, the model discards virtually all word-order information. We followed the steps that have been empirically shown to produce the most informative bag-of-words representations (Sebastiani 2002). For example, because the contents of a document depend much more on the document's notional words (nouns, verbs, adjectives) than on the functional ones (e.g., articles and prepositions) and punctuation, we removed all functional words from all the documents before computing the independent variables. As most of the words in a collection of documents occur very infrequently, we collapsed multiple related words into one (e.g. 'protested', 'protesters', 'protests', and 'protesting' to 'protest') using a specialized tool called a stemmer. In addition to word and phrase counts of the bag-of-words representation, we derived other independent variables; e.g. we counted the number of times European and common non-European country and city names occurred in the document. We built the representation of each news report from the title and the lead sentence as well as all the sentences that contain a keyword from the search query (such as 'attack', 'protest', 'demonstrate'). We manually classified about 7,500 documents into relevant (i.e. mentioning recent protest events in Europe) and non-relevant ones and fitted a regularized logistic regression to their representations.[5]

Having tested the resulting model on a set of withheld documents, we estimated that we would still be left with an impractically large number of false-positive documents, were we to apply the model as is to all the unclassified documents. This would translate to more work during manual coding. To increase the model's precision (at the expense of a slight drop in the model's recall of true positives), we raised the threshold at which the logistic regression model predicts the positive outcome, i.e. the relevance of the documents.[6]

The document classifier excluded almost 86 per cent of all the remaining documents. Unlike the previous step, which used a simple set of rules matching metadata to filter out documents, this step required a careful examination of potential biases introduced by our statistical model. Accordingly, we compared the proportions of non-relevant documents and counts of events for each event from above and below the threshold (Figures 2.1 *and* 2.2). The tests were based on the manual coding of 1,000 documents randomly drawn from all the documents classified as non-relevant for three countries: Hungary, Spain, and the United Kingdom. We chose one country per region analysed in this book, as we anticipated variations in the reporting on protest events across the three regions. For each country, we considered two years: one pre-crisis (2004) and one during the crisis (2012). These two criteria correspond to our cross-regional comparative design and to our specific interest in comparing the pre-crisis period with the Great Recession.

Figure 2.1 shows that there were almost no relevant documents below the threshold for the three countries selected for the test. Moreover, above the threshold, the share of non-relevant documents rapidly declines for all the countries. This is an indication that the document

[5] We fitted the model with stochastic gradient descent implemented in scikit-learn, a machine learning library (Pedregosa et al. 2011). We regularized logistic regression with elastic net (Zou and Hastie 2005), a technique for cases in which there are more independent variables than training samples. In addition, this penalty has the effect of automatically identifying the most informative independent variables for the inclusion into the classification model and setting the parameters of the remaining variables to zeros.

[6] Recall that with a binary logistic regression, one predicts the positive outcome if its conditional probability is estimated as being equal to or greater than 0.5. However, one is free to change the threshold of 0.5 if an application calls for a higher precision of the model (in which case one would increase the threshold) or a higher recall (in which case one would lower the threshold).

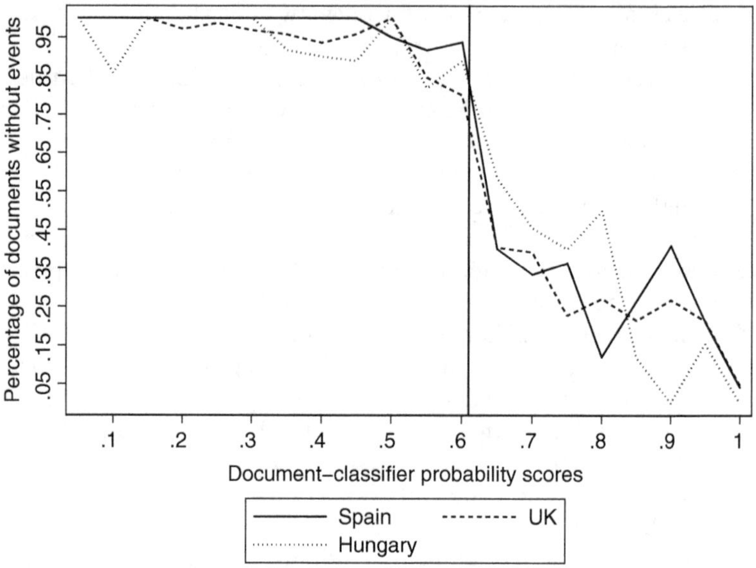

Figure 2.1 Share of non-relevant documents above and below the document classifier threshold. The test covers data on Hungary, Spain, and the United Kingdom for the years 2004 and 2012.

classification model was confident about whether documents reported protest events irrespective of the country.

Using the same set of documents, we assessed potential biases concerning forms of action. Figure 2.2 shows the distribution of events found at the various probability levels for different forms of protest action – demonstrations, strikes, violent actions, and a residual category covering all other forms. Again, for each action form we found very few events in the documents classified below the threshold. Moreover, the number of events increases rapidly above the threshold for demonstrations, strikes, and violent actions. Across these three forms, most events were found when the document classification model was highly confident that the document reported on protest events (probability scores above 90 per cent). The trends are similar across the three main forms of action. They differ only for the residual category covering all other actions, which contains a large variety of forms and was therefore more difficult for the document classifier to identify. As this category is of the least interest for our analysis,

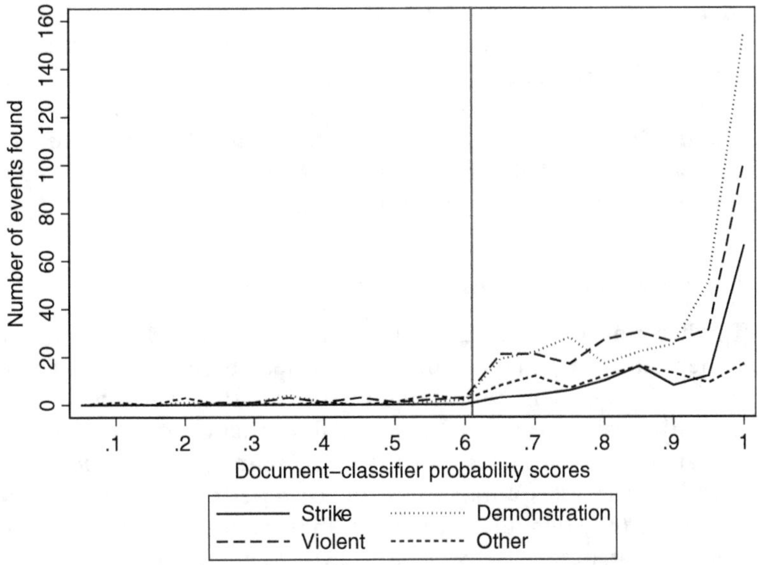

Figure 2.2 Number of events found above and below the document classifier threshold by form of action. The test covers data on Hungary, Spain, and the United Kingdom for the years 2004 and 2012.

we accepted the lower degree of precision. In general, the results indicate that the document classification model is not biased against any specific form of action.

2.2.5 *Near-Duplicate Removal*

Full duplicate documents can be quickly removed based on document identifiers. However, we also face the problem of very similar reports that differ only in the wording of one or two sentences – the so-called near-duplicates. A large part of near-duplicates is due to news agencies rewriting the same news story over the course of the day as events unfold. We consider near-duplicates as noise: First, they rarely contain information about new relevant events; and second, we ultimately aim to code as few documents per relevant event as possible.

We removed near-duplicates with the SpotSigs algorithm (Theobald et al. 2008), which performs highly efficient comparisons over millions of documents. The algorithm relies on compact document representations and the clever computation of the (multiset Jaccard) similarity between them.[7] The algorithm comes with a hyper-parameter – the similarity threshold. We established its optimal value by checking 100 duplicate pairs, which we obtained from several SpotSigs runs with different threshold values. This step removed approximately 10,000 documents, which is a decrease of about 6 per cent from the number of documents that had passed through the document classifier filter.

2.2.6 *Protest Mention Classification*

To further improve the identification of relevant documents, we implemented a classification model that detects mentions of protest events in the text. Unlike the document classifier, this model relies on carefully designed independent variables that capture much of the immediate context of words most likely signaling protest actions. The independent variables entail the lexical properties of context words (e.g. whether they denote locations, human beings, or organizations), the sentence structure, as well as word-order information that can provide evidence of possible event mentions (Ahn 2006).

Concretely, we manually coded 518 news reports and marked in them single words that most directly named protest actions, e.g. 'demonstration', 'petition', or 'took' (as in the phrase 'took to the streets'). The binary dependent variable in this model is then whether or not a word expresses a protest event. We then fitted a regularized logistic regression[8] to the variables derived from these reports and applied the resulting model to the remaining documents. If the model did not find event mentions in a document, then this document was filtered out. We considered the highest probability that the model assigned to one of the detected event mentions as its estimate of the relevance of that document. As with the document classifier, we raised the threshold from which the model starts predicting the positive class, thereby increasing its precision. Using the protest mention classifier, we excluded almost 50,000 documents – one-third of the remaining documents.

[7] Documents are represented as multisets (i.e. sets with repetitions) of tuples of functional words followed by content words. The Jaccard similarity between two multisets is simply the ratio of the cardinality (= size) of the intersection of the two sets to the cardinality of their union. The simple trick, which SpotSigs explores, is that by considering only the cardinalities of two sets, one can tell if the sets can potentially be similar with some Jaccard similarity *s*.

[8] This is another logistic regression regularized with elastic net and fitted with stochastic gradient descent.

To better understand the performance of the protest mention classifier, we manually worked through documents that the document classifier found relevant but the protest mention classifier considered non-relevant. Following the procedure used to evaluate the document classifier, we manually coded 300 documents for Hungary, the United Kingdom, and Spain.[9] This allowed us to estimate how likely it was that a document filtered out by the protest mention classifier was truly not relevant. We found that it was 2.5 times more likely that a UK document was non-relevant than relevant when it was filtered out and 2.4 times more likely for documents for Hungary. For Spain, however, a document filtered out was equally likely to be relevant or non-relevant. As the protest mention classifier excluded 30 per cent of the documents, we also compared the distributions of action forms in the test sample to those in our final, manually coded dataset. We found that they are virtually the same except for the catch-all 'other action form' category.

2.2.7 *Sampling of Protest-Relevant Documents*

After the six steps, the corpus of relevant documents still remained too large to perform a manual annotation of all of them. Therefore, we sampled the documents. For countries for which we had a very large sample of documents, we manually annotated 25 per cent of the documents[10]; for ones with an average number of documents, we sampled 50 per cent[11]; and for very small countries with only a few hundred news reports, all the reports were manually annotated.[12]

[9] The probability was high that if the document classification model found a document relevant then the event trigger classification model found it relevant too. As a result, there were simply not enough non-relevant documents for Hungary for the years 2004 and 2012. We therefore drew documents from 2004 and 2012 for Spain and the United Kingdom and for 2004, 2005, 2006, 2012, 2013, and 2014 for Hungary. We drew a proportionate stratified sample in which each stratum corresponded to a 0.05-step interval of the conditional probability of the positive class, from 0 to 0.85. Thus, for each country, the number of randomly sampled documents in a stratum was proportionate to the number of the country's documents falling in that interval, but scaled down so that the overall sample did not exceed 300.

[10] CZE, DEU, ESP, FRA, GBR, HUN, IRL, ITA, LVA, and POL.

[11] BEL, DNK, EST, GRC, NOR, PRT, and SVK.

[12] AUT, BGR, CHE, CYP, FIN, ISL, LTU, LUX, MLT, NLD, ROU, SVN, and SWE.

2.3 Manual Coding of Protest Events

In the manual coding, the goal was to retrieve information on all politically motivated unconventional actions in the selected countries and time periods. To this end, we employed a simplified version of the PEA approach established by Kriesi et al. (1995) and further developed by Hutter (2014). The first step in the manual coding procedure was the identification of relevant documents, i.e. documents reporting on protest events that took place in one of the thirty countries that we studied for the years 2000–2015.

Identifying protest events is a challenge. Not only machines but also human coders make errors when extracting information on events (see Ruggeri et al. 2011). The complexity of the task is related to the high degree of interpretation that is required in deciding whether an event is relevant. Our coders did not rely on a theoretical definition of relevant protest actions, which might be conceptually precise but practically very difficult to implement. Instead, they identified relevant actions using a detailed list of unconventional or non-institutionalized political action forms. We instructed them to select all mentions of actions listed in the description in Table 2.2 as relevant. A relevant document may contain references to only one protest event or it may contain references to more than one. Moreover, the same protest event may be referred to several times in the document. For coders to distinguish events and to annotate them only once, we defined unique events using the combination of the form of action, the timing, and the location. Hence, two descriptions of protest events in a document refer to a single event if they occurred on the same day in the same community and with the same form of action. If one or more of these key elements differed, the coders annotated multiple events.

Once the relevant documents were identified and the events singled out, the coders annotated the following variables for each event: (1) the date of the event (the day, month, and year when it took place); (2) the location of the event (if possible not only the country but also the city); (3) the form of action, distinguishing between six main forms – demonstrations, blockades and occupations, strikes, petitions, violent actions, and other action forms used as a residual category; (4) the topic of the protest: economic issues (distinguishing between public and private ones), environmental issues, cultural liberalism, cultural conservatism, regionalism, politics, xenophobia, and again a residual category covering all other issues; and lastly (5) the actors participating in or organizing the protest event. In the case of actors, we were interested in the presence of political parties, trade unions, civil society

Table 2.2. *Forms of action and issue categories used in manual coding*

Form of action	
Demonstrations	Demonstrations, marches, rallies, camps, meetings, vigils, and other non-confrontational gatherings
Strikes	Industrial action of any kind (including work stoppages, pickets)
Blockades and related acts	Blockades, occupations, sit-ins, camps, and other confrontational strategies
Petitions	Petitions, letters, consumer activism, boycotts, symbolic protests (performances)
Violent protests	Sabotage, riots, destruction of private or public buildings, bomb or arson attacks, violence against persons, clashes with police, cyber-attacks
Other protests	All other action forms
Issues	
Economy (private)	Economic claims addressed to firms/employers: dismissal of staff, closure of firm/branch, labor conflict related to pay rise, pay cut, etc.
Economy (public)	Economic claims addressed to public institutions, e.g. welfare, budget policies, agricultural policies, labour regulation, state regulation of the economy more generally
Environment	Environmental protection, nuclear energy, other forms of energy production, infrastructure projects (e.g., transport), animal rights
Cultural liberalism	Peace (questions of war and peace, nuclear and other conventional weapons, military infrastructure, military spending, military service), women's rights (including equal treatment, abortion rights), LGBT (rights and recognition of lesbian, gay, bisexual, and transsexual individuals), international solidarity (development aid, anti-imperialism), anti-racism, rights of migrants more generally, squatter mobilization (for autonomous living and cultural spaces)
Regionalism	Separatism, regional independence, protection of regional interests, anti-regionalist counter-mobilization
Cultural conservatism	Counter-mobilization to all aspects of cultural liberalism except for anti-racism and migrants' rights (which is in xenophobia)
Xenophobia	Right-wing extremism, racist mobilization (against foreigners or ethnic minorities), anti-immigration
Political	Representation, corruption, electoral reform, and institutional issues in general
Other	All other issues not covered by the previous categories

Table 2.2 *(cont.)*

Actors		
Political parties	Left	For example, Social Democrats, Greens, Communists
	Right	For example, Liberals, Christian Democrats, Conservatives, etc.
	Unknown	Unknown or unclear political orientation
Trade unions	Public	Public sector unions
	Private	Private sector unions
	Both	Unions from public and private sectors
	Unknown	Unions for which sector is unknown
Other organizations		
Social groups	Occupational	Workers, teachers, lawyers, etc.
	Students	
	Pensioners	

organizations, and specific occupational or social groups such as students or pensioners (see Table 2.2 for details). We also annotated the number of participants.

We collected inter-annotator agreement scores before and during the coding. More precisely, 14 of the 35 coders received the same 65 documents at different times so we measured the level of agreement on both the identification of events and the coding of the additional event attributes. We focused on the most important attributes, which were the actors, issues, and number of participants. For the identification of the events, we assessed whether two coders agreed on the date, country, and form of action for every event they identified in the same document. As this is an open-ended identification task – theoretically there is an infinite number of possible date–country–action combinations – we report the unweighted F1 score, which indicates the ratio of matched to non-matched events. The average F1 score over all possible pairs of the 14 coders was 0.60, with a standard deviation of 0.06. As for the event attributes, we first aggregated the matches and non-matches for every attribute of each event which two coders had identified in the same document. Second, we calculated Cohen's kappa on these aggregated numbers of agreements. We had a fixed number of classes for every attribute, which implied that our measure of agreement had to be chance corrected. The average of Cohen's kappa for the actors was 0.57 (standard deviation: 0.13), 0.53 (0.13) for the issues, and 0.45 (0.06) for the numbers of participants. It has been claimed that guidelines on how

Cohen's kappa values should be interpreted are sometimes misleading (Gwet 2014). However, values from 0.40 to 0.60 are often defined as fair to good.

In spite of all efforts to filter out non-relevant documents, in the manual coding phase we ended up with 59.0 per cent of non-relevant documents. Of these, 26.3 per cent were false positives that did not contain any events at all. In addition, another 32.6 per cent only contained information on events that were already reported in other documents. Most of these documents containing duplicates of events were identified by the manual coders as they went through the selected documents (27.3 per cent), but a substantial proportion (5.3 per cent) also consisted of duplicates containing only events that were already annotated by different coders from other documents. Overall, only 21,173 of the 45,680 documents sampled included unique information on protest events (see the last column in Table 2.1).

This confirms that even the most sophisticated (semi-) automated selection procedure is not able to eliminate the problem of event duplicates in a satisfactory manner. However, manual coding has a high cost. In our case, 35 undergraduate and graduate students performed the manual coding. One coder annotated at most 3,092 and at least 417 documents. The amount of time required to annotate a document varied greatly across news agencies and coders. Nonetheless, using the coders' self-declared working time we estimated an average processing time of 7 minutes per document. This estimate provided for a rough assessment of the amount of time required for the coding of the whole corpus of 45,680 documents. We invested about 642 working days in annotating our dataset covering 30 countries over a period of 16 years. Even when using automated techniques to reduce the work, the amount of time required for manual coding remained considerable.

2.4 Aggregation and Weighting of the Data

Our main indicator to measure the mobilization of protest is the frequency of events, i.e. the sheer *number of events* per month. However, nothing is really simple in the study of protest, not even an indicator apparently as simple as the number of events. More precisely, an indicator summing numbers of events per month has inherent features that require special measures before it can be used to compare mobilization in different countries. To begin with, recall that we used separate sampling probabilities in small, medium-sized, and large countries. For the numbers to be comparable across countries, we adjusted for the different sampling probabilities. Accordingly, numbers from countries where we drew a 0.25 sample were multiplied by 4, and those from countries where we drew a 0.5 sample were multiplied by 2.

Furthermore, following the example of Beissinger and Sasse (2014), we decided to adjust the number of events according to the country size. The size of the population has important implications for the level of protest we report for a given country. If we do not adjust for country size, we privilege the large countries; i.e. the large countries are the ones that are characterized by the largest numbers of protests. Indeed, if we do not adjust for country size, notoriously unruly France turns out to have the largest number of protests per month (65.8), followed by the United Kingdom (56.9), Spain (52.6), Italy (48.0), and Germany (47.0). We tested different ways of weighting for the country size, and it turned out that a natural logarithmic scale worked best. More precisely, we divided the number of events by the logarithm of the size of the country in which the events took place. Accounting for population size *per se*, as Beissinger and Sasse (2014) do, is overcorrecting the data. The large countries are "punished" too much, and protests in smaller countries become so prominent that all small countries are pushed into the upper half of the average rankings. Weighting with a logarithmic population size scale renders this weight less incisive and the country rankings look more valid. Unfortunately, this adjustment has the drawback that the numbers cannot be straightforwardly interpreted on an intuitive linear scale. However, there is no magic bullet solution to this weighting issue, and after careful thought we considered that the proposed solution offered the best possible compromise.

Lastly, our multisource approach included news agencies focusing on specific countries and we had to correct this focus by using an additional weight. We observed that in our dataset only two small countries have an above average number of monthly protests, namely the Czech Republic (45.3) and Greece (38.2). While Greece is, indeed, a highly unruly country, the high level of protest resulting in the Czech Republic was due to the fact that for this country we relied on a country-specific English-language news agency. It so happens that the same "advantage" applied to some of the large countries, too. Thus, France (AFP), the United Kingdom (PA), and Germany (DPA) were the countries which hosted our most important sources, and we also relied on national news agencies for Italy (ANSA) and Poland (PAP), which means that these countries are probably also over-represented in our data. Consequently, we added another weight to control for agency bias. For every country, we distinguished between the share of documents from general news agencies and the share from news agencies specialized in the country. We defined the specialized agencies as follows: ANSA = Italy, AFP = France, DPA = Germany, BNS = Baltic states, MTI = Hungary, PA = UK (including Northern Ireland) and Ireland, BBC = UK (including Northern Ireland), PAP = Poland and CTK = Czech Republic. To construct the agency weight, we took a mean of 1 and the general news agency share. If all the documents are from a specialized agency, the weight is 0.5; if all are from a general agency, the weight is 1.

Figure 2.3 presents the ups and downs of protest across European countries with the weighted and unweighted data. It shows that the weighting procedures implemented for the country comparisons do not affect the overall trend in protest. During the sixteen years that we analyze, the two lines capturing fluctuations in the amount of protest move together. Importantly, the peaks correspond in both datasets. The main difference lies in the fact that the weighted data accentuate some of these peaks. As an additional control, we calculated the correlation between the two patterns. It is quite close: $r = 0.89$ for the smoothed curves presented in Figure 2.3, and 0.90 for the corresponding raw curves.

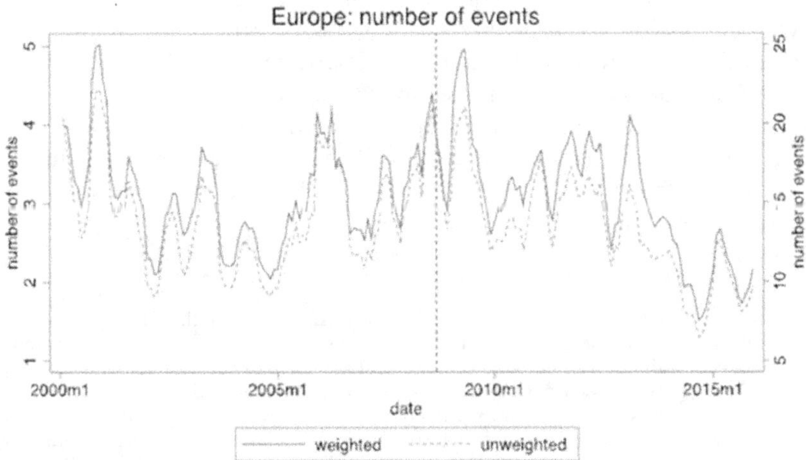

Figure 2.3 Number of events across Europe, 2000–2015: moving averages, weighted and unweighted.

2.5 From Protest Events to the Intensity and Radicalness of Protest

In addition to the frequency of protest, the literature uses other types of indicators to measure the importance of collective action. Tilly (1978: 96) proposed three types of indicators: the frequency, the size, and the duration of protest events. Frequency refers to the number of events in a given period, size to the number of participants in these events, and duration to the number of days the event lasted. We do not have reliable information on the duration of events, but we have information on the number of participants for at least 43 per cent of the events. We have full information on very large events (with 100,000 participants or more) and almost full information (with only 9 per cent missing cases) on large events (with 10,000 to 100,000 participants). By contrast, our information is most scarce for intermediate events with 1,000 to 10,000 participants, for which we lack information in roughly two-thirds of the cases.[13] To avoid losing any cases due to lack of information, we imputed the number of participants: To each event without information on the participants, we attributed the median number of people who participated in an event with the same form of action in the same country. For example, if we lacked information about the number of participants in a demonstration in Germany, we assumed that the number of participants in the demonstration corresponded to the median number of participants in German demonstrations during the period of coverage.[14] We also capped the number of participants at 1 million participants per event. This corrects for over-reporting and prevents individual events from distorting the overall pattern of mobilization. Finally, we weighted the number of participants as we did for the number of events, but with the difference that we applied a special treatment to "big events:" We weighted "big events" equally across all the countries; i.e. we assumed that we had found all the "big events" even in the countries in which we applied a lower sampling probability.[15]

[13] The events in this size category, for which we lack information on the number of participants, are mostly strikes (49 per cent) and demonstrations (43 per cent), and they took place predominantly in Greece (18 per cent), France (16 per cent), Italy (13 per cent), Spain (10 per cent), Germany (9 per cent), and the United Kingdom (6 per cent).

[14] In twenty cases, there was no median for a given form of action in the country, because none of the reports on this form of action in the country report the number of participants. This occurred, for example, in the case of strikes in Malta. In these cases, we set the number of participants at 0.

[15] For countries with fewer than 5 million inhabitants, we define 'big events' as events that have a number of participants which is larger than two standard deviations above the mean participation across all events in a given country. For small countries

The importance of a protest event depends not only on its size, however, but also on its newsworthiness. As Rochon (1990) and Koopmans (1995) point out, in addition to its magnitude, an event's radicalness and its originality also make for news. Thus, violent events, even if they do not involve many participants, are likely to be newsworthy, as are original events such as environmentalists sitting in trees to prevent them from being cut down, Greenpeace activists setting out in rubber boats to protest against whaling, or the early sit-ins by black students in the south of the United States. We were able to pick up many confrontational and violent events with our keyword search and we constructed an indicator of the radicalness of protests. This indicator summed all the confrontational and violent events in a given period, weighting violent events twice as much as confrontational ones.

The frequency and radicalness of protest are closely related ($r = 0.81$), as both are based on the count of events, but also because violent and confrontational events are quite numerous in our dataset – they account for 8.4 and 20.1 per cent respectively of all the events. Not surprisingly, by contrast, size measures a very different aspect of protest to frequency. There are many small and few very large events, but the large events contribute most of the participants. Therefore, the correlation between the monthly indicators of frequency and size is rather low ($r = 0.44$). The correlation between radicalness and size is even lower ($r = 0.19$), which is not surprising either: Radical events are the preserve of small groups. However, while radicalness and size measure very different aspects of protest, they both increase its newsworthiness and indicate unusual intensity. In fact, we combined the indicators for size and radicalness into a single indicator of the intensity of mobilization. To do this, we standardized both of the original indicators and added the standardized numbers. To avoid negative numbers, we shifted the mean of the combined indicator of intensity so that the minimum for this indicator became 0. The intensity indicator measures whether an event is large, confrontational/violent, or both. It is closely correlated with the monthly frequency of events ($r = 0.81$).

such as Iceland, this threshold is very high (several tens of thousands of participants), while it is much smaller for large countries (it is the lowest for Germany, where it corresponds to roughly 2,000 participants). This is why we define big events differently for countries with more than 5 million inhabitants. For these countries, big events are simply events with 100,000 participants or more. Overall, 775 events or around 2.6 per cent of all the events we identified are thus defined as 'big events'. For these events, we disregard the lower sampling probabilities.

2.6 Conclusion

In this chapter, we have presented our semi-automated procedure for the construction of the dataset covering protest events in thirty European countries over the time period from 2000 through 2015. We described our tools and discussed their evaluation. We first introduced a dataset of more than 5 million documents obtained from LexisNexis using a general protest-related search query. Then, we showed how we discarded exact and near-duplicates, and how we removed a large part of geographically irrelevant documents by filtering using the location information in the metadata of the documents. Next, we presented our statistical classification models that further narrow down the set of documents to just above 100,000 documents. The classification models try to identify protest-relevant documents by using linguistic information at the document level as well as by looking at the immediate context of likely protest event keywords. Finally, we discussed how we drew a country-specific sample of documents, which we manually coded following a well-established approach to protest event analysis. We presented a number of evaluations whose goal is to uncover potential biases due to the statistical classification step. We observed no major biases or losses in terms of protest events missed and their action forms. We presented the inter-coder agreement for the manually coded data, which we found adequate and corresponding to the standards of quality in the discipline.

Finally, we proposed using a combination of three weights to correct for the errors introduced by the data collection method. The weights correct for sampling probability, country size, and the presence of a news agency in a given country. Furthermore, in addition to event counts, we proposed a measure of protest intensity based on the number of participants and the radicalness of an event. Both of these result in greater newsworthiness of events and increase their influence on politics and society.

In the next chapter, we compare our dataset to two other protest event datasets. First, we compare it to another automatically generated dataset. This allows us to get insights about our data in a comparison with a dataset that uses the same or very similar sources (news reports). Second, we compare our data to datasets resulting from the manual coding of national news. This test estimates potential selection biases that we introduce by focusing on English-language news.

3 External Validation of Protest Event Analysis

Bruno Wüest and Jasmine Lorenzini

Protest event analysis (PEA) is attractive to social movement scholars because it is an unobtrusive technique that can cope with unstructured data, that can be adapted to the research context and that can handle large volumes of data (Hutter 2014). However, it is exactly this popularity which also has drawn some major criticisms. The most pressing one, of course, is reporting bias (Weidmann 2016). The sources of our data are news agencies that publish in English, which leads to a multitude of potential problems. Some of these problems are related to event characteristics. It is, for instance, well known that violent events, events organized by established political forces, or events that coincide with important policy decisions carry more news value and are reported more often (Amenta et al. 2009; McCarthy et al. 2008; Oliver and Maney 2000). Other problems are linked to the attention paid by news agencies themselves (Andrews and Caren 2010). Events that take place in a capital – where most foreign journalists have their workplaces – are more likely to become news than events happening in the countryside. A thorough engagement with these issues of external validity is crucial before undertaking the analyses in the following chapters on the substantial aspects of the European protest landscape.

This chapter therefore sets out to discuss the choice of international news agencies as a source of protest event data and to compare the dataset that we have compiled to other datasets. More precisely, we test our dataset against two external datasets in order to identify its strengths and weaknesses.[1] The first data is the Integrated Crisis Early Warning

[1] We have made intensive efforts to find more datasets suitable for comparison. However, many covered too few years or countries. More problematic, other datasets we could identify are based on other measures of contentious action such as the duration of protests. For instance, the International Labour Organization (ILO) strike data (see Vandaele 2016) are available only on a yearly basis and contain the number of days workers were on strike, which is not fully comparable to the number of strike events included in our dataset.

System (ICEWS) data (Boschee et al. 2015). Among other things, the ICEWS data contain information on protest events for all the thirty countries and almost all the years covered by our study. This enables a detailed look into the differences across countries.

The second comparison of our semi-automated dataset is with data derived manually from national newspaper articles and news reports for a selection of western, eastern, and southern European countries (Spain, Germany, the Netherlands, the United Kingdom, Hungary, and Poland). These datasets were collected by different teams of researchers and therefore cover different periods of time. Nevertheless, they allow us to compare the numbers and types of events that we find in the news reports published in English to the national press and to estimate potential biases related to the relative sparsity of our data. This comparison can establish which kinds of events make it into the international press and which events are systematically excluded.

3.1 News Agencies as Reliable Sources for PEA

The advantages and disadvantages of using media data for PEAs have been so thoroughly analysed that we can discuss the quality of our data with the help of a rich literature. Both skeptics and proponents agree that protest events reported in the news are selected based on the characteristics of the events (intensity, size, duration, violence), contextual factors (news holes, proximity to news sources), media structures (corporate interest, attention cycle, political climate), and research processes (research question, resources available). Because of these selection processes, Ortiz et al. (2005) note that not all the events taking place on the streets of a given country or city make the news (considering any media source), and even fewer are included in protest event data. The question is whether these selection processes are known and consistent so they can be taken into account (Earl et al. 2004), or whether they are unstable and therefore difficult to correct when using news sources for PEAs (Ortiz et al. 2005).

However, even sceptics concede that adding sources is a solution, which brings us to the multisource approach advocated by Jenkins and Maher (2016).[2] While we cannot solve the dispute between proponents

[2] However, this solution comes with a price, which is the multiplication of false-positive events, as we discuss in Chapter 2.

and opponents of media data for the study of protest events, we can provide evidence that including multiple news agencies allows reaching accepted standards of quality for PEA.

In this study, we code protest events in ten different news agencies. Previous research on media biases agrees about the importance of the presence of news agencies (Earl et al. 2004; Ortiz et al. 2005), and research on international news coverage also shows that the presence of a news agency is the second most important predictor of news reporting (Wu 2000). Therefore, in a first step, we verify that the news agencies included in our study cover not only the three regions but also all the countries we analyse. Table 3.1 documents the presence of news agencies and their partners in different European cities. It shows that news agencies have their offices in the capitals (sometimes also in other large cities) of all the countries included in our study except two. In Cyprus and in Luxembourg, we do not have a news agency office. Furthermore, in most countries, there is more than one news agency operating. There are five countries with only a single news agency office; all of them are small countries (Estonia, Iceland, Ireland, Lithuania, and Malta). This shows that our multisource approach ensures an adequate coverage of most, if not all, countries included in our study.

A second important question relates to the accuracy of the selection of protest events by these news agencies. Strawn (2008) highlights that relative media biases are critical in evaluating the accuracy of a particular news source. In his comparison of news agencies to newspapers, he finds that news agencies cover the whole country more extensively. They also cover more events that target the national government. He concludes that news agencies retain more protest events because these agencies are retail sources – the agencies sell news to other media and gain from an extensive coverage. News is a commercial product with which they compete against each other and also against protesters, who increasingly report events directly on social media (Deuze 2008). Furthermore, news agencies (unlike newspapers) have unlimited space for publication – they can cover protest events extensively because they report news online only.

To conclude, the news agencies that we include in our analyses allow us to pursue a multisource approach, cover the different countries under study, and appear to offer equivalent if not better coverage of protest events than other media outlets. In the remainder of the chapter, we assess this idea by comparing our data to other data using similar or different sources.

Table 3.1. *Location of news agencies in the thirty countries under study*

Country	City	News agencies
Austria	Vienna	AFP, APA
Belgium	Brussels	AFP, ANSA, AP, DPA
Bulgaria	Sofia	AFP, APA (via BTA), DPA
Croatia	Zagreb	AFP, APA (via HINA)
Cyprus	—	—[a]
Czech Republic	Prague	APA (via CTK), CTK, DPA
Denmark	Copenhagen	AFP, DPA
Estonia	Tallinn	BNS
Finland	Helsinki	AFP, DPA
France	Paris	AFP, ANSA, AP, BBC, APA (via AFP), DPA
France	Strasbourg	DPA
Germany	Berlin	AFP, DPA
Germany	Cologne	BBC, DPA
Germany	Frankfurt	AFP, APA (via DPA & Minds), DPA
Germany	Hamburg	APA (via DPA), DPA
Greece	Athens	AFP, DPA
Hungary	Budapest	AFP, APA (via MTI), DPA, MTI
Iceland	Reykjavik	DPA
Ireland	Dublin	DPA
Italy	Milan	AFP, ANSA
Italy	Rome	AFP, ANSA, AP, APA (via ANSA), DPA
Latvia	Riga	BNS, DPA
Lithuania	Vilnius	BNS
Luxembourg	—	—[a]
Malta	Valletta	DPA
Netherlands	Amsterdam	DPA
Netherlands	The Hague	AFP
Norway	Oslo	AFP, DPA
Poland	Warsaw	AFP, APA (via PAP), BBC, DPA, PAP
Portugal	Lisbon	AFP, DPA
Romania	Bucharest	AFP, APA (via AGERPRES), DPA
Slovenia	Bratislava	APA (via TASR), DPA
Slovenia	Ljubljana	APA (via STA)
Spain	Barcelona	AFP
Spain	Madrid	AFP, ANSA, DPA
Sweden	Stockholm	AFP, DPA
Switzerland	Bern	APA (via ATS)
Switzerland	Zurich	AFP
Switzerland	Geneva	AFP, DPA
United Kingdom	London	AFP, ANSA, AP, BBC, DPA, PA, APA (via AFX)

AFP, Agence France Press; ANSA, Agenzia Nazionale Stampa Associata; AP, Associated Press; APA, Austria Presse Agentur; BBC, British Broadcasting Corporation; BNS, Baltic News Service; BTA, Bulgarian Telegraph Agency; CTK, Česká Tisková Kancelář; DPA, Deutsche Presse Agentur; HINA, Hrvatska Izvještajna Novinska Agencija.
[a] No news agency based in this country.

3.2 Comparison with the ICEWS Dataset

The ICEWS data report on demonstrations[3] until 2014, whereas our time period extends to 2015. In the ICEWS annotations, events are derived from both multiple English and foreign language (Spanish, Portuguese, and French) news sources, the latter of which are machine translated into English prior to the analysis. Compared to our data, the ICEWS data are built from similar types of sources, but the number of sources is larger and the set includes sources in languages other than English as well. Furthermore, in the ICEWS dataset the event detection is performed fully automatically. More precisely, the news reports are processed using the commercial software BBN ACCENT, which employs a range of natural language tasks and dictionary lookups in the automated recognition of events.

The starting assumption with respect to the following comparisons is that both the ICEWS and our own data are imperfect. Unfortunately, annotation errors always leave us with an imperfect picture of the 'reality' of protests. This is why the relevant question is not whether a dataset is perfectly correct, but whether it is a valid enough approximation of the subject under study. We have shown in the internal validations in Chapter 2 that our data were produced with some uncertainty. Very similarly, the authors of the ICEWS dataset report a precision of 84.5 per cent and a recall of 72 per cent for the recognition of protest events (Boschee et al. 2015). This is respectable, but again shows that content analysis data are unavoidably imprecise to a certain extent.

Subsequently, the validation of our data with the ICEWS data will be conducted as follows. In a first step, we establish the general trends in the datasets concerned and examine whether different weighted averages are beneficial to the validity of the data. In a second step, we show that the datasets compare very differently across the thirty countries and that general country characteristics cannot explain the reasons for these differences. Finally, in a third step we present an in-depth qualitative analysis of the time periods for which the two datasets deviate most heavily in terms of the numbers of events they report.

[3] In both datasets, demonstrations are defined as politically motivated public gatherings such as marches, rallies, camps, meetings, vigils, etc.

All the comparisons will be conducted in two ways. First, all the events annotated as demonstrations in the two datasets are compared. This allows an assessment of the general differences between the two datasets. For the second comparison, both datasets are restricted to events collected from sources that are available in both data sets. More precisely, only events from BBC Monitoring, Agence France-Presse (AFP), Associated Press (AP), Česká Tisková Kancelář (Czech News Agency, CTK), the Baltic News Service (BNS), and Agenzia Nazionale Stampa Associata (ANSA) are included. As the sources are the same, the comparison might better reveal differences in the annotation methods. Pretests of the analyses that follow indicated that the deviations in the ICEWS data are even greater if we compare them with our fully weighted data as described in Chapter 2. The comparisons will therefore be conducted using the original event counts with only the sample weights applied.[4]

The most important question, and the one with which we therefore start, is whether the overall levels and the dynamics of the time series are similar. With this aim, the trends in the two time series over all the countries are plotted in Figure 3.1. On the left-hand side, the monthly aggregated numbers of protests are shown, while on the right the 5-monthly moving averages are shown.

First, it is clear that the level of the full ICEWS time series is far lower than in our data. There can be different reasons for this. Our data may significantly over-report the numbers of protests or the ICEWS data might under-estimate the number of protests. Later on, we will present the results of a qualitative evaluation of these differences that will show that the latter is most likely the case. Most notably, the ICEWS data even contain many duplicated events and violent demonstrations, the latter which, according to the ICEWS codebook, should have been categorized as a different form of action (violent protests instead of demonstrations). The restricted datasets,

[4] The documents for Hungary, France, Germany, Spain, the United Kingdom, Italy, Latvia, Poland, the Czech Republic, and Ireland were sampled with a probability of 0.25, so they are given four times more weight in the regression. The documents for Greece, Slovakia, Portugal, Estonia, Denmark, Belgium, and Norway were sampled with a probability of 0.5, so they are given two times more weight in the regression. For all the other countries, all the documents were sampled, which is why the documents from these countries are given value 1.

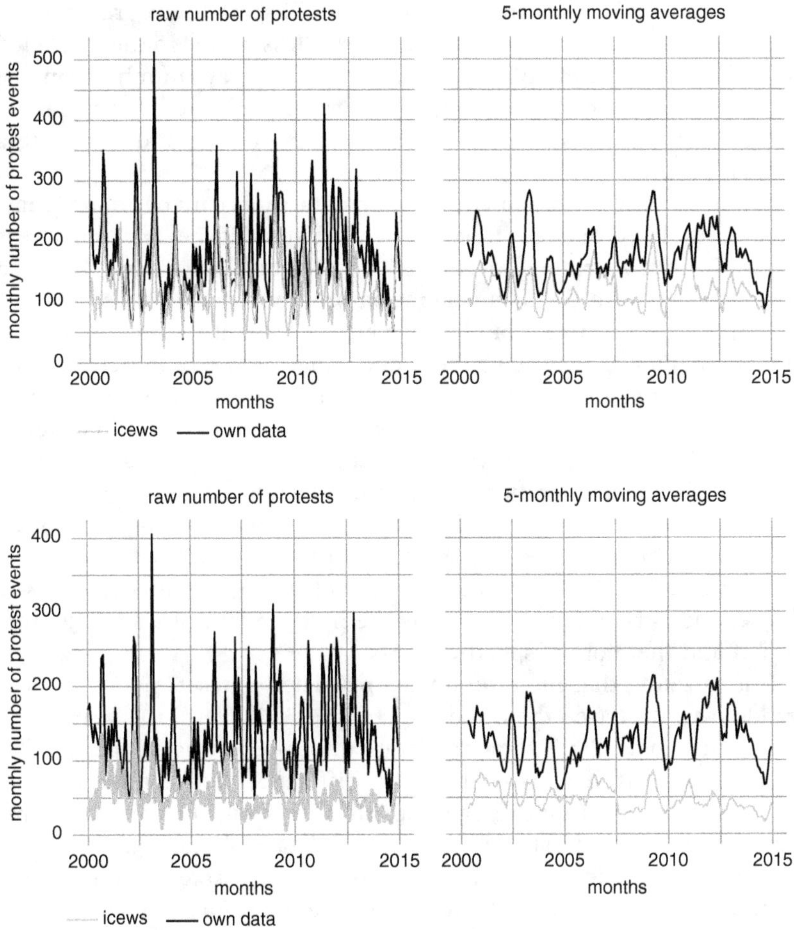

Figure 3.1 Monthly number of protest events in the full (top) and restricted (bottom) datasets for the ICEWS and our own protest data.

in contrast, differ much less. For many months, both datasets report similar levels of protest. Second, the ICEWS data show regular peaks, while our data show only three substantial ones: the Iraq war demonstrations in 2003, the protests following the meltdown of the global financial system in 2009, and the protests during the eurozone crisis in the years after 2010. For the restricted data set, these patterns are less pronounced. Nevertheless, our data still seem to accurately show the three major peaks, while they are again less visible in the restricted ICEWS dataset. Finally, a comparison of the raw numbers on the left and the 5-monthly moving averages on the right shows that for descriptive and visual analyses the data should be standardized to a certain extent.

It has already been shown that our data report many more events than the ICEWS data do. It would be worrisome if the deviations were not uniformly distributed over time, as this would mean that there is a systematic error in the data generation process for one of the datasets. A dropout of a source, could, for example, constitute such a systematic error. Figure 3.2 shows these deviations as the ratio between the monthly aggregated numbers of protests in the two time series for all the countries. There are peaks where ICEWS reports five times fewer events. These peaks, however, are exceptions and in general the development of the ratio is stationary.[5] There is therefore no extended period for which the reporting of the ICEWS is much below or above the average of 0.7, which is surprising given that there are 21,777 events in the ICEWS and 31,719 in our data. In sum, at least for the full datasets, the discrepancies between the two sets are independent of a specific time period and therefore of specific events.

It is puzzling that the ratio for the restricted datasets points to clear trends over time (see the bottom of Figure 3.2). Here, the years from 2001 until about 2007 show moderate under-reporting in the ICEWS data. Afterwards, in stark contrast, the differences between the ICEWS and our data are constantly large, with an average ratio between the numbers of protest in our data and the ICEWS data of about 0.3. The reason for this might be found in changes in the set of sources used to generate the ICEWS data. Indeed, the documentation explicitly mentions two such changes in the sample of sources (Boschee et al. 2015). In our data, almost all the sources are available for the whole research period.

3.2.1 *Country-Specific Comparisons*

So far, we have established that we need a certain level of standardization, i.e. moving averages or similar approaches such as local regressions, in order to make the two datasets comparable. Furthermore,

[5] This is confirmed by a unit root test (augmented Dickey–Fowler test) on both the ratio as well as the two time-series separately. In general, the unit root signals non-stationarity only in one country (Ireland) in the ICEWS data.

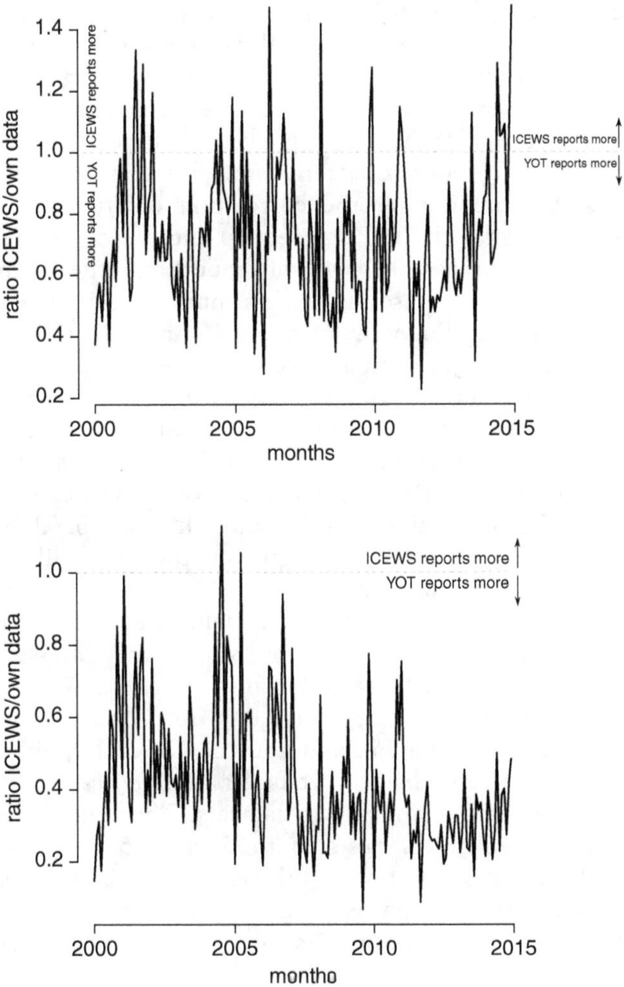

Figure 3.2 Difference between the ICEWS and our own data over time for the full (top) and restricted (bottom) datasets. The figures show the ratio in monthly aggregated numbers of protests.

it has been shown that the differences over time are constant and thus most likely not a concern for the external validation of our data compared to the ICEWS. In contrast, however, in the following we show that the external validity indeed differs heavily depending on the single countries.

Figure 3.3 shows the distribution of correlation coefficients for the numbers of protests across the thirty countries under consideration for different levels of aggregation and varying strengths of smoothing. *On average*, we can achieve a better congruence between the two datasets for both a higher level of aggregation and more smoothing. If we compare quarterly time series instead of monthly time series, the median for the correlation coefficients increases from 0.50 to 0.54 for the full datasets (at the top of Figure 3.3). If we additionally increase the level of smoothing, the median correlation coefficient increases to a maximum of 0.56 for the time series with 5-quarterly moving averages. By increasing the smoothing and the level of aggregation, we can therefore assume that some of the annotation and selection errors are straightened out and the datasets become more comparable. The correlations for the restricted datasets behave very similarly. Quite surprisingly, however, they are generally lower, despite the fact that the two datasets start from the same sources. For the majority of the countries, the correlation coefficients are weak, i.e. below 0.6. However, they are still strong for about a third of the countries.

Nevertheless, while the average congruence increases, so does the *spread* among the countries. A comparison of the time series with 10-quarterly moving averages is the most extreme. While the two datasets correlate with an impressive 0.98 for Greece, the correlation is clearly negative for Finland and the Czech Republic (−0.24 and −0.25 respectively). Hence, we face a *trade-off between the average level and the variation* in the two datasets. The comparison of the monthly aggregated time series smoothed with a 5-monthly average seems to offer the best solution to this trade-off. The correlation for Finland is still virtually non-existent (0.07), but besides this singular odd result, no other country has a correlation coefficient lower than 0.20.

The variation in the difference between the two datasets seems to systematically correlate with general country characteristics. Table 3.2 illustrates this by showing the results of regressions on the difference in the 5-monthy averaged times series for the full and restricted data. The dependent variable is the monthly difference between the ICEWS data and our dataset.[6] As explanatory factors, we include the regions as

[6] As the data are stationary, no transformations such as de-meaning or de-trending are necessary.

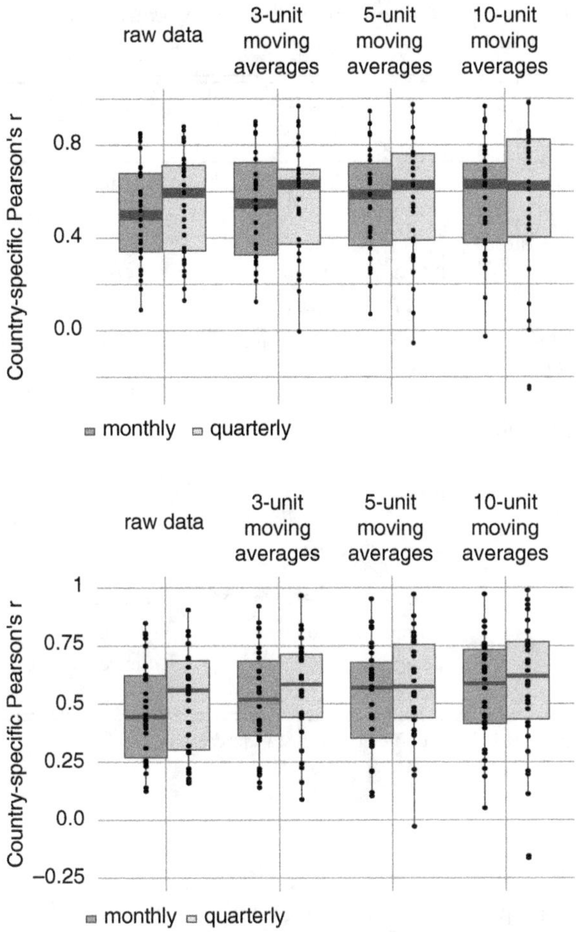

Figure 3.3 Country-specific correlations between the ICEWS and our own data for different levels of aggregation (monthly, quarterly) and different types of moving averages (3, 5, or 10). Comparisons between the full datasets are shown at the top; comparisons between the restricted data sets are shown at the bottom.

defined in Chapter 1 (central-eastern [CEE], north-western [NWE], and southern [SE] Europe), the size of the population (in millions), a binary indicator of whether a country in our sample is a self-declared focal country for one of the news agencies in our sample, and three of our four time periods (normal times, the shock period, and the

Table 3.2. *Random-effects GLS regression on the difference between 5-monthly averaged ICEWS and our own data*

	Full dataset			Restricted dataset		
	Coef.	Std. err.	$P > \|z\|$	Coef.	Std. err.	$P > \|z\|$
(Intercept)	−0.255	0.820		−0.064	1.017	
Region (ref = central-eastern)						
North-western	0.860	0.974		0.412	1.205	
Southern	−0.576	1.227		−2.393	1.519	
Average population (in million inhabitants)	−0.050	0.021	*	−0.049	0.025	*
Agency focus	−2.613	1.004	**	−3.369	1.237	**
Period (ref. = normal)						
Shock	−0.789	0.205	***	−0.885	0.171	***
Euro crisis	−0.264	0.125	*	−0.908	0.105	***
N observations	5,280			5,280		
N countries	30			30		
Wald test	43.64	df = 6	***	114.71	df = 6	***
R^2	Within:	0.00		Within:	0.02	
	Between:	0.54		Between:	0.52	
	Overall:	0.19		Overall:	0.27	

Notes: Unstandardized GLS coefficients and standard error.
Significance codes: $^{***}p \leq 0.001$; $^{**}p \leq 0.01$; $^{*}p \leq 0.05$.

eurozone crisis period; see Chapters 1 and 4 for detailed discussions of our periodicity). We show the results of a random-effects model in order to account for uneven variance across months and countries.

First, the size of the differences does not depend on the region. Compared to the reference category, CEE, the differences are non-significant for NWE and SE. Furthermore, the country size is negatively correlated with the differences between the two datasets. This is not surprising, as it can be assumed that international news agencies are more present in larger countries, which most likely increases the number of protest events indicated in both datasets and thus potentially leads to smaller differences. In addition, the agency focus is related to smaller differences. There is most probably some underreporting for some countries which are not in the spotlight of our international news agencies. Hence, we have most likely introduced some bias into the data, which is why we weight for this in the analyses in the following chapters. Finally, there is also a relationship between the periodicity and the differences in the two datasets. The differences in the shock and Euro-crisis periods are substantially smaller than before the Great Recession. This can be explained by the fact that the crisis years in general might be better covered by international news agencies – more public attention is given to protests, to which news agencies have to cater. In consequence, the selection bias in the sources of both datasets is smaller, which should lead to smaller differences between the time series.

3.2.2 Qualitative Comparison

The general comparison of the two time series so far has revealed little about the actual reasons for the differences. It is, however, crucial to know more about the substantive differences in the two datasets. Otherwise, we cannot confidently start with our analysis, especially for the countries which show a low overall correlation. To shed more light on the substantial differences, we conducted a qualitative examination of the time periods during which the deviations between the two time series are most pronounced. More precisely, we compiled our set of problematic time periods for this check as follows. First, we looked at the highest monthly differences per country in the raw data between the ICEWS and our own data. From these periods with the highest monthly differences, we chose a case from one country in each of the four regions. For these cases (see Table 3.3), we calculated the duplicates in terms of location and date and tried to assess the difference in the number of protests by means of a study of country reports, yearbooks, newspaper articles, Wikipedia entries, and general web searches.

In the first case, Denmark in December 2009, our search through external sources found only a few demonstrations, as our dataset reports. We also found many events that we included in other categories, such as blockades, petitions, and violent protests. Such protests should have been included in other categories in the ICEWS data as well. However, the even bigger reason for the differences is duplicated events. While we systematically filter them out in our dataset, the ICEWS contains seventy in this case. Such demonstrations that take place on the same day in the same place as other already annotated demonstrations make up the lion's share of the difference. The same holds true for Hungary in September 2006, where many duplicates can be found and many violent protests took place. The third case,

Table 3.3. *Selected cases for the qualitative evaluation*

Month	Country	*N* protests own data	*N* protests ICEWS	Difference	Duplicated events ICEWS
Dec. 2009	Denmark	6	86	−80	70
Sept. 2006	Hungary	34	153	−119	131
Dec. 2014	Ireland	2	28	−26	18
July 2001	Italy	14	97	−83	75
Mar. 2003	Ireland	13	3	+10	0
Mar. 2007	Norway	4	0	+4	0
Jan. 2012	Romania	74	56	+18	36
May 2011	Portugal	11	2	+9	1

Ireland in December 2014, was less clear. There are many duplicates here too, but there remains a substantial amount of over-reporting in the ICEWS data. Even after a very extensive search, we could not find more than the two events reported in our dataset. These are related to the 'right 2 water' protests in Dublin. For Italy in July 2001, we also did not find more events than are reported in our data. There is much reporting on police violence related to the events mentioned, so maybe these are falsely counted as separate events by the ICEWS. As for the four cases in which our dataset reports more events than the ICEWS, we found most of the events that are reported in our dataset with the exception of Portugal in May 2011. March 2011 was a major protest month in Portugal (organized by the 'Movimento 12 de Março'), so we suspect that our coders had problems finding the correct dates related to these protests. So, in these four cases, the ICEWS seems to under-report protests. However, compared to the cases in which the ICEWS data report more events, these cases are rare and the differences are not very large.

Hence, this qualitative assessment of the largest differences between the two datasets yielded the impression that the ICEWS data contain duplicates and events that would have been classified in other categories by our coders. The ICEWS data are compiled from many more news sources than our dataset, which most probably also leads to many more duplicated entries of the same protest event. Sometimes, however, events such as police violence, which should not be counted as protests, are reported by the ICEWS.

3.3 Comparison with Data Based on National News Sources

In this second part of Chapter 3, we compare our dataset to datasets based on the annotation of national news sources. Similar to what Strawn (2008) has done, our goal is to discuss relative media biases and to present variations in the types of events covered by international news as contained in our data with respect to national news, for which we rely on datasets based on national newspapers (for southern[7] and western Europe[8]) or news reports from national news agencies (for eastern Europe[9]), all published in the relative national language.[10] Following what we did in the comparison with ICEWS, in the comparisons that follows we weight the data only according to the sampling probability used to select documents annotated for the individual countries.

3.3.1 *Forms of Action and News Sources*

We start our comparison with the share of different forms of action found in the datasets based on the annotations of international and national news sources. This comparison is important for our subsequent analyses, in particular for the study of action repertoires and how they evolve during economic and political crises. Table 3.4 shows that demonstrations are the most common type of protest events across the datasets and countries. For Germany, the United Kingdom, Hungary, and Poland, demonstrations represent more than half of all events, while for Spain and the Netherlands they amount to 40 per cent of all events.

[7] For the Spanish dataset, the source is El Pais and the data cover the years 2007–2015. We would like to thank Martin Portos for sharing this protest data that he collected with us.

[8] For the western European countries, the sources are quality newspapers (for the United Kingdom, *The Guardian*; for Germany, *Frankfurter Rundschau*, and for the Netherlands, *NRC/Handelsblad*) and the dataset is based on annotations of Monday editions only. For the north-west, we have data for the period from 2000 to 2011. We would like to thank Swen Hutter for sharing the protest data he collected for the north-western countries with us.

[9] For CEE, the data cover the same period as ours – 2000–2015 – and the sources are national news agencies: MTI (Hungarian News Agency Corporation) for Hungary and PAP (Polish Agency Press) for Poland. We would like to thank Ondrej Cisar for sharing the protest data that he collected for central and eastern Europe.

[10] The national datasets cover different periods of time: our whole period of interest (for the central and eastern European countries), finishing before the end of our period (north-west), or not starting at the beginning of the 2000s (south). To account for these variations, we include in the comparison only data for the same time periods as are available in the national news.

Table 3.4. *Forms of action by news source for the six countries for which we have manually annotated protest event data (frequencies)*

			Demo.	Strike[b]	Violent	Other	Total[c] (N =)
North-western	Germany	International	**60.5**[a]	—	**31.2**	8.3	5,908
		National	48.6	—	19.7	**31.7**	1,697
	Netherlands	International	44.2	—	42.2	13.7	351
		National	41.6	—	36.4	**22.0**	341
	United Kingdom	International	53.2	—	**31.5**	15.3	6,988
		National	**60.1**	—	22.1	17.8	449
Central and eastern	Hungary	International	50.0	**19.2**	19.2	**11.6**	2,104
		National	52.6	5.1	**33.9**	8.5	3,716
	Poland	International	48.0	**15.4**	**20.6**	16.0	3,376
		National	**61.0**	6.4	14.6	18.0	6,713
Southern	Spain	International	44.8	**14.1**	**30.1**	11.0	5,404
		National	45.0	10.4	19.8	**24.8**	2,002

[a] Numbers in bold indicate higher adjusted residuals than expected (>1.96).

[b] Strike data are not available for the north-western national news datasets.

[c] The total number of events is multiplied by the sampling probability. We multiply the events found for Germany, the United Kingdom, Hungary, Poland, and Spain by 4. For the Netherlands, we coded all the documents found so the total number of events is not corrected for sampling probability.

Concerning the share of demonstrations across news sources, we find the same share for three countries (Hungary, Spain, and the Netherlands). For Poland and the United Kingdom, the share of demonstrations is greater in the national news, while for Germany it is greater in the international news.

The second form of action we are interested in is strikes. Unfortunately, we do not have data on strikes for the NWE countries so we exclude them from all our comparisons between national and international news for the north-west. We notice that strikes account for a smaller share of all events, less than 20 per cent. Regarding the comparison of interest to us, that between national and international news, strikes account for a larger share of the events in the international news. For Hungary, there are four times as many strikes in the international news (19 per cent) as in the national (5 per cent). Similarly, for Poland the ratio is one to three, with 15 as opposed to 6 per cent). Lastly, in Spain the difference is smaller (14 vs. 10 per cent) but also biased in favour of international news.

Surprisingly, violent events account for a larger share of events than strikes. They represent between a third and a fifth of all events depending on the type of news source and the country. In the case of violent events, as we found for strikes, they tend to be over-reported in the international news. This is the case across regions, for Germany, the United Kingdom, Poland, and Spain. For the Netherlands, no difference across sources is observed, while for Hungary violent events are over-reported in the national news. Less surprising is over-reporting of other action forms – the residual category – in the national news compared to the international news. National newspapers have more space to report on other, perhaps more innovative or less conventional, forms of action than do international news sources.

Our comparison of forms of action across news sources reveals no unexpected biases in the way international news sources report on protest events. They tend to over-report protest events deemed newsworthy – in particular, violent events. The newsworthiness of a protest event is set at a higher level in the international news than in the national. Therefore, events including violence are more likely to be reported. This appears for four of the countries we used in the test and we should therefore be careful when analysing processes of radicalization in the next steps of our analyses. More surprisingly, the international news over-reports strikes. This might be related to the fact that during the crisis economic protest events were a core focus of attention in the international press, more so than in the national news. We will keep this bias in mind when comparing pre- and post-crisis periods, but for cross-national comparison it does not appear to be a problem because we find a similar bias in the two regions for which we have data, the south and the east.

3.3.2 Location and Size of Protest Events

Next, we turn to specific characteristics of protest events that might explain why they are reported in the international press. In particular, the location and the size of events are key variables to explore. In Table 3.5, we see that the international news agencies are biased in favour of events taking place in the capitals or in the whole country and large events with more than 10,000 participants.

First, regarding the location of the events, we find that the international news is more likely to feature protest events taking place in capitals. This finding holds across all the countries but there are variations in the amount of over-reporting of protest organized in capitals. For Germany, the percentage of events in the capital is twice as large in the international as in the national news. For Hungary, Poland, and the United Kingdom, the share is 50 per cent higher in the international news than in the national. For Spain and the Netherlands, the differences are smaller. When considering large cities instead of focusing on the capital, we find a more diverse picture. In this case, sometimes we find that events taking place in large cities are more likely to be reported in the national news. This is the case for Germany, Hungary, and Spain, while for the Netherlands and the United Kingdom the share of events taking place in large cities is higher when using the international press than the national.

Apart from these two types of location, it is interesting to look at the share of events taking place throughout the country – which are also more likely to gain the attention of the international press. In fact, in this case they are consistently more likely to be featured in the international press than in the national. Furthermore, the differences can be very large but may also be due to the lack of a clear code for nationwide events in the NWE and SE national datasets.

Looking at the size of events, we investigate the share of events with more than 10,000 participants reported in both news sources. Large events represent a larger share of all events in the international press than in the national press. This difference is greatest for small countries and CEE countries. The Netherlands, Hungary, and Poland display larger differences across news sources with regard to the share of events attracting large crowds. In these cases, the percentages of large events are four times larger in the international news.

Table 3.5. *Location and size by news source for the six countries for which we have manually annotated protest event data (frequencies)*

			Capital	Large cities[c]	Nation-wide[d]	Total[e] ($N =$)	Large events (>10,000)	Total[e] ($N =$)
North-western	Germany	International	**23.0**[a]	22.5	11.2	5,908	19.7[b]	3,576
		National	11.6	**33.1**	**18.2**	1,697	12.2	1,238
	Netherlands	International	**31.9**	**29.3**	**23.1**	351	16.0	187
		National	23.5	20.8	7.6	341	3.8	211
	United Kingdom	International	**47.2**	**11.3**	**15.2**	6,988	13.2	3,360
		National	32.7	7.8	7.6	449	21.0	224
Central and Eastern	Hungary	International	**57.6**	4.2	**28.3**	2,104	17.9	896
		National	36.6	**8.5**	3.3	3,716	4.8	1,770
	Poland	International	**40.2**	13.6	**17.9**	3,376	14.4	1,472
		National	25.9	15.3	7.2	6,713	2.5	4,664
Southern	Spain	International	**33.9**	16.0	**22.3**	5,404	25.2	2,236
		National	27.3	**31.1**	0.1	2,002	16.1	1,363

[a] Numbers in bold indicate higher adjusted residuals than expected (>1.96).

[b] Underscores indicate a *t*-test confirming that the two samples have different means.

[c] Large cities exclude the capital and comprise cities >500,000 inhabitants for (Hamburg, Munich, Cologne, Frankfurt am Main, Essen, Stuttgart, Dortmund, Düsseldorf, and Bremen), for Poland (Kraków, Łódź, Wrokław, Poznań, and Gdańsk), and for Spain (Barcelona, Valencia, Sevilla, Zaragoza, and Malaga); >300,000 inhabitants for the Netherlands (Rotterdam, Utrecht, and The Hague) and the United Kingdom (Birmingham, Liverpool, Leeds, Sheffield, Bristol, Manchester, Leicester, Glasgow, and Edinburgh); and >100,000 inhabitants for Hungary (Miskolc, Nyíregyháza, Debrecen, Kecskemét, Győr, Szeged).

[d] For north-western and southern Europe, the data resulting from annotation of national news do not include a specific code for protest events taking place in the whole country. We create a proxy using a code to identify events occurring on the same date, addressing the same issues, but taking place in different locations.

[e] The total number of events is multiplied by the sampling probability. We multiply the events found for Germany, the United Kingdom, Hungary, Poland, and Spain by 4. For the Netherlands, we coded all the documents found so the total number of events is not corrected for sampling probability.

The differences are much smaller for Germany and Spain, and virtually absent for the United Kingdom. It is not surprising that the international news focuses on big events, especially those taking place in specific countries that are not of focal interest to international audiences.

3.3.3 Issues and Actors in Protest Events

Lastly, we look at issues and actors to identify biases in substantial characteristics of the events included in our analysis. We are interested in knowing whether the events we find focus on specific issues or are led by specific actors, as this may have implications for the analyses that we present in the following chapters.

For the issue addressed by protesters, we compare events focusing on economic issues, and for the CEE countries also on issues related to democracy (for the other regions, this was not included in the list of issues annotated). For the economy, we find important variations across countries. However, there is no prevailing trend in the over- or under-reporting of economy-related protest in the international press. In Germany and the United Kingdom, the international press reports a larger share of events focusing on the economy than does the national press. However, the contrary is true for Hungary and Spain. For the Netherlands and Poland, there are no differences with regard to the prevalence of economic issues across news sources. In the CEE countries issues related to democracy tend to be over-reported in the international press.

In Table 3.6, we compare actors and we observe that the composition is very similar for the events reported in the national and the international press. There is an overall tendency in the national press to include more information about the actors engaging in a protest. Furthermore, we find that the reported share of events organized by parties tends to be larger in the datasets based on national sources in the three NWE countries and Spain but not for the two CEE countries. For trade unions, the frequency is also higher in the national press than in the international, but only for Poland and Spain. For civil society organizations (CSOs), a similar tendency appears for Germany, the Netherlands, and Spain. Therefore, the national news often conveys more information about the presence of parties and to some extent also trade unions and CSOs across regions and countries. However, the overall composition – the share of actors of each kind – is consistent across the two types of sources.

Table 3.6. *Issues and actors by news source for the six countries for which we have manually annotated protest event data (frequencies)*

			Economy	Democracy[b]	Parties	Trade unions	CSO	Total[c] (N =)
North-western	Germany	International	**17.7**[a]	12.9	10.4	7.9	16.1	5,908
		National	6.1	—	**15.8**	7.7	**28.7**	1,697
	Netherlands	International	16.5	15.6	3.1	4.0	19.9	351
		National	12.6	—	**11.4**	6.8	**27.9**	341
	United Kingdom	International	**26.5**	8.8	3.5	9.9	27.0	6,988
		National	10.0	—	**6.9**	8.5	31.6	449
Central and eastern	Hungary	International	42.0	**29.3**	12.2	17.9	13.5	2,104
		National	**61.4**	16.7	11.7	15.7	12.5	3,716
	Poland	International	51.9	**18.4**	8.8	36.3	19.9	3,376
		National	52.4	4.3	9.1	**42.8**	17.4	6,713
Southern	Spain	International	50.4	11.1	3.0	12.4	21.3	5,404
		National	**70.1**	—	**10.6**	**51.2**	**48.9**	2,002

[a] Numbers in bold indicate higher adjusted residuals than expected (>1.96) and underscore indicates adjusted residuals smaller than expected (<−1.96).

[b] The issue 'democracy' was not available in the north-western and southern national news datasets.

[c] The total number of events is multiplied by the sampling probability. We multiply the events found for Germany, the United Kingdom, Hungary, Poland, and Spain by 4. For the Netherlands, we coded all the documents found so the total number of events is not corrected for sampling probability.

3.3.4 Predicting the News Sources as a Test of Differences

As a last test in this comparison between national and international news sources, we are interested in the explanatory power of different sets of predictors. To more formally test differences between the two types of data sources, national and international, we run a regression in which we predict the news sources using the different characteristics of protest described earlier. We use a stepwise approach in order to evaluate changes in the variance explained. We start with the location, and then we include the size, form of action, timing (year), issues addressed, and the actors involved in the event. This allows us to check for systematic variance in the kind of events reported in the national and in the international news.

Table 3.7 summarizes our findings by presenting the explanatory power of our different sets of predictors across the six countries. First of all, it appears that for the three western European countries, the predictive power of the model is lowest. The six different sets of predictors do not account for the variations between the national and the international news. The variation explained lies between 12 per cent for Great Britain and 17.8 per cent for the Netherlands. Similarly, for another CEE country, Poland, we find a low R^2 value (18.8 per cent). When the variation explained is low, it means that there are no major differences across the two datasets – at least no systematic differences that can be associated with the variables of interest to us for our subsequent analyses.

In two countries, the R^2 value is considerably higher. For Spain, we explain as much as 45.9 per cent of the variation and for Hungary 31.6 per cent. Looking at specific sets of variables, we observe that in these two countries, the locations of the events and their sizes carry a strong explanatory power. This corresponds to specific characteristics of the international press, which follows specific patterns for the inclusion of protest events. The events covered are more likely to take place either in the capital or in the whole country. Furthermore, large events are more likely to be reported in the international news. These two characteristics of events retrieved from international news sources are not surprising and they do not introduce important biases into the data. They are related to methodological choices and considerations related to the resources available for annotation.

Next, we look at the average explained variance by the predictors included in the model and the increase in terms of explained variance that the next set brings. We find that on average location explains 9 per cent of variance and that each subsequent set brings between 2 and 3

Table 3.7. *Explanatory power of different sets of predictors across countries for which we have manually annotated protest event data (R^2 based on stepwise logistic regressions)*

	Location	Size	Action form	Action form X location	Year	Issues	Actors	Full model
Spain	**0.148**	**0.197**	0.228		0.251	0.282	0.452	0.459
Hungary	**0.184**	**0.200**	0.210	0.262	0.289	0.301	0.310	0.316
Poland	0.043	**0.102**	0.135		0.150	0.178	0.159	0.188
Netherlands	0.090	**0.107**	0.122		0.148	0.148	0.175	0.178
Germany	0.026	0.045	0.121		0.127	0.144	0.139	0.155
Great Britain	0.046	0.063	0.067		0.086	0.115	0.091	0.120
Average (added) explained variance	0.09	0.03	0.03		0.03	0.02	0.03	0.02

additional percentage points of explained variance. The low numbers hide some variations across countries. Nevertheless, they show that these predictors do not account for large variations across the two datasets and allow us to assume that most divergence is random, or at least not related to any important biases that our methodological choices carry.

For issues and actors, in the descriptive analyses we noted variations across the data sets that may have implications for our analyses in the next chapters. Protest events about economic issues tend to be over-reported in the international news. However, we do not find that issues carry a large predictive power when already considering the location, the size, the year, and the form of action of the event. Similarly, we find that the international news tends to under-report actors, especially political parties and other CSOs. But again, these characteristics of protest carry a weak predictive power and do not point to important biases in our dataset resulting from the sources that we use – the international news.

Overall, these analyses show that a dataset based on international news slightly differs from one based on national news, but mostly in ways that are expected, i.e. in relation to location, size, and to some extent the form of action. However, they also show that other characteristics are not important in explaining variations across datasets. Hence, our dataset based on annotation of international news appears to be convincingly capturing trends in the types of protest events taking place in the different countries and regions included in our dataset. When compared to national sources, the most variation appears with regard to the location of the event and its size. By choosing international news for our protest event analysis, we find fewer small events and fewer events taking place outside the capital. Furthermore, we have shown that the location and size of the event do not introduce major biases in terms of the kinds of events that are reported in the news.

3.4 Conclusion

The evidence provided in the first part of this chapter first established that 5-yearly moving averages provide the best solution for the trade-off between the average level and the variation in a comparison between our data and the ICEWS dataset. Second, we found that our dataset is more precise than the ICEWS data. Compared to this comparable data source for demonstrations, our data show no trend in over-reporting. In contrast to the ICEWS data, our dataset does not suffer much from duplicated events and misclassifications of the protest form.

A consequence of these imprecisions in the ICEWS data is that they do not indicate the major waves of demonstrations across Europe, which were related to opposition to the Iraq war in 2003, the global financial meltdown in 2008 and 2009, and the Euro crisis from 2010 onwards. Hence, our considerable efforts in selecting as many documents as possible from ten different news agencies seem to have paid off. In addition, we find improved quality in our semi-automated PEA compared to fully automated approaches. The manual steps embedded in our annotation procedure certainly led to fewer problems with misclassifications and duplicates. This is not to say that our dataset is second to none for all research on protests in Europe. As the results for Finland show, our data are not always above reproach for small countries for which we collected only very few protest events. This also underlines the need for a certain level of aggregation in the analysis.

The analyses presented in the second part showed that our data based on the annotation of international news differ from datasets based on the annotation of national newspapers, but these differences are mostly related to diverging newsworthiness selection criteria for the national and international press. First and most importantly, the differences are small. Second, the differences show that the international press tends to cover larger events and events taking place in the capital or in several places throughout a country. These are all expected differences when comparing the international and national press. In terms of the form of action, the issue addressed, and the actors involved, we found some variations but no systematic bias that runs across countries and time periods. Relating our findings to the analyses in the following chapters, it is worth stressing that we do not over-report protest events focusing on economic issues. Furthermore, although we find differences related to the action repertoires – more violent events and strikes in the international news – as well as the actors – fewer actors are reported in the international news these biases are not systematic across the different data sources. Hence, although we have to conclude that our data differ from datasets based on annotation of the national press, the differences are due to the different sources chosen for the annotation and, if at all, will lead to underestimation of the correlations and effects in the following chapters.

In general, our findings pertain to the quality of our data. Our choice of sources – international news publishing in English – does not bias the data in important ways. Moreover, our data generation process conveys more precise information than other datasets that are available for as many as thirty countries and as many as fifteen years. Of course, we must remain alert for potential biases in the following chapters.

Our data collection is only an approximation of the reality of contentious politics, and, after all, its quality crucially relies on the limited attention that news agencies devote to political protests (Andrews and Caren 2010). Hence, a certain number of events as well as some information on the events identified is surely missing in our dataset. In general, however, we are confident that the data provide enough robust evidence to draw more empirically substantial conclusions in the subsequent analyses. Most importantly, we have not found biases that would lead to an over-valuation of the main arguments of the book.

Part II

Trends of Protest in the Great Recession

4 Overall Trends of Protest in the Great Recession

Hanspeter Kriesi

Crisis like the Great Recession can be viewed in two ways (Kahler and Lake 2013) – as moments of great uncertainty, i.e. as unstable situations of great danger and punctuations of a pre-existing equilibrium, or as turning points which give rise to changes in the overall direction of the regime and replace the old equilibrium by a new one. If it is too early to tell whether the Great Recession was a turning point in the second sense of the term, it certainly was a crisis in the first sense – a moment of great instability and uncertainty. Even if it did not fundamentally reorient the political trajectories of European countries, as a moment of great uncertainty it opened up a window of opportunity for political agency in general and for mobilization of protests in particular. This chapter asks about the overall development of political protest in this moment of uncertainty. Has this profound economic crisis given rise to a wave of protests across Europe? Did the collapse of Lehman Brothers constitute a historical triggering event that unleashed a massive wave of protest mobilization in the different parts of Europe? Did the Great Recession see a sequence of collective mobilization of protests of unprecedented proportions? This chapter gives a first answer to these questions by presenting the overall trends of protest across Europe from 2000 to 2015. We shall present the data in three steps: for Europe as a whole, for the three regions of Europe: north-western Europe (NEW), southern Europe (SE), and central and eastern Europe (CEE), and for the thirty individual countries covered by our study.

We know that political protest is 'highly unequally distributed across time and space, and that much of it is concentrated in intense waves of contention with a broad scope in geographical and social space' (Koopmans 2004: 40). Protest waves as periods of intense and widespread contention are characteristic for times of crisis. While political protest is rare and intermittent in normal times, in times of crisis, uncertainty and contingency are likely to give rise to positive feedback processes, i.e. endogenous processes of reinforcement and suppression that spread protest across time and space (see Biggs 2003; Koopmans 1993, 1995; Tarrow 1994, 1989).

In the Great Recession, all European countries were initially hit by the economic crisis. In a short period lasting roughly up to the end of 2009, we shall call it the 'shock period', governments countered the economic impact of the crisis by relying on some version of 'liberal' (Pontusson and Raess 2012) or 'emergency Keynesianism' (Hall 2013). However, with the Euro crisis, which started to evolve soon after the beginning of 2010, all European governments reverted to austerity measures. As austerity became the only game in town (Hall 2013), it met with widespread opposition among the populations of different countries. Moreover, during the Euro crisis, all countries of the eurozone were involved in the management of the crisis as either debtor or creditor countries, and the populations of the debtor countries in particular were confronted with similar challenges in the course of this crisis. The similarity of conditions and the interconnectedness of the European countries in the crisis are likely to have contributed to similar reactions in terms of political protest, which may have led to a wave-like character of protest across Europe.

However, we also know that political protest responds to highly contingent stimuli. From this perspective, it is important to keep in mind that the economic crisis hit the countries to a varying extent – the countries in the north-west of Europe were generally hit much less than the countries in the south and in the east of Europe. Moreover, the countries in the north-west and in the east of Europe recovered much faster from their original setback than the countries in the south of Europe. In addition, the political conditions under which the crisis hit the national economy varied from one country to the other, as did the packages of policy measures that were adopted to counter the effects of the crisis. Austerity may have become the only game in town, but the game played out very differently in the different parts of Europe. Thus, even if European decisions such as imposing a bailout with drastic conditions for the national economic policy constituted the ultimate triggering event of a series of protests in several national contexts, the impact of such decisions has been filtered by domestic politics, and political protest has ended up targeting domestic authorities just as much as European decision-makers. Small, local events may have large consequences, depending on the reaction of other actors in the particular context. While similar conditions may stimulate the parallel rise of protest in different countries at one and the same time, and while processes of diffusion from one country to another may contribute to the wave-like character of contention across Europe, it is more likely that the stimuli that unleash a sequence of protest are of a highly specific national and even local origin. In the final analysis, protest is organized in specific localities, about specific issues, against specific targeted actors who react in specific ways. The pattern of interaction that develops in such specific locations is typically highly context dependent and the dynamics of the corresponding contentious episodes are determined more by these local conditions than by the context of an overall wave. Based on these considerations, we do not expect the same wave-like pattern of protest to have occurred across all three regions, nor across all the countries of Europe. We much rather expect to find waves of protest at the regional, or even more so at the country level. As this chapter will show, these expectations are indeed borne out by the data.

In spatial terms, our unit of analysis in the present study is the country. The nation-state constitutes the setting where the contingent events take place that are giving rise to the collective mobilization of political protest covered by our sources – international and national newswires. Given that such newswires are not very sensitive to local or regional events and focus mainly on important events at the national level, we make virtue out of necessity and focus on the individual countries and not on sub-national units. There is one exception. In addition to our thirty countries – the 27 EU members before the accession of Croatia in 2013, as well as Iceland, Norway, and Switzerland – we also include Northern Ireland as a separate unit of analysis. Although not a separate country, for our purposes it is important to distinguish Northern Ireland from the rest of the UK, because the 'troubles' in this part of Britain follow their own dynamics, which would not become apparent if we did not treat it separately. One might argue that for similar reasons, it would also have been advisable to treat Catalonia and the Basque country separately. But we considered these two cases of regional separatism as less self-contained than the case of Northern Ireland and therefore did not treat them as separate units of analysis.

In terms of time, our unit of analysis in the present chapter is the month. This means that we aggregate the protest events and their characteristics for each region and country to monthly figures. For the 16 years from 2000 to 2015 there are 192 months, which are roughly evenly divided by the collapse of Lehman Brothers in September 2008 into the period before the crisis and the crisis period. For our analysis, we shall, however, not only distinguish between pre-crisis and post-crisis periods. Instead, we shall break down the period covered into four sub-periods:

- The 'pre-crisis period' running from January 2001 to September 2008
- The 'shock period' covering the initial period after the 'historical event' of the collapse of Lehman Brothers from October 2008 up to and including January 2010
- The 'Euro-crisis period' lasting from February 2010 (the beginning of the troubles in Greece) up to and including July 2015 (the Greek referendum on the third bailout)
- The short period of the 'refugee crisis' covering the last five months of 2015

The distinction between the 'shock period' and the 'Euro-crisis period' seems obvious, although one might take issue with our decision to have the Euro-crisis period end only in summer 2015. Another option might have been to let this period end with the ratification of the renewed Stability and Growth Pact in the first half of 2012 (see Kriesi and Grande 2016). Our choice of July 2015 is based on the long drawn out repercussions of the Euro crisis in SE, which reached another climax with the Greek referendum in summer 2015. In summer 2015, however, Europe experienced not only the climax of the Greek referendum, but also the beginning of what came to be known as the 'refugee crisis', which definitely shifted public attention away from the implications of the Great Recession and marks, for our purposes, the end of the Euro-crisis period.

4.1 The Mobilization of Protest across Europe, 2000–2015

We begin by presenting the development of the pattern of protest at the most aggregate level, i.e. the European level. We first present the pattern based on the number of events, and then the one based on the intensity of protest. Our basic indicator for the mobilization of protest will be its frequency, i.e. the *number of events* per month. Let us just briefly recall that we use a weighted indicator for the number of events, which takes into account the varying country-specific sampling probabilities, the (log of the) population of the different countries, as well as the presence of national English-speaking news agencies in a given country (see Chapter 2). Although we do not achieve full comparability between countries, we introduce these weights to make the country-specific mobilization levels as comparable as possible.

To arrive at the indicator for the number of events at the European level, we have simply averaged the weighted number of monthly events across countries. Figure 4.1 presents the development of the number of monthly protest events for the whole of Europe across the period covered. The collapse of Lehman Brothers in September 2008, which marks the beginning of the Great Recession, is indicated by a vertical dashed line. The figure presents the overall development across Europe

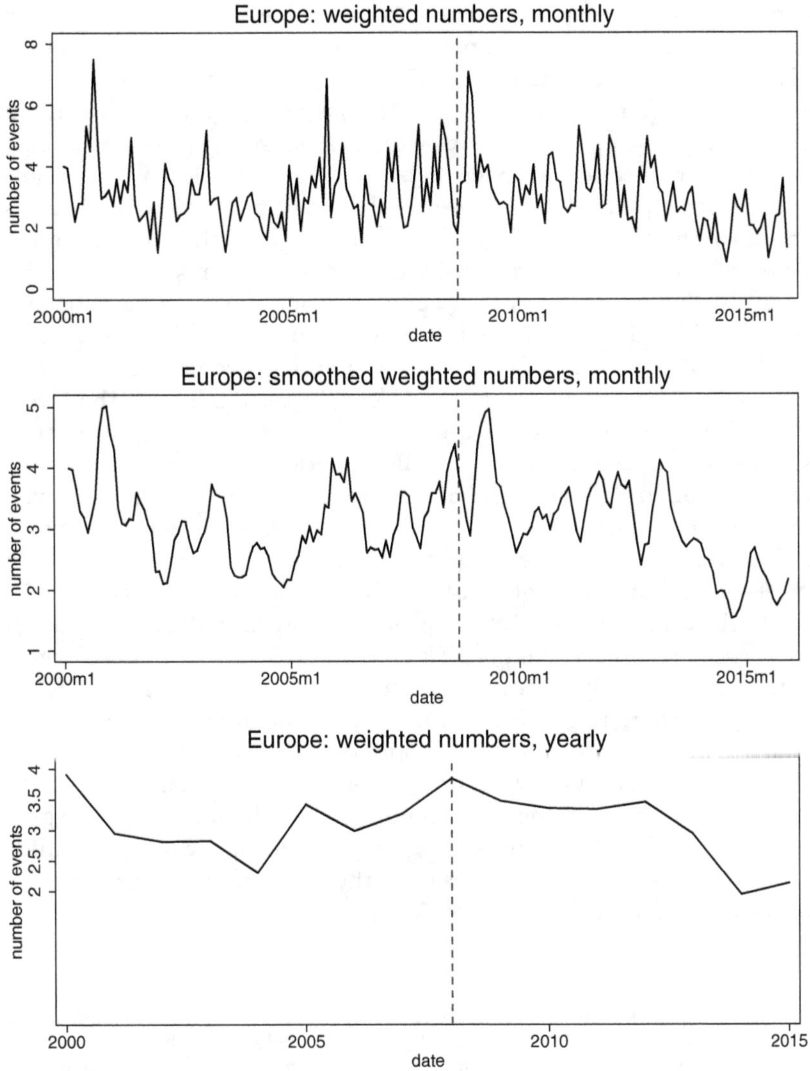

Figure 4.1 Number of events across Europe, 2000–2015.

in three ways: first as a raw monthly count, then using 5-monthly moving averages (which, as we have seen in Chapter 3, provide an optimal pattern), and finally as yearly counts.

From this figure, three points become immediately apparent. First, monthly European protest events follow a rather jagged pattern. Even when we apply moving averages to obtain a smoother development, the resulting pattern is still anything but smooth. To be sure, this jagged pattern is partly a result of our sources: As we have seen in Chapter 3, the international newswires mainly pay attention to highly visible events, neglecting the build-up and decline of mobilization before and after such events. But the jagged pattern also confirms the notion that protest responds to local stimuli, which are highly variable across time and space. Second, there is no clearly discernible trend in this pattern. The ups and downs of protest proceed across the entire period covered and there is no break at the moment of the onset of the Great Recession. In the technical terms of time-series analysis, the pattern of protest across Europe proves to be quite stationary.[1] Nor did the Great Recession lead to a lasting increase in the level of protest across Europe. If anything, we witness a decline in protest towards the end of the Great Recession. Third, the Great Recession does seem to have given rise to two waves of protest, a short one that characterizes the shock period immediately after the fall of Lehman Brothers, and a second, more drawn out and less visible one that marks the Euro-crisis period. There were also two or three short waves during the pre-crisis period. These waves become most visible for the smoothed monthly numbers, which correct for the build-up and the decline of protest before and after the peaks of the waves. The yearly counts pick up the same waves, but if we aggregate the number of protests to entire years, the waves appear to be moving much more gently and they seem to be much less impressive. Indeed, in the European 'movement societies' (Meyer and Tarrow 1998), there is always a basic stock of protest that remains fairly constant across time. Taking into account this basic overall level of protest, what is most striking is the long drawn out wave that builds up in the pre-crisis period, peaks in the shock period, and subsides towards the end of the Euro crisis.

[1] This is confirmed by the result of the Dickey–Fuller test for the raw data series, which takes a value of −8.931 (−5.216 for the smoothed series), which is statistically highly significant and indicates that the series of protest (as well as the smoothed series) at the European level is, indeed, stationary.

4.1.1 *The Intensity of Protest*

As we have already pointed out in Chapter 2, in addition to the frequency of protests, the literature also uses other types of indicators for measuring the importance of collective action. Thus, we have introduced indicators for the size of protest (the number of participants) and for the radicalness of protest (the degree to which it is violent and/or confrontational). The frequency and radicalness of protest are closely related ($r = 0.81$ for the raw data/0.83 for the smoothed data), as both are based on the count of events, but also because violent and confrontational events are quite numerous in our dataset – respectively they account for 8.4 and 20.1 per cent of all the events. Not surprisingly, by contrast, size measures a very different aspect of protest than frequency. There are many small and few very large events, but the large events contribute most of the participants. Accordingly, the correlation between the monthly indicators of frequency and size is rather low ($r = 0.44$ and 0.55 respectively for raw and smoothed data). The correlation between radicalness and size is even lower ($r = 0.19$ and 0.28), which is not surprising either: Radical events are the preserve of small groups. However, while radicalness and size measure different aspects of protest, they both have in common that they increase its newsworthiness and indicate unusual intensity (Koopmans 1995: 149ff.; Rochon 1990: 108). In fact, as we have argued in Chapter 2, we can combine the indicators for size and radicalness to a single indicator for the intensity of mobilization by adding up the standardized figures of each. This procedure implies that the resulting index is equally influenced by its two components. It measures whether an event is large or violent/confrontational or both.

Figure 4.2 presents the development of participation (size), radicalness, and intensity across Europe. In each case, we add the frequency pattern (in dashed lines) for comparative purposes. With respect to participation, three points are important. First, we find once more a jagged pattern, even for participation measured in moving averages as is the case here. Second, there is again no clearly discernible trend in this pattern. The ups and downs of protest proceed across the entire period covered and there is no break at the moment of the onset of the Great Recession. Third, however, there is a discernible difference between the size and the frequency pattern with respect to the waves. Thus, the most sizeable wave in terms of participation occurred in 2003, long before the Great Recession set in. It is linked to the European-wide mobilization against the Iraq war. The peak we found in the shock period for the number of events, however, is not visible at all in terms of

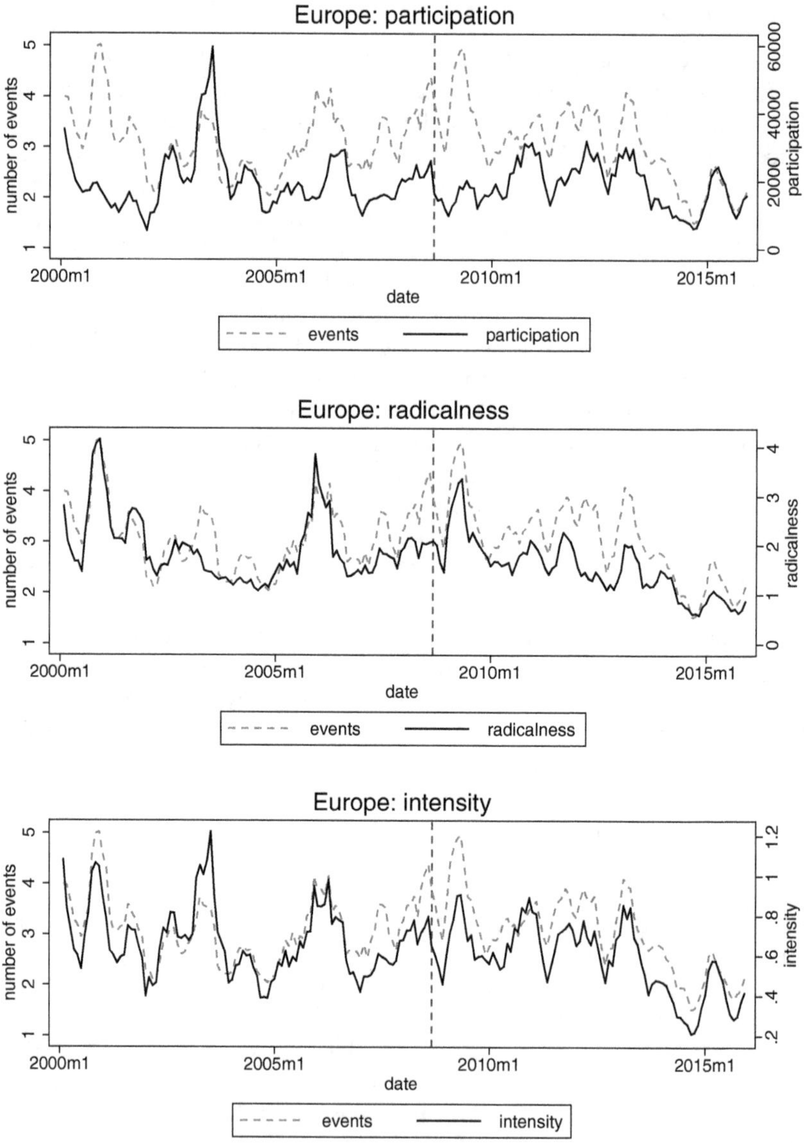

Figure 4.2 Intensity of the events across Europe, 2000–2015: smoothed indicators for size, radicalness, and intensity.

size, which suggests that the initial shock of the Great Recession gave rise to a large number of relatively small events.

The second part of the figure shows that size and radicalness develop quite differently over time. While size peaks in 2003 and fluctuates otherwise more or less randomly, there are three clearly discernible peaks in terms of radicalness – two occur in the pre-crisis period, while one coincides with the shock period. Moreover, this part of the figure indicates that radicalness followed a declining trend throughout the Euro-crisis period – a remarkable result which will be analysed in more detail in Chapter 5. A more detailed analysis shows that the three peaks in radicalness depend on three countries only, which vividly documents the importance of country-specific context conditions. The early peak in the year 2000 is mostly the result of the combined violence linked to regionalism in Spain (Euskadi Ta Askatasuna [ETA]) and Northern Ireland (the 'troubles'). The 2005 peak is related to Northern Ireland in particular: In January 2005, the murder of a Catholic, Robert McCartney, in a Belfast bar by the IRA led to a campaign initiated by the victim's sisters, which, among other events, greatly contributed to the extraordinary radicalness of protest in Northern Ireland over the following months. By contrast, the third peak of violence, the one in the shock period, is almost entirely attributable to Greece, where extreme violence broke out in the aftermath of the shooting of a teenager by the police in December 2009, even before the highly confrontational mobilization against austerity measures started to pick up in early 2010. Figure 4.3 illustrates the very specific development of radicalness in these three countries.

The pattern for intensity, finally, is a mixture of the patterns for size and radicalness: It picks up both the peaks of participation and the peaks of radicalness. It resembles the frequency pattern more closely than the patterns of its components, which is reflected in its close correlation with the monthly frequency of events (participation: $r = 0.81$ and radicalness: 0.88).

4.2 Regional Patterns

As discussed in the introduction, we shall distinguish between three European regions: NWE, SE, and CEE. We shall present the same two indicators for frequency and intensity for each one of the three regions. Similarly to what we did at the European level, in calculating these indicators we take the average across the countries in a given region. This implies that small countries (e.g. Malta or Cyprus) contribute equally to the regional pattern as large countries (e.g. Italy or Spain).

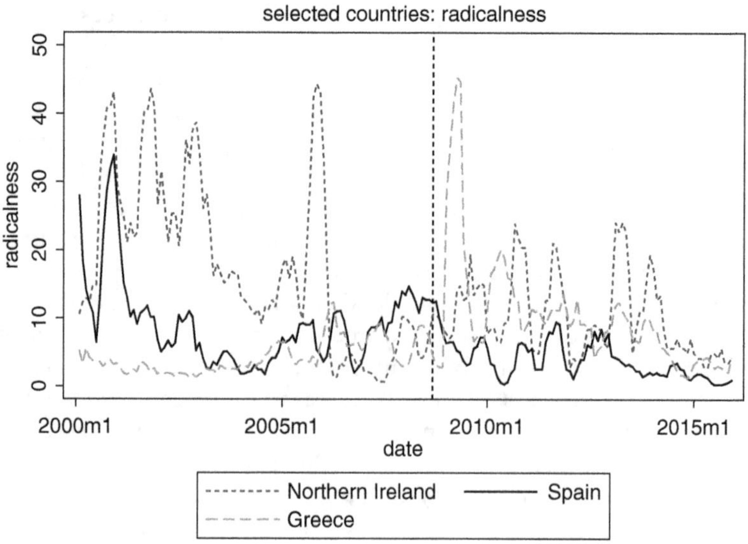

Figure 4.3 The development of radicalness in three selected countries: Northern Ireland, Spain, and Greece, 2000–2015.

What we show is an average national pattern for each region. We only present the 5-monthly moving averages.

As we can see from Figure 4.4, protest develops quite differently in the three regions across the period covered. Except for the fact that the number of protest events peaks in every region during the shock period in the immediate aftermath of the collapse of Lehman Brothers the regional patterns clearly differ from each other. In NWE, protest peaks in the early 2000s with an early wave in 2000, the wave around the Iraq war mobilizations in 2003, and a wave in fall 2005/spring 2006. These peaks are linked to events we have already discussed, but additional events in other countries contributed to them as well. Thus, in addition to events in Northern Ireland, French events significantly contributed to the last pre-crisis wave. First, suburban riots broke out in fall 2005 in France which led to the declaration of a state of emergency. Then, in spring 2006, massive demonstrations mobilized students against the labour market reform of the de Villepin government (le Contrat première embauche). The pre-crisis peak of protest in 2005–2006 was never reached again in NWE during the entire crisis period. After the shock period, the Great Recession did not make much difference

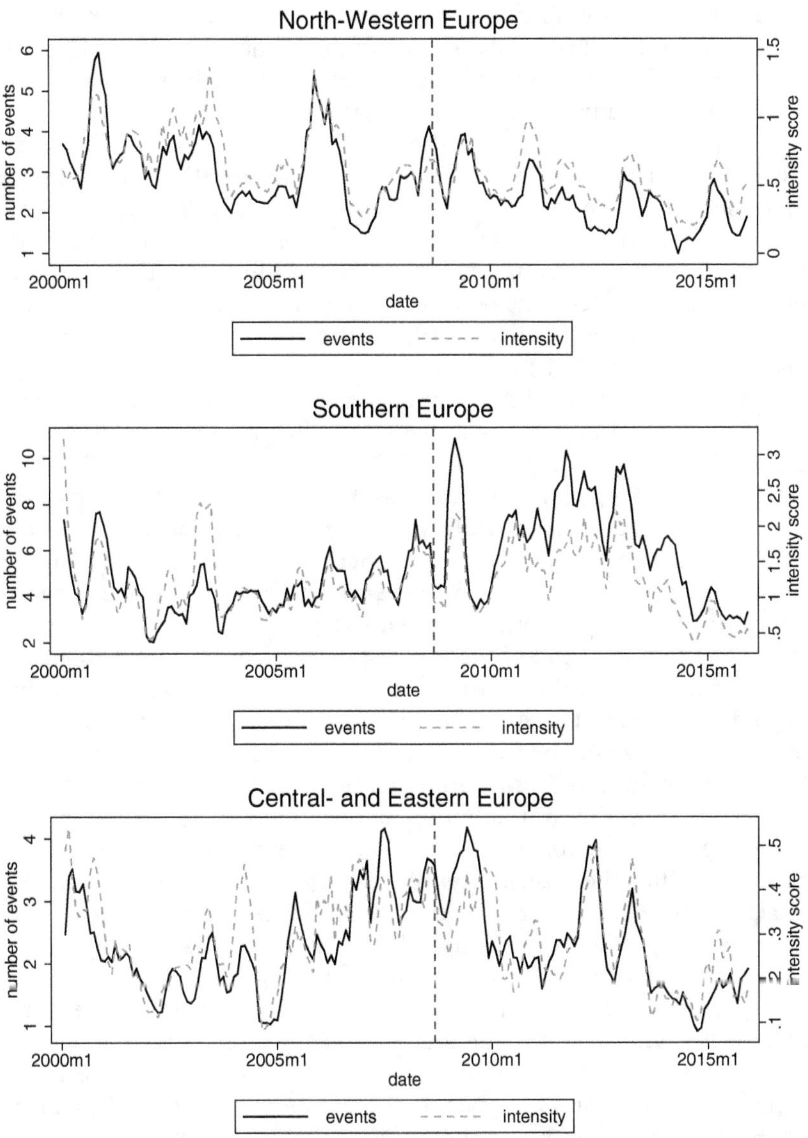

Figure 4.4 Number of events and intensity per region, smoothed monthly data, 2000–2015.

in terms of the overall number of events or their intensity in NWE. Throughout the Euro-crisis period, protest follows a declining trend in this part of Europe, and it picks up again only at the very end of the period covered, during the refugees' crisis.

The pattern in SE is very different. Contrary to NWE, the Great Recession did give rise to massive protest waves in SE. Protest already increased in the run-up to the crisis and it peaked for the first time during the shock period, as we shall see above all as a result of a series of very intense protests in 2008/9 in Greece. Moreover, there is a sustained wave of protest during the Euro crisis in SE, which is interrupted only by a lull in the aftermath of the ratification of the revised Stability and Growth Pact (SGP) in summer 2012.

In CEE, the pattern is different once again: In this part of Europe we find an extended protest wave that spans the pre-crisis and the shock period. It takes off in 2005 and peaks four times – in fall 2006, in 2007, 2008, and 2009 – before it subsides at the beginning of the Euro crisis. These peaks had at first hardly anything to do with economic issues, but depended on country-specific political and cultural issues. Thus, in fall 2006, a series of massive anti-government protests organized by the opposition (Fidesz) swept through Hungary, after it had been leaked to the public that the head of the socialist government had lied about the state of the economy during the preceding election campaign. In spring 2007, Estonia experienced the worst crisis since its independence, when ethnic riots broke out because of the government's decision to remove a Soviet war memorial. In the fall of the same year, neighbouring Latvia saw the mobilization of the 'umbrella revolution' against the rampant corruption in the country, which forced the resignation of the government. In 2008, the Czech Republic was the site of widely publicized attacks against the Roma minority, of clashes between neo-Nazis and anarchists and of attacks against a US military radar site. Only during the shock period, protest increasingly turned against economic issues. Thus, Latvians mobilized massively against the austerity measures and the bailout by the International Monetary Fund (IMF) in January 2009, and the Czechs organized the biggest protests since the fall of communism against austerity and corruption in spring 2009. During the Euro crisis, we observe a shorter wave that is also interrupted in the aftermath of the ratification of the revised SGP.

To be better able to identify the waves at the regional level, we have created a 'wave index'. According to Hutter (2014: 68), there are four key components to a wave: It is characterized by an increasing and then decreasing number of interrelated collective actions and reactions, which extend over a longer period of time and include more than a single movement covering the whole territory, and it is transformative in terms of frames, issues, alliances, or identities. For our purposes, we use only the first two characteristics to identify the waves. At the regional level, our wave index simply corresponds to the moving average of the sum of the standardized number and intensity of events. To identify the larger picture, we extend the smoothing and take moving averages over the six months preceding and the six months following the month in question, also including the latter. Figure 4.5 presents the three regional developments in one single graph with a common scale.

From Figure 4.5, it becomes immediately apparent that, during the period covered, SE has been much more unruly than the other two regions. As a result, the overall European development is very much shaped by the development of protest in SE. In the pre-crisis period, the initial two peaks in 2000 and 2003, which are linked to regional violence and to the Iraq war, become visible both in SE and in NWE, while the third pre-crisis peak in 2005 is mainly due to NWE and to French events in particular. In SE, events peak for a first time at the moment when the Great Recession breaks out. Then, southern protest subsides to some extent, only to explode with the start of the Euro crisis and to reach unprecedented heights during this crisis. It peaks at the end of 2011 and starts its impressive decline in fall 2012 to reach its lowest level

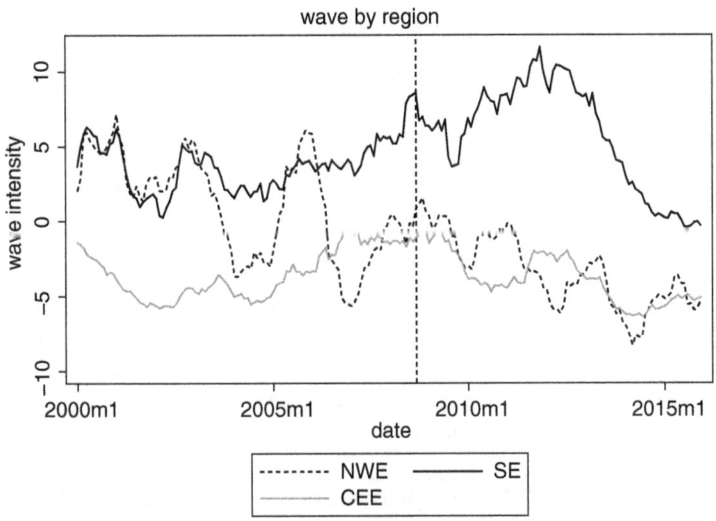

Figure 4.5 Wave intensity – across Europe and by region, extended smoothed monthly data, 2000–2015.

as in the other two regions by the end of 2015. The sustained wave of protest during the Euro crisis in SE is the clearest example of a protest wave at the regional level. In the other two regions, we can identify a wave in NWE which extends from 2005 to 2006, and an extended wave in CEE that starts its rise in 2005 and, after having reached an extended plateau, begins to decline in 2009. As we have already seen, this wave is at first not at all or only indirectly related to economic problems, but it becomes more closely intertwined with the economic crisis once the shock of the Great Recession hits the respective countries.

If the overall European development is very much shaped by the developments in SE, the overall development in SE is very much dependent on the events in Greece. This is shown by Figure 4.6, which presents the wave intensity for SE without Greece and compares it to the wave intensity in Greece. With the exception of the summer 2012, the weighted protest in Greece was more intense than in all the other countries of SE taken together during the entire crisis period. The early peak of protest in SE during the shock period is entirely due to Greece. While Greece has experienced a prolonged period of protest that lasts more or less uninterruptedly from fall 2008 to at least the end of 2012, in the rest of SE the protest wave started to take off only with the beginning of the Euro crisis in early 2010 and it dropped off more rapidly than

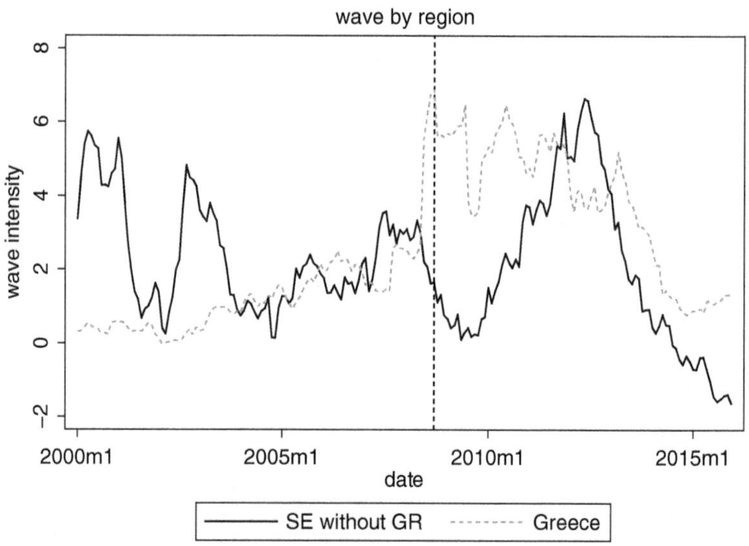

Figure 4.6 Wave intensity – in southern Europe, Greece versus the other countries, extended smoothed monthly data, 2000–2015.

in Greece after it had peaked in summer 2012. Figure 4.6 documents perhaps most strikingly the exceptional case of Greece. Within Greece, December 2008 was exceptional again. This is the month with the maximum number of events and maximum intensity in a single country during the entire period. On 6 December 2008, riots broke out in Greece after a fifteen-year-old student had been killed by two special officers in the Exarcheia district of central Athens. The killing of the young student resulted in large protests and demonstrations, which escalated into widespread *rioting*. From Athens, demonstrations and rioting soon spread to several other cities. It may be important to recognize that this event occurred before the economic crisis hit Greece in earnest.

Most scholarly accounts of the Greek events focus on the 2010–2012 period and typically treat it as a single unit (Aslanidis and Marantzidis 2016; Diani and Kousis 2014; Kanellopoulos et al. 2017; Karyotis and Rüdig 2018; Petropoulos 2014). However, following Altiparmakis (2019b), we can break down this period into three phases. The first phase is the 2010 wave, which consisted mostly of protests from the 'usual suspects' of unions and the radical left. The massive protests of this phase were narrowly focused on economic issues and spearheaded by traditional actors. The next wave of protest occurred in summer 2011, when the Greek Indignados made their appearance and semi-spontaneous, peaceful demonstrations occurred in all major urban centres. This phase is marked by much more innovative protest forms, such as the occupation of the Parliament square and repeated verbal and physical attacks on politicians. In this phase, the claims against the bailout became fused with grievances against the political class. The third phase covers the period October 2011–February 2012 and is a continuation of the previous protest waves but, as Altiparmakis (2019b) shows, is also characterized by the intensification of low-level union action and the spillover of protest into uncharted terrains.

We can analyse the regional data with simple time-series models. For each one of the three regions, we have a panel of 192 months, in total 576 observations. The dependent variables in these models are based on the averages of the weighted monthly events and intensity (averaged over the countries of a given region). The models include one and two period lags of the dependent variable for the number of events and one period lags only for intensity,[2] as well as a time-trend and one dummy variable for each one of the relevant periods – the initial shock period

[2] The best ARIMA model has two lags for each region in the case of the number of events and one lag for each region in the case of intensity.

and the Euro-crisis period (with the pre-crisis period as reference category) – and regions – SE and CEE (with NWE as reference category). We estimate a baseline model including these independent variables, as well as a second model allowing for region-specific developments in the three periods of interest. In addition, we also estimate a third model that takes into account the exceptional character of the Greek case. This third model will show to what extent Greek is really different and to what extent SE is different from the other regions once we control for the case of Greece. The models are estimated with ordinary least squares (OLS) regressions.[3] The results are presented in Table 4.1.

The baseline model for the frequencies (model 1) confirms that protest events were generally more numerous in SE as well as during the first period in the crisis – the shock period. As we have seen previously, during the shock period, protest events increased across all three regions, even if there was a real wave only in SE. However, we do not find a similar general increase for the Euro-crisis period. Allowing for region-specific developments in the number of events (model 2), we find that protest events were, indeed, particularly numerous in SE both during the shock period and during the period of the Euro crisis, but not in the other two regions. In terms of intensity (models 4 and 5), SE sticks out, too, but in this respect only during the Euro crisis, when protest in SE was particularly intense. By contrast, protest in CEE countries turns out to be least intense, not only less intense than in SE, but also significantly less intense than in NWE. In terms of intensity, we also find a long-term trend of decreasing intensity, which reflects the already observed decline in radicalness over time. Finally, note that the effects of the lagged dependent variables are of very limited size, even if they are highly significant in the case of the number of events, and somewhat significant in the case of intensity. This means that the effects of protest in terms of frequency and intensity carry over only to a limited extent from one month to the next. The same is true if we analyse the data at the national level. This confirms the notion that protest is a reaction to highly context-specific conditions and hardly diffuses across the countries of a given region.

The additional models (models 3 and 6) taking into account the special case of Greece show that Greece is, indeed, special. Once we

[3] Given that we are dealing with count data in the case of the frequency models, the appropriate estimation method would have been a negative binomial regression. However, because the results of the two estimation methods are virtually identical and the OLS results are easier to interpret, we report OLS results only.

Table 4.1. *Development of protest per region, number of events, and intensity (OLS-regression coefficients and t-values)*

	Number of events			Intensity		
	(1)	(2)	(3)	(4)	(5)	(6)
L.DV	0.298***	0.254***	0.219***	0.111**	0.095*	0.125***
	(7.150)	(6.041)	(6.014)	(2.671)	(2.274)	(3.464)
L2.DV	0.164***	0.122**	0.060			
	(3.951)	(2.889)	(1.660)			
Trend	−0.003	−0.003	−0.003	−0.002*	−0.002**	−0.002
	(−1.234)	(−1.465)	(−0.530)	(−2.580)	(−2.640)	(−1.099)
Shock	0.781*	0.166	0.141	0.188	0.008	0.005
	(2.453)	(0.327)	(0.089)	(1.948)	(0.051)	(0.013)
Euro crisis	0.412	−0.279	−0.377	0.146	−0.019	−0.024
	(1.457)	(−0.769)	(−0.347)	(1.702)	(−0.168)	(−0.086)
South	1.352***	0.792**	0.564	0.503***	0.360***	0.293
	(6.014)	(3.073)	(0.716)	(7.964)	(4.557)	(1.455)
CEE	−0.227	−0.462	−0.535	−0.300***	−0.373***	−0.361
	(−1.180)	(−1.832)	(−0.680)	(−4.999)	(−4.735)	(−1.789)
Greece			2.110**			0.322
			(2.648)			(1.595)
Shock_CEE		0.615	0.718		0.171	0.166
		(0.883)	(0.328)		(0.795)	(0.294)
Shock_SE		1.502*	−0.169		0.378	−0.137
		(2.145)	(−0.077)		(1.752)	(−0.243)

Table 4.1 *(cont.)*

	Number of events			Intensity		
	(1)	(2)	(3)	(4)	(5)	(6)
Euro_CEE		0.425	0.493		0.154	0.149
		(1.044)	(0.386)		(1.231)	(0.456)
Euro_SE		1.874***	1.152		0.350**	0.138
		(4.318)	(0.900)		(2.770)	(0.420)
Shock_Greece			11.020***			3.028***
			(4.860)			(5.273)
Euro_Greece			6.138***			1.205***
			(4.577)			(3.632)
Constant	1.524***	2.099***	2.390***	0.670***	0.756***	0.727***
	(6.120)	(7.407)	(3.444)	(9.464)	(9.718)	(4.150)
Observations	570	570	760	573	573	764
AIC	2333.63	2320.13	4839.34	990.27	989.12	2786.56
BIC	2368.39	2372.28	4908.84	1020.72	1036.98	2851.50
R^2	0.41	0.43	0.40	0.32	0.33	0.26

Significance levels: $^{*}p = 0.05$, $^{**}p = 0.01$, $^{***}p = 0.001$.

control for the case of Greece during the two periods in question, all the period-specific effects for SE vanish. By contrast, all interaction effects for Greece are highly significant. In other words, the specificity of SE during the shock-period and during the Euro crisis is largely due to the especially intense protests in Greece.

4.3 Country-Specific Development of Protest

In addition to Greece, we find some pronounced waves in some other countries. The selective existence of such waves at the country level confirms the expectation that the impact of the Great Recession is filtered by country-specific conditions, that protest reacts to context-specific stimuli and that there is only a limited diffusion of protest from one country to the other. Based on the wave index, Figure 4.7 presents the development across the period covered for twenty-one out of the thirty-one countries. The graphs present weighted yearly data of the wave index, which are smoothed so as to bring out a possible wave-like character of the development at the country level. We shall describe these patterns in some detail to give the reader an idea of the country-specific factors that contributed to the developmental patterns in the different contexts.

The first row of graphs refers to NWE countries, the second and third rows refer to countries of SE and CEE. Let us first consider NWE. The first sub-graph describes two countries with a clear-cut wave – France and Great Britain – as well as three small countries – Ireland, Iceland, and Denmark, two of which did experience a wave, too. Confirming our previous interpretations, we find a clear-cut pre-crisis wave in France which spans 2005 and 2006. We have already described this wave previously, as it decisively contributed to the shape of the NWE pattern during this period. During the crisis, there is a small resurgence of protest in France, which is related to the mobilization against Sarkozy's pension reform and which took place in fall 2010. This reform was part of the first package of austerity measures introduced by the French government. It consisted mainly of the proposal to increase the normal retirement age for public pensions from sixty-five to sixty-seven and the anticipated retirement age from sixty to sixty-two. The main challengers were the major French labour unions, which asked for the modification or withdrawal of the reform at all stages of the decision-making process and finally tried to prevent the signature of the Presidential Decree. They mobilized in the form of large-scale demonstrations and strikes. Strikes were first organized in the public sector, but in October the challenger coalition extended

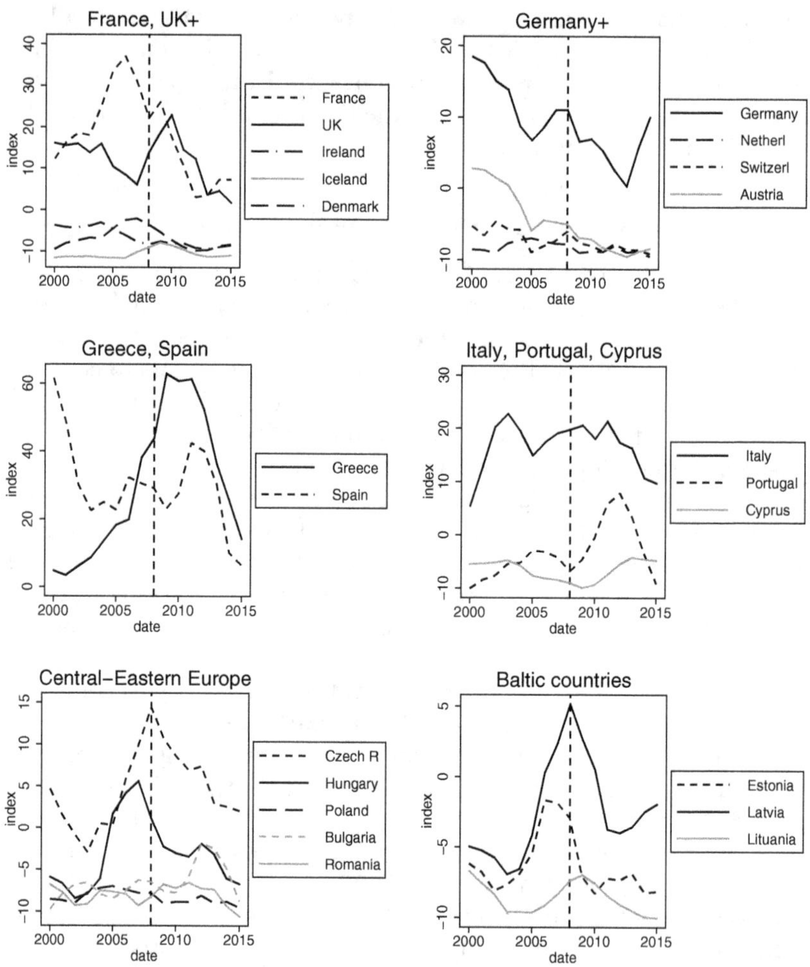

Figure 4.7 The development of protest at the country level: wave index, yearly values.

to and covered other sectors as well such as student unions and high school students, who organized blockades. The action repertoire of the challengers became more radical with the multiplication of unlimited strikes, in particular in oil refineries and garbage collection centres, leading to an important gasoline shortage and to the piling up of garbage in the streets in several cities. The government repeatedly rejected all the demands of the protesters, in a way that was considered by many as an abuse of power. When the law was finally enacted, the labour unions stopped to call for demonstrations and the challenger coalition fell apart. As we see from the graph, after this specific mobilization, which did not reach the previous pre-crisis levels anyway, France seems to have demobilized.

The British wave of protest is one of only two clear-cut protest waves related to the economic crisis in NWE. It was a reaction to the austerity program of the new Conservative government in 2010 and 2011. In fall 2010, it was mainly students who protested against the spending cuts in higher education, while large demonstrations turned against the government's spending cuts more generally in 2011. Thus, in 2011 London saw the largest demonstrations since the anti-Iraq war protest in 2003 and the largest union-organized rally since World War II.

Compared to these two large countries, all Scandinavian countries generally have seen very low levels of protest. Except for Iceland, protest hardly reacted at all to the economic crisis in this region. In addition to the United Kingdom, Iceland is the only other NWE country with a clear-cut protest wave during the Great Recession, but given its small size, this wave is barely visible in Figure 4.6. Iceland was, arguably, the first country to have taken the full hit of the crisis. Its three banks collapsed and had to be nationalized already in October 2008. At the same time, its economy imploded. In November 2008, it had to be bailed out by the IMF and thus became the first western European country since 1976 to receive an IMF loan. The country had to take drastic austerity measures to arrive at fiscal consolidation in the medium term. As the economic crisis deepened and thousands began losing their jobs, public anger grew. Public outcry at the failure of politicians and officials to accept responsibility for the crisis reached its peak in January 2009 when the Parliament assembled after the Christmas holiday. For Iceland, the protest wave was massive and violence reached a level never seen before in Icelandic politics (Hardarson and Kristinsson 2010: 1011). On 20 January, a mob of riotous protesters pounded on the walls of Iceland's parliament building, denouncing the government for its incompetence. The riot, which involved some 2,000 demonstrators, was only the beginning of a sequence of events that had a major impact on Icelandic politics.

Denmark, the other Scandinavian country portrayed in the figure, saw a protest wave, too, but like the French wave it took place in the pre-crisis period, as a combined result of the so-called Danish cartoon crisis (which led to large-scale Muslim demonstrations abroad and to the boycott of Danish goods by Arab countries) and of mobilization related to a youth centre in Copenhagen.

Although it was also hit very hard by the economic crisis, Ireland did not experience a protest wave. This does not mean that the Irish public did not protest in reaction to the economic crisis. Thus, in February 2009, the imposition of a 'pension levy' on all public servants as the main plank of the recovery plan triggered a one-day strike by civil servants, the first industrial action of its kind in Ireland in almost twenty years, and a huge demonstration with about 100,000 participants in Dublin. Protesting continued in fall 2009, with thousands of workers around the country taking to the streets in a series of marches in early November to protest against proposed government cuts in pay and services. November 2009 also saw the largest student protest for a generation taking place outside the Dail in Dublin. Finally, one year later, in November 2010, when Ireland became the third western European country after Iceland and Greece to have to accept a rescue package from the European Union and the IMF to recapitalize its banks and meet the government's budget, one of the largest demonstrations in the history of the Irish Republic brought more than one hundred thousand people onto Dublin's streets in protest over the bailout and four years of austerity ahead. However, these protests remained isolated events, had no impact at all, and what rather characterizes Ireland in contrast to Iceland is the ensuing stoic resignation of the hard-hit population.

By contrast, Northern Ireland (not shown in the graph because the extreme size of its protest would dwarf protest in all the other countries) saw a very intense protest wave which peaked in the early 2000s, and then again a more contained wave during the Great Recession. Both of these waves were, however, almost exclusively focused on the very specific 'troubles' in this part of the United Kingdom and did not in any way react to the Great Recession.

The second sub-graph for NWE presents the development of protest in Germany and in three of its neighbouring countries – Austria, the Netherlands, and Switzerland – all of which got amazingly well through the Great Recession. In line with the benign development of the economic crisis, we do not find any sign of a protest wave in these countries. In Germany and Austria, protest almost linearly declines from a comparatively high level in the early 2000s, while the protest curves remain rather flat at a very low level in both the Netherlands and Switzerland. We should point out that in Germany, protest resumed after the end of the Great Recession, in late 2014, with the mobilization of Pegida, and, more importantly, with the intervention of the refugee crisis in summer 2015, which led not only to an enormous increase in the frequency of events, but also to an increase of violent events in particular.

Turning to the countries of SE, which are presented in the second row of Figure 4.7, we find that four out of the six countries experienced a wave of protest during the crisis. As we already know from the previous analysis, it is Greece which has produced the ultimate protest wave, a wave that started already in the early 2000s, accelerated in spring 2008, peaked in 2010–2012, and then declined until summer 2015. It has been said that Greece has a 'deep-rooted culture of resistance' of which protesting, rioting and resisting authority formed a part (see Andronikidou and Kovras 2012). Note, however, that Greece's level of protest was quite average at the beginning of the millennium (close to 0, which is the overall average value), and that it reached such levels again after the extended wave. The finding of Rüdig and Karyotis (2014) that previous protest involvement was the most important predictor of participation in the 2010 protests in Greece does not necessarily point to the existence of such a 'deep-rooted culture of resistance' either, but rather to the fact that the wave had already reached an impressive level before the start of the Euro crisis in 2010, and that, accordingly, protest experience was widespread because of the opportunities of protest provided by the earlier stages of the wave, which, as we have already seen, were not directly related to the economic crisis, but were triggered by the killing of a young student. To be sure, the protest in the crisis period was accentuated in Greece, but it was essentially a continuation and intensification of protests that were already underway at very high levels before the crisis. As we shall see in later chapters, the very impressive proportions of the Greek protest wave can be explained as a reaction to the double economic and political crisis, which hit Greece more severely than any other European country during the Great Recession.

The other three SE waves occurred during the Euro crisis. The Spanish wave was shorter and mostly visible in terms of intensity. It took off in spring 2011, when the Indignados burst on the scene, and it peaked in 2012, under the new government led by the Partido Popular that had come to power in fall 2011. Spain is a high protest country and, compared to the experience in the early 2000s, when it was hit by ETA violence, the mobilization related to the Indignados looks less impressive than the Greek wave. Also note the very strong demobilization of Spanish protesters at the end of the Great Recession. Spanish protest fell to unprecedentedly low levels by 2015.[4] The Portuguese

[4] Portos-Garcia (2016: 54), who has manually coded protest events from Spanish newspapers, essentially finds the same wave for Spain, with the only difference that, according to his data, the level of protest was already quite low before the wave took off in 2011.

wave preceded the Spanish one, but it was much more limited and more moderate. As shown in the second sub-graph related to SE, it took off in 2010, at the beginning of the Portuguese financial crisis and peaked in 2012–2013. The 12 March 2011 demonstration, when 200,000 took to the streets in the name of Portugal's 'Desperate Generation' (Geração à Rasca), marked the beginning of the wave, which peaked with the largest demonstration two years later, organized by the Que se Lixe a Troika ('Fuck the Troika' – QLT) platform. After this peak, the frequency and intensity of protests declined (see Accornero and Ramos Pinto 2015). In Cyprus, there was also a minor wave which took off in 2011 and peaked after the bailout in 2013.

Malta and Italy are the exceptions without a protest wave in SE. Italy is characterized by a generally rather high level of protest, but while it experienced a series of intermittent crisis-related mobilizations, it did not see a clear-cut protest wave develop during the Great Recession. This is not for lack of trying. As a matter of fact, in the fall 2011, Italian activists tried to mobilize for a replication of the Indignados success in Italy. But, as Zamponi (2012) argues, what ought to have been the identity-providing big event, the 15 October demonstration, utterly failed. Zamponi invokes at least two reasons for this failure: First of all, the political context was unfavourable in the aftermath of the demonstration, because the focal point of the previous protest – the Prime Minister Silvio Berlusconi – disappeared with the fall of his government in mid-November 2011. The new government was strong and supported by a grand coalition including the centre-left and an air of 'national unity' prevailed in public opinion. Second, the timing of the big event had been badly chosen in the first place, because, at the time of its mobilization, the Italian activist scene had already been divided by previous processes of politicization and was not ready to build an encompassing coalition as the Indignados had successfully done.

Let us finally turn to the patterns of the CEE countries. In the first sub-graph, we present three Visegrad countries – the Czech Republic, Hungary, and Poland – plus two south-eastern countries – Bulgaria and Romania – while the second sub-graph refers to the Baltic countries. Two of the Visegrad countries – the Czech Republic and Hungary – experienced a protest wave, while Poland, a traditionally rather unruly country, did not.[5] The waves in Hungary and the Czech Republic have in common that they started out in the pre-crisis period and peaked either before the crisis or in the earliest stages of the crisis. Their origin was essentially related to political and cultural issues and the economic

[5] Nor did Slovakia or Slovenia, which are not shown in the graph.

crisis contributed to the wave only during its declining phase. The wave in the Czech Republic culminated in 2008 and the previously mentioned large-scale mobilizations against the government's austerity policies occurred in 2009, when the wave was already declining. In Hungary, as already mentioned, the wave took off after the 2006 elections and subsided in 2010 when Fidesz came to power. After the 2006 elections, the incumbent socialist prime minister Ferenc Gyurcsány, whose party had won the elections, admitted in a party meeting he had lied about the state of the country's economy during the election campaign. When his talk was leaked to the public, the reaction was immediate: The conservative opposition and the radical right started protesting and rioting at Parliament Square. Subsequently, the opposition under the leadership of Victor Orbán (Fidesz) launched no less than seven carefully framed referendum proposals. Against the backdrop of the very unpopular austerity measures, which the government had to adopt already before the global crisis, the opposition triumphed in the vote in March 2008 (Pallinger 2012). As the global crisis hit Hungary half a year later, the weakness of its economy became unsustainable, the government had to resort to an IMF bailout, and its fate was sealed. The much smaller wave of protest that followed during the Euro-crisis period corresponds to the mobilization by the opposition against Fidesz, now the governing party, and was equally politically motivated.

The first sub-graph also shows a smaller wave of protest for Bulgaria, a wave which refers mainly to two series of anti-government protest that occurred in summer and fall 2013, when the general public and later on the students took to the street on a daily basis to articulate their protest against the shady practices of two consecutive governments. The Polish exception can be accounted for by the fact that, as we have shown in Chapter 1, Poland got through the Great Recession exceptionally well. Indeed, in Poland, political satisfaction hit its lowest point before the crisis and actually increased throughout the crisis.

Turning to the second sub-graph, we observe that the three Baltic countries also experienced protest waves which started out already in the pre-crisis period. In Latvia this wave was most sustained and lasted from 2006 to 2010. It began with protests against government corruption; peaked in early 2009, as a direct reaction to the austerity measures to which the government had to agree in exchange for the bailout by the IMF; and then subsided when the incriminated government fell. In Estonia the protest wave already peaked before the crisis and subsided rapidly as the Great Recession set in. As we have already seen, it was related to the ethnic conflict between Estonian and Russian speakers. The Lithuanian wave followed the Latvian example, but on a much more reduced scale.

4.4 Conclusion

We started this chapter with the idea that protest occurs in waves and we formulated two competing hypotheses with respect to the level at which we would be most likely to find such waves. A first hypothesis suggested that given the parallel incidence of the Great Recession in all European countries, the similarity of the policy reactions of the national governments, and the interdependence of the countries' experiences as a result of the way the crisis was managed at the European level, we would find the crisis to have given rise to a sweeping protest wave across Europe. The competing hypothesis suggested that we would be more likely to find waves at the national level, because protest reacts to national or even local stimuli and develops in highly context-specific ways, even if it is triggered by similar types of economic hardship.

In fact, we did not find much evidence for the first hypothesis of a European-wide wave of protest triggered by the Great Recession, even if we specified it with respect to sub-periods of the Great Recession in Europe. We did find some systematic increase of protest across Europe at the beginning of the crisis, but this wave proved to be rather short lived and only partially related to the onset of the Great Recession. Viewed from the perspective of Europe as a whole, the great economic crisis did not make much of a difference in terms of protest. If anything, counter-intuitively it contributed to the pacification of protest in the long run.

By contrast, the second hypothesis was better corroborated by our evidence. When adopting a regional and even more so when adopting a country-specific perspective, we could find wave-like patterns of protest that are related to the crisis, in line with the notion that the impact of an economic crisis such as the Great Recession on protest is filtered by regional and national political conditions. Thus, we did find two period-specific protest waves in SE – one for the shock period and one for the Euro-crisis period, which were, however, mainly due to the developments in Greece. In Greece, the crisis gave rise to a sustained wave of protest that covered both the shock and the Euro-crisis period. But even in the case of Greece, this wave had already been under way once the economic crisis really hit the country. Moreover, while the crisis also gave rise to protest waves in Cyprus, Portugal, and Spain during the Euro crisis, it did not do so in all SE countries. There were no waves to speak of in Italy and Malta during any part of the Great Recession. In NWE, with the exception of Iceland and the United Kingdom, protest seems to have developed largely independently of the economic crisis, while we have found some country-specific waves in CEE.

But the eastern European waves, too, had either already accelerated before the intervention of the Great Recession, which only contributed to their peaks (Latvia, Lithuania), delayed their decline (Czech Republic, Hungary), or was actually unrelated to the protest (Bulgaria, Estonia).

A lot of protest during the Great Recession responded to country-specific conditions which were entirely unrelated to the crisis. The best illustrative example is the case of Northern Ireland, which was preoccupied by its 'troubles' independently of the crisis. Political and cultural issues with only a tenuous or no relation to the crisis were just as important triggers for protest during the period covered. The following chapters will show in more detail the role the different types of issues (Chapter 6), grievances (Chapters 7–9), as well as political context conditions (Chapters 10–11) have played in the mobilization of protest during the Great Recession. Before we turn to these questions, however, the next chapter will be more specifically concerned with the question of the radicalization of protest, or the lack of it, during the Great Recession.

5 All Quiet on the Protest Scene? Repertoires of Contention and Protest Actors During the Great Recession

Sophia Hunger and Jasmine Lorenzini

5.1 Introduction

In times of economic and political crisis, diverse social actors resort to protest in order to make their claims and grievances heard. Attempting to gain political influence, protesters use repertoires of contention which consist of 'limited numbers of historically established alternative performances linking claimants and the objects of their claims' (McAdam, Tarrow, and Tilly 1996: 23). The choice of specific action repertoires allows protesters to increase their visibility and to attract participants to support their claims. In this chapter, we examine the types of protest events and protest actors that prevail over time in the three regions that we study. In so doing, we ask whether and how the Great Recession transformed customary action repertoires in southern (SE), north-western (NWE), and central and eastern Europe (CEE).

As we have seen in Chapter 4, during the Great Recession some countries in the south of Europe saw a rise in protest that corresponds to the idea of a protest wave. These heightened phases of protest often come along with a qualitative expansion of the conflict (Tarrow 1989). The qualitative expansion can take two forms: changes in the action repertoire and a growing diversity of actors involved in protest.[1] Because public attention is limited, social movements need to innovate in order to gain visibility – particularly so, when new social actors enter the protest scene simultaneously. The movements need to renew the ways in which they perform their protests in order to gain social and political attention. Another way to attract media attention is to use illegal or violent actions. These transformations can also take place when governments remain unresponsive to the demands or oppositions

[1] Chapter 4 presents three indicators of expansion: size, radicalness, and originality. In this chapter, we are not interested in the first one, which corresponds to the quantitative expansion of conflict. Instead we consider the other two criteria, radicalness (use of violence) and originality (innovations in the action repertoire), as well as actors involved.

emerging from society. Hence, changes in the contention repertoire are more likely to happen where economic and political crises are at play, but also in countries and regions that have a burgeoning civil society. The Great Recession provided several of these triggers which may lead to changes in action repertoires: increased levels of contention and protest in some countries, new social actors entering the stage in others, and at times unresponsive governments pushing for austerity policies. Hence, we examine contentious repertoires across the three regions to analyse the prevailing forms of action, to see if new modes of action emerged during the crisis and whether protesters used violence.

Repertoires of contention are also important in establishing the collective identity and ideology of given groups of protesters (Taylor and van Dyke 2004). Some movements are known specifically for the type of action that they adopt. Among others, the ecology movement is known for non-violent illegal action such as blocking train convoys or accessing nuclear plants, some new feminist groups are known for subversive action using nudity (showing their breasts) or inversion of stigma (slut walks), and radical right extremist groups are known for their displays of physical violence against immigrants or minority groups. During the Great Recession, research has shown that loose networks prevailed over established organizations (Anduiza, Cristancho, and Sabucedo 2014). Therefore, we analyse the presence of different types of actors to see which actors dominate the protest scene during the Great Recession. We consider the possibility that organized actors appeared later in the protest scene as an indicator of institutionalization.

Using newspapers to code protest events limits the variation in terms of forms of action. This also applies to international news agencies as sources (Taylor and van Dyke 2004). Hence, we explain variations in the use of commonplace and widespread action forms, i.e. demonstrations, strikes, confrontational and violent actions, instead of looking at more fine-grained categorizations of action repertoires. We show how their prevalence changes across different contexts and time periods. Moreover, we would like to note that, contrary to recent research on contention repertoires, we are not interested in the growing role of the internet in transforming repertoires of action. In a digital era, e-political activities range from online activities that support political mobilization offline to online activities that exist solely on the internet (Earl and Kimport 2011; Theocharis and van Deth 2016; Van Laer and Van Aelst 2010). It would be interesting to combine research on protest events taking place offline and e-movements – social movement activities that exist only online (digitally enabled activities) – to understand the degree of protest digitalization during the Great Recession. However, given our choice to code protest events from media content we focus on offline protest events.[2] The study of online protest requires the use of other sources, in particular, organizations' websites (Kousis and Paschou 2017) and new social media (Theocharis et al. 2015) which allow identifying these forms of actions better than traditional media sources.

In the chapter, we first introduce repertoires of contention and how they transform over time. We account for the prevalence of demonstrations and strikes over other forms of contention across regions and time periods. Then, focusing on transformations observed during the crisis, we show that innovation and revolutionary processes, in the form of violent events, took place only in some parts of the south and they were short lived. Lastly, we turn to actors and show that protest events increasingly feature social groups without formal organizational structures. We conclude by arguing that contention repertoires remained largely unaffected by the Great Recession; demonstrations were and remained the prevailing form of protest across regions and time periods.

5.2 Repertoires of Contention

Protest takes multiple forms, be it a march down the street, a political gathering in a park, a sit-in in front of a public building, or a general strike paralyzing a city. Sometimes it also resorts to illegal or violent action, with some or all of the protesters engaging in a display of strength against authority, destroying property, or clashing with the police. Repertoires of contention are resources used to defend rights, oppose changes, express grievances, or make claims. The forms that protest events take are historically and contextually bound. Past protests, political opportunities, and interactions with other protesters transform action repertoires (Tilly 2008). The organizers' collective identity and ideology also shape action repertoires (Taylor and van Dyke 2004). Furthermore, we explore the possibility that some slight modifications to action repertoires happened in relation to the Great Recession and protest waves.

5.2.1 Demonstrations as the Modular Action Form

Tilly's work on repertoires of contention shows how limited and regularly repeated social movements' performances are (Doherty and Hayes 2018; Tilly 2008). Since the establishment of representative democracies, street

[2] To illustrate the fact that our coding strategy does not capture online activism, we can look at the number of online events that our dataset includes. This corresponds to 7.8 per cent of all the events coded. These online events exclusively take the form of hacking and mail bombings.

demonstrations have become a major form of protest in NWE (Tilly 2008). The nineteenth century came with the establishment of democracies in Europe and important socio-economic transformations such as the rise of the working class and the development of trade unionism. Both contributed to the growing importance of demonstrations. In democracies, the parliament appeared as a new political institution centralizing political power, and citizens developed repertoires of political action allowing them to make their political claims on this institution. Demonstrations enable citizens to demand or oppose changes while showing their strength with regard to what Tilly calls their WUNC – worthiness, unity, numbers, and commitment to a cause. Demonstrations offer an important advantage: They are modular, that is, they offer the possibility of addressing multiple issues and making claims on the political institutions, which can decide to legislate on the issue(s) at play (Tarrow 2011 [1994]). For these reasons, demonstrations prevail over other forms of action and, up until this day, constitute the main form of contention on the streets. Given the modularity of demonstrations and their widespread usage across countries, our first hypothesis is that despite the economic and political crises demonstrations were and remained throughout the Great Recession the prevailing form of contention on the streets in the three regions (H1).

5.2.2 *From Strikes to the More Encompassing General Strikes*

Contention repertoires change only under exceptional circumstances (Fillieule 2010). In the action repertoires of the twentieth century, together with demonstrations, strikes prevailed. However, in the last decades, two parallel trends shaped labour movement activism.

First, the number of economic strikes has been declining (Hamann, Johnston, and Kelly 2013). This can be linked to waning trade union membership (Visser 2013). The decline in strike activities is more pronounced in the north-west of Europe, while in the south trade unions remain stronger – strike activities are common in Spain, Greece, and Italy. Scholars have also pointed out that their number even grew during the crisis (Vandaele 2016). France belongs to this group of countries with high strike rates, while Portugal has a more moderate but still vivid strike scene (Hamann, Johnston, and Kelly 2013). Quite on the contrary, in post-communist countries, the decline of trade unions is even stronger than in the north-west and south (Crowley 2004). In eastern Europe, trade unions have lost members dramatically after the fall of the Soviet Union. They also lost trust and credibility among large shares of the population and workers. Trade unions represent the old communist regimes and they are one of the few political institutions that survived the transition period (Crowley 2004). Research shows a decline in the number of strikes (Greskovits 2015) even in the period of the Great Recession (Beissinger and Sasse 2014). However, in some countries, trade unions were able to mount protest and organize strikes as a response to austerity (Varga 2015).

Second, there is a growth in the number of general strikes (Hamann, Johnston, and Kelly 2013) or, as some call them, political strikes (Gall 2013; Lindvall 2013). In general or political strikes, protesters addressed their claims to the government and different groups of workers or segments of the population participate in these protest events. The goal of a political strike is to discredit the government, enforcing political and not economic pressure (Gall 2013). The growth in the number of general strikes is associated with widespread cuts in public spending, dismantling of the welfare state, loosening of labor protection, and worsening of working conditions. It is also associated with the government's exclusion of trade unions from legislative procedures (Hamann, Johnston, and Kelly 2013) and with the fading alliance between trade unions and social democratic parties (Gall 2013). The growth in general strikes is most likely in cases in which the unions are neither very strong nor very weak, but rather when they have a moderate power and mobilizing capacity (Lindvall 2013). Among the countries analysed in these studies, Greece appears as an outlier with an exceptionally high number of general strikes (in the data presented by Hamann, Johnston, and Kelly 2013, they represent thirty-three of the seventy-two political strikes analysed).

The decline in strikes and the growth of more encompassing general strikes illustrate the idea that there are instances when institutional or socio-economic changes transform contention repertoires (Taylor and van Dyke 2004). In the late twentieth century, the neoliberal turn reinforced the prevalence of demonstrations over other action forms. As neoliberal reforms challenged the power of citizens and the state, workers built on more inclusive repertoires of action than those of the labour movement. In addition to strikes, they increasingly used demonstrations to make claims related to citizens' rights, not only focusing on workers' rights (Gentile and Tarrow 2009). These union-led demonstrations often took the form of general strikes (Gall 2013; Hamann, Johnston, and Kelly 2013). During the Great Recession, austerity policies reinforced cuts in the welfare state and aggrieved large segments of the population. As the government adopted austerity measures, protests grew across SE (Altiparmakis and Lorenzini 2018). The dismantling of socio-economic rights angered citizens, who took to the streets to express their grievances (Galais and Lorenzini 2017). General strikes display opposition to the government's adoption of laws detrimental to the principles of social justice, social protection, and workers' rights defended by trade unions. Hence, we expect that the economic crisis with its implementation of austerity policies fostered strike activity as a response to worsening working conditions and loosening of social protection. Our second hypothesis states that we see a rise in strikes, more specifically of general strikes aiming at mobilizing broad segments of the population, during the Great Recession in the south of Europe (H2). We anticipate that in CEE, the economic crisis did not trigger a growth in strike activity because of the weakness of trade unions. In the north-west, because the economic crisis was more limited, we also advance that there would be no increase in strike activity.

5.2.3 Innovations in Action Repertoires

Chapter 4 has shown that the Great Recession resulted in a protest wave in four SE countries, namely Greece, Cyprus, Portugal, and Spain, whereas in NWE and CEE only some countries saw a rise in protest but there were no protest waves. During phases of heightened protest, social movements aim to draw attention to their actions, and the most efficient way of doing so is innovation: using new forms of action that capture media attention and put the spotlight on their mobilization (Tarrow 1989). As protest grows, changes in the action repertoire are more likely. This leads us to postulate that economic and political crises have a transformative influence on action repertoires when a quantitative expansion of conflict happens. Our third set of hypotheses deals with transformations in the action repertoire and focuses on the south of Europe, where protest increased.

We are especially interested in examining the kinds of transformations taking place during phases of heightened contention. The choice of a form of action is always torn between innovation and repetition (McAdam, Tarrow, and Tilly 2001). The former brings surprise, catches opponents off guard, and may trigger media attention, while the latter benefits from widespread recognition and the actors' familiarity with it. In addition, a process of radicalization might take place (Tarrow 1989). As some fringes of social movements radicalize over time, others turn to institutional modes of action. We examine three types of transformation: (1) innovations in the shape of new forms of action designed to mobilize citizens during the Great Recession; (2) the use of violence in attempts to trigger revolutionary processes; and (3) institutionalization of protest with a growing involvement of organizations.

Often novelties build on slight modifications of existing action forms. Sometimes, they adopt or adapt protest events from other social movements (Soule 2004). During the economic crisis, one of the main innovations relates to the establishment of protest camps in the main squares of large cities (Castells 2015). The Arab Spring started a movement that soon took place in many countries around the world under the name of 'occupy'. The camps used in some of the major protest events organized during the crisis served to express grievances, to attract visibility, and also to express agreement with alternative modes of political participation that require time, sustained engagement, and deliberation (Polletta 2014). The occupation of squares served as a way to express both economic and political dissatisfaction. We hypothesize that the major innovation in the action repertoire took the form of occupations and happened only in the region experiencing increased levels of protest, SE (H3a).

The second transformation we analyse relates to violence. Protest wave theory postulates that violence happens at the end of a protest wave, when protest dies out and some social movement actors take the institutional path. For instance, at the end of the protest wave led by new social movements, some environment activists founded Green parties (Kitschelt 1989). In parallel, more radical fringes of social movements resort to political violence to sustain protest and capture media attention (della Porta and Tarrow 1986; Tarrow 1993). Yet, other scholars postulate that violence is an early component of revolutionary processes. Disorderly and violent protest takes place at the beginning of contention before established forces take over the grievances and normalize political actions (Piven and Cloward 1977; Scott 2012). These two theories disagree about the timing of political violence. They lead us to consider two alternative hypotheses on the timing of political violence. We hypothesize that political violence takes place at the beginning of the crisis, before institutional actors take over and normalize protest, again, only in the south of Europe (H3b1). Furthermore, we consider the possibility that violence takes place at the end of the protest wave together with institutionalization (H3b2).

Lastly, we study processes of institutionalization in relation to protest actors. Political violence theories share the assumption that a process of institutionalization and normalization is at play either in parallel with (Tarrow 1989) or after the outbreak of violence (Piven and Cloward 1977). We look at institutionalization regarding the presence of specific types of actors on the streets. When protest grows, it opens political opportunities – elites are more divided, they seek new alliances, and they become less repressive (Tilly 2008). New actors are drawn to the streets to make claims on the government (Tarrow 1989). Then, in a second phase, a process of institutionalization might follow. This takes place when organizations replace unorganized social groups. For the years of the Great Recession, we expect to see a growing diversity of political actors on the streets where we observe increased levels of protest. Our last hypothesis is that in the south of Europe during the early phase of the crisis the share of unorganized social groups grew and that, later on, organizations prevailed (parties, trade unions, and civil society organizations), hinting at a process of institutionalization (H3c).

5.3 Demonstrations and Strikes: Stability in the Action Repertoires

Turning to the empirical part of our study, we present descriptive analyses to provide an overview of the compositions of action forms. We begin by investigating the development of action repertoires over time by region. Thus, we focus on the qualitative expansion of conflict, and more specifically for this first part on changes in the action repertoire. We also pay special attention to SE countries which experienced a protest wave, i.e. Greece, Portugal, and Spain. Although Italy did not experience a protest wave, we also include it in these additional analyses to give a more complete picture of the south.[3]

5.3.1 Demonstration as the Prevailing Action Form

Figure 5.1 shows the percentage shares of the various forms of action from 2000 to 2015 by region. We use different scales for demonstrations on the left-hand panel, and strikes, confrontations, and violence on the right-hand one, to give more visibility to changes in the less frequent action forms. Although we use a different scale for demonstrations, the attentive reader will already have noticed that demonstrations prevailed during the whole period. They represented roughly two-thirds of the events, with 62 per cent in the north-west, 58 per cent in the south, and 69 per cent in the CEE countries.

The relative shares of demonstration in the three regions changed little over time. The stability of the share of demonstrations in NWE is most striking. In this region, demonstrations represented the same proportion of events when aggregating the three periods. We see only

[3] We do not include additional analyses for Cyprus and Malta because of the small number of protest events included in our dataset for these countries.

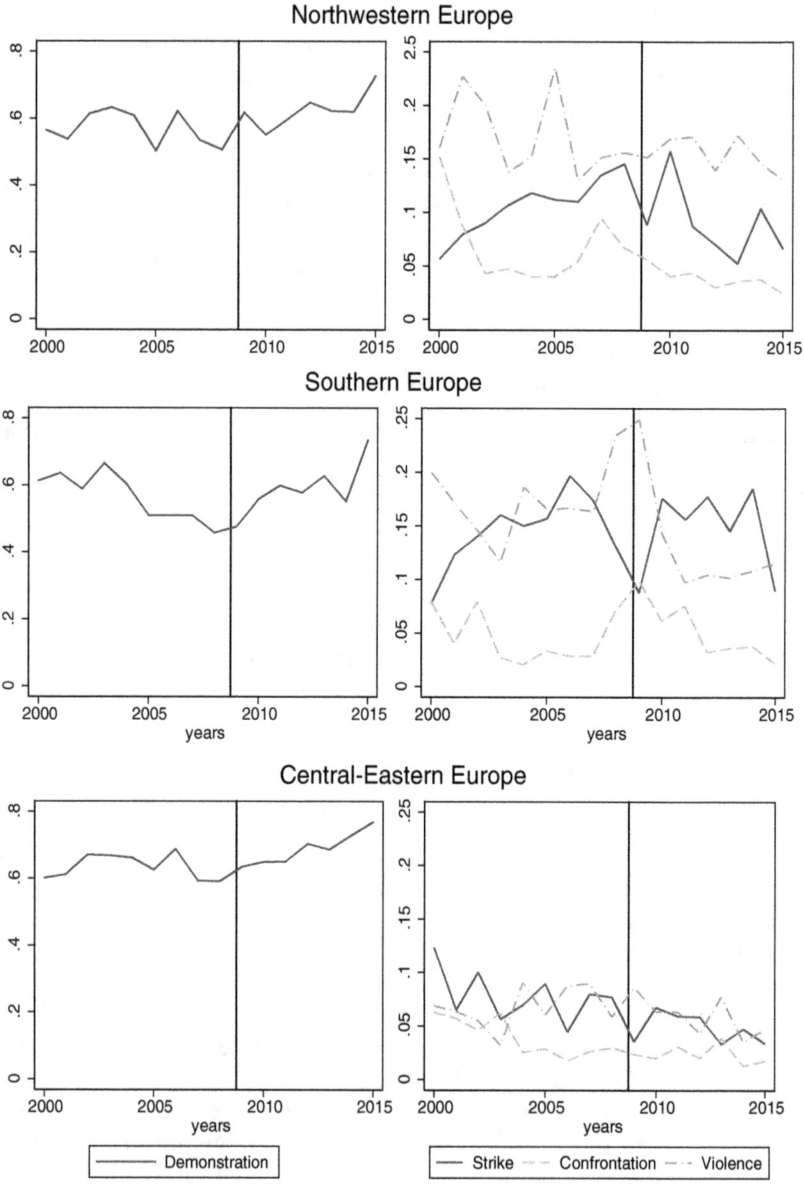

Figure 5.1 Share of demonstrations (left) and other action forms (right) for the three European regions.
Note: The scales for demonstrations and for the other action forms differ to account for the fact that the share of demonstrations is much higher than the ones of strikes, confrontations, and violence.

slight changes in the share of demonstrations in these distinct periods, for instance, a marginal decline before the onset of the crisis in 2008. Most notably, we see an increase in the share of demonstrations when the refugee crisis kicks off at the end of our period of interest. In this region, only Finland and the Netherland stick out with an overall smaller share of demonstrations.

For CEE, Figure 5.1 reveals a steady increase in the share of demonstrations over the sixteen years analysed here. At the beginning of the 2000s, demonstrations represented 63 per cent of all events, while at the end of the period they represented 79 per cent. During the refugee crisis, demonstrations constituted by far the prevailing form of action in the CEE countries. This share is slightly higher than in the northwest and the south of Europe. Turning to country-level data, this trend is very homogeneous across all countries in CEE.

In the south of Europe, stability in the share of demonstrations also prevailed. However, we observe the lowest share of demonstrations during the shock period – the early phase of the crisis. This corresponds to the moment when other forms of action kicked in and gained relative importance in the action repertoire. We will look at this in more details for our third set of hypotheses. In spite of intraregional variance with regard to the intensity of the crisis, no specific country leads the SE pattern. It is mostly consistent across countries. In Figure 5.2, focusing on four SE countries, we see that the share of demonstrations oscillates between 40 and 80 per cent of the action repertoire. In Spain and Portugal, the corresponding share reaches an all-time low before the onset of the Great Recession. While demonstrations steadily increase towards the end of the Great Recession in Spain, there is a decline in Portugal – a country with a less established protest culture (Accornero and Ramos Pinto 2015). In Greece, the share of demonstrations declines right after the beginning of the crisis, in September 2008, when other forms become more important, but then steadily increases during the crisis. Even in this country which experienced an important protest wave, demonstrations prevail over all other action forms. In Italy, the share of demonstration is most stable and fluctuations are unrelated to the Great Recession. These findings suggest that our expectations about demonstrations as a dominant action form hold even in countries most strongly hit by the crisis or where there was a protest wave.

These observations confirm our first hypothesis: Demonstrations were the dominant form of action across the three regions during the whole period. Despite varying trends in the relative share of demonstrations across the regions, demonstrations remained the most common form of protest in Europe, even during the Great Recession. We observe only slight changes in their relative share, such as a drop in

Greece during the shock period. By contrast, although we only cover its beginning, we observe that during the refugee crisis, the share of demonstration increases in all three regions.

5.3.2 Strike as an Important Action Form in the South During the Crisis

Turning to the other forms of protest in the right-hand panel of Figure 5.1, we present the development of strikes compared to political violence and confrontational actions. Here, the scale ranges from 0 to 25 per cent. Generally, and referring to the whole period of observation, NWE and SE are characterized by a more diverse repertoire of action than CEE.

When considering strikes, we see that they represent between 5 and 15 per cent of all events in the north-west of Europe. In the pre-crisis period, we observe an upward trend for strikes, with a sharp decline in 2008 as the crisis hits Europe and a peak in 2010 when the eurozone crisis kicks in. The year 2010 was marked by numerous industrial actions in many European countries. The organizers were as diverse as Lufthansa pilots in Germany, gas station owners in Cyprus, or doctors in the Czech Republic. However, these strikes fell into a few months of 2010 and culminated in a coordinated European day of protest on 29 September 2010, with 50,000 workers protesting in Brussels.[4] Even in countries with few strikes, we see the relation to the Great Recession, i.e. with judges and prosecutors threatening to walkout as they claimed to be understaffed for the challenges that the bank- and business-related crisis imposed on them in Austria. By the end of the period that we analyse, in 2015, the level is back to the low levels of the early 2000s. Notable outliers are Finland and Belgium, with a steady increase in the relative shares of strikes after September 2008. In the CEE region, in line with the idea that trade unions are weak and that strikes are not a prominent form of action even during the Great Recession, the share of strike is much lower (ranging from 5 to 10 per cent). Furthermore, in this region, we observe a declining trend throughout the whole period.

In the south, the situation is similar to the north-west but there are two notable divergences. The peaks are higher in the south, here the share of strikes ranges from 5 to more than 20 per cent on average. Furthermore, the increase is stable throughout the whole crisis period and it declines only towards the end of the period that we analyse. Figure 5.2 displays the specific situation for the four countries in

[4] Many countries – in the three regions that we analyse here – participated. For instance, there was a general strike in Spain and other industrial actions in Greece, Portugal, Ireland, Slovenia, and Lithuania.

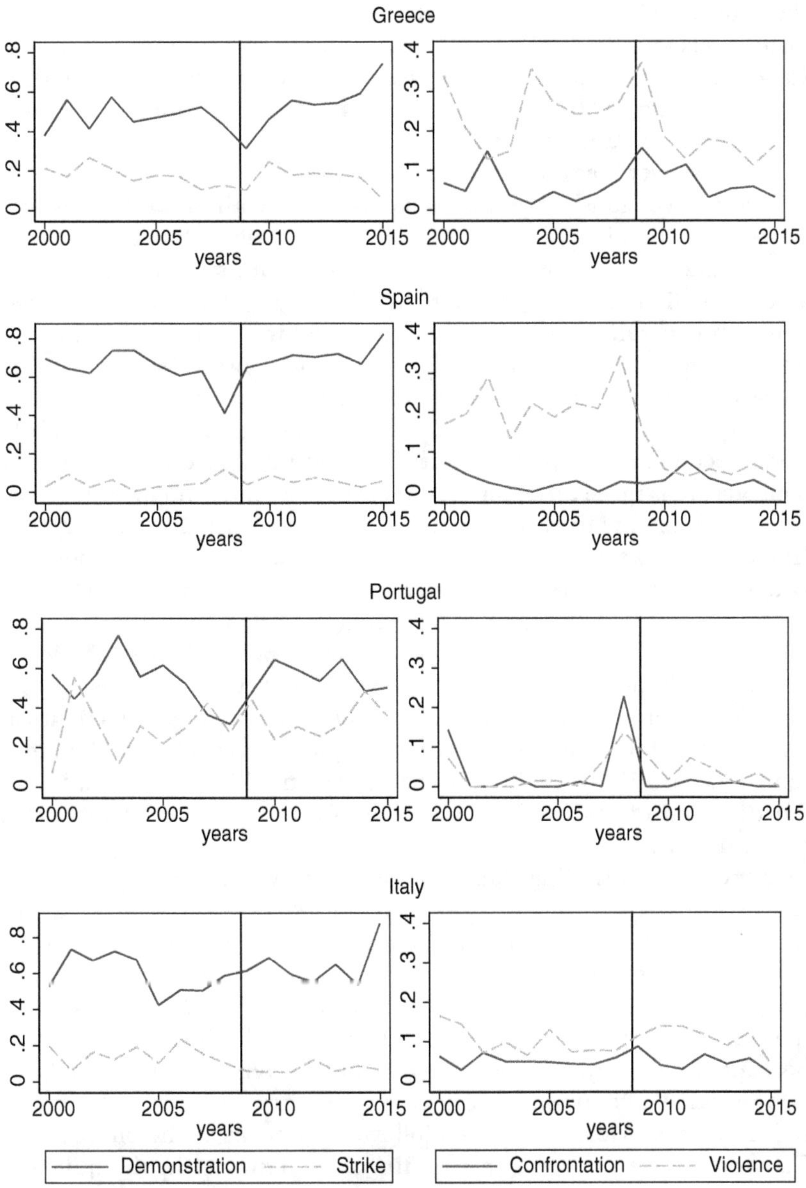

Figure 5.2 Share of demonstrations and strikes (left) as well as violent and confrontational events (right) for four southern European countries.

the south. In Portugal, strikes seem to be nearly on a par with demonstrations and the time trend is rather stable. By contrast, in Greece, Italy, and Spain, strikes play a rather subordinate role compared to other action forms. In Greece, strikes peak at the beginning of the Euro crisis, when the unions initially led the opposition against the government's austerity measures (Altiparmakis 2019a).

So far, we considered all strike activity without distinguishing between economic and general (or political) strikes. Further analyses of our data show that strikes addressing political issues[5] represent only a very small share (2.7 per cent) of all strikes (results not presented here). In general, the share of strikes that address only political issues does not vary over time in NWE or CEE. We observe a very flat line in eastern Europe and a minor peak in the north in 2006. In both regions, the share of strikes addressing political issues, or a combination of economic and political ones does not increase during the crisis. The picture is quite different in the south, where we find more fluctuations over time, with two peaks prior to the crisis (in 2003 and 2007). Interestingly, we observe an increase in strikes that address political issues during the Great Recession. Strikes addressing either political issues or a combination of economic and political issues peak in 2011. There is no difference in the number of political strikes between countries with and without a protest wave. However, Greece is again a notable outlier here. The country faced up to 17 per cent of all political strikes during the Euro crisis, confirming previous findings (Hamann, Johnston, and Kelly 2013). This serves as an additional validation of our data and of our operationalization of general strikes as strikes on political issues.

Our empirical findings fail to support our second hypothesis, which suggests that there is an increase in the relative share of strikes in the south of Europe during the Great Recession. Instead, what we observe is a sharp decline before the beginning of the crisis and a return to the pre-crisis level during the shock period. A majority of these strikes focus on economic issues, we find limited evidence supporting the idea that general strikes grow over time. Our analyses also revealed a common pattern across the three regions, a decline in strike activity prior to the crisis followed by peaks at the onset of the Euro crisis. We interpret this finding as a sign that in the build-up

[5] The coding used for action forms does not distinguish general strikes from economic ones. To compare the two types of events, we consider the issue addressed and we distinguish between strikes addressing only economic issues, only political ones, and those that combine the two issues.

of the crisis workers and unions refrain from going on strikes, but once the crisis unfolds with its economic and political responses strike activity regain intensity.[6] In the north-west, the whole period is characterized by fluctuations in strikes, whereas a steady decline appears in the CEE region.

5.4 Transformations of Action Repertoires During Protest Waves

Our next set of hypotheses address changes in the action repertoires taking place during a protest wave. We pay special attention to the south of Europe and to the period of the Great Recession. First, we consider innovations in the action repertoire. Then, we analyse the timing of violence. Lastly, we turn to protest actors.

5.4.1 *Innovation in the Form of Confrontational Actions*

We explore changes in action repertoires by examining confrontational actions, which comprise blockades, protest camps, and the occupation of squares. Confrontational actions represent the smallest share of protest actions in the three regions (see Figure 5.1). In the north-west, there are two peaks in confrontational actions in the early to mid-2000s but otherwise their share remains stable at around 5 per cent throughout the period covered. In contrast, in CEE, confrontational actions are in decline throughout the whole period. They decrease from 7 to 3 per cent. Similarly, in the south, confrontational events are only of minor importance, representing between 3 and 10 per cent of all protest events. We also observe a first peak in the early 2000s but more interesting for us, confrontations peak at the onset of the Great Recession and stay at a relatively high level until 2011.

In Figure 5.2, we present separate graphs for four SE countries. The increase at the onset of the Great Recession is mostly driven by the Greek case. There are some early events connected to the Great Recession in September 2008, when airport personnel blocked runways and main roads in Athens. However, the biggest share of this peak is

[6] Strikes are heavily related to the business cycle (Gall 2013). However, researchers disagree about the timing of strikes in the business cycle. Some argue that strikes are more likely to be associated with growth (raising demand for work as an opportunity to set claims) or with recession (when pressure increases on wages and the risk of cuts in jobs occurs).

related to the street riot that broke out after Alexandros Grigoropoulos, a fifteen-year-old student, was shot by police forces. Mass protest and rioting spread to other Greek cities and lasted more than three weeks, with protesters blocking streets and occupying buildings, such as radio stations. In Italy, we find a minor increase in confrontations at the beginning of the crisis. This captures an extended series of sit-ins and blockades against education cuts. Students and faculty in Italian universities and schools protested against the Berlusconi government austerity plan for education. In Portugal, confrontational actions peak prior to the crisis and, in Spain, confrontational actions peak in 2011, at the time of the mobilization by the Indignados. Even in the south, among countries with and without a protest wave, confrontational action remains rather limited.

Figure 5.3 presents a more detailed categorization of confrontational events in six selected countries. For this purpose, we used a refined coding scheme and choose two countries per region – Greece and Italy in the south, Germany and the United Kingdom in the north-west, and

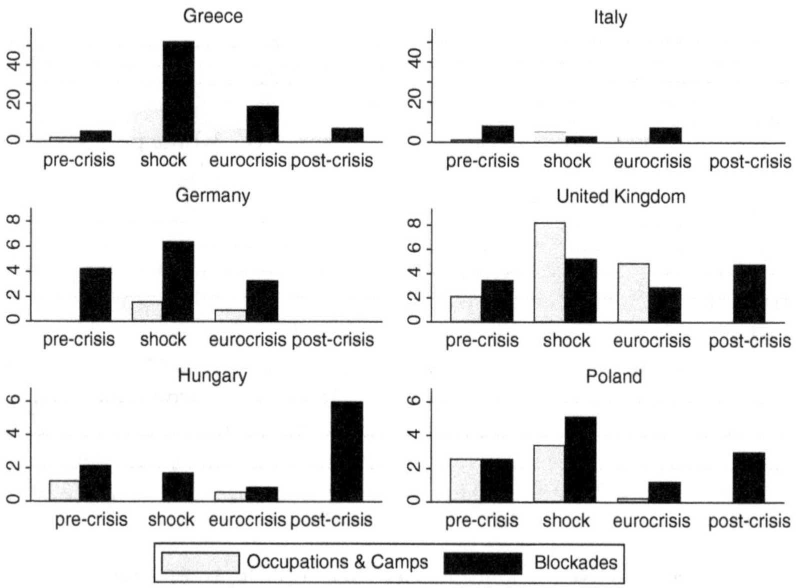

Figure 5.3 Confrontational action forms in six selected countries. *Note:* Here, we report numbers of events instead of shares. The scales differ by regions.

Hungary and Poland in the east.[7] This allows us to compare the occurrence of blockades to both protest camps and occupations in countries heavily and less heavily hit by the Great Recession.[8]

Except in the United Kingdom, blockades prevail as the traditional form of confrontational actions, while more innovative forms such as occupations and protest camps amount to only a small number of events. Unsurprisingly, we find most blockades in Greece, where the number of blockades increases during the shock period and the Euro crisis. Protest camps and occupations represent a much smaller number of confrontational events in Greece, but we observe a small peak in 2012, after the Indignados movement took place in Spain. In Italy, there is hardly any change in the use of occupations, blockades, and protest camps.

Interestingly, we notice a sizeable increase in occupations and protest camps in the United Kingdom. In this north-western country, not strongly hit by the crisis but facing a protest wave, we see some incidents of occupy-flavoured actions. These incidents stem from a broad array of motives and participants, among others foreign policy matters, i.e. Gaza and Kurdistan, environmental and workers claims, tuition fees, and resistance against tax avoidance. Only in October 2011, we find a series of Occupy Wall Street–inspired protest in the United Kingdom. In Poland, blockades and other confrontational actions are used either for economic protests, medical personnel, i.e. nurses and doctors seeking pay raises, or for environmental ones. The increase in Hungary in the post-crisis period refers to protest events regarding the refugee crisis.

We find limited evidence to support the hypothesis that innovations take place at the beginning of the crisis in the form of occupations (H3a). Looking at confrontational actions overall, we observe a peak at the onset of the crisis in SE. However, looking more specifically at four southern countries, we find a mixed pattern. Confrontational actions peak in Greece in September 2008 as reaction to the killing of a schoolboy by police forces and in 2011, when a series of blockades of infrastructure (e.g. airports, harbours, and highways) and public buildings, such as ministries and the parliament, hit the country. Moreover, the 'Indignant Citizens Movement' held a protest camp at the Syntagma

[7] As there are several studies on the *Indignados* in Spain, we choose not to study it and rather to analyse whether *Indignados*-flavored protest spilled over to other southern countries.

[8] We subsumed occupations and protest camp into one category, as they are innovations associated with the Great Recession.

Square during the summer of 2011. We also observe a small peak in confrontational action in Spain that coincides with the Indignados movement in 2011. Nevertheless, Greece seems to be an outlier with its important and lasting increase in confrontational actions. Moreover, only few confrontations took the form of occupations or protest camps. Turning to the other regions, these specific action forms did not travel to other countries not experiencing a protest wave and they were used (more prominently sometimes) prior to the crisis period. The relative importance of protest camps and occupations is modest even in countries strongly hit by the crisis. This shows the value of comparing different cases and including long periods of time when analysing changes and innovations in action repertoires.

5.4.2 *Violent Protest Events as Early Drivers of Protest?*

Violence is an integral part of contentious repertoires; hence, we analyse the timing of violent events. We examine whether they increased at the beginning of the protest wave when unorganized citizens take to the streets to express their grievances (hypothesis 3b).

As Figure 5.1 shows, violent political events constituted the second most common form of action in the north-west and south of Europe. Although its share is much lower than for the share of demonstrations, violence accounted for an average of 16 and 17 per cent of all protests respectively. By contrast, in CEE, the share of violent events was much lower, accounting for fewer than one-tenth of all protest events in the region.

Turning to fluctuations over time, in NWE, where we do not observe a quantitative expansion of protest, the share of violent events was stable over time. It remained at around 16 per cent throughout the entire time period covered here. Focusing on specific countries, some display a higher share of political violence compared to the others in NWE. Most importantly, this is the case for Northern Ireland, where the conflict between Catholics and Protestants resulted in violent events until the final peace agreement in 2007. In CEE, at a low level, the share of violent events declined over time across the countries in the region. Only Bulgaria (17 per cent in the Euro crisis) and Hungary (12 per cent in the shock period) diverged from this pattern. In Bulgaria, these violent actions result from the protests against the Borisov cabinet and their government austerity measures in 2013 and from the protests against the Oresharski cabinet in 2013 and 2014, which were more targeted towards a general dissatisfaction with the legitimacy of the government and its corruption. In Hungary, most violent events are related to a series of murders and violence towards Romani people that began in mid-2008 and lasted for more than a year.

Most interesting for us is the timing of violent events in SE, where most of the protest took place. In this region, we observe a peak of violent events in the early phase of the crisis, when protest events became more numerous. During the shock period, the share of violent events went from the 17 per cent during the pre-crisis period to 25 per cent. Later on, during the second phase of the protest wave, violence declined and accounted for only 11 per cent of all events. This share then remained stable throughout the refugee crisis. As can be seen in Figure 5.2, the increased share of political violence observed in the south was mostly driven by events in Greece, where violent actions were skyrocketing to 35 per cent in late 2008. These developments are related to the 2008 street riots in Athens mentioned earlier. While political violence decreases in Spain, we find a small peak of violence in Portugal during the Euro crisis, which results from clashes between police and protestors on the sideline of several mass protests in 2012.

Our empirical finding lends support to the hypothesis based on Piven and Cloward's (1979) claim that violent events are part of an early phase of protest waves. They happen at the beginning of a protest wave, when citizens' strong dissatisfaction is voiced but not channelled through organizations and institutional politics. A movement is more radical at the beginning, before organized actors enter the protest scene and pacify the political conflict.

5.4.3 Institutionalizations of Protest During a Protest Wave

As a last step, we consider the possibility that a process of institutionalization takes place at the end of a protest wave. The institutionalization hypothesis predicts that protest events called by organizations replace those led by unorganized social groups during a protest wave (H3c). We study the share of events in which organizations were present and compare it to the share of events with only social groups mentioned. Additionally, we present the share of events in which both groups of actors participated. Then, we zoom in on the share of events led by trade unions, parties, and other civil society organizations (CSO) relative to all events. This strategy allows us to detect when and where the involvement of institutionalized actors increases.

We coded actors if they had called for, taken part in or organized an event. Excluding all protest events with no or only vague information on actors, such as mentions of 'protesters' or 'people', leaves us

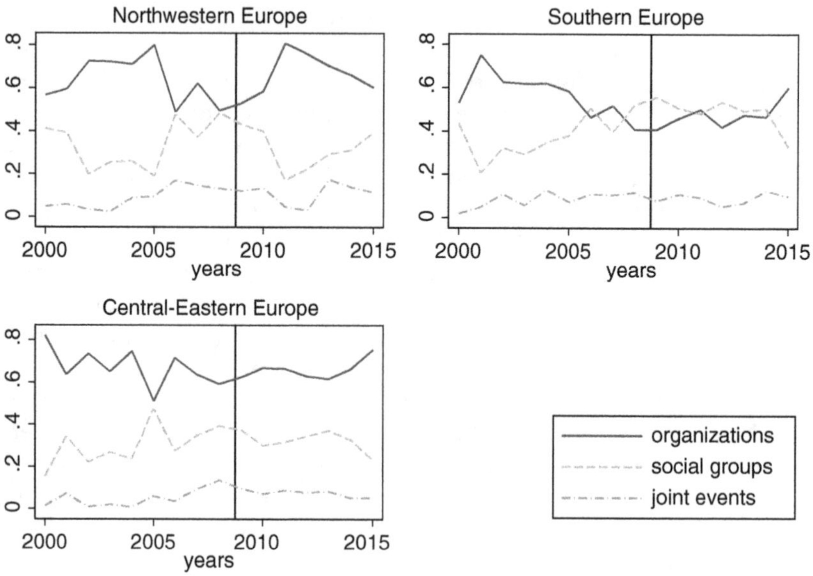

Figure 5.4 Shares of events led by institutionalized and non-institutionalized actors including joint events of both actor groups, relative to all events with information on actor types.

with 14,799 observations.[9] For our analyses, we aggregated categories to their more general level, e.g. left- and right-wing parties were subsumed under 'parties' and public and private sector unions were combined. This leaves us with six actor categories – three organized actors (parties, unions, and other civil society organizations) and three social groups (occupational groups, pensioners, and students).

Figure 5.4 shows the share of events with and without organizations by region. First, we see that, in the north-west and in the east, events with organizations prevail. They represent 50 per cent or more of all events in the north and around 60 per cent in the east. The south differs importantly with respect to this trend. There, organizations prevail prior to the crisis but their involvement steadily declines from 2005 onwards. The share of events carried by organizations reaches the lowest level in 2007 and only picks up again after the onset of the crisis. The engagement of social groups (with no mention of organizations

[9] This is around 50 per cent of all observations (total of 30,941).

being present) in protest follows a different trend. Social groups are increasingly present in the streets from the early 2000s onward and their activity steadily grows until 2014. This reflects the idea that digital tools and online activism facilitates the organization of protest (Earl and Kimport 2011). As noted for the Indignados (Anduiza, Cristancho, and Sabucedo 2014), organizations have generally become less central for protest in SE – their resources, infrastructure, and knowledge are less crucial to gather citizens in the streets.

Focusing on SE countries (results not presented here), we observe similar trends in the four countries – a growing presence of social groups that persists until the refugee crisis. In Italy, we see a steady growth from 2002 onwards. In Greece and Spain, the growth appears closer to the crisis period and is most visible in the early phase of the crisis. In Portugal, the share of events with organizations plummets in 2008 (prior to the crisis) while those with social groups skyrocket. Most of these events are related to truck drivers' protests against raising fuel prices taking the form of road blockades and torching vehicles. These events were not limited to Portugal; similar actions were taken in Spain, Greece, and even in Poland. Otherwise, in Portugal, organizations are involved in a majority of events (between 60 and 80 per cent).

Figure 5.5 shows the specific organized actors on the left-hand side. We present the share of union, party or CSO-led actions relative to all events with actor information in our dataset. On the right-hand side, we include the shares of events led by the different social groups, i.e. pensioners, students, and occupational groups. We observe that, in the north-west of Europe, unions are the organizations most often present in protest events. They are present in 30–50 per cent of the events. Their share grew slightly during the Great Recession – from 35 per cent in the pre-crisis period to 42 per cent during the eurozone crisis. Other types of CSOs are present in 10–20 per cent of the protest events. In 2005 – prior to the crisis – we find a peak in CSOs' activities due to a heterogeneous set of protest in some north-western countries.[10] Parties are present in 5–15 per cent of protest events. Their presence reached a low point in 2005. Then it increased steadily during the whole period

[10] It mostly captures events in Denmark, Belgium, and Northern Ireland. In Denmark, these events are manifold and do not cover any overarching trend. The events happening in Belgium are unrelated to domestic politics and happen in Brussel as the heart of the EU, covering several issues such as Turkey's EU membership, protest again US president George W. Bush, and so forth. The events in Northern Ireland are mostly related to the ongoing conflict between Protestants and Catholics, with 2005 marking Belfast's most widespread riots in a decade.

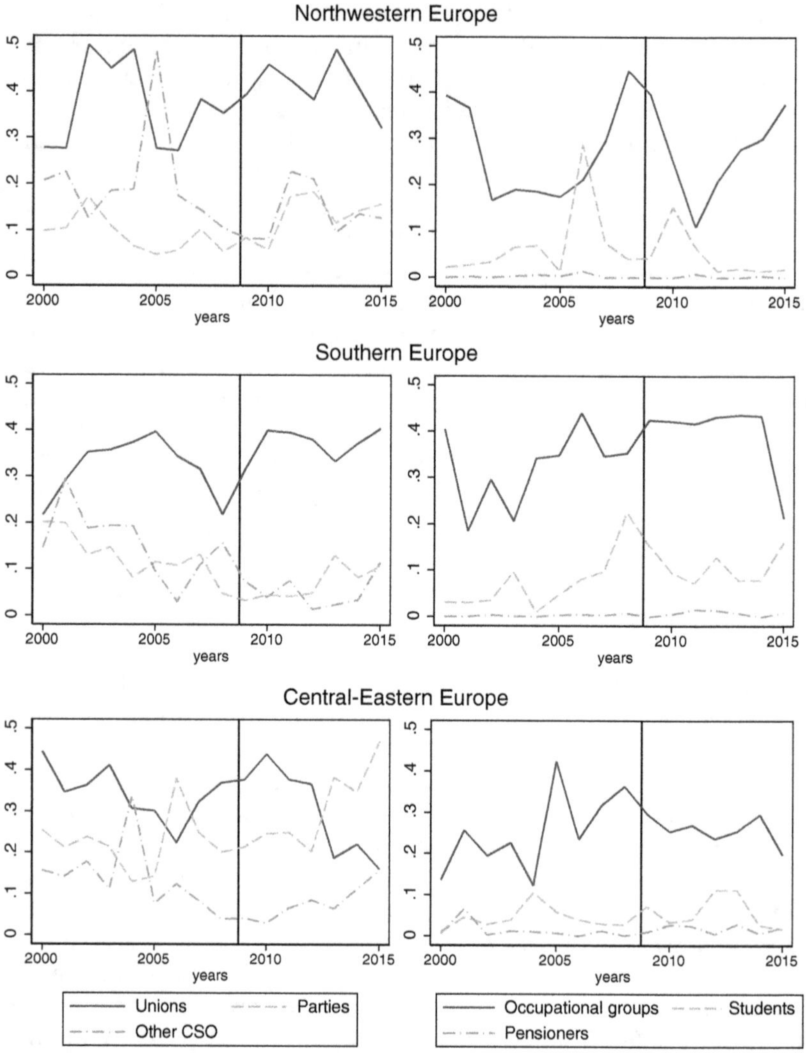

Figure 5.5 Share of actions led by different actors across regions, left: unions, parties, civil society organizations, right: occupational groups, students, and pensioners.

of the Great Recession. Chapter 11 will return in more detail to the specific role of parties for protest mobilization. Social groups are most often occupational groups; more rarely they are students or pensioners. The relative share of protest events involving occupational groups varies considerably across time.

In eastern Europe, it is trade unions that are most present in the streets. Their relative share of protests is stable throughout the pre-crisis period and most of the Great Recession (around 35 per cent) but it declines drastically after 2012 and during the refugee crisis (14 per cent). In contrast, the relative presence of civil society organizations increased modestly during the crisis (from 4 to 14 per cent), while that of political parties grew massively (from 23 to 53 per cent) and reached unprecedented levels during the refugee crisis. In eastern Europe, parties combine electoral and protest strategies when dealing with issues that are central in their political agenda. Turning to social groups, occupational groups also predominated in CEE and their relative share of protest is rather stable throughout the crisis period (from 26 to 32 per cent).

In the south of Europe, we find again that unions are very active with the highest relative share (between 20 and 40 per cent), while parties and CSOs display equivalent shares (between 20 and 5 per cent). Regarding the timing of their presence, parties and unions were less present during the shock period than later on during the crisis. As protest picked up, organized political actors constituted a smaller share of all the actors on the streets: The relative presence of parties dropped from 13 to 4 per cent and that of unions from 33 to 24 per cent. In parallel, students became more active in the protest scene before the collapse of Lehman Brothers' and during this early phase of the protest wave. Their relative share multiplied fivefold. Students accounted for only 5 per cent of all actors in the pre-crisis phase while they represented as much as 25 per cent of all actors during the shock period. This, however, was a rather short-lived phenomenon. As the protest wave unfolded in the south of Europe, organized actors were increasingly present on the streets. The presence of parties did not recover to pre-crisis levels (7 per cent only), whereas trade unions gained visibility on the streets, accounting for a larger share of all actors during the eurozone crisis (38 per cent).

Regarding institutionalization, we find little support for our hypothesis 3c. The growing presence of social groups in protest events corresponds to changes that take place in the longer term; their presence grows already prior to the crisis, and is not associated specifically with the Great Recession. In turn, the presence of organizations grows slightly during the eurozone crisis in Greece and Portugal, but the patterns are less stable in the other two SE countries.

5.5 Conclusion

How did the Great Recession shape and change protest repertoires? Which actors became more active in the protest arena? In this chapter, we described the contentious repertoires across three European regions – north-western, southern, and central and eastern Europe – and in the four different periods related to the Great Recession. Our findings show that stability prevails in action repertoires across regions and even in countries facing a protest wave. Protesters use mainly demonstrations and strikes, few innovations have made it to the protest scene, early signs of political violence were limited, and the growing presence of (unorganized) social groups reflects longer-term trends. Overall, we observe business as usual in the streets of Europe.

One feature common to all three regions is that demonstrations were the most widely used form of political protest. This customary form prevailed not only during the pre-crisis period but also during the recession, from 2008 to 2015. We observed only minor shifts in the general repertoires across the three regions. Demonstrations are most widespread in the three regions, while strikes were declining in NWE and CEE. In the south, the share of strikes dropped during the shock period but then recovered during the Euro crisis. We observed an outburst of confrontational and violent events in the south, but this development was not only short-lived – it happened during the shock period and was soon replaced by traditional repertoires of action, but also mainly confined to Greece, where it was, moreover, largely unrelated to the economic crisis. Innovations in contentious repertoires were limited to a short period of increased confrontational events. This period was accompanied by growing political violence, but it was also limited in time. Hence, we conclude that stability prevailed in contentious repertoires during the 2000s in the three regions.

Our findings show that the contentious repertoires in the younger democracies of CEE mainly resembled those of NWE and SE. In the CEE, demonstrations were the customary form of protest over time. The Great Recession, in turn, manifested itself in a brief outburst of protest early in the shock period rather than in a continuous wave of protest.

In NWE, our data reveal the prevalence of standard repertoires and a trend towards the pacification of conflicts in the streets. In eastern and southern Europe political violence peaked at the beginning of the Great Recession. This finding is at odds with the literature on protest waves and radicalization (Tarrow 1989). Instead, it supports the idea that violent events take place in early phases of protest waves, prior to the mobilization of organized actors (Piven and Cloward 1977). We have not found evidence of a revolutionary process at play during the Great Recession. Violent action increased early in the protest waves but soon died out.

Even in the south, where a protest wave took place, we have uncovered surprisingly little evidence of transformations in the action form used. We did not observe an important and lasting increase in occupations and protest camps. However, it is important to mention one limitation of our study, i.e. we do not analyse online activism. Our data does not allow us to consider e-protest during the crisis. Some innovations in the action repertoires may have taken place online during the crisis, not only actions enabling offline protest but also actions taking place solely online.

We observed limited evidence for the proposed institutionalization, i.e., organizations taking over protest started by social groups. To the contrary, we have found some evidence of a growing involvement of social groups over time, including during the early phase of protest in the south. However, trade union and political party activities only declined in the early phase of the protest wave and they picked up during the shock period. The declining presence of organizations in the streets of SE seems to be a long-term trend. The growing involvement of social groups without organizations began already in the early 2000s.

In this chapter, we have identified differences and commonalities in the action repertoires and the presence of actors in regions facing a protest wave and those not. The next chapter deals with the different sets of issues addressed in these protest events. It asks whether the Great Recession mainly triggered economic protest or whether it fostered protest addressing multiple issues in addition to economic ones.

6 The Return of the Economy?
Issue Contention in the Protest Arena

Theresa Gessler and Julia Schulte-Cloos

6.1 Introduction

For the past decades, studies of protest and social movements have focused mostly on new social movements: Scholars have argued that since the 1970s, citizens have used protest primarily to address claims associated with cultural liberalism. This includes the peace movement, alter-globalization protests, and a wide variety of socio-cultural issues. Yet, with the arrival of the global financial crisis, more recently, attention has turned back to anti-austerity protests across Europe. A broad body of literature, including but not limited to the chapters in this volume, has investigated numerous protests centred on economic issues (Bermeo and Bartels 2014a, 2014b; Giugni and Grasso 2015; Quaranta 2016). These protest events include small, local protests with few participants as well as spectacular mass events such as the anti-austerity demonstrations in Portugal in March 2011, the largest demonstrations in the democratic history of the country. Given the dissonance between our established view of the issue agenda of protest and the renewed importance of economic protest, this chapter explores the issues involved in protests before, during, and since the Great Recession. We contribute to the emerging research agenda on economic protest by comparatively studying the trajectory of contention around different policy domains in the protest arena during the period covered.

As Europe experienced one of the most severe economic crises over the past decades, this chapter's main question is whether the return of hard times changed the distribution of contention over the different policy domains in the protest arena. Bridging social movement theories about the role of grievances with explanations on political behaviour in times of economic crises, we expect that the prevalence of economic protest increases during the financial crisis. Austerity packages imposed hardship, socio-economic inequalities gained salience, and established economic paradigms could be called into question. Thus, we posit that economic protest increased during the

Great Recession and expect that this effect was greatest in the countries most heavily affected by the austerity measures.

As outlined in the first chapter, the structural impact of the economic crisis is mediated by the national political context that conditions the resilience of the economy as well as citizens' willingness to tolerate hardship. Similar to other chapters in this book, we adopt a regional perspective, given the variation in the impact of the Great Recession from one region to another. We argue that varying crisis experiences also served to channel economic grievances into issue domains other than purely economic ones: Governments deflected blame for austerity packages onto international institutions and right-wing challengers mobilized economic fears by promising more exclusive welfare benefits. Hence, the economic crisis was also addressed in political and cultural terms. Furthermore, towards the end of our period of observation, the refugee crisis also had an impact on the protest arena. Accordingly, we focus on the economic but also the political and cultural issues included in the dataset to address the wider impact of the Great Recession on the distribution of protest in Europe.

In what follows, we outline our reasoning about the development of economic, cultural, and political protest during the Great Recession for each of the regions under study. We start by reviewing the literature on the relationship between political, economic, and cultural protest and proceed by describing the changes we expect to occur during the Great Recession for each region. We then continue with the empirical analysis by first outlining our categorization of issues and describing our dataset. Subsequently, we present the development of protest by issue over time and test the proposed hypotheses by comparing the change in salience of the different issues in each region across the periods covered.

6.2 The Relation between Economic Cultural and Political Protest

Early social movement studies considered protest as a rather indiscriminate expression of frustration and grievances that could align with almost any issue. The primary question was, as the title of a classic book posits, 'why men rebel' (Gurr 1970). With the re-conceptualization of protest as a rational form of political participation, some scholars have started to emphasize that individuals' willingness to participate in protests is less a general 'protest potential' (Barnes and Kaase 1979) than an issue-specific propensity to engage in protest activities (Kriesi, Saris, and Wille 1993: 155).

However, this attention to the mobilization potential of different issues has found little reflection in event-based studies, given that the issue-specific protest potential has typically been conceptualized as an attitudinal phenomenon. So far, studies either failed to consider the issues involved in the ebbs and flows of protest or they focused on specific issues or even specific movements without adopting a comparative perspective. Thus, many of our theories are ill suited to understand variation in the salience of various issues in the protest arena. While our analysis is unable to address latent mobilization potentials, it contributes to a comparative understanding of the mobilization regarding different issues, an important outcome of issue-specific mobilization potentials.

Scholars rely mostly on the concept of grievances to explain protest in general or to specifically tie it to economic issues. As mentioned, grievances have originally been a major explanatory factor in the study of popular protest and social movements. The concept of 'relative deprivation' captures a deviation of individuals' resources from their expectations and is 'practically as old as sociology itself' (Gurney and Tierney 1982). According to this line of thinking, citizens turn to protest if their expectations are disappointed (Gurr 1970). This holds particularly under conditions of crisis in which economic affluence rapidly declines, leading to 'suddenly imposed grievances' (Davies 1962; Walsh 1981).

As already mentioned, in the past decades, much of the literature on protest has focused on *cultural* issues. This was due to a criticism of the traditional grievance literature as well as to empirical developments in the issue agenda of protests in the post-industrial societies typically studied by the social movement literature. On the one hand, with the emergence of alternative identity- and resource-based theories, grievance theories have lost standing in social movement studies (Gurney and Tierney 1982). Critiques of grievance-based approaches contend that grievances are always present and citizens require an additional impulse or certain resources to actually act on their grievances and engage in protest. On the other hand, with the rise of new social movements in western Europe (Kriesi et al. 1995), there has been an increase in protest on cultural issues. After the first transformation of the political space in western Europe in the 1970s, scholars started studying these emerging movements. With the fragmentation of traditional cleavages of class or religion in advanced industrialized societies, new issues linked to post-materialist values gained in salience, particularly among the new middle class. Social movement theories 'followed the reality of the streets' (Van Aelst and Walgrave 2001: 462) and turned their attention to studying 'new social movements' as a specific movement family with distinct characteristics.

The second value transformation in the 1990s led to a rise of 'new right' parties in the electoral arena (Bornschier 2010), which also focused on cultural issues, but these new actors did not articulate their conservative position on these issues to the same extent in the protest arena as the new social movements. This is in part due to a preference for more orderly forms of mobilization among organizations on the political right (Hutter 2014; Hutter and Kriesi 2013). Positions close to the traditional, authoritarian, or nationalist side of the political spectrum such as anti-immigration sentiments have mostly been mobilized in electoral politics, as opposed to the protest arena. Thus, for the past decades the protest arena has been dominated by left positions on cultural issues. Regarding the share of events, different kinds of cultural issues have continuously accounted for around half of the protest events in western Europe since the 1970s and left issue positions have dominated in these events, whether on culturally liberal issues or on immigration (Hutter 2014: 82, 91).

However, the importance of these new cultural issues depends very much on the strength of traditional cleavages (Kriesi et al. 1995: 3–25). Thus, the importance of these topics is most evident in north-western Europe, while we have little evidence from the other regions. Even in north-western Europe, however, economic issues have not disappeared with the growing mobilization for culturally liberal issues after the 1960s. 'The bread-and-butter issues of the past, such as employment, have remained and have been supplemented by new concerns such as peace, anti-racism and the environment' (Van Aelst and Walgrave 2001: 462). Thus, the overall protest potential grew through the mobilization of new social groups and their demands. Hutter (2014) found that in terms of salience, the new cultural issues exceeded the traditional economic issues in the protest arena. However, economic issues have joined cultural issues in terms of average participation rates as participation in protests on cultural issues has decreased since the 1980s (Hutter 2014: 82–83). Thus, the relation between cultural and economic protest changes over time, depending on the salience of issues within a society. As we shall discuss in the next section, the Great Recession may have marked another turning point in this relationship.

Beyond cultural and economic protest (with the former including both liberal and conservative positions), we also include political protest in our analysis, i.e. protest addressing problems with the quality of democracy and political representation. While political protest is a frequent occurrence in many democracies, there is less comparative theory about it, given the strong mediating role of domestic institutions and political dynamics. Our only references are studies of the electoral arena (Hutter and Kriesi 2019) which suggest that political issues are primarily salient in eastern and southern Europe, depending on the performance of the political system. The Great Recession provides a unique opportunity for gaining comparative evidence because it triggered political crises with a similar timing across different countries.

6.3 The Issue Agenda of Protest During the Great Recession

As we have argued, the economic crisis may have reduced the dominance of cultural issues. Thus, recent papers often proclaim to bring economic grievances and the political economy 'back in' to the analysis of protest (Kern, Marien, and Hooghe 2015; Tejerina et al. 2013). Across Europe, the austerity programs, the retrenchment of welfare states, and fears of unemployment have again taken centre stage in political conflicts. Policy measures to come to terms with the economic crisis as well as company-specific cuts (such as lay-offs and reduced hours) have increased economic grievances among many citizens. In many countries, the downturn interrupted a period of economic growth and led to suddenly imposed economic grievances. Importantly, the economic crisis also triggered a series of highly salient policy measures such as bailouts and austerity packages that allowed focusing grievances on political issues.

Given the strong impact of the crisis on southern Europe, we expect a particularly pronounced rise in economic protest in these countries. The same holds for eastern Europe, although several of the countries under study in this region had already signed International Monetary Fund (IMF) standby agreements and implemented austerity programs before the financial crisis affected the rest of Europe. Across all of Europe, we argue that, given the nature of the crisis, protest mostly mobilizes against the crisis management by public policies rather than against individual companies. Protest is expected to run parallel with the strong electoral punishment to which incumbent governments have been subjected (Hernández and Kriesi 2016).

> *H1a: The Great Recession led to an increase in the salience of economic protest, directed primarily against the state (public economic protest).*
> *H1b: The salience increase of economic protest is strongest in the regions that were hardest hit by the Great Recession.*

However, the crisis did not only increase grievances regarding the economy. Much of the literature on the political consequences of the Great

Recession has highlighted the connection between political and economic crises across Europe (Hernández and Kriesi 2016; Roberts 2017). In some countries, the Great Recession not only hit the economy but also triggered a lasting political crisis. Arguably, political institutions experience a 'democratic crisis' because neoliberal reforms reduced the capacity to protect citizens' rights (Della Porta et al. 2017: 14). Furthermore, electorally unaccountable institutions imposed many of these reforms. Several studies of public opinion analyse the impact of the crisis on satisfaction with democracy (Armingeon and Ceka 2014; Armingeon and Guthmann 2014; Cordero and Simón 2016). They found that whenever governments have bowed to international pressure to implement austerity programs, this has led to electoral de-alignment and government crises. Electoral upheavals may have been triggered by preceding increases in political protest (see Chapter 11). Many countries have experienced a wave of protest against incumbent governments. Particularly in southern Europe, the kind of crisis management and the electoral punishment of successive incumbent parties has fundamentally altered the structure of political competition. In short, the packaging of austerity measures and rampant political mismanagement and corruption are likely to have often fueled not only economic but also political protest against decision-making procedures.

Thus, we expect the economic crisis to have increased political protest. To be sure, political grievances were already present before the Great Recession. Thus, in southern Europe, corruption was a problem already before the crisis, but a widespread feeling of impunity prevailed as long as the economy flourished (Royo 2014: 1585). In southern Europe, the economic crisis brought an end to public tolerance of corruption and a new focus on political grievances. In eastern Europe, political scandals have dominated the political agenda of some countries for an even longer period. In this part of Europe, the crisis has built on existing political crises and dissatisfaction, further aggravating mistrust among citizens. We would like to suggest that in the first shock period, the attention generally shifted from political to economic issues, temporarily silencing protest against corruption, government mismanagement, and similar issues during the immediate shock period. But with the beginning of the Euro crisis and the accompanying focus on state debt and state capacities, we expect political issues to have gained traction again.

H2a: In the first phase of the Great Recession, the salience of political protest temporarily decreased.

H2b: The salience of political protest increases in the second phase of the Great Recession after 2011.

Furthermore, the Great Recession may also have had an impact on cultural issues in the protest arena. Generally, the concept of issue-specific political opportunity structures (Kriesi et al. 1995: 83–84) also suggests an increasing potential for cultural protest. During crises that impose strong economic constraints, particularly on debtor countries, cultural issues are likely to have a relatively low profile. In the hard hit countries, there are two possible directions of change. First, the increasing importance of economic issues may shift attention away from culturally liberal issues. Such issues may lose relative salience in comparison to the rise of economic issues. However, we may see increasing culturally conservative protest as social movements may try to benefit from the increased openness of the political system on cultural issues. Some countries, mostly in north-western Europe, were only indirectly affected by the economic crisis, as most of them experienced less economic hardship. In these countries, rather than as a domestic crisis the economic crisis entered political discussions in terms of international solidarity and obligations towards crisis-ridden debtor countries. Some governments and political parties have chosen to frame the crisis in cultural conservative or even xenophobic terms (Fourcade et al. 2013), not least to escape punishment by voters. Studies of the electoral arena have also pointed to the growing importance of defensive nationalism in eastern Europe (Hutter and Kriesi 2019) and to the increasing salience of the economic impact of immigration during the Great Recession (Dancygier and Donnelly 2014). We expect an increase in culturally conservative issues in north-western and eastern Europe in particular, given that populist right parties which are most likely to attempt to channel economic dissatisfaction into culturally conservative issues are far less present in southern Europe (see, e.g. on Spain: Alonso and Kaltwasser 2015).

> *H3: During the Euro crisis after 2012, the salience of culturally conservative protest increases in north-western and eastern Europe.*

6.4 Issue Categorization

Conceptually, our analysis distinguishes between five different issue domains. While the dataset offers a categorization on a slightly finer level (including nine different issue areas), for the purpose of the present analysis, we restrict ourselves to five domains. These include two types of economic protest (respectively targeting the state and private enterprises), political, cultural liberal, and cultural conservative protest, with the latter also including xenophobic protest. In addition, the dataset also includes regionalist, environmental, and a residual category of other protest.

According to our coding scheme, a protest event targets a public economic issue when people are taking to the streets and voice their (dis-)content with economic policies of the government or other political institutions, such as the European Troika. These economic policy measures include, for instance, welfare or budget policies, agricultural policies, labour regulation, and public regulation of the economy more generally. Similarly, a protest event is related to private economic issues when people are directing their economic claims and demands against firms or employers and protest, for instance, against the dismissal of staff, the closure of a firm or branch, and labour conflicts related to a pay rise or to a pay cut. Cultural liberal protest, by contrast, includes any protest events related to the promotion of human rights, women's rights (including equal treatment and abortion), gay rights, etc. It also includes peace, international solidarity, opposition to racism, and events demanding autonomous living and cultural spaces. A protest event, in turn, relates to cultural conservativism when protesters take to the streets to oppose any proposal promoted by new social movements. For our analysis, this category also includes xenophobic protests, i.e. racist or anti-immigration demands, right-wing extremism, or protest against foreigners or ethnic minorities. We have separated environmental issues, given that they follow a different dynamic and are heavily influenced by natural disasters and related globally salient events. Though many economic and cultural protest events are also inherently political, we consider a protest event explicitly as political when it relates to the political system and its performance itself, rather than to the policies it produces. Political protest includes mostly mobilization related to corruption, electoral reform, democratic representation, and other institutional issues. Hence, while not every protest that criticizes a government's decisions is political, all grievances related to the political system fall into this category. As a separate category, we also include regionalist protests and counter-mobilization against regionalism as they challenge the boundaries of the existing political system. However, given that such protest also follows a dynamics of its own, we do not aggregate regionalist protest events into our indicator for protest events on political issues.

6.5 The Distribution of Issues

The majority of protest events relate to (at least) one issue domain: Only 4 per cent of all events do not explicitly refer to any issue at all. The five issue domains we focus on make up roughly two-thirds (70.3 per cent) of all events covered. Before we focus on these areas in our analysis, we

Table 6.1. *Distribution of protest events across issue areas*

Issue domain	*N*	Per cent
Economic public	7.662	25.9
Cultural liberal	4.318	14.6
Political	4.004	13.5
Economic private	3.601	12.2
Other issues	3.356	11.3
Cultural conservative (incl. xenophobic)	2.473	7.4
Regionalism	2.175	7.4
Environment	1.999	6.8
Total	29.588	100.0

give a short overview over the weight of all nine issue categories coded in the dataset. The distribution of these eight issues (see Table 6.1) shows that public economic issues, that is, economic claims addressed to the government, are voiced roughly a quarter (25.9 per cent) of the protest events in our dataset. Furthermore, 12.2 per cent include economic claims addressed to employers. This clearly diverges from previous findings on the predominance of cultural liberal issues, which amount to only slightly below 15 per cent of the events we cover. Even also considering environmental issues, which are often mobilized by new social movements (Kriesi et al. 1995), does not change the balance in favour of cultural liberalism: Together, cultural liberal and environmental issues account for only 21.4 percent of the protest events, compared to the 38.1 per cent of economic protest events. As found by previous literature, conservative claims are relatively scarce. This also applies to the somewhat more common protests on xenophobia, which are still less salient than culturally liberal or environmental protests. Hence, we aggregate xenophobic and cultural conservative protests for the rest of the analysis. Together, they make up 7.4 per cent of protest across Europe. Political issues, by contrast, are relatively salient, making up almost 13.5 per cent of protest events. As already pointed out, we distinguish them from regionalist events (7.4 per cent), which we exclude from our analysis to avoid a potential bias stemming from separatist militant groups in a few countries. While the majority of events focuses on a single issue (88.3 per cent), some protest events simultaneously address more than one issue (11.7 per cent). Most often, these events address political claims, next to economic or cultural claims.

6.6 Issue Contention During the Crisis

We start by showing the quarterly moving averages of each issue domain in the three regions to discuss briefly the development of protest over the course of the Great Recession in a comparative way. Next, to test the proposed hypotheses, we analyse the average shares of issue-specific protests in the three regions across the three periods of interest – the pre-crisis period up until September 2008, the shock period until early 2010, and the Euro-crisis period ranging from February 2010 to July 2015. Following the general framework of the book, we assess the findings by region to account for the different crisis experiences across Europe. To substantiate the findings from the three regions, we 'zoom in' to selected countries to discuss the country-specific trajectories of protest events during the crisis and discuss the parallel development in participation numbers where appropriate.

Figure 6.1 shows the quarterly moving averages of all protest events that relate to public economic and political issues across the

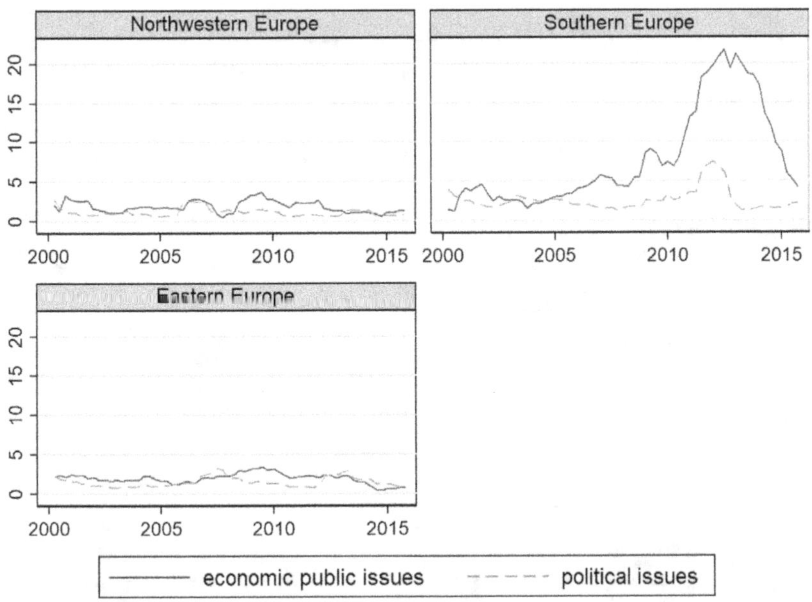

Figure 6.1 Quarterly moving average number of protest events related to public economic and political issues across three regions.

three regions. It provides first evidence of a rise in economic protest targeting the government during the Great Recession. In particular, in southern Europe, we observe a slow but steady rise of public economic protest events from 2010 on until 2013. We also observe a certain surge in economic protest events in eastern Europe during the shock period in 2008, although there was already a period of similarly heightened contention during the early 2000s. In all three regions, economic claims dominate over political protest. Moreover, there is no substantive increase of the latter during the Great Recession. In southern Europe, we observe a period of slightly heightened contention early in the Euro-crisis period, while in eastern Europe, political protest seems to follow its own dynamic, reflecting greater latent dissatisfaction with the political system (Pop-Eleches 2010).

Regarding cultural issues, we observe the influence of specific events on the trajectory of protest, even regarding cultural liberalism as a typical domain for social movement protest (Figure 6.2). In particular, we observe a peak during the anti-war mobilizations in the early 2000s that is visible across the regions, though slightly less pronounced in

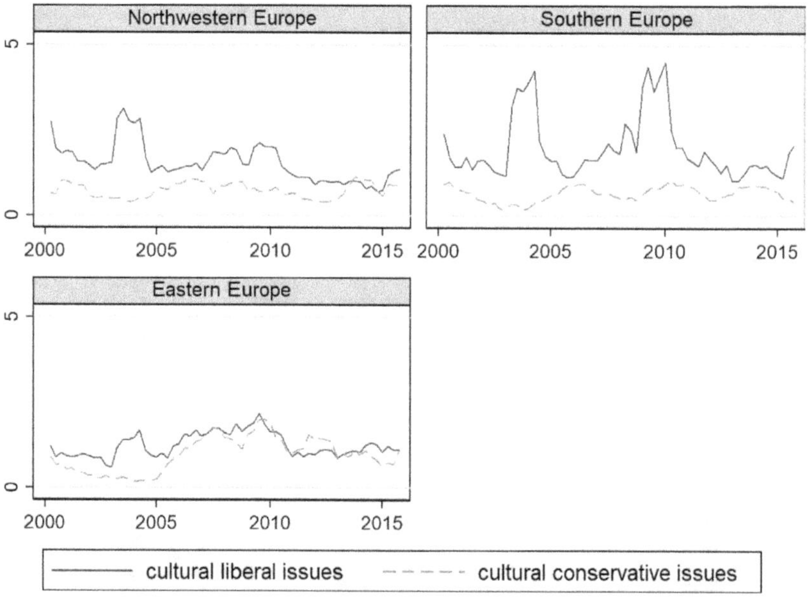

Figure 6.2 Quarterly moving average number of protest events related to cultural issues across three regions.

eastern Europe. We observe a second peak in southern Europe in 2008 and 2009. However, this peak does not affect the whole region equally. It is due to protests and riots after the death of a fifteen-year-old in a conflict with police in Greece and a series of protests on a variety of culturally liberal topics including alter-globalization in Italy in 2009. Furthermore, it is notable that this issue domain is similarly salient across all of Europe and not merely a topic relevant for north-western European social movements. By contrast, from 2006 onward the level of culturally conservative protest is substantially higher in eastern Europe. Nevertheless, remarkably, the economic crisis does not seem to trigger an increase in culturally conservative protest. Though the literature on radical right-wing parties considers socio-structural factors at the macro-level a key demand-side variable to explain the support for radical right parties in a given political system (Jackman and Volpert 1996), the protest arena does not seem to follow this logic in any of the regions.

In southern Europe, the difference in the number of public economic protest events in the pre- and post-crisis period is statistically significant (see Figure 6.3). Compared to the pre-crisis level of economic protest in southern Europe, in the midst of the eurozone crisis, citizens started to voice their (dis-)content with economic policies of the government significantly more often, supporting hypotheses *H1a* and *H1b*. The number of participants involved in these protest events mirrors this finding.

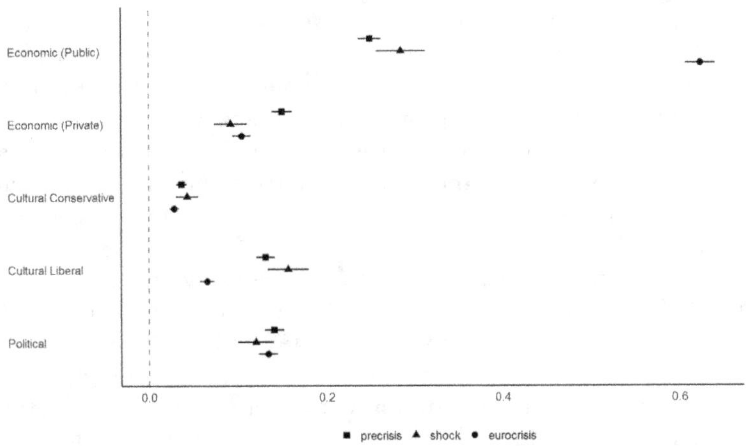

Figure 6.3 Average share of protest events across issue domains in southern Europe.

During the Euro crisis, public crisis management turned into a mass mobilizing issue: During this period, public economic protest amounts to roughly two-thirds of all the protest in southern Europe (62.2 per cent), compared to average levels of such protest that prevailed also in this part of Europe during the pre-crisis (24.9 per cent) and the shock periods (28.4 per cent). This finding suggests that citizens not only punished the government parties in the electoral arena for the austerity measures they adopted during the financial crisis, but also expressed their economic discontent and grievances in non-conventional political participation. Yet, especially regarding participation numbers, this protest only gradually started to increase in the aftermath of the global financial crisis. Thus, in Greece and Spain, two of the southern European countries that were affected most heavily by the financial crisis, although the surge of public economic protest began during the shock period, it reached its peak only during the Euro crisis in 2012. In Spain, this surge roughly coincided with the rise of the 'Indignados' movement.

Regarding hypothesis *H2a, positing* an initial decrease of the salience of political protest, we observe mixed results in southern Europe. There are no statistically significant differences across time in terms of the average number of protest events, though the salience of political protest decreases in terms of participation during the shock period. Regarding hypothesis *H2b*, we do not observe an increase of the *relative* salience of political protest either once the immediate shock period of the Great Recession had passed (see Figure 6.3). Given that public economic protest became overpowering, the absolute salience of political protest might have increased nevertheless. This is partly illustrated in Figure 6.1, where we see the small surge of political issues during the Euro crisis. Yet, when focusing only on political protest that also had an economic dimension (i.e. protest directed against both private economic policies and government measures), we do observe an increase of economic protest in southern Europe during the shock period and during the Euro crisis, which is statistically significantly higher than the pre-crisis level.

Concerning protest related to culturally conservative demands, in southern Europe we do not find any systematic relation to the economic crisis. The high unemployment rates and the severe recession during the global financial crisis and the Euro crisis seemingly did not prompt a higher level of culturally conservative protest in southern Europe. This means that the protest arena did not turn into a forum for the voicing of a potential radical right demand that might have arisen in response to high unemployment rates or the economic crisis more generally. In line with the discussion in the theory section, culturally conservative protest was already at a remarkably low level prior to the onset of the crisis. The share of protest events relating to xenophobic, anti-immigration, or culturally conservative claims even marginally decreased during the Euro-crisis period. This decrease is, however, only statistically significant for the number of participants involved in cultural conservative protest.

Given that many eastern European countries were not (yet) members of the eurozone and had in some cases already started to implement austerity measures before the Great Recession, the impact of the two phases of the crisis on the issue profile of protest events in eastern Europe is less notable and concentrated in the shock period (see Figure 6.4). This moderate reaction is in line with previous research on the relative patience of eastern Europeans regarding economic hardship that studies of the post-transition period have found (Greskovits 1998). While there was an initial increase in public economic protest in the shock period after 2008, compared to the pre-crisis level, the number of protest events related to public economic issues decreased slightly starting from 2012. When considering the number of citizens involved in economic protests directed against the government, we do not observe any statistically significant difference regarding either of the two crisis phases. Yet, participation numbers are somewhat lower during the shock period. This supports our hypothesis *H1a* that economic protest

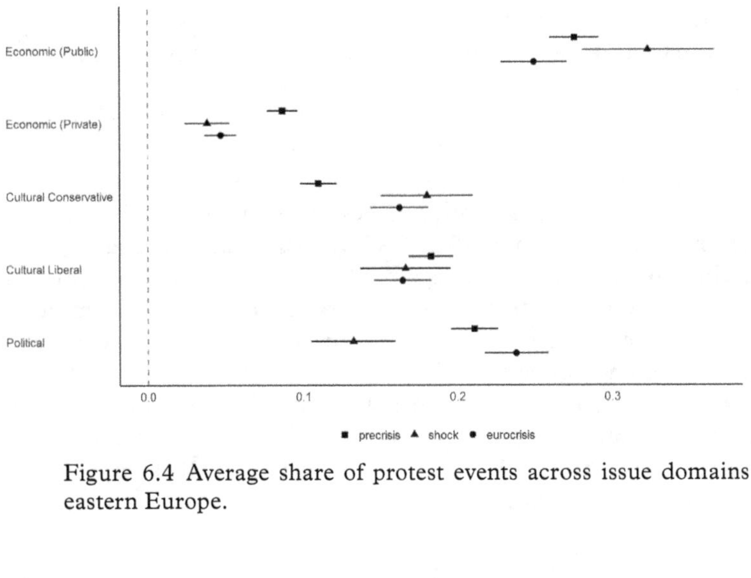

Figure 6.4 Average share of protest events across issue domains in eastern Europe.

increased only in those regions most strongly affected by the austerity measures. As the eastern European countries signed IMF agreements and implemented austerity measures early in the crisis, the impact of the Euro crisis was less pronounced. Thus, we do not observe an increased salience of economic protest stemming from suddenly imposed grievances.

Regarding the salience of political protest in eastern Europe, the trajectory of protest events over time supports the proposed relationship in hypotheses *H2a* and *H2b*. While the number of protest events and the related number of participants significantly decreased during the immediate onset of the crisis, these issues gained more salience during the Euro crisis. Yet, the average share of political protests was already at a comparatively high level in the region before the crisis, given that several countries experienced waves of anti-government protests (e.g. Hungary or Latvia) or a populist party coming to power (e.g. Poland). Thus, the relative salience of political issues during the Euro crisis does not significantly exceed the pre-crisis level. Instead, the temporary acquiescence during the shock period deviates from what appears to be the norm. Hence, the protest arena mirrors the generally high political discontent in eastern Europe that is also visible in electoral politics (Pop-Eleches 2010). Some of these new political mobilizations may also be connected to the rise in cultural liberal demands, given political mobilizations were often connected to environmental demands or protests for housing rights. Consider, for instance, the Romanian movement against the Rosia Montana mining project and the 'United We Save Romania' party that channelled environmental and anti-corruption claims into political protest.

Yet, in eastern Europe, we see a stark increase in the salience of culturally conservative protest regarding both the number of events and the number of participants (see Figure 6.4), which supports hypothesis *H3*. In light of the gradual surge of such protest events after 2005, their rise may relate to the onset of the economic crisis, but may also reflect a trend of cultural conservative protest in the region. Political conflict in the region was heavily influenced by issues around religion, nation-building and ethnic minorities already before the crisis (Rovny 2015). This corresponds to the overall higher salience of cultural conservative protest in the eastern European region compared to the countries of southern and north-western Europe. While the share of culturally conservative protest increased in most of the individual countries in eastern Europe, we caution against interpreting this finding as evidence that economic hardship in those countries further fuelled protest against outgroups. While this hypothesis might hold for some countries, the steady surge of culturally conservative protest already prior to 2008 (see Figure 6.2) suggests that the political disenchantment, and the various domestic political crises that the region faced, contributed to the appeal of national-populist demands in the electorate and related contention in the protest arena. Remarkably, the level of culturally liberal protest in eastern Europe is also high and accounts for a similar share of protest events in the region. These mobilizations may be equivalent to culturally liberal protest in other regions or may present a countermobilization from an emerging new left to the strong culturally conservative or xenophobic protest within those countries.

Given the rapid recovery of north-western European countries during the financial crisis, the prevalence of public economic protest events increases significantly only in the immediate shock period but not during the Euro crisis (see Figure 6.5). Yet, in terms of the number of mobilized participants, the salience of the issue did not even increase during the shock period. In view of the north-western Euro-crisis experience, this supports our hypothesis *H1b* positing that the salience of economic protest increases more within regions that have been strongly affected by the crisis. Parallel to the moderate increase of economic discontent directed against government actors, economic protest directed against private companies was partly crowded out, which is a statistically significant result regarding the number of participants involved, but not for the number of protest events.

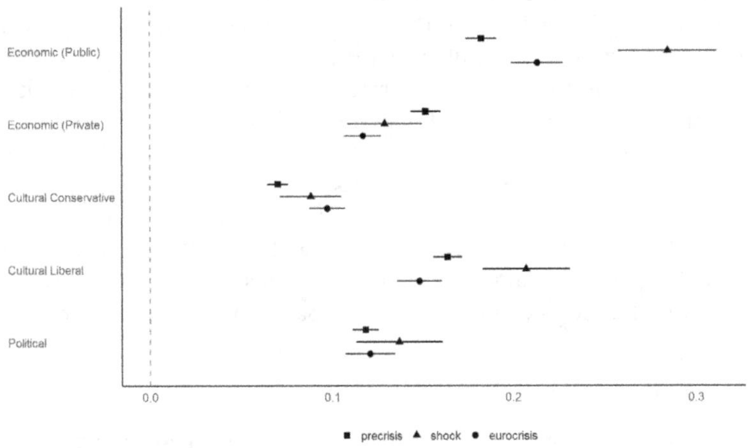

Figure 6.5 Average share of protest events across issue domains in north-western Europe.

When looking at the overall share of culturally conservative protest within the region, we see a significant increase in the share of conservative, racist, and anti-immigration demands during the Euro crisis. In addition to the increase in the share of the number of protest events related to such demands, the issue also mobilized more citizens. A look at the time-line of culturally conservative protest event, however, suggests that those protest events did not gain in importance during the shock period (see Figure 6.2). It was rather the onset of the migration and refugee crisis in 2014 that fuelled the salience of cultural conservative protest in the north-western European region. The sequential development of culturally conservative protest, e.g. in Germany, a country where the migration issue was strongly politicized, highlights the close temporal relationship with the onset of the migration crisis. The observational window of our study includes the populist radical right (PEGIDA) movement that reached peak numbers of protest events across Germany during late 2014 and early 2015. Accordingly, and mirroring the north-western European picture, Germany's protest arena sees a sharp increase in the number of anti-immigration related protest events. Prior to this peak, cultural conservative protest only reached such a high level during the early 2000s. The high salience of cultural conservative protest in the early 2000s corresponds to the influx of refugees from the western Balkan countries during the civil wars in former Yugoslavia (Decker, Kiess, and Brähler 2015).

Thus, the recent increase in cultural conservative protest in the north-western region might have occurred even in absence of the global financial and Euro crisis, leaving us cautious in interpreting the findings as support for hypothesis H3. Yet, the arrival of the economic crisis provided for a renewed appeal of populist rhetoric in most north-western creditor countries. During the onset of the refugee and migration crisis, cultural conservative protest substantially gained in salience in their domestic protest arenas. Furthermore, the German case suggests that similar increases in culturally conservative protest may also occur outside the context of an economic crisis. Finally, let us add that, in line with previous research on new social movements (Hutter 2014; Kriesi et al. 1995), we also find the highest share of culturally liberal protest in this region, especially when considering the average number of participants in such protest events.

6.7 Conclusion

In line with our theoretical arguments, the empirical analysis of the salience of protest domains (regarding both the number of protest events and the numbers of participants involved) finds evidence for a reinvigoration of economic protest within those parts of Europe that were most strongly affected by the economic crisis, namely the southern European region. Citizens channelled their economic discontent with their governments and the austerity measures not only in the electoral arena, but also took to the streets to voice their grievances in the protest arena. The number of protest events against economic policy measures increased massively over a period of several years within southern Europe. Simultaneously, protest against corruption or the form of democratic representation increased significantly during the crisis whenever it was related to economic grievances. Our analyses also show that there was a small increase in cultural conservative protest, particularly in north-western and eastern Europe. When the Euro crisis ended, the migration crisis began to affect the protest arena. Given that our data extend only to the year of 2015, we might even underestimate the full impact of the migration crisis on culturally conservative protest in north-western and eastern Europe. Similar to the economic crisis, there is great variation in the experience of the migration crisis across the three different regions. Just as the economic crisis has significantly altered issue contention during the shock period and the Euro crisis, in the longer run, the migration crisis might alter issue contention in the European protest arenas. The initial evidence of this chapter also suggests that cultural liberal protest might gain in salience in all three regions as a counter-mobilization strategy to culturally conservative or xenophobic protest. Particularly within those regions that had a noticeable protest culture related to cultural issues prior to the crisis, those issues might regain salience in non-conventional political participation.

Part III

Sources of Protest

7 Economic Grievances, Political Grievances, and Protest

Hanspeter Kriesi, Chendi Wang, Thomas Kurer, and Silja Häusermann

7.1 The Relationship between Economic Grievances, Political Grievances, and Protest

Against the backdrop of widespread economic hardship during the Great Recession, the obvious starting point for this chapter is to ask whether there is a direct link between *economic grievances* and political protest. In line with grievance theory, many studies argue that there is no straightforward direct link between the experience of material hardship and political reaction. The type of link between the two has been contested in the literature for a long time, as both demobilizing and mobilizing effects are possible. Based on Jahoda's (1982) latent deprivation model and Rosenstone's (1982) 'withdrawal hypothesis', part of earlier research, argued that, for socio-economic and psychological reasons, economic grievances demobilize participation both in the electoral and in the protest arenas. At the individual level, citizens who struggle with everyday economic hardship may suffer from stigmatization and a depressed self-concept, or simply be preoccupied with making ends meet, thereby lacking the capacity for political engagement. In other words, the experience of unemployment can lead to *withdrawal* from political engagement (Solt 2008). At the aggregate level, scholars such as Mair (2006), Offe (2013), and Streeck and Schäfer (2013) have argued that the economic crisis alienates citizens politically not only via their own experience of hardship, but also by way of a collective experience of disempowerment. Accordingly, they have shown that the existing evidence of a generally demobilizing effect of economic grievances also holds at the aggregate level. Conversely, economic hardship is *more* conducive to political mobilization when citizens perceive the economic situation as unfair or unjust, when they believe that the situation can be changed (Klandermans et al. 2008), and when they blame others, for example the government, for economic outcomes (Arceneaux 2003). The very same economic condition may be *activated for* protest if citizens attribute the causes to factors outside their own control, and if they believe that the authorities could do something about the situation (Incantalupo 2011; Aytaç et al. 2016). Such perceptions of political action capacity and blame-attribution are most likely influenced by political entrepreneurs and organizations (Kriesi et al. 1995), which reinforce demonstration and band-wagon effects of protest mobilization (Kuran 1991; Kurer et al. 2018; Tarrow 1994). Social research also finds that demobilization is less pronounced when individuals experience a generalized, more widespread impact of grievances in their occupational peer group (Brand 2015; Oesch and Lipps 2013). In other words, the impact of economic grievances on protest – both at the individual and the aggregate level – crucially depends on the social and political context, which is often missed by analyses inspired by grievance theories which only examine the direct link between economic grievances and (de)mobilization.

The widespread protest activities across the advanced democracies in the wake of the Great Recession have revived a keen interest in these questions, i.e. in the extent to which – and the conditions under which – economic hardship has the effect of mobilizing contestation, as theorized early on by Geschwender (1968), Gurr (1970), and Schlozman and Verba (1979). Several more recent studies have indeed found evidence for direct mobilizing effects both at the macro- and the micro-level (Bernburg 2015; Burden and Wichowsky 2014; Charles and Stephens 2013; Galais and Lorenzini 2017; Kern et al. 2015; Lim and Sander 2013), in particular in reaction to a sudden and massive deterioration of the economic situation, which is precisely what occurred in the context of the Euro crisis (Kurer et al. 2018; Rüdig and Karyotis 2014). 'Movements of crisis' (Kerbo 1982) have mobilized the economic grievances of their constituents, which are related not only to unemployment, but also to financial strain and worsening working conditions more generally, as Galais and Lorenzini (2017) have shown for the case of Spain.

In our analysis, which is located at the aggregate level, we rely on unemployment as the one indicator that most directly translates macroeconomic performance to individual economic hardship for citizens and their families. With respect to the mobilization of protest, we have seen in Chapter 6 that it is relevant to distinguish different types of protest in terms of the issues articulated. In the present chapter, we start from the assumption that the link between economic grievances (as measured by unemployment) and protest depends on the type of protest considered. In an economic crisis, we expect a closer relationship of economic grievances with economic protest than with non-economic protest. This is by no means a self-evident expectation, as economic hardship could

Table 7.1. *Correlations between unemployment rates (economic grievances) and number and type of protest events (logged population weights), overall and by region*

Type of protest event	All countries	North-western Europe	Southern Europe	Southern Europe (without Greece)	Central and eastern Europe
All types of protest	0.23	0.14	0.45	0.43	−0.03
Public economic	0.38	0.19	0.52	0.53	0.19
Economic	0.36	0.22	0.52	0.53	0.18
Private economic	0.10	0.13	0.25	0.25	−0.02
Non-economic	−0.25	−0.14	−0.52	−0.51	−0.12
N	954	442	192	160	320

just as well be mobilized and channeled in cultural terms, e.g. against immigration. Moreover, in the Great Recession, during which it was above all the public crisis management which was at issue, we expect an even closer relationship between economic grievances and *public* economic protest, i.e. with protest which is addressed to public authorities and refers to their crisis management (austerity policies in particular and economic and social policies more generally), than with *private* economic protest, which is addressed to firms and private employers (mostly labour conflicts or conflicts about the closure of plants). We shall also systematically distinguish between the three European regions, given that they have been quite differentially affected by the Great Recession (see Figure 1.1) and given that, during the Euro crisis, public economic protest increased above all in southern Europe (Figures 6.1 and 6.3). We shall analyse the case of Greece separately, because of its exceptional status that we have already identified repeatedly in the previous chapters.

Table 7.1 provides a first idea of the relationship between economic grievances and protest. It presents the bivariate correlation coefficients for the relationship between economic grievances and the various types of protest, overall and per region, based on biannual data.[1] As is shown by the first row in the table, the relationship between the economic grievances and all types of protest is positive overall and in north-western Europe (NWE) and southern Europe (SE), but not in central and eastern Europe (CEE), where it turns out to be slightly negative.

[1] We use biannual instead of monthly data in this analysis because our indicator for political grievances is available only biannually (see the text that follows).

While the positive relationship is rather modest in NWE, it is quite sizeable for SE (with and without Greece). Turning to the various types of protest, the relationship becomes positive and more sizeable for public economic protest in general and in every region, while it is negative for non-economic protest in all the regions. In other words, during the economic crisis, economic protests have crowded out non-economic protests across Europe. These preliminary results also show that in SE, the 'movements of crises' were most clearly related to economic grievances, while the corresponding relationships are only modest in the two other regions. The relationship for private economic protest is situated in between the two extremes, generally and in each region. That is, economic grievances gave only to a limited extent rise to private economic protest.

As argued more generally in Chapter 1, we expect particularly strong protest mobilization when economic and political grievances occur together. More precisely, we expect the impact of economic grievances on protest mobilization to be *mediated, as well as conditioned by political grievances.* By 'political grievances' we refer to negative evaluations of political actors and institutions by citizens, which are typically measured by the citizens' dissatisfaction with the performance of political actors, institutional distrust, and the dissatisfaction with the way democracy works. Our argument emphasizes both causal pathways, indirect and interactive, as political grievances are to some extent a logical consequence of economic grievances, but they can also be an exogenous factor. The first, indirect, link refers to the fact that economic grievances are likely to *produce* political grievances to the extent that political actors are held responsible for the poor economic performance of a given country. Many studies have shown that distrust of the government and dissatisfaction with the way democracy works increase if citizens are dissatisfied with the economic performance of their country (see, e.g., Polavieja 2013; Quaranta and Martini 2016; Torcal 2014).

However, political grievances do not arise only from economic hardship. Political grievances may also be the result of poor political performance more generally (see Cordero and Simón 2016; Kriesi 2017). As a matter of fact, poor economic performance may not at all be the best predictor of political grievances. For example, Torcal (2014) shows for the cases of Spain and Portugal during the Great Recession that the main sources of political grievances (distrust in parliament) were the lack of responsiveness of their political institutions as well as the perceived corruption of the political elites. More generally, Magalhães

(2014) has demonstrated that, in democracies, political grievances are above all linked to government effectiveness, and Dahlberg and Holmberg (2014) have also shown that popular satisfaction with political institutions is closely linked to the quality of government performance.

Hence, we argue that, more than anything else, it is the *combination* of an economic and a political crisis that fuels economic protest in a country. The reason for this argument is that we expect economic grievances to result in protest only if citizens hold their governments responsible for the macroeconomic and political management of the crisis, and if they see their expectations unmet.

Analogous to economic grievances, we shall first analyse the bivariate relationship between political grievances and the various types of protest to check the direction of the direct link in Europe as a whole and in the three regions we consider. We measure political grievances with the share of citizens who are fairly/very dissatisfied with the way democracy works in their own country. This often-used indicator may have its disadvantages, but it is not so bad after all (Ferrin 2016).[2] We take this indicator from the Eurobarometer, which in principle provides biannual measures for it.[3] Table 7.2 presents the bivariate relationship between political grievances measured in this way and the various types of protest.

The first row again demonstrates the relationship for all types of events. This relationship is strongly positive in NWE, where protest has generally increased with political dissatisfaction during the Great Recession. By contrast, it is close to zero for SE including Greece, and negative for SE without Greece and also negative for CEE. Turning to the various types of protest, we find that, with the exception of CEE, the relationship is positive for economic protest in general and for public economic protest in particular. For public economic protest the relationship is strongest in SE. For private economic and non-economic protest, however, the relationship with political dissatisfaction is generally

[2] We obtain very similar results if we use the share of citizens who distrust political institutions such as the national parliament instead.

[3] In some years, it has been included in the corresponding surveys only once or not at all. Thus, for the eastern European countries, the series only begin in 2003 or 2004 with their accession to the EU. For the non-EU members Iceland, Norway, and Switzerland, we do not have any data at all, and hence they have been removed from our analysis. This leaves us with 804 half-yearly data points for the change in satisfaction with democracy.

Table 7.2. *Correlations between dissatisfaction with the way democracy functions in one's own country (political grievances) and number and type of protest events (logged population weights), overall and by region*

Type of protest event	All countries	North-western Europe[a]	Southern Europe	Southern Europe (without Greece)	Central and eastern Europe
All types of protest	0.13	0.55	0.06	−0.13	−0.24
Public economic	0.23	0.27	0.38	0.29	−0.01
Economic	0.21	0.35	0.37	0.27	−0.02
Private economic	0.00	0.31	0.06	0.02	−0.07
Non-economic	−0.08	0.10	−0.39	−0.29	−0.24
N	804	380	177	145	247

[a] Without Iceland, Norway, and Switzerland.

inexistent or even negative, with the exception of NWE, where it remains slightly positive. This is to suggest that public economic protest in particular was driven not only by economic grievances, but also by political ones.

7.2 The Role of Context Conditions

In line with insights from the social movement literature, we expect that the political and economic context affects the extent to which economic and political grievances translate into protest mobilization. This idea is not new: Early on, scholars of social movements have pointed to the role of political opportunities in turning grievances into voiced protest (e.g. Kitschelt 1986; Kriesi et al. 1995). Building on this literature and following other more recent contributions (Grasso and Giugni 2016; Marx and Nguyen 2016; Solt 2015b),[4] we introduce several aspects of a country's political and economic context that are likely to condition the relationship between economic and political grievances on the one hand and protest on the other hand. More specifically, we expect two types of political context characteristics – low state capacity and

[4] Beyond such political context effects, the socio-structural distribution of economic hardship should also matter, as unemployment may not affect all individuals equally. We analyse these interactions with demand-side conditions elsewhere (e.g. Kurer et al. 2018) but refrain from it here for reasons of space.

international interventions – to amplify the extent to which economic grievances translate into political grievances. Furthermore, we expect that the joint effect of these two grievances on political protest was particularly pronounced during the Euro-crisis period.

Figure 7.1 presents the overall structure of our model for the explanation of protest, which we shall discuss in more detail in the text that follows. In this model, economic grievances are the exogenous factor. Their effect on protest is assumed to be partly, but not completely, mediated by political grievances. In line with the bivariate results, which we have already presented, the effect of both types of grievances is expected to be stronger for economic protest than for non-economic protest, and particularly strong for public economic protest, given that the governments were held responsible for the management of the economic crises. Most importantly, we not only expect that the effect of economic grievances on protest is partly mediated by political grievances (indicated by the indirect link via "political grievances I"); we also expect that economic and political grievances reinforce each other in determining protest (indicated by the interaction with "political grievances II"). We expect the combination of the two types of grievances to have a particularly strong effect on the mobilization of protest. In addition, we expect the effect of economic grievances on political grievances to be conditioned by two types of context characteristics – state capacity and international interventions, while the joint effect of economic and political grievances on political protest is expected to be enhanced in the Euro-crisis period.

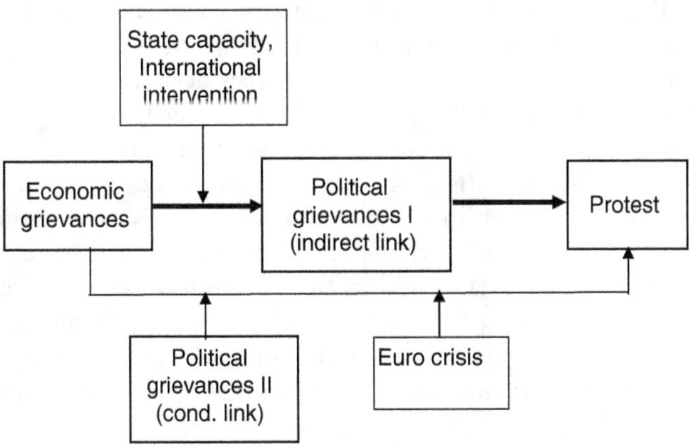

Figure 7.1 Economic grievances, political grievances, and protest.

7.3 How Context Moderates the Effect of Economic on Political Grievances

With respect to the conditioning of the effect of economic on political grievances, we contend that mobilization is reinforced (a) when governments are unwilling or unable to respond to the hardship of citizens and (b) when international interventions impose harsh economic conditions on the national government. When governments and policymakers are captured by the constraints of existing institutional, political, and politico-economic legacies, they may be incapable of enacting decisions that could either relieve hardship or initiate the necessary adjustment to engage in economic recovery. Consequently, when economic grievances raise expectations among citizens vis-à-vis national governments to relieve their pain and when these expectations are not met, protest may erupt with particular force.

This expectation mainly concerns SE, where political grievances rapidly increased during the crisis (see Figure 1.1) and where structural problems, policy errors, and misconceptions predated the Euro crisis and left the countries particularly ill-prepared to respond to the crisis. As we have argued in Chapter 1, the SE countries are characterized by rather weak fiscal state capacity (Beramendi et al. 2015a: 13), and this limited capacity has been additionally undercut by a weak administrative capacity indicated by clientelistic practices and political corruption. As Royo (2014) argues for Spain, we cannot understand the real estate bubble, the loss of competitiveness or the financial crisis without taking into account what he calls the 'institutional degeneration' in Spanish politics. However, as he also argues, civil society tolerated such behaviour before the economic crisis hit the country. Only when the crisis exposed an unsustainable economic model was the public outraged by the actions of its elites. The increased perception of corruption was coupled with growing distrust towards both domestic and European political institutions (Muro and Vidal 2016). As the economic crisis deepened and the overall sense of frustration with the political elites captivated a large share of the population in SE, we expect the weak state capacity to have become a factor reinforcing the effect of economic grievances both on political grievances and on protest in this part of Europe. This expectation holds both as compared to NWE, where state capacity is generally high, as we have seen in Chapter 1, and within SE. As we have seen in Chapter 1 (see Figure 1.7b), among SE countries, Greece certainly has the lowest administrative and fiscal capacity, with both major parties having established a system of party patronage (Pappas and O'Malley 2014), followed by Italy and Cyprus, while Portugal and Spain have comparatively stronger state capacities (for the case of Portugal, see Afonso et al. 2015: 6).

Eastern European countries also entered the economic crisis ill-prepared, but, as a result of the low levels of political and administrative performance and the corresponding high levels of corruption in these countries (Pop-Eleches 2010: 232, Linde 2012), public dissatisfaction with domestic politics was already very high before the economic crisis struck. At the same time, the populations of these countries also had a considerable experience with economic hardship. As has been shown by Coffey (2013) in her discussion of economic voting in the Czech Republic, poor past economic performance increases the citizens' tolerance with respect to poor current performance (and vice versa for good past performance). In line with this finding, the citizens of Central and East European countries in general have been expected to have greater tolerance with respect to poor economic performance than citizens of Western European countries. This would suggest not only that economic grievances have contributed little to political grievances during the crisis, but also that the weak state capacity is unlikely to have reinforced the effect of economic on political grievances in this part of Europe. Alternatively, as argued by Beissinger and Sasse (2014), it is also possible that patience may run out, especially if one's own country is doing much worse than comparable other countries in one's neighbourhood. In other words, it may also be that economic grievances have indeed contributed to political grievances in CEE as well and that the weak state capacity may also have reinforced the effect of economic on political grievances in this part of Europe.

Moreover, in the current European context, it is important to keep in mind that economic and political grievances both have strong domestic and European components. Thus, for understanding the impact of both economic grievances on political grievances and of political grievances on protest, it is important that Europe has developed into a multilevel political structure and that, given the close economic interdependence of the EU member states, the economic crisis in Europe has developed into the Euro crisis (Copelovitch et al. 2016). This crisis has been mainly driven by economic imbalances between different members of the eurozone, which led to the intervention of supranational actors in the crisis management of 'debtor' countries. It was under the pressure from the EU (represented by the 'Troika') that the national governments of the worst hit countries had to adopt austerity policies that were harsh for large parts of society. The model case is Greece, where the Troika intervened most heavily and with most dramatic consequences for the country's economy and its party system (e.g. Hutter and Kriesi 2019; Verney 2014). However, under the impact of the crisis, other countries in our sample became the object of supranational interventions as well.

As a result, the governments' maneuvering space in macroeconomic policy-making was severely restricted and they were not able to adopt the reforms they had originally promised. The supranational conflict, where it is present, obviously is about austerity, too, but it also turns on the defence of the nation-state, national pride, and humiliation, and addresses the democratic deficit at the European level. As Armingeon and Guthmann (2014) have shown, the imposition of policies by international actors contributes to political grievances in the affected countries, independently of other factors.

In this chapter, we focus on national political grievances, given that the crisis management during the Great Recession and especially during the Euro crisis crucially involved national governments, which became the focal point of public attention in the countries hardest hit by the crisis. Chapter 8 will take up the international dimension in more detail and study its impact on protest. In this chapter we shall focus on the effect of international interventions on political grievances and test whether or not international interventions have amplified the effect of economic grievances on political ones. On the one hand, one might expect international interventions to increase the effect of economic grievances on political ones. International interventions put the failure of national authorities to come to terms with the economic crisis into a particularly glaring light. This is also the reason why national governments usually make every attempt to avoid international interventions and deny that they are required to accept them until the very last day before these interventions are imposed. On the other hand, however, the citizen public may react strongly to the national humiliation and the hurt national pride that result from such an intervention, which means that the independent impact of the economic grievances on political dissatisfaction may actually be reduced once such international interventions occur.

7.3.1 The Conditioning of the Effect of Economic and Political Grievances on Protest

As already indicated, we expect the political grievances not only to mediate the effect of the economic grievances on protest, but also to add to their impact and to condition it as well. A straightforward mechanism can account for this expectation: Economic grievances are likely to contribute to public economic protest, i.e. to the most important type of protest during the Great Recession, under the condition that the government is blamed for the management of the economic crisis. If the economic crisis is not blamed on the government, i.e. if the citizens are not dissatisfied with the way the government is managing the economic crisis, economic grievances are not expected to have any effect on the main type of protest. We expect the combined effect of the two types of grievances to be of particular importance in SE, because, as we have argued in Chapter 1, it was hit by a double crisis during the Great Recession – the combination of an economic and a political crisis.

Moreover, we expect economic and political grievances to have had a greater effect during the Euro-crisis period. During the shock period, the citizen public may have given the government the benefit of the doubt: All countries were hit hard by the Great Recession and all governments tried to counter the economic impact of the economic crisis with stimulus programs. However, once Europe had entered the Euro crisis, the economic hardship increased in some countries, especially in the SE, while the economy recovered in some other countries, especially in the NWE. The comparison with NWE made the economic hardship in SE particularly difficult to bear, which is why we expect economic grievances to have had a stronger effect on protest during the Euro crisis, especially in SE. Moreover, as the policy approach of the governments across Europe changed to austerity, governments were increasingly blamed for the economic hardship and it is most likely that these political grievances were increasingly expressed in protests on public economic issues. Again, this effect may have been particularly strong in SE, where the austerity programs were especially harsh.

Finally, the mobilization of public protest also depends on the political opportunity structure. We therefore introduce four components capturing the political environment as controls in this second part of the analysis. First, because political grievances are also expressed in the voting booth, i.e. because elections provide an alternative outlet for political dissatisfaction, we expect that the level of protest is generally lower during election times, when the voters have a more conventional option to express their dissatisfaction. Second, given that protest mobilization is mainly a domain of the left, we expect it to be enhanced, if the left is in the opposition (Kriesi 1995: 59). In the opposition, the left benefits from the mobilization of protest against the government and is likely to support it. When it is in government, it not only does not support the protesters, but the latter also tend to be more likely to give the government the benefit of the doubt and to be more hesitant to attack it in the streets. Following this argument, people are less willing to express their economic and political grievances in the streets when the left is in power. However, as mentioned earlier, the policy of austerity has been playing an important role in contentious politics since the crisis. Following the 'new politics' argument, retrenchment is generally assessed as an unpopular policy choice for all political parties and will always induce discontent from the public, irrespective of the government's color (Pierson 2001; Pierson and Smith 1993), which suggests that there might not be any impact of government composition on public economic protest after all. Third, we expect the polarization of the party system to be negatively related to the mobilization of protest in the streets. If polarization in the party system decreases as a result of the convergence of the mainstream parties on the economic dimension, then the opposition is likely to be articulated not only by challenger parties within the party system, but also by challengers outside of the party system. Finally, we also include International Monetary Fund (IMF) conditionality as a political control variable because the imposition of policies by supranational actors has directly contributed to political protest at the national level, independently of their effect on political grievances.

7.4 Operationalization and Estimation Procedures

In order to test the hypotheses of our model presented in Figure 7.1, we continue to measure economic grievances with the level of unemployment and political grievances with the share of citizens who are fairly/very dissatisfied with the way democracy works in their own country. For the independent variables, we have two measures of state capacity, which we introduced in Chapter 1 – a measure each for administrative state capacity, operationalized by clientelistic practices, corruption and rule of law, and fiscal state capacity, operationalized by the size of the shadow economy. We operationalize the control variables by a dummy variable for countries which have become the object of IMF conditionality in a given period, by a dummy variable for the occurrence of elections in a given six-month period (any kind of elections), by the average left–right position of the parties in government, weighted by their seat share,[5] and by Dalton's (2008) polarization measure. Our dependent variable is the protest frequency, weighted by sampling probability, agency bias, and logged population.

Our estimates are based on biannual data. We shall apply a dynamic model which will be able to take into account the development over time of the relationship between grievances and protest. We begin by checking the stationarity of all the time series variables used in our

[5] This indicator ranges from a minimum of 1 (left-dominated) to a maximum of 8.4 (right-dominated government).

analysis and conclude that our dependent variable is stationary. By contrast, our main independent variables, the unemployment rates and the share of dissatisfied citizens, are non-stationary. We rely on ADL models (so-called autoregressive distributive lag models) with country-fixed effects to explain the half-yearly level of protest mobilization by the corresponding change in economic and political grievances. We use error correction models (ECMs) when political grievances are the dependent variable because they are not stationary.[6] For model specification, we follow a general-to-specific approach. Starting with a general ADL or ECM model to capture the characteristics of the data-generating-process, we then test whether the coefficients for some independent variables can be restricted to zero and select the best fitting model.[7] For estimation, we use ordinary least squares (OLS) estimators.[8] We shall present only the best fitting models.[9] Given its exceptional character, we exclude Greece from the general analysis and come back to it only at the end of Section 7.5.

7.5 Results

7.5.1 Explaining Political Dissatisfaction

Proceeding with the presentation of our results, we start with the ECM for political dissatisfaction. Table 7.3 presents the results for Europe as a whole and for the three regions in our study. As this table shows, political grievances are strongly dependent on previous unemployment levels and on change in unemployment levels. In other words, economic grievances are strong determinants of political grievances. This applies

[6] As Grant and Lebo (2016) argued, all ADL models and ECMs must satisfy the equation balance requirement. To ensure that we have equation balance, we followed the guide provided by Philips (2018) and differenced both political grievances and unemployment rate when explaining protest level, and checked whether all independent variables, including interaction terms, of each equation are collectively stationary, i.e. whether there is a linear combination of these non-stationary variables that is stationary.

[7] All models have been tested for white noise residuals based on the Arellano and Bond (1991) m_2 test or test for OLS as suggested by Wooldridge (2002). We also tested each fixed-effects model against the pooled model and concluded that fixed effects are appropriate.

[8] A well-known problem of analysing dynamic panels with OLS with fixed effects for a small T is the so-called Nickell bias (1981). However, as we have a decent $T = 31$, we use OLS to estimate (Beck and Katz 2011; Beck et al. 2014). We ran robustness checks with the Bayesian orthogonal re-parameterization (OPM) approach (Lancaster 2002), which have led to the exact same results.

[9] Our selection criteria are Bayesian information criterion (BIC) for OLS, deviance information criterion (DIC) for OPM, and significance levels of variables.

Table 7.3. *Change of political grievances, overall and by region: OLS-effect parameters, standard errors, and significance levels*

	ΔPolitical Grievances$_t$				
	Whole Europe	Whole Europe	Southern Europe	North-western Europe	Central and eastern Europe
Political Grievances$_{t-1}$	−0.134***	−0.139***	−0.424***	−0.136*	−0.158*
	(0.040)	(0.040)	(0.104)	(0.056)	(0.068)
Political Grievances$_{t-2}$	−0.110**	−0.103**	−0.185*	−0.130*	−0.048
	(0.038)	(0.038)	(0.088)	(0.053)	(0.068)
ΔUnemployment	0.983***	1.125***	4.463***	1.733	0.808**
	(0.166)	(0.194)	(0.846)	(1.521)	(0.244)
Unemployment$_{t-1}$	0.527***	0.488***	1.804***	1.195*	0.299**
	(0.069)	(0.087)	(0.345)	(0.508)	(0.112)
State Capacity$_t$	−0.384	−1.502	−6.526	5.740	0.517
	(1.282)	(1.575)	(6.577)	(5.525)	(2.214)
IMF$_t$	−0.340	1.352	−0.421	−3.226	−7.441
	(1.391)	(4.372)	(4.112)	(3.182)	(18.565)
IMF$_{t-1}$	1.885	10.960*	−30.084	−2.019	66.450**
	(1.406)	(4.823)	(88.925)	(3.120)	(23.675)

ΔUnemployment*State Capacity$_t$		−0.208	−7.413***	−0.612	−0.259
		(0.343)	(1.664)	(2.405)	(0.449)
Unemployment$_{t-1}$*State Capacity$_t$		0.130	−0.232	−1.034	−0.090
		(0.139)	(0.380)	(0.801)	(0.206)
ΔUnemployment*IMF$_t$		−0.689	−2.865		−0.611
		(1.355)	(2.395)		(2.033)
ΔUnemployment*IMF$_{t-1}$		−1.611*	27.327		1.841
		(0.732)	(84.861)		(1.671)
Unemployment$_{t-1}$*IMF$_t$		−0.130			1.237
		(0.429)			(2.685)
Unemployment$_{t-1}$*IMF$_{t-1}$		−0.655			−8.954*
		(0.403)			(3.522)
R^2	0.196	0.207	0.446	0.232	0.207
Adj. R^2	0.156	0.160	0.367	0.184	0.122
Num. obs.	666	666	113	326	227
Fixed effects	Yes	Yes	Yes	Yes	Yes
White noise residuals	Yes	Yes	Yes	Yes	Yes

IMF, International Monetary Fund; CLS, ordinary least squares.

***$p < 0.001$; **$p < 0.01$; *$p < 0.05$.

to all three regions, but the effects are strongest in SE and weakest in NWE, with CEE taking an intermediate position. In NWE, the crisis was generally not deep enough for economic grievances to result in rising political dissatisfaction. If political dissatisfaction rose in this part of Europe during the period covered, it was for other than strictly economic reasons. In CEE, pain tolerance may, indeed, have limited the impact of economic grievances on political grievances, but it did not reduce them to insignificance (or 'patience may have run out', in the words of Beissinger and Sasse 2014). As a matter of fact, during the Great Recession the effect of economic grievances on political ones has been stronger in CEE than in NWE.

The direct effect of state capacity on political grievances is insignificant and, in general, it does not have the expected enhancing effect of economic on political grievances either. We show here only the findings for administrative state capacity, but fiscal state capacity does not yield any direct explanatory power over political grievances either. Only in SE does the lack of administrative state capacity enhance the effect of economic on political grievances (this does not hold for the fiscal state capacity, as an indicator of which we used the size of the informal economy, and which is therefore closely linked to macroeconomic grievances, while the administrative state capacity is less interdependent with economic performance). If we plot this effect for SE against administrative state capacity as in Figure 7.2, we see that the effect is substantively important. At an administrative state capacity of around 0 as in Italy or Cyprus (see Figure 1.7), a half-yearly increase of unemployment by 0.5 per cent (which corresponds to a yearly increase of 1 per cent) implies an instantaneous increase of political dissatisfaction of about 2.5 per cent. By contrast, in a country with an administrative state capacity of around 0.5 as in Portugal or Spain, an increase in unemployment does not lead to any increase of political dissatisfaction at all. The same pattern applies to the long run as well. In SE, as a result of the increasing economic difficulties, it seems that the citizen public has, indeed, become less tolerant of the administrative deficiencies in its own country. But, beyond Royo's (2014) claims about the single case of Spain, the declining tolerance seems to have been even more consequential in Italy and Cyprus than in Spain or Portugal.

International interventions do not have a general direct effect on political dissatisfaction either, but they do interact with unemployment in determining political dissatisfaction, too. In their case, however, the interaction effects are all negative and partly significant for Europe as a whole. This means that international interventions tend to reduce the effect of economic grievances on political grievances.

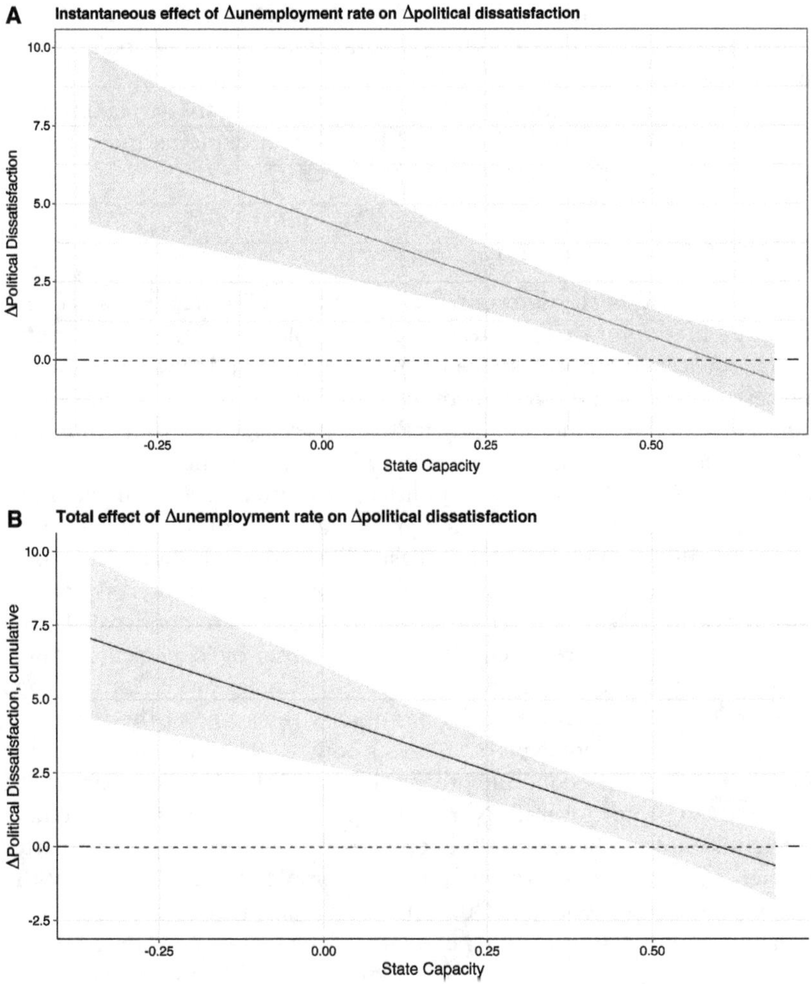

Figure 7.2 Instantaneous and total effects of change in unemployment on change in political dissatisfaction, conditioned by state capacity, for southern Europe (Table 7.3).

In countries in which international interventions impose austerity measures on the national government, the direct effect of economic grievances on political dissatisfaction is to some extent counteracted by the national humiliation linked to international interventions which act as a substitute for economic grievances in contributing to political grievances. This substitutive effect is particularly clear-cut in CEE, which is another indication of the tolerance for economic pain in this part of Europe.

As is indicated by the R^2 values, the model for the explanation of political grievances works best for SE, where it explains more than a third of the variance. It is least adapted to CEE.

7.5.2 Explaining the Level of Protest

For the analysis of the determinants of the level of protest, we start with the presentation of three ADL models in Table 7.4. This table presents two models each for protest overall, for economic and for non-economic protest – a model (a) without interactions and a model (b) with interactions between economic and political grievances. A first finding is that the factors explaining economic and non-economic protest are very different. While economic and political grievances are of considerable importance in the determination of economic protest, they have no impact at all for non-economic protest. This may not be surprising after all, because non-economic protest has long been attributed to 'movements of affluence', i.e. movements which typically are not driven by the grievances of their direct beneficiaries, but rather by 'conscience adherents' who mobilize on behalf of some beneficiaries or collective goods (Kerbo 1982: 655). However, it does qualify the scope of the argument that grievances cannot explain protest, a point that has mostly been made on the basis of non-economic protest, but (mistakenly, as it seems) with reference to protest overall. Nor do the political control factors we take into consideration have any effect on non-economic protest. As a matter of fact, non-economic protest is almost completely determined by the autoregressive component of the model, which means that it develops in a path-dependent way, independently of the factors considered in our model. By contrast, changes in economic and political grievances each have a positive, but weak instantaneous effect on economic protest. In addition, instantaneous and lagged interactions between the two types of grievances also have an influence on economic protest. Given the prevalence of economic protest during the Great Recession, the pattern of the factors determining overall protest is similar to the one for economic protest, although the effects are generally weaker.

The second important finding refers to the models for the most important form of protest during the Great Recession, economic protest. While the introduction of interactions between economic and political grievances neither improves the models for protest overall nor for non-economic protest, it does so for economic

Table 7.4. *Level of protest events, overall OLS-effect parameters, standard errors, and significance levels*

	Protest (overall)$_t$		Protest (economic)$_t$		Protest (non-economic)$_t$	
	Model 1a	Model 1b	Model 2a	Model 2b	Model 3a	Model 3b
Protest (overall, economic other)$_{t-1}$	0.253***	0.256***	0.230***	0.221***	0.897***	0.895***
	(0.033)	(0.033)	(0.037)	(0.037)	(0.013)	(0.013)
ΔPolitical grievances$_t$	1.768*	0.413**	1.052*	0.282***	0.266	0.004
	(0.765)	(0.134)	(0.490)	(0.085)	(0.218)	(0.038)
ΔPolitical grievances$_{t-1}$	−1.151	−0.126	−0.077	−0.029	−0.355	0.010
	(0.770)	(0.135)	(0.494)	(0.085)	(0.220)	(0.038)
ΔUnemployment$_t$	0.354**	1.624*	0.234**	0.915†	−0.002	0.256
	(0.131)	(0.770)	(0.084)	(0.487)	(0.037)	(0.220)
ΔUnemployment$_{t-1}$	−0.069	−0.744	0.019	−0.110	0.011	−0.245
	(0.131)	(0.846)	(0.084)	(0.535)	(0.037)	(0.241)
IMF$_t$	5.297	5.293	5.198	5.942†	−0.490	−0.635
	(5.056)	(5.067)	(3.240)	(3.204)	(1.439)	(1.445)
IMF$_{t-1}$	2.465	2.644	−0.031	0.442	−0.753	−0.818
	(5.100)	(5.106)	(3.270)	(3.231)	(1.452)	(1.457)
System Polarization$_t$	−2.314†	−2.315†	−0.541	−0.480	−0.373	−0.396
	(1.396)	(1.396)	(0.891)	(0.879)	(0.397)	(0.398)
Cabinet Position$_t$	0.413	0.413	0.494*	0.500*	0.059	0.061
	(0.372)	(0.372)	(0.240)	(0.236)	(0.106)	(0.106)
Election Month$_t$	−1.775	−1.766	−1.658†	−1.658†	−0.262	−0.270
	(1.344)	(1.344)	(0.860)	(0.849)	(0.382)	(0.383)
Election Month$_{t-1}$	1.805	1.797	1.159	1.174	0.377	0.366
	(1.349)	(1.350)	(0.865)	(0.854)	(0.383)	(0.384)

Table 7.4 *(cont.)*

	Protest (overall)$_t$		Protest (economic)$_t$		Protest (non-economic)$_t$	
	Model 1a	Model 1b	Model 2a	Model 2b	Model 3a	Model 3b
ΔUnemployment$_t$*ΔPolitical Grievances$_t$		0.053		0.403**		−0.043
		(0.203)		(0.128)		(0.058)
ΔUnemployment$_t$*ΔPolitical Grievances$_{t-1}$		0.037		0.212		−0.033
		(0.239)		(0.151)		(0.068)
ΔUnemployment$_{t-1}$*ΔPolitical Grievances$_t$		−0.194		−0.271**		−0.004
		(0.141)		(0.089)		(0.040)
ΔUnemployment$_{t-1}$*ΔPolitical Grievance$_{t-1}$		0.136		0.151		−0.009
		(0.182)		(0.115)		(0.052)
R^2	0.121	0.128	0.114	0.144	0.882	0.882
Adj. R^2	0.074	0.075	0.066	0.092	0.875	0.875
AIC	5,686.9	5,689.7	5,047.9	5,031.3	3,882.7	3,888.4
Num. obs.	718	718	718	718	718	718
Fixed effects	Yes	Yes	Yes	Yes	Yes	Yes
White noise residuals	Yes	Yes	Yes	Yes	Yes	Yes

AIC, Akaike information criterion; IMF, International Monetary Fund; OLS, ordinary least squares.
$^{***}p < 0.001$; $^{**}p < 0.01$; $^{*}p < 0.05$; $^{\dagger}p < 0.1$.

protest. This is indicated by the improved predictive power of the interaction model for economic protest, as well as by the reduced Akaike information criterion (AIC) values. For the interpretation of the complex pattern of direct and interaction effects for the explanation of economic protest we turn to Figure 7.3. The two graphs in this figure show the instantaneous and total effects of changes in

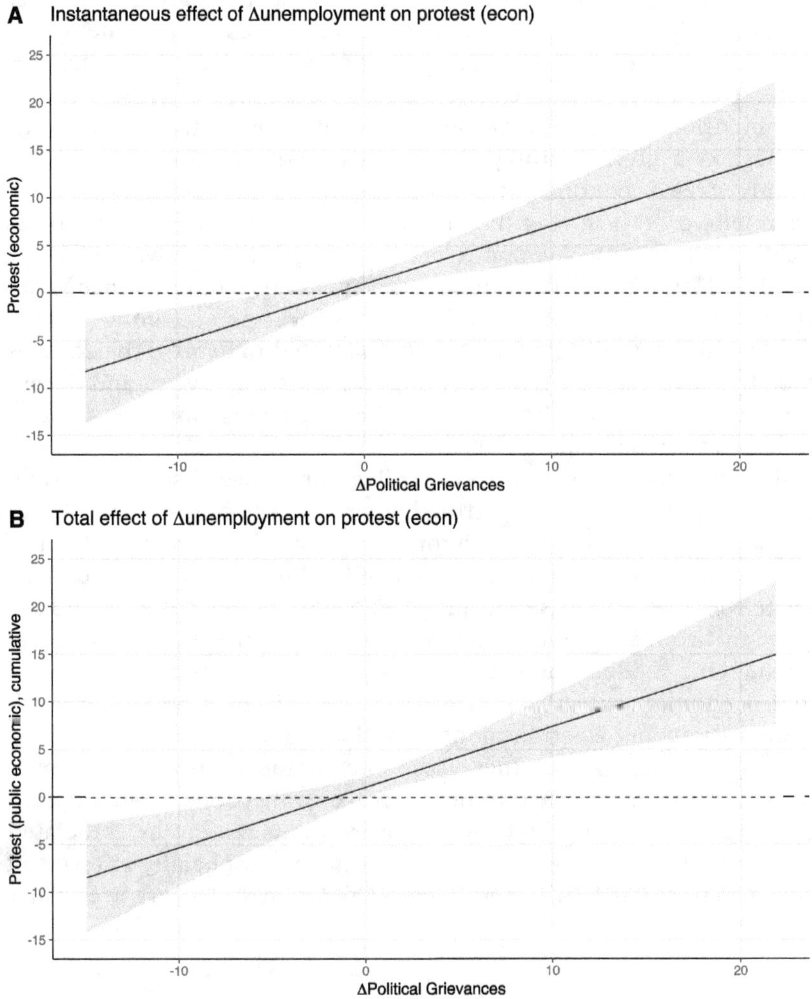

Figure 7.3 Interaction between economic and political grievances (economic protest model 2 from Table 7.4).

unemployment, i.e. economic grievances, on economic protest for different changes in political dissatisfaction, i.e. political grievances. As is immediately apparent, there are increasing effects of economic grievances on protest when change in political dissatisfaction is increasing. Changes in unemployment thus have significant effects on economic protest, depending on changes in political dissatisfaction: While increasing unemployment reduces the amount of economic protest when political dissatisfaction decreases, it increases the amount of economic protest when political dissatisfaction goes up. At stable levels of political dissatisfaction, changes in unemployment do not have any impact on economic protest at all. This is a perfect illustration of the idea that it takes a *double crisis* – i.e. the combination of an economic with a political crisis – to fuel economic protest in a given country. More than anything else it is the co-occurrence of economic and political grievances that led to a rise in economic protest during the Great Recession. Economic grievances hence contribute to economic protest in two distinct ways: On the one hand, they increase political grievances, and, on the other hand, they reinforce the effect of political grievances on economic protest. Regarding temporal dynamics (not illustrated in detail), the effect is mostly instantaneous, i.e. occurring in the first half year, and decays rapidly, which is why the pattern in the long run is much the same as the instantaneous one for Europe as a whole.

Turning to the effect of the control variables, we observe that IMF conditionality, on average, strongly increases the overall level of protest as well as the level of economic protest. However, the effect of IMF interventions seems to vary considerably from one target country to the other, because, in spite of the very strong effect, we do not see significance. The next chapter will analyse these effects in more detail. Our models for overall and economic protest (but not for non-economic protest) also confirm that the level of protest, indeed, decreases during election months, and that it generally decreases as the level of polarization increases. The composition of government does have an effect in our model for overall protest and on economic protest too, i.e. right-wing governments tend to be associated with more protest than left-wing governments, especially in terms of economic protest.[10] All the effects of the control factors are rather

[10] We also ran general models including interaction between cabinet position and political grievances, and we did not find significant interaction terms.

weak. Moreover, note that judging by the within R^2 values (0.07 and 0.09 respectively for economic and overall protest), our capacity to predict the levels of economic and overall protest over time is rather limited.[11]

7.5.3 Explaining Public Economic Protest

In the next step of our analysis, we focus on *public* economic protest, which, as we have argued, is most likely to be influenced by the combination of economic and political grievances. Table A7.1 presents the detailed results of the models for the levels of public economic protest, overall and by region. Again we present only the best fitting models. For the whole of Europe, the pattern of effects is very similar to the pattern we found in the previous table for economic protest in general. At the European level, public economic protest, just like economic protest in general, depends on a complex pattern of instantaneous and lagged interactions between the two types of grievances. The left-hand side of Figure 7.4 illustrates these interaction effects. These effects are very similar to the ones presented for economic protest in general in the previous graph: Change in unemployment has a significant, mostly instantaneous, effect on public economic protest, if political dissatisfaction increases at the same time.

Turning to the regional patterns, it becomes apparent that the overall pattern reflects to a large extent the pattern in SE, as shown in the second set of graphs in Figure 7.4. In SE, although the confidence interval of the short-run effect crosses 0, possibly due to a smaller sample size, the pattern is the same as for Europe as a whole. Moreover, the scale of the total long-run effect of change in unemployment on public economic protest in interaction with political dissatisfaction is much larger (almost two times larger) than the overall effect for the whole of Europe. Additional analyses (not illustrated in detail) demonstrate that the impact of unemployment on protest in SE decays less rapidly than in the other regions, which is the reason why it results in larger cumulative total effects. In CEE, we also find a similar pattern (see third set of graphs in Figure 7.4), but the scale of the interaction

[11] Given that our models include fixed effects, the R^2's in the table refer to the explanation of over-time variation. The overall R^2 actually lies above 0.30, which indicates that the largest part of the variation is due to differences between and not within countries.

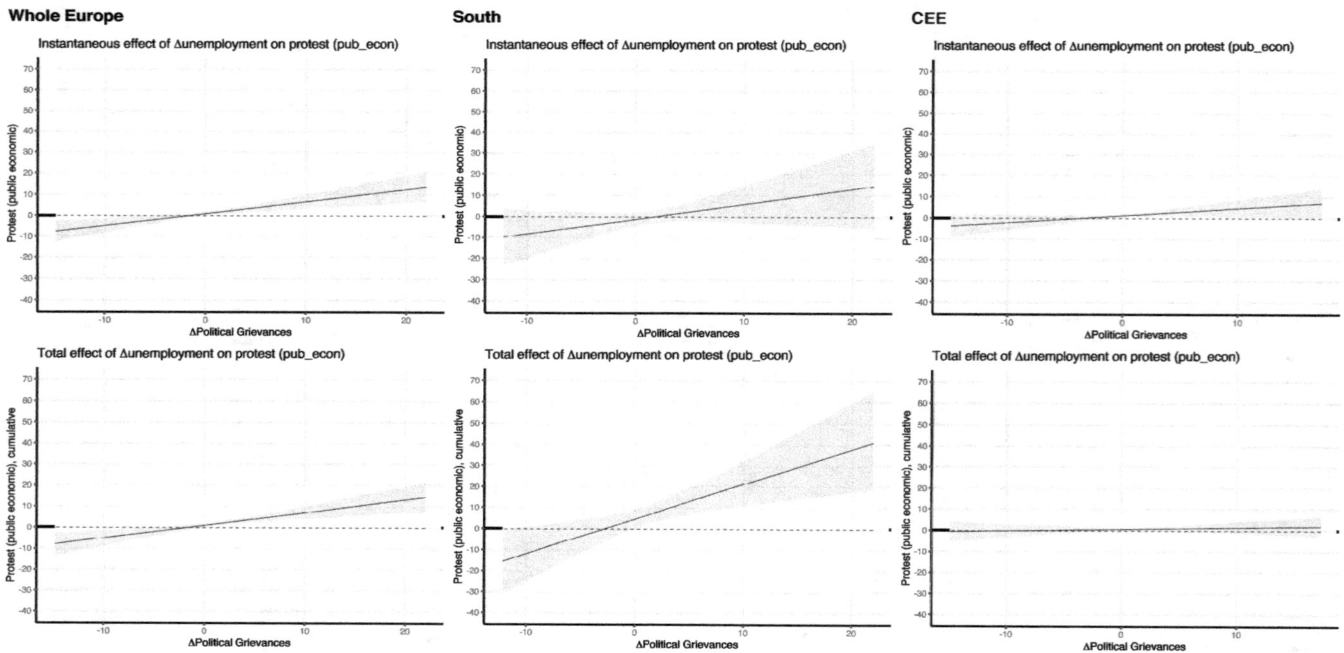

Figure 7.4 Interaction effect of change in unemployment on public economic protest, conditioned by change in political dissatisfaction (whole of Europe, southern and central and eastern Europe models from Table 7.5).

effect is much smaller, and there is hardly any long-term impact on public economic protest levels. By contrast, in NWE, there is hardly any indication of an interaction between economic and political grievances, nor of some direct effect of either one of them. In other words, the strong overall interaction effect of economic and political grievances on public economic protest (and by implication on economic protest more generally) is driven mainly by the events in SE. While the model explains virtually nothing of the over-time variance of public economic protest in NWE, it is able to explain more than a third of the corresponding variance in SE.

As for the control variables, their effects are once again generally weak. We can confirm that right-wing governments are more likely than left-wing governments to be opposed by public economic protest in the streets, but the effect is significant only for NWE. We also find that, during election times, the level of public economic protest is reduced in all regions, but the corresponding effect is weak and hardly significant at all. The effect of system polarization is generally insignificant, and it has the expected negative sign only in SE. IMF interventions, by contrast, have a strong impact on the mobilization of protest in SE and NWE, but the effect varies again heavily from one country to the other, which implies that it reaches conventional significance levels only for SE. In CEE, IMF interventions do not lead to immediate increases in protest.

Finally, we test for *period-specific effects* of the two types of grievances on the level of public economic protest. We specify a general model with interaction terms between political and economic grievances, on the one hand, and a period dummy on the other hand. In line with our hypothesis, we use 2010 as the dividing point.[12] The first period includes the pre-crisis and the shock period, while the second covers the Euro crisis. Table A7.2 presents the detailed results for Europe overall and for each one of the three regions. These results are most complex, because they involve a three-way interaction. Figure 7.5 illustrates the period effect on the interplay between the two types of grievances. As these figures show, the combined effect of economic and political grievances is, indeed, characteristic of the period of the *Euro crisis* – for Europe as a whole and, more specifically, for SE which is again responsible for the overall effect. Before the Euro crisis, the

[12] We tested alternative periodizations – one with the three periods that we used throughout this volume, and one with two periods (pre-crisis [up to 2008] and crisis [2009–2015]), but based on model selection criteria (BIC), the model we present here provides a better fit to the data.

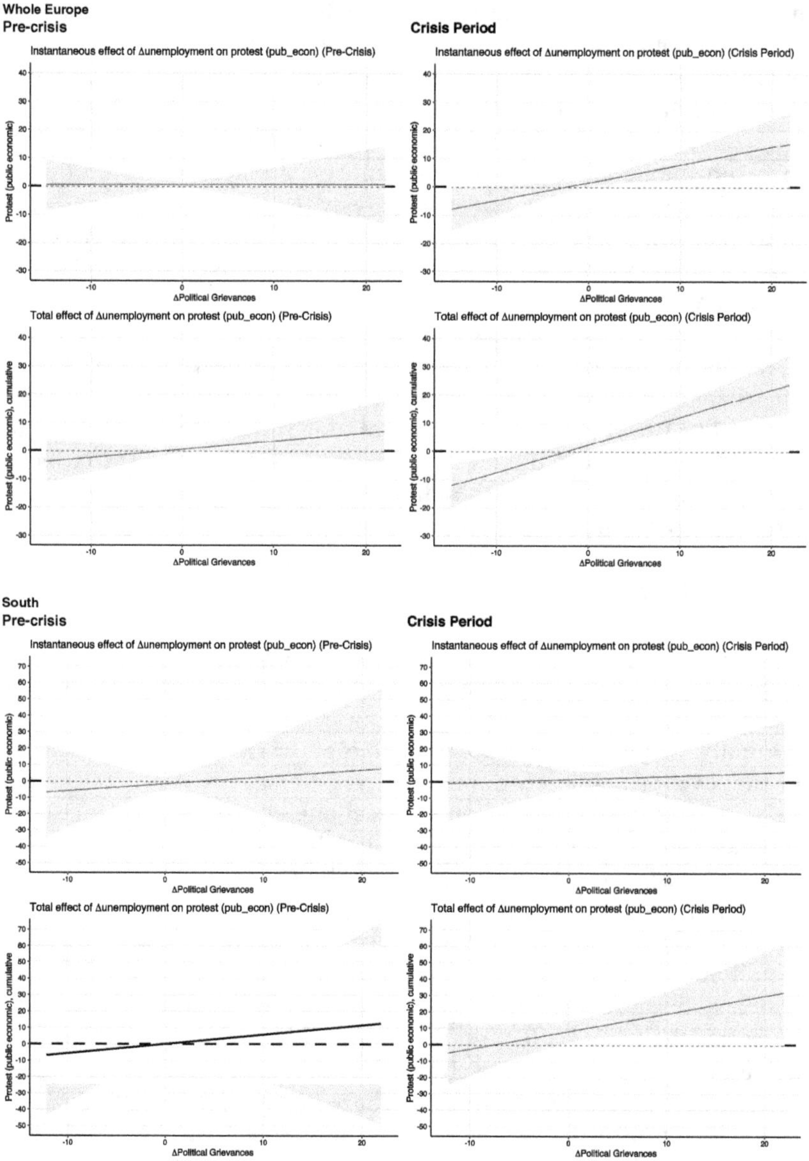

Figure 7.5 Interaction between economic and political grievances in pre-crisis and crisis periods (whole of Europe from Table A7.2).

combined effect is somewhat visible overall and in SE (and also in NWE (not shown), but it turns out to be much weaker and hardly significant in the pre-crisis period.

7.6 The Perfect Storm: Greece as a Special Case

Throughout this study, Greece proved to be a special case and has thus been excluded from the pooled analysis. The main reason for this is that the combination of an exceptional economic with an exceptional political crisis sets Greece apart, even within SE, where the countries typically experienced a double crisis. The combination of the two types of crises during the Euro crisis is illustrated by the parallel explosion of the economic and political grievances in Greece during the Euro-crisis period. As we can see in Figure 7.6, the explosion of the political grievances preceded the one of the economic grievances by about a year, but from 2010 onwards the two essentially moved in lockstep to create 'a perfect storm' (Altiparmakis 2019a), which is reflected in the exceptionally high correlation ($r = 0.91$) between the level of the two types of grievances.[13] Greece is also special to the extent that its protest explodes during the Euro crisis, which means that the protest series for Greece are not stationary. Moreover, the pattern of relationships between public economic protest and the two types of grievances is characterized by a clear structural break in Greece. This is shown by a Markov-switching model applied to the relationships between the two types of grievances and the level of public economic protest for Greece.[14]

Table 7.5 presents the coefficients from the Markov-switching regression.[15] We can see that there are two states for Greece. In the crisis periods (2008 and the Euro-crisis period), change in political grievances has a highly significant and strong effect on public economic protest, while in the previous period change in political grievances hardly played a role

[13] The correlation between political and economic grievances has been checked for other panels as well. Only Greece is characterized by an extremely high level of correlation.

[14] We checked other panels and concluded Greece is a special case which has undergone a structural break.

[15] For the Markov-switching model, p11 = 0.813, p12 = 0.187, p21 = 0.160, and p22 = 0.840. p11 denotes the probability of staying in state 1 in the next period given that the process is in state 1 in the current period. Likewise, p22 denotes the probability of staying in state 2. p12 and p22 are one step transition probabilities which are the probabilities of transitioning from one state to another in a single step.

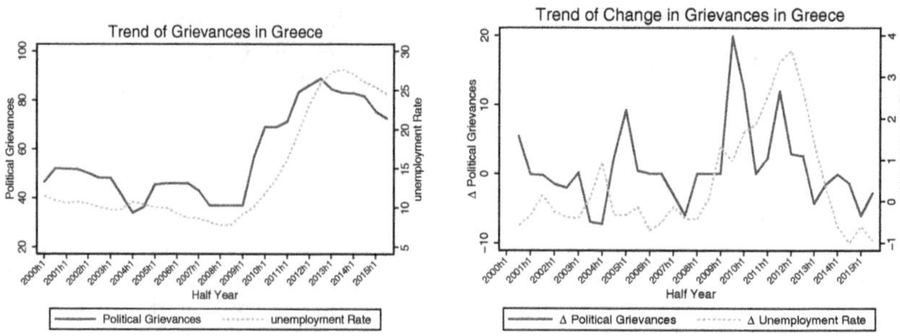

Figure 7.6 Development of political and economic grievances in Greece.

Table 7.5. *Markov-switching model for Greece*

	Protest (Public Economic)$_t$	
	Crisis period (2008 and 2010–2015)	Non-crisis period (2000–2007)
ΔPolitical Grievances$_t$	3.037***	0.743†
	(0.608)	(0.390)
ΔUnemployment$_t$	14.226***	9.877**
	(2.186)	(2.430)

***$p < 0.001$; **$p < 0.01$; *$p < 0.05$; †$p < 0.1$.

at all. Unemployment, however, has a very strong effect on protest in both periods, with the effect in the crisis period being even bigger. This means that, contrary to the other countries in SE, economic grievances have already driven public economic protest in Greece before the crisis, and the size of their effect has become much bigger during the crisis. During the crisis, however, we see the same combination of effects of the two types of grievances as in the rest of SE. Figure 7.7 presents transitions between the two regimes over time. In 2008, when protest exploded because of the incident with the killing of a student in Athens, the regime switched to State 2, which corresponds to the coefficients in the crisis period but did not stay there and went back to State 1, which corresponds to the coefficients in the non-crisis period. However, once the Euro crisis hit Greece, the regime switched to State 2 again and stayed there for most of the time until 2015.

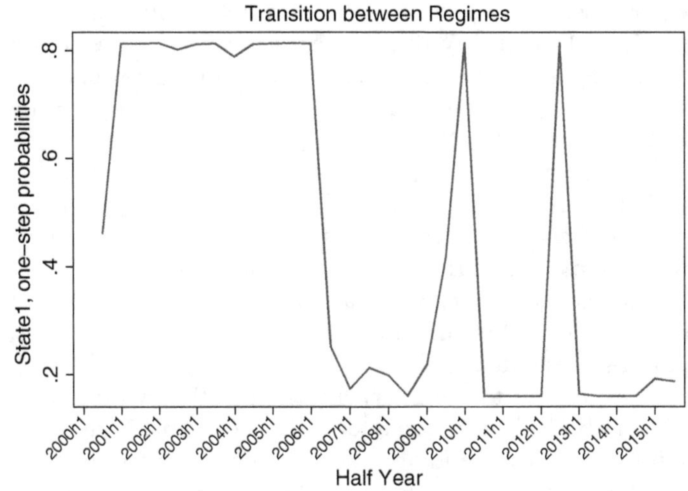

Figure 7.7 Transition probabilities in Markov-switching model for Greece.

7.7 Conclusion

In this chapter, we have analysed the relationship between economic and political grievances as well as their joint role for the determination of the mobilization of protest during the Great Recession in Europe – the overall level of protest and the level of public economic protest in particular. In a preliminary analysis, we considered the direct bivariate relationships between each type of grievances and the level of diverse types of protest. We found economic grievances to be most closely related to public economic protest, the most important type of protest during the Great Recession, while they have been crowding out non-economic protest. The relationship proved to be strongest in SE. Similarly, we found a strong link between political grievances and public economic protest, again most clearly in the European south.

Having established that economic and political grievances matter for economic protest in general and public economic protest in particular, we proceeded with the more detailed analysis of the relationship between the two types of grievances. As expected, political grievances have been strongly influenced by economic grievances across Europe during the period covered. However, the relationship proved to be the closest in SE, while it was much weaker in NWE, with CEE constituting an intermediate case. While the rapid recovery of the countries of NWE and the pain tolerance in the countries of CEE probably served to limit the impact of the economic grievances on political dissatisfaction, the fact that the SE countries not only were hard hit by the economic crisis, but also experienced a relative decline with regard to the other parts of Europe most likely enhanced the impact of economic on political grievances in this part of Europe. Moreover, it is also above all in SE, that the effect of economic on political grievances was conditioned by state capacity and IMF interventions: While weak state capacity enhanced the effect of the former on the latter, IMF interventions attenuated it.

Finally, we turned to the interplay between the two types of grievances. A core finding of this chapter is that economic protest was most heavily influenced by the joint effect of economic and political grievances. Protest mobilization was particularly pronounced whenever dire economic conditions and dissatisfaction with the political system rose together and reinforced each other. This joint effect proved again to be strongest in SE, where it manifested itself in particular during the Euro crisis. In other words, in SE, the sharp increases in economic grievances during the Euro crisis not only contributed to the rise of political grievances, but they also enhanced the effect of political grievances on (public) economic protest. The double economic and political crisis of SE was the key determinant of the protest wave that we have identified in Chapter 4, and the absence of such a combination of crises explains the absence of a corresponding wave in the other parts of Europe. It is also noteworthy that neither economic nor political grievances, whether separately or jointly, did have any impact at all on non-economic protest.

Throughout this chapter, we have treated Greece separately. While Greece shares the SE pattern of the double crisis and its impact on economic protest, in this case of an extraordinary conflagration of the two crises, the combined grievances had an extraordinary impact on protest during the crisis period (which also includes the year 2008). Moreover, economic grievances already drove protest in Greece before the crisis period.

Appendix: Additional Tables

Table A7.1. *Level of public economic protest, overall and by region: OLS-effect parameters, standard errors, and significance levels*

	Protest (Public Economic)$_t$			
	Whole of Europe	Southern Europe	North-western Europe	Central and eastern Europe
Protest (Public Economic)$_{t-1}$	0.202***	0.332***	−0.010	0.117†
	(0.037)	(0.076)	(0.054)	(0.070)
ΔPolitical Grievances$_t$	0.241**	0.188	0.154	0.289***
	(0.079)	(0.245)	(0.124)	(0.081)
ΔPolitical Grievances$_{t-1}$	−0.061	−0.067	−0.295*	−0.105
	(0.079)	(0.254)	(0.124)	(0.089)
ΔUnemployment$_t$	0.980*	−1.052	0.540	1.290***
	(0.453)	(1.689)	(0.988)	(0.376)
ΔUnemployment$_{t-1}$	−0.099	4.226*	0.028	−0.590
	(0.498)	(2.088)	(1.048)	(0.397)
IMF$_t$	5.711†	18.068*	7.875	−0.673
	(2.982)	(7.838)	(7.352)	(2.528)
IMF$_{t-1}$	1.499	−10.424	−0.131	2.973
	(3.008)	(8.018)	(7.439)	(2.653)
System Polarization$_t$	0.137	−2.224	0.212	0.211
	(0.819)	(4.393)	(1.024)	(1.073)

Table A7.1 *(cont.)*

	Protest (Public Economic)$_t$			
	Whole of Europe	Southern Europe	North-western Europe	Central and eastern Europe
Cabinet Position$_t$	0.470*	0.434	0.798*	0.150
	(0.220)	(0.557)	(0.363)	(0.240)
Election Month$_t$	−1.432†	−3.394	−1.604	−1.275
	(0.790)	(2.689)	(1.144)	(0.801)
Election Month$_{t-1}$	1.533†	7.099*	0.295	0.714
	(0.795)	(2.776)	(1.151)	(0.798)
ΔUnemployment$_t$*ΔPolitical Grievances$_t$	0.360**	1.059**	−0.055	0.375*
	(0.119)	(0.355)	(0.255)	(0.156)
ΔUnempl$_t$*ΔPolitical Grievances$_{t-1}$	0.215	−0.354	0.224	−0.044
	(0.141)	(0.399)	(0.388)	(0.138)
ΔUnempl$_{t-1}$*ΔPolitical Grievances$_t$	−0.233**	−0.547**	−0.138	−0.289*
	(0.083)	(0.175)	(0.192)	(0.138)
ΔUnemployment$_{t-1}$*ΔPolitical Grievances$_{t-1}$	0.147	0.941*	0.388	0.028
	(0.107)	(0.463)	(0.270)	(0.082)
R^2	0.141	0.459	0.063	0.196
Adj. R^2	0.089	0.370	−0.011	0.100
Num. obs.	718	135	356	227
Fixed effects	Yes	Yes	Yes	Yes
White noise residuals	Yes	Yes	Yes	Yes

$^{***}p < 0.001$; $^{**}p < 0.01$; $^{*}p < 0.05$; $^{\dagger}p < 0.1$.

Table A7.2. *Level of public economic protest, overall and by region with interaction of political grievances and period (2000–2010; 2010–2015)*

	Protest (Public Economic)$_t$			
	Whole of Europe	Southern Europe	North-western Europe	Central and eastern Europe
Protest (Public Economic)$_{t-1}$	0.162***	0.248**	−0.022	0.127†
	(0.037)	(0.087)	(0.054)	(0.069)
ΔUnemployment$_t$	0.722	−1.234	0.400	1.607**
	(0.609)	(2.265)	(1.170)	(0.514)
ΔUnemployment$_{t-1}$	−0.148	1.366	1.067	−0.621
	(0.799)	(3.092)	(1.365)	(0.697)
ΔUnemployment$_t$*Period (2010–2015)	0.959	2.914	−0.524	−1.264
	(0.992)	(3.825)	(2.268)	(0.839)
ΔUnemployment$_{t-1}$*Period (2010–2015)	0.536	3.230	−0.982	0.214
	(1.036)	(4.599)	(2.322)	(0.842)
ΔPolitical Grievances$_t$	0.129	0.015	0.342*	0.120
	(0.103)	(0.326)	(0.173)	(0.100)
ΔPolitical Grievances$_{t-1}$	−0.354**	−0.038	−0.533**	−0.604***
	(0.115)	(0.370)	(0.177)	(0.140)
ΔPolitical Grievances$_t$*Period (2010–2015)	0.272†	0.316	−0.197	0.188
	(0.158)	(0.539)	(0.253)	(0.172)
ΔPolitical Grievances$_{t-1}$*Period (2010–2015)	0.532***	−0.175	0.539*	0.800***
	(0.160)	(0.575)	(0.250)	(0.177)
ΔUnemployment$_t$*ΔPolitical Grievances$_t$	0.290*	1.038	−0.039	0.711***
	(0.146)	(0.874)	(0.305)	(0.186)

Table A7.2 *(cont.)*

	Protest (Public Economic)$_t$			
	Whole of Europe	Southern Europe	North-western Europe	Central and eastern Europe
ΔUnemployment$_t$*ΔPolitical Grievances$_{t-1}$	−0.286	−0.613	0.396	−0.945***
	(0.292)	(1.070)	(0.605)	(0.279)
ΔUnemployment$_{t-1}$*ΔPolitical Grievances$_t$	−0.205*	−0.376	−0.575*	−0.545***
	(0.098)	(0.283)	(0.256)	(0.160)
ΔUnemployment$_{t-1}$*ΔPolitical Grievances$_{t-1}$	0.445†	0.396	1.156*	0.488*
	(0.234)	(1.308)	(0.451)	(0.210)
ΔUnemployment$_t$*ΔPolitical Grievances$_t$	0.055	−0.400	−0.036	−0.879*
*Period (2010–2015)	(0.263)	(1.016)	(0.572)	(0.352)
ΔUnemployment$_t$*ΔPolitical Grievances$_{t-1}$	0.565†	0.177	−0.297	1.119***
*Period (2010–15)	(0.334)	(1.173)	(0.805)	(0.323)
ΔUnemployment$_{t-1}$*ΔPolitical Grievances$_t$	0.448†	0.093	0.494	0.826*
*Period (2010–2015)	(0.250)	(0.643)	(0.574)	(0.330)
ΔUnemployment$_{t-1}$*ΔPolitical Grievances$_{t-1}$	−0.502†	0.487	−1.168*	−0.579*
*Period (2010–2015)	(0.266)	(1.470)	(0.583)	(0.229)
IMF$_t$	5.160†	11.024	10.191	−0.910
	(2.952)	(8.544)	(7.578)	(2.390)

IMF_{t-1}	0.705	−16.377†	0.803	2.572
	(2.994)	(8.582)	(7.564)	(2.527)
System $Polarization_t$	0.261	−2.583	1.214	−0.036
	(0.831)	(4.550)	(1.153)	(1.024)
Cabinet $Position_t$	0.469*	0.494	0.775*	0.252
	(0.217)	(0.591)	(0.363)	(0.229)
Election $Month_t$	−1.517†	−2.582	−1.512	−1.602*
	(0.778)	(2.778)	(1.140)	(0.762)
Election $Month_{t-1}$	1.225	7.414*	0.419	0.557
	(0.791)	(2.887)	(1.158)	(0.771)
Period (2010–2015)	0.235	3.015	−1.377	−0.614
	(0.633)	(2.388)	(0.898)	(0.705)
R^2	0.184	0.498	0.107	0.319
Adj. R^2	0.123	0.366	0.009	0.203
Num. obs.	718	135	356	227
Fixed effects	Yes	Yes	Yes	Yes
White noise residuals	Yes	Yes	Yes	Yes

$^{***}p < 0.001$; $^{**}p < 0.01$; $^{*}p < 0.05$; $^{\dagger}p < 0.1$.

8 Bailouts, Austerity, and Protest
Representative Democracy and Policy-Making in Times of Austerity

Argyrios Altiparmakis and Jasmine Lorenzini

8.1 Introduction

As the economic crisis unfolded over European countries after the Greek debt exploded in late 2009, supranational bailouts became a prominent and controversial topic in the countries they were imposed upon. A supranational actor, the Troika – the triumvirate composed of the European Commission, the European Central Bank, and the International Monetary Fund (IMF), which gained broad media attention and political power – enforced these decisions. The growing importance of the Troika during the economic crisis relates to its key role during the negotiation processes over bailout packages and their profound impact on economic prospects. The bailouts and Troika institutions lacked popularity among citizens. They were often viewed as a form of technocratic power imposing the cost of financial misdeeds on them. Furthermore, the Troika only indirectly benefited from democratic legitimacy yet it played a major role in shaping austerity policies in European countries strongly hit by the crisis. As such, it posed important questions about the future of democracy and so opens interesting avenues of research in relation to protest politics.

Chapter 7 has shown the importance of both economic and political grievances in triggering protest. Here, we study how political events associated with the Great Recession contributed to protest. More specifically, we focus on bailout agreements as potential sources of economic and political grievances because they were major political events for the countries in which they took place. They conditioned the socio-economic future of countries through the specific austerity measures agreed on during the different rounds of negotiations. They challenged democratic procedures – in particular, the capacity of future governments to take policy decisions that differed from the choices taken by the current government (Mair 2013). Moreover, they gained high visibility in the media. For all these reasons, political opponents can easily politicize bailout agreements and, in so doing, trigger protest. In this chapter, we analyse the effects of bailouts on protest, but we are mostly interested in understanding why bailout agreements contributed to protest.

First, we explore the direct effects of bailout agreements on protest. The previous chapters have already hinted at the influence of these agreements on protest when working on the thirty countries included in our dataset. Here, we narrow our analyses down to the countries in which a bailout agreement was signed with supranational institutions.[1] Focusing on these seven countries still allows us to include countries belonging to the three regions studied in this book. Thus, it gives us the opportunity to work on cross-regional differences related to the adoption of bailout agreements.

After having established the impact of bailout agreements on protest in the different regions, we speculate on the mechanisms through which a bailout fosters protest. The mere fact that a bailout triggers protest does not help us understand why citizens protest in reaction to a bailout agreement, and in particular whether this is due to the associated economic or political grievances analysed in this book. Therefore, in a second step, we analyse the mediating role of prospective economic sentiment to see whether the effects of bailout agreements are associated with fears of a worsening economic situation. If the effect of bailouts on protest is mostly an artefact of widening economic dissatisfaction, it could mean that citizens are mostly concerned with the economic consequences of bailouts, such as widespread austerity and financial hardship. Therefore, protest can be explained by a turn in economic sentiment, while the bailout itself might only be epiphenomenal in regard to protest.

Alternatively, in a third step, we consider citizen dissatisfaction stemming from procedural aspects – dissatisfaction with how socioeconomic policies were decided in agreement with supranational institutions and not through national channels of democratic decision-making. We test this idea by replicating our analyses using austerity measures. This allows us to see whether national decision-making adopting restrictive socioeconomic policies (1) triggers protest and (2) is mediated by economic dissatisfaction. If we find different effects for bailout agreements and national austerity measures, we can argue that the mechanisms at play relate to specific political grievances associated with supranational intervention in national politics.

[1] We focus on seven countries involved in bailout agreements: Cyprus, Greece, Hungary, Ireland, Latvia, Portugal, and Romania.

The chapter is structured as follows. First, we discuss our theoretical model. Then, in the empirical part of our study we present visual evidence on the relationship between protest and bailouts and austerity measures – or the lack thereof – across the three regions. Lastly, we use panel data to estimate the effect of supranational and domestic political austerity events on protest. To conclude the chapter, we summarize our research, explore possible caveats, and open up avenues for future research.

8.2 Bailouts as Drivers of Contention on the Streets

Why is a supranational intervention in the form of a bailout expected to trigger protest? Supranational interventions can foster protest because citizens are afraid of the economic consequences of the bailout. They can also trigger protest due to the amount of attention they receive, which facilitates the politicization of the issue, either as a domestic failure in the management of the economy or as a supranational intervention in national politics. Political opponents in the institutional system (political parties) and other civil society organizations might seize the opportunity to mobilize this discontent and to foster protest against government pacts with supranational institutions. In fact, existing research shows that IMF intervention triggered protest in central and eastern Europe (CEE) during the Great Recession (Beissinger and Sasse 2014). Similarly, in Latin America during the 1990s IMF interventions triggered broad protest (Walton 1987), as in many developing countries (Auvinen 1996; Walton and Ragin 1990). In particular, IMF interventions generate protest in democratic settings with high levels of urbanization and economic development (see Auvinen 1996 for a literature review and findings on developing countries).

In a previous study focusing on southern Europe (SE), we found that austerity measures associated with bailout agreements triggered protest (Altiparmakis and Lorenzini 2018). The inclusion of countries from different regions in a single analysis adds to our study of bailout and protest. It allows us to test whether the effects of bailouts on protest identified were idiosyncratic to SE countries. Differences in the impact of bailout agreements on protest might be related to the intensity of the economic and the political crises concerned. As we might not find the same effects when including countries from northwestern Europe (NWE) or CEE, we first verify that bailouts foster protest across European countries and regions. Therefore, our first hypothesis is

H1: The adoption of bailout agreements with supranational institutions fosters protest across all regions in spite of differences in the intensity of the economic and political crises observed in the previous chapter (Chapter 7).

8.3 Anticipated Economic Downturn or Conditionality on Decision-Making?

Bailouts have an impact on decision-making processes. In particular, they constrain socio-economic policies. We consider two mechanisms related to socioeconomic policies through which bailout agreements contribute to increased protest. We examine the relationship between bailout agreements and attitudes towards the economy, and also their influence on decision-making processes, to see whether bailout-related protest is partially a product of worsening economic prospects or political grievances.

A bailout agreement sets in motion a process of austerity: the adoption of restrictive socioeconomic policies by national representatives. In the first place, a bailout already reflects declining economic performance and therefore it can provide a trigger for accumulated economic pessimism to lead to protest. However, citizens may also prospectively fear that these austerity measures will worsen the national economy. In periods of widespread austerity, public sector wages are cut, layoffs take place, and living standards fall as the state reduces social subsidies. All these can be potential sources of economic dissatisfaction that trigger protest (Galais and Lorenzini 2017). We expect some of the increase in protest to be due to growing economic pessimism.

Citizens are not only afraid of the economic consequences of the supranational intervention but are also dissatisfied with the decision-making process. Here, we build on the idea of a legitimation crisis (Langman 2013) and on the fact that globalization poses a challenge to democracy as we know it (Kübler and Kriesi 2017). Research shows that citizens are critical of supranational decisions that tie the hands of their governments. In countries that face a bailout, citizens are less likely to blame their government for mismanagement and less dissatisfied with democracy at the national level (Cordero and Simón 2016). In times of economic crisis, their main concerns relate to their socioeconomic situation and they expect their national representatives to defend their interests in this respect – be it at the national or at the supranational level. However, as the government and the parties in charge fail to do so they lose credibility. In the long run, when governments cannot take their own decisions in the best interest of the people, it might hinder degrees of satisfaction with democracy (Magalhães 2014). Roberts (2008b) notes a coupling of demands for social and political rights in the anti-neoliberal protest in Latin America. Citizens associated their worsening socioeconomic situation and the absence of political alternatives to the dominant neoliberal paradigm. Democracy failed to sustain the emergence of alternative political projects. In the course of these unfolding of events, a learning process is at play and citizens learn that democratic institutions are weak and unable to defend their interests. Quite the contrary, some argue that supranational management of the economic situation pacifies political contention at the national level (Genovese, Schneider, and Wassmann 2016).

During an economic crisis which threatens the prevailing means of gaining a living, the economic system loses legitimacy and so do the associated political leadership and political ideology. A critical economic situation in a country triggers a bailout, and the reaction to the bailout encapsulates an already sour mood caused by the declining economy, but most importantly a bailout reveals (1) the inadequacy of the current management of the economy by the national political elite and (2) that new economic policies will be decided in agreement with supranational institutions and not by a newly elected government. Both dimensions may trigger political dissatisfaction, which in turn leads to protest.

Summing up, the first path that we consider builds on the idea that bailouts constrain socio-economic policies. We anticipate that bailout agreements trigger fears that the economy will suffer from the bailout. Therefore, the impact of bailouts on protest runs through a dire assessment of the economy and its prospects. To capture this interplay between economic fears, bailouts, and protest, as a control we use economic sentiments[2] measured at the time when the bailout is voted on. If an anticipated worsening of the economy accounts for the effects of bailouts on protest, the effects of bailout should disappear when we introduce prospective economic sentiment as a control in our model (full mediation), or at least they should be reduced (partial mediation).

> H2: The effects of bailouts on protest are mediated (dampened) by a fall in economic prospects as measured by changes in the consumer confidence index.

[2] We measure prospective economic sentiment using the Eurostat consumer confidence indicator, combining four questions on (1) the financial situation over the next twelve months; (2) the general economic situation over the next twelve months; (3) unemployment expectations over the next twelve months; and (4) savings over the next twelve months.

Our second path posits that bailouts challenge democratic decision-making because they constrain the choices available to democratically elected governments (Alonso 2014). In this alternative path, the effect of bailouts on protest relates to democratic institutions and results from dissatisfaction with how representative channels work under bailout regimes. Considering the relationship between economic intervention by supranational actors and protest, we explore the idea that citizens protest not only because of the dire economic prospects they foresee but also as a reaction to supranational intervention in national processes of decision-making.

To account for the supranational intervention, we replicate our analyses on austerity legislation passed as a domestic initiative without the involvement of a foreign actor. If citizens are mostly concerned about the economic consequences of the bailout, to a degree the same effect should be found for austerity legislation. If instead they are also protesting against the process through which the bailout is imposed, we should find that the effect of bailouts on protest is greater in supranational cases. This can be seen if austerity episodes have a more limited effect on protest than bailouts. We compare the effects of bailouts on protest to those of two sets of austerity measures: Austerity measures adopted under a bailout regime and austerity measures adopted without conditionality.

There is an important caveat here concerning a degree of bias in the comparison. Bailouts are triggered by declining economic circumstances and increasing yields which a domestic austerity package cannot contain or reverse. As such, bailouts are applied to the most economically constrained countries and therefore naturally involve much more austerity than other legislation initiated at the domestic level which has neither the urgency nor the constraints of bailouts. Moreover, as the authors of bailouts are agents outside the domestic political system, they have no incentive to avoid political costs and 'soften' their proposals. All this suggests that bailouts should be associated with greater economic distress and more negative sentiments than domestic legislation because they logically contain deeper and more severe cuts. However, if citizens perceive this and the bailout worries them more than domestic austerity packages, this should be reflected and captured by greater changes in the consumer confidence index and/or objective measures of the economy such as unemployment. Because we control for these factors, we believe that our comparison between domestic austerity and supranationally agreed austerity/bailouts is a meaningful one.

H3a: Bailout agreements and austerity measures involve similar economic policies and therefore they trigger protest events equally.

H3b: Austerity measures decided by national governments are unrelated to protest; only bailout agreements involving supranational interventions in decision-making processes trigger protest.

8.4 Bailouts, Austerity and Protest across Europe: Empirical Evidence

We start our inquiry with a descriptive analysis of the interplay among bailouts, different sets of austerity measures, and protest. We consider the impact of nine bailout agreements on protest across seven countries belonging to the three regions studied (see Table 8.1). As can be seen at first glance, the number of bailouts varied importantly across regions. In the north-west of Europe, only Ireland faced a bailout,[3] Furthermore, this country did not live very long under the bailout agreement. There was no bailout in the continental core of the eurozone, neither during the initial shock period nor during the subsequent eurozone crisis. However, in the south of Europe not only did more countries face a bailout but some, like Greece, faced more than one agreement and are still under supranational financial control. Lastly, in CEE we observe bailouts in three countries with varying durations. Although the CEE countries were the first ones to have to deal with bailout agreements already during the shock period, they were also short lived in Hungary and Latvia. However, Romania's recovery took longer.

To measure the effect of bailouts on protest, we operationalize our dependent variable as the weighted number of public economic protest events. We choose public economic protest events because they are the most likely to track protest reactions to the crisis and the political management of it. Focusing on public economic protest allows us to filter out events that are not directly related to the Great Recession, such as intra-firm conflict, regionalist issues, and/or particularistic political events in each country.

In addition to bailout agreements, we consider the influence of major austerity measures on protest. We compile a list of austerity events according to expert opinion, selecting between one and six instances of contentious episodes per country where austerity became a focal point of

[3] We exclude Iceland because of a lack of data on prospective economic sentiments.

Table 8.1. *Timing and duration of bailout agreements in the seven countries involved in bailout agreements*

Country	Bailout start (vote in parliament)	Bailout end (end of treaty)
North-western Europe		
Ireland	December 2010	December 2013
Southern Europe		
Cyprus	April 2013	March 2016
Greece	May 2010	March 2012
Greece	March 2012	June 2015
Greece	August 2015	June 2018
Portugal	May 2011	June 2014
Central and eastern Europe		
Hungary	October 2008	November 2010
Latvia	December 2008	January 2012
Romania	May 2009	September 2015

Source: EU Financial assistance information as provided by the European Commission. https://ec.europa.eu/info/business-economy-euro/economic-and-fiscal-policy-coordination/eu-financial-assistance_en.

attention across political arenas (Hutter et al. 2017). A pool of national experts annotated austerity measures as part of a study of contentious episodes. Contentious episodes are moments when institutional politics and protest engage in heated dialogue. These experts searched the international press for the most important instances of austerity-related decision-making in their country of expertise. Then, in a second step, they read all the articles in the national press related to the most important austerity measures identified in the first step, thus confirming that they were relevant instances of austerity at the national level.[4]

The result is a list of twenty-four episodes of austerity taking place in the seven countries included in our analysis. Table 8.2 presents

[4] Information on Cyprus was not included in the dataset constructed by this pool of experts. Therefore, we collected data on austerity in Cyprus using a different procedure. Instead of reading the international press, we read the European Commission economic adjustment program reviews, which present all the steps taken in compliance with bailout agreements. These reports are available at: https://ec.europa.eu/info/business-economy-euro/economic-and-fiscal-policy-coordination/eu-financial-assistance/which-eu-countries-have-received-assistance/financial-assistance-cyprus.en. This allowed us to find the conditional austerity measures for Cyprus. For the austerity measures adopted before or after bailout agreements, we asked national experts to identify them.

Table 8.2. *Timing and conditionality of austerity measures in the seven countries involved in bailout agreements*

Country	Austerity measures	Timing	Rel. to bailout
North-western Europe			
Ireland	Emergency budget/First austerity package	April 2009	Prior
Ireland	Second austerity package	November 2009	Prior
Ireland	Third austerity package (Kenny)	November 2010	Conditional
Ireland	Fourth austerity package (Kenny)	December 2012	Conditional
Southern Europe			
Cyprus	Austerity package (AKEL)	August 2011	Prior
Cyprus	Fiscal Responsibility Budget System Law	February 2014	Conditional
Greece	Austerity package	March 2010	Prior
Greece	Multi-law bill	October 2011	Conditional
Portugal	PEC 1	March 2010	Prior
Portugal	PEC 2	May 2010	Prior
Portugal	PEC 3	September 2010	Prior
Portugal	Austerity package	September 2012	Conditional

Central and eastern Europe			
Hungary	First austerity package	April 2009	Conditional
Hungary	Pension nationalization	November 2010	Conditional
Hungary	Szell–Kalman plan 1	March 2011	Post
Hungary	Szell–Kalman plan 2	April 2012	Post
Hungary	Internet tax	November 2014	Post
Latvia	Austerity (Dombrovski)	March 2009	Conditional
Latvia	Extraordinary austerity	June 2009	Conditional
Latvia	Austerity budget	December 2009	Conditional
Latvia	Austerity budget	December 2010	Conditional
Latvia	Austerity budget	December 2014	Post
Romania	Austerity package	May 2010	Conditional
Romania	Tax reform	February 2015	Conditional

Note: Data are based on the annotation of contentious episodes as identified in the international and national press by a pool of national experts. These annotations were done in the framework of the ERC POLCON project. AKEL, Progressive Party of Working People (Cyprus); PEC, Programa de Estabilidade e Crescimento.

these episodes, which include, for instance, two austerity packages in Cyprus, Greece, and Romania but as many as five in Hungary. These austerity-related contentious episodes take multiple forms. In the south, they often came as labour market reforms – reducing work protection or social rights. In some eastern European countries – Hungary and Poland – they took the form of pension reforms. While some of the measures were amendments and/or extensions of (conditional) bailout agreements, others were decided before or after a bailout agreement, as indicated in the last column in the table. Cross-regional variation is visible. Post-bailout-agreement austerity mostly happened in the CEE countries, whereas in the north-west and south, non-conditional austerity packages were introduced prior to bailout agreements.

The relationship between bailouts, austerity measures, and protest is depicted in Figures 8.1–8.3. These figures plot the level of economic protest aggregated by semester over time for north-western, southern, central, and eastern European countries and Greece. We treat Greece separately because of the high number of protest events in the country and its repeated bailout agreements, and also because our panel treatment is unsuitable for a

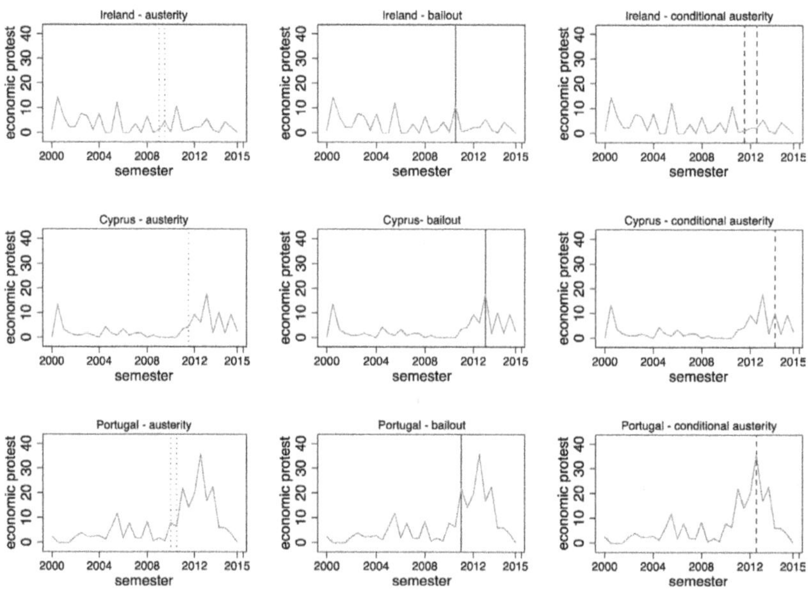

Figure 8.1 The timing of political events and protest in north-western and southern Europe during the 2000s.

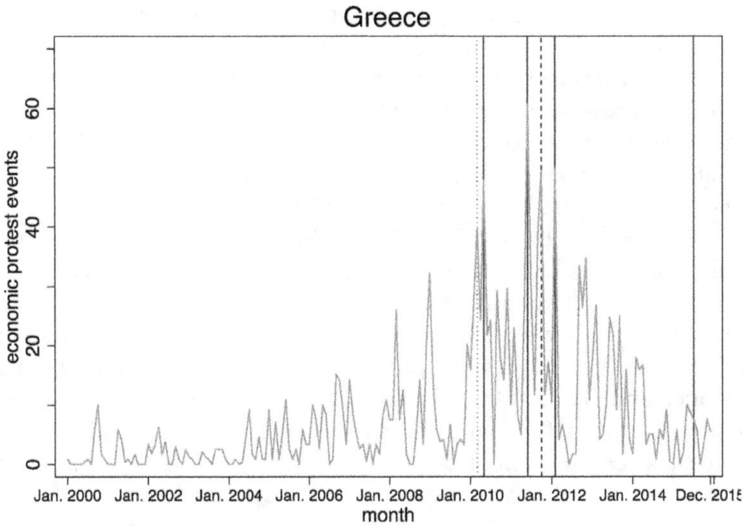

Figure 8.2 The timing of political events and protest in Greece during the 2000s.

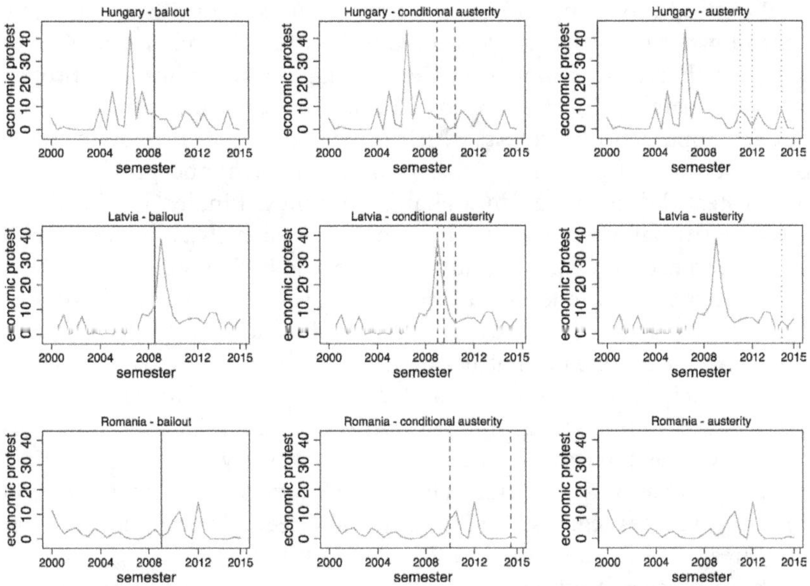

Figure 8.3 The timing of political events and protest in central and eastern Europe during the 2000s.

country for which almost all the economic, political, and protest indicators are non-stationary. This offers us the opportunity to replicate our analyses with a higher degree of detail, working on monthly levels of protest. In the three figures, bailouts are indicated by a vertical solid axis, whereas austerity measures are depicted with a dashed vertical axis (conditional austerity) or a dotted vertical axis (non-conditional austerity).

The figures suggest a varying correspondence between the timing of bailouts and increases in protest. In NWE and SE, the correspondence between the timing of protest and bailout agreements is stronger than in CEE.

Comparing regions and periods, we observe that bailouts prior to the eurozone crisis were mostly introduced in eastern Europe and triggered protest unequally (see Figure 8.3). In Hungary, contrary to what Beissinger and Sasse (2014) find, there seems to be only a moderate increase in protest following the bailout in 2008. The slight increase in protest after the bailout does not reach the extent of earlier peaks of protest. In Latvia, the bailout causes an outburst of protest relative to the country's low level of protest in general, but it subsided quickly afterwards. In Romania, the timing of protest does not appear to be correlated with that of the bailout, even if after the bailout there is a clearly elevated amount of protest compared to the period before.

Moving to SE, depicted in Figure 8.1, in Cyprus the bailout appears in the middle of a period of protest outbursts, coinciding with one peak of protest. In Greece, presented in Figure 8.2, and also to a lesser degree in Portugal, bailouts seemed to trigger a wider wave of protest that was sustained over a period of time. The last bailout in Greece is not accompanied by protest, which indicates that there may be some bailout fatigue at play as the change of government and previous bailout protest did not result in a change of policy. Finally, in NWE, we consider the bailout in Ireland. For Ireland, we can observe only a small increase in economic protest at the moment of bailout adoption.

While there is a tendency of increased protest around the bailouts, although not in all the cases, the timing, duration, and intensity vary significantly. It appears that national reactions to the crisis depend on the specificities of the country and do not follow a universal pattern, perhaps accounting for different severities, frames, and timings of bailouts, as well as the protest tradition of each country.

Turning to austerity measures, in Figure 8.1 we observe more variation within and across regions. For Portugal and Greece, conditional austerity measures correspond to important peaks of protest. For Portugal, in fact, the momentum of protest on the streets corresponds to the timing of a vote on austerity related to the bailout agreement of 2012. For Cyprus, the conditional austerity captures only a smaller outburst of protest subsequent to the peak which corresponds to the timing of the bailout agreement. In Ireland, the adoptions of two austerity measures under the bailout regime do not correspond to peaks in protest. They instead come in moments displaying low levels of protest. The pattern for Greece can be seen in Figure 8.2. Here, we see that conditional austerity coincides with a peak in protest even when working at a lower level of disaggregation, with monthly data. Austerity measures unrelated to bailouts, those taken prior to supranational agreements, appear in the building up of the protest wave in SE.

In Figure 8.3, which presents trends for CEE countries, we see a different picture. In this case, the bailouts come first, then conditional austerity, and lastly unconditional austerity adopted after the end of bailout agreements. We observe that for Romania and Latvia conditional austerity corresponds with peaks in protest. But this is not the case for Hungary, where the bailout agreement and conditional austerity happen at the end of periods of heightened protest. In Hungary and Latvia, the two countries for which we have post-bailout austerity, we do not find any correspondence with high levels of protest.

The next step is to create models that give statistical estimates of the effects of bailouts and austerity measures on protest in our seven cases. As previously, we work with data aggregated at the semester level. Therefore, the structure of our data is based on observations for country-semesters and we have twenty-nine observations for NWE, fifty-eight for SE, and eighty-seven for CEE. We codify votes for a bailout treaty in national parliaments and additional dichotomous variables that indicate austerity measures taken under bailout regimes or without conditionality. We build three models, one for each region. In our models, we control for the period and unemployment to account for variations in the intensity of the crisis. This allows us to estimate the effects of bailouts and austerity net of the effect of potentially different situations in terms of economic downturns and political turmoil. Furthermore, we control for prior protest levels, with a lagged variable for economic protest to account for mobilization that simply 'leaks' from previous peaks of protest. Lastly, we use country fixed effects to account for time-invariant elements such as different protest cultures and corresponding different protest levels across countries.

When estimating the impact of bailouts in a regression model, we find that they have a positive effect on protest in NWE and SE – a bailout agreement increases the number of protest events in a given country in a given semester (see Table 8.3) – while they have no effect in CEE. The coefficient fails to reach conventional levels of statistical significance owing to the high confidence interval. Nevertheless, it is interesting to note that bailout agreements have – if anything – negative effects on protest in eastern Europe. These first results lend partial

Table 8.3. *Regression on economic protest with absorption of country variance, by region with and without prospective economic sentiment*

	North-western Europe		Southern Europe		Central and eastern Europe	
	W/o ESI	W/ ESI	W/o ESI	W/ ESI	W/o ESI	W/ ESI
Bailout agreement	8.910*	8.665*	13.218***	13.237***	−0.879	−4.422
	(2.280)	(2.190)	(4.203)	(4.217)	(−0.194)	(−1.048)
Austerity no conditionality	1.497	2.989	0.320	−0.239	0.274	−2.590
	(0.342)	(0.623)	(0.096)	(−0.071)	(0.082)	(−0.828)
Austerity under conditionality	−0.477	−0.464	15.353***	15.776***	1.320	0.783
	(−0.182)	(−0.175)	(5.038)	(5.144)	(0.466)	(0.304)
Lagged economic protest	−1.374***	−1.370***	−0.675***	−0.663***	−1.060***	−1.018***
	(−7.124)	(−7.037)	(−6.539)	(−6.405)	(−10.045)	(−10.534)
Change in unemployment rate[a]	−0.732	−1.167	0.940	0.638	3.315***	2.735***
	(−0.582)	(−0.845)	(1.455)	(0.908)	(4.098)	(3.646)
Periods (ref. 2001–2004)						
2005–2008	−1.699	−1.998	1.494	1.632	5.151**	4.364*
	(−0.968)	(−1.104)	(0.951)	(1.038)	(2.684)	(2.482)
2008–2010	−2.197	−2.341	−1.939	−1.398	2.274	1.747
	(−0.568)	(−0.599)	(−0.948)	(−0.665)	(0.661)	(0.557)
2010–2015	−3.128+	−2.945	2.694	3.046+	3.305+	4.431*
	(−1.737)	(−1.607)	(1.559)	(1.736)	(1.815)	(2.636)

Change in economic sentiment		−0.073		−0.107		-0.362^{***}
		(−0.796)		(−1.086)		(−4.081)
Constant	5.851^{**}	5.874^{**}	0.994	0.796	1.967	1.870
	(3.849)	(3.827)	(0.894)	(0.708)	(1.463)	(1.527)
Observations	29	29	58	58	87	87
AIC	155.83	156.87	334.73	335.29	566.58	551.14
BIC	168.13	170.55	353.27	355.90	588.78	575.80
R^2	0.78	0.79	0.67	0.68	0.58	0.66

Note: For each region, we present two models. The first one (W/o ESI) does not include prospective economic sentiment, while the second (W/ESI) controls for prospective economic sentiments measured as citizens' expectations about the economic situation in the country in the next twelve months. AIC, Akaike information criterion; BIC, Bayesian information criterion; ESI, Economic Sentiment Index.

[a]We measure changes in the half-yearly unemployment rate.

t statistics in parentheses.

$^{+}p < 0.10$; $^{*}p < 0.05$; $^{**}p < 0.01$; $^{***}p < 0.001$.

support to our first hypothesis: Bailout agreements triggered protest in NWE and SE; in the CEE countries they had no effect.

We provide tentative explanations for the null findings for the CEE; in particular we advance two alternative explanations. On the one hand, citizens might anticipate that supranational interventions will bring improvements to the economic situation and the quality of governance in the region. In these countries, supranational interventions might be viewed from a different perspective given the low degree of satisfaction with democracy observed in these countries throughout the 2000s (see Chapter 7). In these contexts, a bailout might appear as an opportunity to implement decision-making in a more efficient way. This might be the case because of high levels of corruption, which normally hinder policy-making processes (Klašnja, Tucker, and Deegan-Krause 2014) or because of endemic low satisfaction with democracy (see Chapter 7). This democratic dissatisfaction in the region results in high electoral punishment and the rise of new parties (Haughton and Deegan-Krause 2015) or a hyper-accountability of parties in these countries (Roberts 2008a). On the other hand, the lack of protest may result from citizens choosing exit over voice (Hirschman 1970). Many CEE countries were plagued with high levels of emigration after the outbreak of the economic crisis. Citizens who decide to leave a country due to a lack of positive economic prospects no longer express their dissatisfaction through protest on the streets. This might account for the low correspondence between bailouts and protest that we find.

8.4.1 *Fear of a Worsening Economy or Dissatisfaction with Decision-Making Processes*

Next, we compare the effects of bailout agreements that we find in the models not controlling for prospective economic sentiment with ones including this additional control. To control for economic sentiment, we include a continuous measure capturing citizens' evaluation of the economic situation in their country for the next twelve months. More specifically, we consider changes in prospective economic sentiments. We clearly see no sign of mediation. Not only do the coefficients for bailout agreements remain roughly the same, but there are no statistically significant effects of economic prospects on protest in NWE and SE. Only in CEE are prospective economic sentiments associated with protest. The more positive citizens feel about the future economic situation of their country, the less they protest. Our empirical analyses do not lend any support to our second hypothesis. The effects of bailout on protest are unrelated to prospective economic sentiments.

Next, we turn to the alternative idea that citizens protest because they are dissatisfied with decision-making processes being constrained by supranational institutions. To gain a better understanding of the mechanism through which bailouts interact with protest, we test whether our finding that bailouts, at least in SE, trigger protest holds for other political events, such as votes for austerity bills in parliament without supranational agreements. The idea is to see whether the adoption of austerity measures through national decision-making processes encounters the same opposition that bailout agreements face. Similar effects of austerity and bailouts would indicate that the main triggers of protest are not supranational interventions but instead the adoption of restrictive economic policies – be it through national or multilevel decision-making processes.

For this last empirical test, we return to a model not controlling for economic sentiment, as models without it present a better fit with our data (as can be seen from the BIC and AIC criteria presented at the bottom of the table) and we compare the effects of bailouts with those of austerity measures. Austerity measures have no effect on protest in the north-west and east of Europe. Only in the south of Europe do austerity measures trigger protest and only conditional austerity does so. Interestingly, the magnitudes of the effects of conditional austerity and bailouts are very similar. That of conditional austerity is even slightly higher, implying that conditionality affects protest positively, both in cases where it is a new agreement and when it is an extension of a previous one. These findings partially confirm our H3b: Citizens are specifically dissatisfied with austerity when it is related to supranational interventions – be it in the form of a bailout agreement or of austerity measures adopted in compliance with a supranational agreement (conditional austerity).

8.4.2 *Focusing on Greece*

We treat Greece separately for both substantive and methodological reasons. Substantively, Greece is an extreme case. It has received three bailouts, with an intermediate extension of the first bailout, and is concurrently a country with a traditionally high level of protest. These substantive differences also give rise to methodological problems, as the inclusion of Greece in either a general or a regional model alters the results significantly with its protest scene dominating that of other countries. We therefore separate Greece from the other countries and focus on it, which gives us the chance to change our time unit to the monthly level and to capture more finely grained differences. It also

Table 8.4. *Regression on economic protest for Greece with and without prospective economic sentiment*

	Greece			
	W/o ESI		W/ ESI	
First bailout agreement	32.831***	(4.559)	30.766***	(4.422)
Mid-term agreement	45.433***	(6.301)	42.151***	(6.046)
Second bailout agreement	38.021***	(5.294)	33.406***	(4.761)
Third bailout agreement	−3.398	(−0.470)	−4.408	(−0.630)
Austerity under conditionality	28.451***	(3.648)	24.700**	(3.244)
Austerity no conditionality	24.032**	(3.327)	23.449**	(3.335)
Lagged economic events	−0.776***	(−13.244)	−0.838***	(−13.958)
Periods (ref. 2000–September 2008)				
October 2008–January 2010	4.418*	(2.244)	2.324	(1.115)
February 2010–July 2015	6.695***	(4.939)	2.541	(1.157)
August–December 2015	0.668	(0.205)	−4.717	(−1.285)
Change in unemployment rate[a]	1.216	(0.819)	0.670	(0.457)
Change in economic sentiment			−0.463***	(−3.844)
Lagged economic sentiment			−0.156*	(−2.574)
Constant	2.754***	(3.766)	−1.857	(−0.984)
Observations	191		191	
AIC	1,303.13		1,289.43	
BIC	1,342.16		1,334.97	
R^2	0.59		0.62	

Note: For Greece, we present two models. The first one (W/o ESI) does not include prospective economic sentiment, while the second (W/ESI) controls for prospective economic sentiments measured as citizens' expectations about the economic situation in the country in the next twelve months. AIC, Akaike information criterion; BIC, Bayesian information criterion; ESI, Economic Sentiment Index.

[a] We measure changes in the quarterly unemployment rate.

t statistics in parentheses.

$^{+}p < 0.10$; $^{*}p < 0.05$; $^{**}p < 0.01$; $^{***}p < 0.001$.

allows us to examine what happens as bailouts succeed each other. Our unit of analysis is the country-month and we have 191 observations.

When we do this, it is directly apparent (see Table 8.4) that protest in Greece is significantly correlated with bailouts. The first bailout, its extension (the mid-term agreement) and the second bailout all have strong and statistically significant effects on protest. The same is true for the consumer confidence index, indicating that the bailout effect persists even after we control for declining economic prospects and political dissatisfaction, although the effect diminishes slightly. However, despite diminishing, the bailout effect is in fact at least five times as strong as the next biggest factor correlated with protest, particularly for the first two bailouts and it is also greater than the protest associated with the austerity incident prior to the commencement of the formal bailout regime, which only acted as a foretaste. The whole period of bailouts is punctuated by increased protest (as shown by the significant effect the period factor has for the eurozone crisis period) and this possibly indicates that continuous and succeeding bailouts might be the key to understanding the protest wave that swept Greece after 2010. As legislation was continually channeled to parliament at the behest of the Troika, protest intensified and rekindled in each instance, sustaining a large protest wave between 2010 and 2012 that eventually subsided somewhat after the 2012 elections and finally ended after the January 2015 election.

This is confirmed by the fact that the third bailout, signed by the new Syriza government after a semester of turbulence in the country's relations with the EU, can be seen to have no correlation with increased protest, something that is also apparent from Figure 8.2. Many potential reasons can be suggested: A combination of protest fatigue and frustration that things did not change despite a radical left-wing party coming to power on a mandate to end bailouts might be enough to explain why protest never resumed during the reign of Syriza. Because Syriza could not end austerity and no other party presented a more credible path towards the same goal, the protest efforts of previous years that were channeled towards Syriza could find no new institutional representation and now in retrospect seem to have been frustrated.

What we can take away from Greece, therefore, is that, somewhat paradoxically, supranational intervention had an effect on the dates when it was voted for in the national parliament, above and beyond the effects of political and economic grievances generated by poor economic prospects and political dissatisfaction. However, this only yielded greater protest as long as a gap in representation persisted, and it subsided after the Syriza alternative first emerged in 2012 and governed in 2015. The bailout effect does not persist if all the alternatives seem 'closed' at some moment in time, indicating a link between the lack of protest at the end of the bailout period in Greece and the lack of protest in the CEE countries, where a period of political resignation continued through the crisis years.

8.5 Discussion and Conclusion

In this chapter, we have linked protest with political events such as bailout agreements and the adoption of austerity measures. We have asked not only whether a bailout agreement triggers protest but also why this is the case. In so doing, we have explored two potential mechanisms linking bailout and protest: through economic grievances in the form of prospective economic sentiments and through political grievances in the form of dissatisfaction with decision-making processes conditioned by supranational intervention.

Our study has shown that bailouts increase protest in some countries but not in others. In the south of Europe, the effect of bailouts is strong and supports the idea that supranational interventions in the form of a bailout trigger protest. However, in the CEE countries, which faced bailouts earlier during the crisis, we do not observe a similar effect. Contrary to what Beissinger and Sasse (2014) found, we have not discovered a consistent impact of bailouts on protest. In the north-west, only Ireland faced a bailout. There, the bailout agreement also triggered protest. Although the effects of bailouts on protest are mostly an SE story, they are confirmed by empirical evidence from NWE.

In CEE, we have found no effects of bailout agreements on protest. We noted a potentially detrimental effect which fails to reach conventional levels of statistical significance and we advanced tentative explanations for this finding. Future research on eastern Europe accounting for the perception of supranational interventions in national economies and for the impact of emigration on protest would greatly contribute to the understanding of protest during the Great Recession in the region.

Concerning the question why, we have found that the effects of bailout agreements on protest are unrelated to negative economic sentiments. Not only do the effects of bailout on protest remain the same when we control for economic sentiment, so there is no mediation at play, but prospective economic sentiments do not account for protest. We conclude that the story of bailouts and protest cannot be reduced to an entirely economic story, even if economic deterioration is certainly a part of the story, but it is possibly not a sufficient trigger of protest. Our findings support the idea advanced by Roberts (2008b) that anti-neoliberal mobilization is a response to diverse insecurities on the market but also a reaction to the depolitization of alternatives.

We have also analysed austerity measures in order to see whether supranational interventions have some specific effects that the adoption of restrictive economic policies only by national institutions might not have. This additional analysis showed that bailout agreements have some effects that can only be replicated by conditional austerity measures. Citizens protest when the government adopts a bailout agreement or when it passes an austerity bill implementing a bailout agreement. However, when the government passes austerity measures unrelated to bailout agreements – either before the agreement or after the conditionality ends – we have found no effects of austerity on protest. This may be due to the fact that austerity measures are taken in economic situations that are not as dramatic as those featuring a bailout; yet, because we control for periods and unemployment levels, we argue that bailouts have an effect that goes beyond the economic one. It is the extra importance given to a supranational intervention in the national management of the economy which has the capacity to trigger protest.

The main limitation of our study relates to the panel regression method we have employed. Our panel series regression estimated whether protest coincides with specific political events and prospective economic sentiment. It did not tell us whether an accumulation of several months of economic pessimism has an accumulating effect on protest, which is a reasonable assumption. It is highly unlikely a bailout itself and the bailout conditionality would have such an effect on protest if it were not accompanied by the precipitous pessimism and dissatisfaction witnessed in SE. Instead, our panel regression methods mostly speak about the rhythm and timing of protest: They indicate that protest does not occur in moments when a decline in attitudes towards the economy is the greatest. Instead, it is structured around focal events, such as bailouts, that provide an opportunity for activists to descend on the streets and organize protest around them.

Our chapter has shown the importance of political events in accounting for protest. Bailout agreements and conditional austerity triggered protest in the south of Europe and, to some extent, also in the northwest. In the east, the ups and downs in protest follow a different logic. The next chapter deals with the diffusion of protest within and across regions.

9 Diffusion of Protest

Bruno Wüest and Matthias Enggist

9.1 Introduction

The previous chapters in this book have convincingly shown that when it comes to protest mobilization, the impact of the Great Recession was largely mediated by specific national characteristics such as the governments' reactions to and the peoples' grievances provoked by the crisis. Accordingly, it does not seem that the economic shock in 2009 has provoked one large, encompassing wave of political protests in its aftermath. Such moderate expectations contrast earlier notions in the social movement literature of a sustained wave of protests in the aftermath of the global financial and economic crisis (e.g. della Porta and Mattoni 2014a; Mason 2012). A prominently featured argument is that the most visible social movements of the past decades, such as the *Indignados*, the *Occupy* movement, or the Arab Spring uprisings, are so closely interwoven with autonomous, Internet, and mobile phone – based communication networks that they can mobilize at an unprecedented scale and speed (Castells 2015). This might be true, but these movements seem to be rather the exception than the norm, as the evidence provided especially in Chapter 4 suggests.

Ultimately, the question whether the extend of protest diffusion is large or small can therefore be answered only by explicitly studying the dynamic interplay between the many single instances of political protests. In other words, a study of protest waves needs to start from a theoretical and empirical perspective that assumes collective action as inherently interdependent across countries. This chapter centres on this interdependence, or diffusion, of political protests. The results will show that there regularly is protest diffusion across the European countries, but it is restricted to specific shared border diffusion. To the best knowledge of the authors, the study in this chapter is the first to assess protest diffusion on a quantitative dataset that includes countries from all regions of Europe and encompasses virtually all forms and issues of protest. Accordingly, this puts us in a good position to draw generalizable conclusions about the spillovers of contentious mobilization in Europe in the shadow of the Great Recession.

There is a long tradition of research on transnational protest in Europe (e.g. Tarrow 2005), most notably the study of cross-nationally organized protests that contribute to the politicization of the European integration process. Studies on protest diffusion in a narrower sense – interdependence or horizontal influence among protests in different locations – are, however, mostly restricted to comparative case studies (e.g. della Porta and Mattoni 2014a) or to the subnational level (e.g. Braun and Koopmanns 2010). This is surprising, as the manifold and complex linkages among European countries provide a fertile ground for large-n studies on diffusion processes in general (Wasserfallen 2016). In addition, a study of horizontal diffusion seems particularly feasible for the analysis of the recent wave of economic protests. Contrary to the Global Justice Movements at the turn of the millennium, which were characterized by a significant globalization of the organization of protests as well as the focus on single, internationally important events (della Porta et al. 2009), the newer protests under the impact of the Great Recession were primarily targeting the national level of policy making and were scattered across the centres of hundreds of different cities.

In the following, we will first develop the notion of protest diffusion and clarify our expectations on the influence of geographical proximity on the likelihood of protests. Subsequently, we will present the design of the spatial panel data analysis, before we discuss the findings on the relationship between European, regional, and cross-border diffusion of protests overall as well as for different time periods, regions, and forms of protests.

9.2 Diffusion of Protests

The literature conveys ample empirical evidence on the influence of protest mobilization in one location on mobilization in other locations (Andrews and Biggs 2006; Beissinger 2007; Givan et al. 2010; McAdam 1995; McAdam and Rucht 1993). Koopmans (2004) even goes as far as claiming that the 'most fundamental aspect about collective action is its connectedness, both historically and spatially'. Moreover, as della Porta and Mattoni (2014a) maintain, protest activity in the aftermath of the financial and economic crisis actually is substantially transnationalized, with shared claims, similar tactics, and mutual recognition among the different sites of protests. Mason (2012) even goes as far as speaking of a new global wave of protests, which will have similarly far-reaching consequences as the Spring of Nations in 1848. As already mentioned, we do not necessarily share this view and expect that the processes of protest diffusion are not sustained enough in order to speak of continent-wide waves of protests in Europe from 2005 to 2015. Most importantly, we can show that the aforementioned claims of a global protest wave, at least for Europe, are due to a selective focus on the few large-scale events organized by the Indignados and *Occupy* movements in the southern European (SE) countries from 2010 on (see, e.g., Castells 2015; della Porta and Mattoni 2014a; or Gerbaudo 2013). If more protest forms in nearly all European countries are considered, the interconnectedness of political protests looks far weaker. Of course, this does not mean that we do not observe limited waves of protests. However, our study of diffusion among the recent protests shows that it is restricted to specific forms, regions, and time periods.

Social movement actors do not 'reinvent the wheel at each place and in each conflict' (McAdam and Rucht 1993: 58). Hence, protest events are not singular responses to grievances and external opportunities – rather, one event changes the likelihood of many subsequent events (Oliver and Myers 2002). 'Diffusion' therefore denotes the influence of prior events on the future probability of similar events, both in positive and negative terms as 'non-diffusion'. While most political protests stay within local parameters, diffusion mechanisms may sometimes result in the integration of new participants, claims, and identities (McAdam, Tarrow, and Tilly 2001). During such mobilization, diffusion shifts the level of protests from loosely coordinated local actions to sustained and more widespread actions.

There are two necessary conditions for such a protest diffusion. First, a movement needs an innovative element in its tactical, organizational, or ideological imprint in order to generate notice from opponents, competitors, and the broader public (Tarrow 1994). Second, a movement needs to be able to disseminate the relevant information on its actions and claims. Such channels for information can be direct or indirect. Direct channels denote *personal networks* or organizational ties between movements (Andrews and Biggs 2006). Hence, the diffusion of protests can be brokered among like-minded activists in networks that span beyond borders or single movements. Indirect mechanisms describe the *mediated* transfer of information on social mobilization (Braun and Koopmanns 2010). The mass media (press, television, and radio) and activist websites as well as mailing lists were originally singled out as the primary indirect channels of protest diffusion. From 2008 on, however, more and more attention has turned to social media such as Facebook and Twitter that increasingly complement traditional media as facilitators of protest diffusion (della Porta and Mattoni 2014a). Through these channels, information on prior occurrences of collective actions, on action repertoires, collective identities, interpretive frames, or organizational forms is transmitted from one place to another. The presence of either direct or indirect information dissemination, however, is not enough for diffusion to take place. At the receiving end of the information, social movement actors that are willing to take over the protests are necessary. Such 'spin-off' movements, as McAdam (1995) has named them, are either able to learn from the successes and failures of other movements, or they emulate other movements because they resonate well with their own predispositions and cultural context (Beissinger 2007; Oliver 1989; Tarrow 1998). In his account of the 'colour revolutions' in Serbia, Georgia, Ukraine, and Kyrgyzstan, Beissinger (2007) offers a telling example of such diffusion processes. One of the keys of the successful export of contention was the critical role played by the Serbian student group 'Otpor'. Their non-violent challenge of the rigged elections in 2000 was so effective that they were able to rapidly disseminate this protest template to like-minded student groups in other countries.

The mere fact that many protest events in different countries take place at the same time does not automatically signify that these events are related one another (Myers 2010). They may also be independent reactions to the same external shocks such as the global financial crisis. In this chapter, we therefore develop an approach that builds on the notion of geographical distance (see Andrews and Biggs 2006). In other words, if the clustering of protests does reflect geographical proximities, we can assume that diffusion in one or another form actually has taken place. Countries which share a border or which are located in the same region or on the same continent at least partly have a common cultural, political, and macroeconomic past, which should be related to increases in the likelihood of protest spillovers (Gunitsky 2013). We define geographical proximity on three layers. The top layer is the European level of protests. More specifically, we investigate whether the dynamic of the single countries' protests is systematically related to the overall dynamic of protests on the continent. This would be the clearest signal for the existence of large-scale protest waves in Europe. Subsequently, we introduce a regional layer into the analysis. More precisely, we pay attention to more fine-grained groups of countries that share similar cultural, political, and economic pathways such as Scandinavia or the Visegrád Four (Poland, Hungary, Czech Republic, and Slovakia). With the assumption that Europe is not one coherent historical space, it seems plausible that the countries attached to the same region possibly influence each other in terms of political contestation. Finally, we test for cross-border diffusion. The transmission of information on protests and the development of organizational linkages between protests is certainly facilitated by a shared border.

We are particularly interested in the differences of the influence of geographical proximity on protests between the time periods and regions as defined in Chapter 1. This enables us to study whether the spread of protest varies in line with the dynamic of the financial and Euro crisis, and whether the different patterns of grievances and protest across the three regions also matter in terms of diffusion. We will present separate models for the three regions and three time periods. In addition, we can expect the forms of protest to be differently affected by diffusion processes. Demonstrations are the preferred action form of most social movement actors in Europe (Beissinger 2007; Hutter 2014). Also, Van Laer (2010) can show that activists organizing peaceful demonstrations benefit especially from the new digital communication channels provided by social media. Hence, diffusion should play a role, which means successful demonstrations are expected to be quickly adopted elsewhere. As the labour movement can be assumed to be better organized at the European level than other movements (Gajewska 2008), information on strikes can disseminate comparatively well through direct channels. Hence, we expect to see a significant diffusion of strike activity across Europe. As for confrontational and violent protest, they usually receive a lot of media attention, but this attention mostly revolves around episodic and not thematic coverage that would help to advance a movement (Smith et al. 2001). Diffusion can thus be expected to play a less prominent role for these forms of protests.

9.3 Data and Estimation

As described in the previous section, we postulate interdependence between the protest levels of European countries based on three different layers of diffusion: We expect European, regional as well as cross-border proximity to increase the likelihood of protest spill-overs. Concretely, we first operationalize cross-border proximity simply by a common border between two countries or not (contiguity).[1] Second, we define regional proximity as a country's membership in one of the following eight regions: Scandinavia (Finland, Sweden, and Denmark),

[1] We do not count maritime borders as shared borders, unless there is a permanent connection such as, for example, the Øresund Bridge between Denmark and Sweden.

the Visegrád Four (Poland, Hungary, Czech Republic, and Slovakia), the Baltic states (Estonia, Latvia, and Lithuania), Ireland and the United Kingdom, south-eastern Europe (Bulgaria, Romania, and Slovenia), southern Europe (Malta, Greece, Cyprus, Italy, Portugal, and Spain), the Benelux countries (Netherlands, Belgium, and Luxembourg), and the other continental countries (Germany, France, and Austria). Concerning the European layer, we assume that an increase or decrease of protests in all other European countries influences the likelihood of protests in a given country.

To test these expectations about spatial relationships between the protest levels of European countries, we employ spatial lags, which capture these geographical relationships, as our primary independent variables of interest. These spatial lags represent 'the (weighted) values of the same dependent variable in all other units' (Plümper and Neumayer 2010: 421). Thus, for country k they are the number of protests at time point t in all European countries except country k weighted by the proximity of these countries with k. Information about this proximity is provided by spatial distance matrices. For each of the three layers considered as potential drivers of protest diffusion, we compute such a spatial distance matrix that depicts how close two countries are concerning this layer. In the shared border matrix, for example, neighbouring countries are coded with 1 whereas two countries not sharing a common border are coded with 0. Therefore, only the protest levels of neighbouring countries of k contribute to the shared border spatial lag of k. The same logic holds true for the regional and European spatial lag. Following the recommendations of spatial econometricians (Darmofal 2006; Franzese and Hays 2007; Plümper and Neumayer 2010), we inverse and row-standardize our spatial distance matrices.

To test whether shared borders, common regional membership, and the European level are connected to protest diffusion, we calculate regression models for each of the three spatial lags individually. Because we suggest that protest diffusion might differ between the three regions presented in the introduction of this book (central-eastern, southern, and north-western Europe) and the time periods (normal times, shock period, and Euro crisis[2]), we present additional models of the shared border spatial lag in regional and temporal subsamples. In a last step, we investigate whether diffusion processes correlate to different forms of protest (namely demonstrations, strikes, confrontational, and violent protests) to a varying degree.

[2] The spatial panel regression models require a minimum of time points in order to run properly. Hence, we had to extend the normal times period by 2 months and the shock period by ten months in order to make the estimations possible.

We consider the countries' political opportunity structure as essential correlates describing different patterns of (non-)diffusion (Beissinger 2007; Braun and Koopmanns 2010; Kriesi et al. 1995). Movement actors that wish to adopt exemplars of protests from abroad can be successful only if opportunities are provided by the general political environment of their country. These opportunities are operationalized in the following estimations as union density, the left–right position of the government, a binary indicator of whether a country has a bailout agreement with the International Monetary Fund (IMF), as well as a binary indicator of whether an election has taken place in a specific month. Finally, the country-specific levels of political (trust in government) and economic (unemployment) grievances are included as control variables in all models. The data concerning our control variables unfortunately are not complete for the years from 2000 until 2004 as well as for Switzerland, Norway, Northern Ireland, and Iceland, which is why we are estimating the models with data for twenty-seven countries and the years 2005–2015.

We estimate panel regressions on our outcome, which is the number of protests in a country-month, weighted by sampling probability, the log of the countries' population size as well as an agency penalty (see Chapters 2 and 3 for a thorough discussion on this). This means that we have many time points ($T = 132$ months) for a comparatively small number of countries ($N = 27$), so different estimators will converge and we can simply use OLS for modelling the time dynamics (see Beck, Gleditsch, and Beardsley 2006). For every model, however, we use a one-temporal lag in order to avoid the problem of simultaneity in spatial dependence and to account for different protest levels between countries. Also, we decided to run all models with a fixed effects specification.[3] Finally, we re-ran all models without Greece as the extreme outlier case (most notably with a weighted number of protests of 127 in December 2008). With the exception of two models – the model for the shock period and the model for the number of strikes in Europe, which we will discuss – all coefficients are robust with respect to the inclusion of Greece.

9.4 Three Layers of Protest Diffusion

We start the discussion of the results with an overview on how protests across Europe are interdependent as a function of our three different concepts of geographical proximity. Table 9.1a shows the results

[3] The spatial Hausmann tests (see Millo and Piras 2012) for most models indicated a fixed-effects specification as more useful, and we applied this specification accordingly to all models in order to keep the results as comparable as possible.

of spatial panel regressions on the number of protests for the European, regional, and shared border layers of protest diffusion, controlled by indicators measuring political and economic grievances as well as a series of political context factors. Several points are noticeable. First, the highly consistent relationship of some control variables with the number of protests confirms the results from the previous chapters. Two out of three models indicate that countries under conditionality agreements with the IMF experience substantial increases in protests. Further, the timing of elections is influential as well. Protest activity is substantially lower in election months than in other times. Then, we clearly see the strong connection to political grievances. The level of trust in government is very substantially related to lower numbers of protests. As for unemployment, we find the same negative correlation with the overall level of protests as reported in Chapter 7.[4]

Turning to a comparison of different potential diffusion patterns, only one pattern emerges as a significant correlate of European protest activity. The spatial coefficient for the European lag is positive but not significant. It is therefore not often the case in Europe that protests spread evenly across the majority of countries, let alone that European protest mainly appears in the form of large protest waves that surge over the continent. The waves that have occurred were locally and temporally too confined to overplay all other scattered instances of protests. In other words, the underlying dynamics of protest diffusion do not point to tightly integrated social movements at the European level, and hence also not to a sustained Europeanization of protests. However, with our data, we are not able to research other aspects for Europeanization such as the addressee or actual instances of transnational movements (see Becker and Hutter 2017).

Regional membership is the proximity factor with the weakest relationship. It is clearly not significant as well. Hence, the shared cultural, political, and economic pathways of countries in the same region do not have a substantial relationship with the diffusion of protests in general. As useful as comparative political typologies usually are (e.g. Hall and Soskice 2001), they cannot account for interdependencies of contentious mobilization.

From the general perspective of research on diffusion processes in political science (see Gilardi 2012), it is not surprising that the shared borders spatial lag is the only significant among the three indicators

[4] This might be counter-intuitive at first glance. However, because unemployment has a negative relationship with non-economic protest, and because non-economic protests predominate, the overall correlation becomes negative.

of diffusion. Although conceptually very simple, this spatial lag regularly performs well empirically. For political contention, the result indicates that there are significant processes of learning and emulation between social movements of adjacent countries. Despite nationally divergent grievance structures and political opportunities, protests do regularly spread across the borders of many European countries. This strong finding may come as a surprise. Beissinger (2007), for example, convincingly shows that the eastern European mobilizations against government corruption spread from Serbia to countries such as the Ukraine or Georgia, which are not geographically adjacent but had a similar political constellation – most notably an election with widespread voter fraud.

However, the differentiation of cross-border diffusion by region in Table 9.1b hints at the fact that diffusion is an even less widespread phenomenon than the strongly significant effect of the shared border spatial coefficient in Table 9.1a suggests. Table 9.1b presents the regression results for the relationship of the shared border spatial lag on the number of protests if we restrict our analysis to each of the three regions – which in other chapters in this book have been shown to differ strongly in terms of protest activity and its reaction to the crisis. In fact, we find that the spatial coefficient for cross-border diffusion reaches statistical significance in central-eastern Europe (CEE) only. This is where changes in the protest level are most strongly related to protest activity in neighbouring countries. By contrast, cross-border diffusion seems to be much rarer in southern and north-western Europe. Looking only at these regions, the coefficient is indeed positive but far from significant and compared to CEE relatively small. That geographical proximity in a narrow sense has no influence in SE does not come as a surprise. In terms of shared borders, SE countries actually constitute three confined pairs: Spain and Portugal, Italy and Malta as well as Greece and Cyprus all share a border with each other, but not with any other SE country. Hence, the shared-border lag is not able to pick up the strong diffusion between at least Spain and Greece that was attested in previous studies (see Gerbaudo 2013). While we find some evidence for regional diffusion in SE (not shown here) it fails to reach statistical significance.

Our regional differentiation confirms the general conceptual focus of this book on different patterns of mobilization in the three regions from a new perspective. Not only the mobilization of grievances as we saw in the last three chapters, but also the cross-national diffusion of protests is related by regional affiliations with diffusion being a mainly eastern European phenomenon. To understand these diffusion

Table 9.1a. *Influence of different layers of diffusion: Results from fixed effects spatial panel regressions on the number of protests*

	European lag			Regional lag			Shared border lag		
	Est.	Std. err.	Pr(>|*t*|)	Est.	Std. err.	Pr(>|*t*|)	Est.	Std. err.	Pr(>|*t*|)
Spatial coefficient	0.177	0.249		0.062	0.110		0.663	0.016	***
Spatial error	0.141	0.265		0.017	0.115		−0.664	0.017	***
Dep. var. (*t*−1)	0.236	0.016	***	0.236	0.016	***	0.130	0.011	***
Elections	−1.020	0.436	*	−1.029	0.437	*	−0.576	0.318	
Gov. ideology	0.067	0.056		0.081	0.056		0.030	0.044	
IMF lending	1.086	0.369	**	1.115	0.370	**	0.822	0.293	**
Union density	−0.021	0.018		−0.034	0.017	*	−0.023	0.01	*
Unemployment	−0.106	0.033	**	−0.118	0.033	***	−0.071	0.023	**
Trust in gov.	−3.530	0.906	***	−3.134	0.904	***	−1.766	0.635	**
Pseudo-R^2	0.38			0.38			0.20		
No. obs.	3,564			3,564			3,564		

The units of analysis are country-months.
Levels of significance: $^{*}p \leq 0.05$; $^{**}p \leq 0.01$; $^{***}p \leq 0.001$.

Table 9.1b. *Relationship of shared border diffusion in different regions: Results from fixed effects spatial panel regressions on the number of protests*

	North-western Europe			Southern Europe			Central-eastern Europe		
	Est.	Std. err.	Pr(>|t|)	Est.	Std. err.	Pr(>|t|)	Est.	Std. err.	Pr(>|t|)
Spatial coefficient	0.081	0.125		0.123	0.126		0.401	0.054	***
Spatial error	−0.014	0.13		−0.112	0.129		−0.361	0.059	***
Dep. var. (t−1)	0.252	0.026	***	0.218	0.036	***	0.158	0.024	***
Elections	−0.214	0.634		−2.396	1.392		−0.654	0.403	
Gov. ideology	0.147	0.093		−0.105	0.158		0.035	0.061	
IMF lending	0.428	0.872		2.858	1.015	**	0.528	0.320	
Union density	−0.018	0.025		−0.063	0.069		−0.028	0.012	*
Unemployment	−0.103	0.084		−0.289	0.093	**	−0.068	0.027	*
Trust in gov.	−0.636	1.445		−8.660	2.710	**	−2.106	0.910	*
Pseudo-R^2	0.31			0.37			0.22		
No. obs.	1,452			792			1,320		

The units of analysis are country-months.
Levels of significance: $^{*}p \leq 0.05$; $^{**}p \leq 0.01$; $^{***}p \leq 0.001$.

processes better, in the following paragraphs we differentiate further by time period and protest form. Beside the pan-European perspective, we thereby pay closest attention to CEE where diffusion occurs most strongly.

9.5 Cross-Border Diffusion of Protests by Time Period

The focus of this book is on how the economic crisis affects patterns of protest behaviour and activity. Therefore, we analyse how the strength of cross-border diffusion has evolved between 2005 and 2015. Table 9.2 shows regression results for shared border diffusion for the pre-crisis period ('normal times'), the shock period, and the Euro-crisis period individually. The upper panel refers to entire Europe whereas in the lower panel the results for CEE are shown.

Looking at entire Europe first, it becomes clear that the differentiation between time periods is crucial. Before the crisis, protests in neighbouring countries do not seem to matter much in connection to protest activities. In the pan-European context the spatial coefficient is even negative indicating that domestic causes of contentious mobilization were far more important than protests in adjacent countries before the outburst of the crisis. In the shock period (2008–2010) the spatial coefficient is not only negative but also significant. This result, however, must be taken with a grain of salt: Excluding Greece from the analysis completely reverses the direction of the relationship. The prevalence of protest in Greece especially during the shock period massively outnumbers protests in every other country in Europe. Greece as an exceptional case, where protest activity seems to follow different patterns and rules than in the rest of Europe, is able to overthrow the results for the entire continent during the shock period. Thus, our finding for the occurrence of diffusion during the shock period is ambiguous. On average, we find no cross-border diffusion. However, excluding Greece both as a case and ignoring Greece's influence on its neighbours, the results indicate that already during the shock period, cross-border diffusion has gained importance as a correlate of changing levels of protest activity.

No such uncertainty exists for the period after the initial shock: During the Euro crisis (2010–2015) the interdependence of protests across national borders becomes strong. The spatial coefficient in this period is strongly significant and exceeds in size every other coefficient obtained so far. The time of the Euro crisis is a period of high interdependence in terms of the proximity of economic

Table 9.2. *Relationship of shared border diffusion by time periods in entire Europe and central-eastern Europe only: Results from fixed effects spatial panel regressions on the number of protests*

	Normal times			Shock period			Euro crisis		
Entire Europe	Est.	Std. err.	Pr(>|t|)	Est.	Std. err.	Pr(>|t|)	Est.	Std. err.	Pr(>|t|)
Spatial coefficient	−0.018	0.189		−0.825	0.021	***	0.776	0.014	***
Spatial error	0.073	0.189		0.841	0.017	***	−0.794	0.015	***
Dep. var. (t−1)	0.169	0.028	***	0.043	0.019	*	0.086	0.013	***
Elections	−1.235	0.767		0.198	0.702		−0.353	0.298	
Gov. ideology	0.142	0.159		0.180	0.195		0.029	0.042	
IMF lending	14.376	4.611	**	0.479	0.825		0.375	0.325	
Union density	0.04	0.07		−0.121	0.082		−0.018	0.008	*
Unemployment	−0.186	0.112		0.051	0.146		−0.070	0.028	*
Trust in gov.	−3.395	1.942		−4.127	1.640	*	−0.782	0.721	
Pseudo-R^2	0.33			−0.14			0.25		
No. obs.	1269			702			1782		
	Normal times			**Shock period**			**Euro crisis**		
Central-eastern Europe	Est.	Std. err.	Pr(>|t|)	Est.	Std. err.	Pr(>|t|)	Est.	Std. err.	Pr(>|t|)
Spatial coefficient	0.284	0.112	*	0.206	0.166		0.457	0.070	***
Spatial error	−0.294	0.119	*	−0.109	0.182		−0.360	0.081	***
Dep. var. (t − 1)	0.141	0.043	**	0.185	0.060	**	0.069	0.032	*
Elections	−1.344	0.932		−0.890	0.872		−0.278	0.402	
Gov. ideology	0.091	0.195		0.374	0.236		0.128	0.076	
IMF lending	13.305	3.491	***	1.132	1.032		−0.604	0.539	
Union density	0.067	0.061		−0.047	0.074		−0.026	0.013	*
Unemployment	−0.13	0.083		−0.135	0.085		−0.011	0.049	
Trust in gov.	−3.928	2.301		−7.769	2.447	**	−1.017	1.171	
Pseudo-R^2	0.21			0.39			0.29		
No. obs.	470			260			660		

The units of analysis are country-months. IMF, International Monetary Fund.
Levels of significance: $^{*}p \leq 0.05$; $^{**}p \leq 0.01$; $^{***}p \leq 0.001$.

grievances, and our results suggest that, on average, neighbouring countries experience similar levels of protests during the Euro-crisis period. Hence, protest diffusion developed considerably after the shock in the course of the financial and economic crisis of 2009 and 2010. The spillovers induced by the crisis thus seem to have needed a certain time to fully build up after the onset of the financial and economic crisis.

Restricting the analysis to CEE (Table 9.2, lower panel) – the region where all in all diffusion among neighbouring countries is strongest – a similar although not entirely identical picture emerges. In contrast to the other regions, we already find support for protest diffusion during normal times, suggesting that, regardless of the crisis, the social movement actors in eastern European countries are more prone to increase or decrease their level of activity concomitant with actors in neighbouring countries. The shock of the financial and economic crisis in CEE subsequently led to a slight decrease rather than an increase in protest diffusion across borders. Hence, in the East, experiences of economic and political grievances first seem to have led to a nationalization rather than a regionalization of protest activity. However, during the Euro crisis this process was reversed. As observed for the entire continent, also in the CEE region, during the Euro crisis cross-border diffusion surged.

Taken together, the shared border spatial correlations indicate substantial cross-border diffusion of protests across Europe during the years of the Euro crisis. In the pre-crisis and shock periods, though, protest diffusion is considerably less related to geographic proximity and is more limited to specific regions (such as the East during normal times).

9.6 Protest Diffusion for Different Forms of Protest

The empirical part concludes with an analysis of the question whether different forms of protest are also differently affected by cross-border diffusion. Table 9.3 accordingly reports the results of the spatial panel regressions on the number of demonstrations, strikes, confrontational events, and violent protests. Table 9.3a is concerned with entire Europe whereas Table 9.3b reports the importance of cross-border diffusion for the different protest forms in CEE only.

Turning to the findings for the whole of Europe first, we find that in the models for three out of four protest forms (demonstrations, confrontational, and violent protests) the size and significance of the spatial coefficients are similar if not greater compared to the one estimated for

Table 9.3a. *Influence of cross-border diffusion on different forms of protest: Results from fixed effects spatial panel regressions on the number of protests*

	Demonstrations			Strikes		
Entire Europe	Est.	Std. err.	Pr(>|t|)	Est.	Std. err.	Pr(>|t|)
Spatial coefficient	0.737	0.018	***	−0.781	0.016	***
Spatial error	−0.714	0.021	***	0.759	0.016	***
Dep. var. (t−1)	0.058	0.014	***	0.084	0.014	***
Elections	−0.136	0.179		−0.080	0.098	
Gov. ideology	0.014	0.026		0.014	0.015	
IMF lending	0.078	0.194		−0.003	0.086	
Union density	−0.012	0.005	*	0.002	0.004	
Unemployment	−0.017	0.017		−0.081	0.015	***
Trust in gov.	−0.015	0.434		−0.216	0.247	
Pseudo-R^2	0.20			0.10		
No. obs.	3564			3564		

	Confrontational			Violent		
Entire Europe	Est.	Std. err.	Pr(>|t|)	Est.	Std. err.	Pr(>|t|)
Spatial coefficient	0.819	0.012	***	0.650	0.023	***
Spatial error	−0.839	0.012	***	−0.670	0.025	***
Dep. var. (t−1)	0.053	0.011	***	0.055	0.016	***
Elections	−0.003	0.050		−0.085	0.095	
Gov. ideology	−0.011	0.007		0.024	0.014	
IMF lending	0.140	0.055	*	0.152	0.103	
Union density	−0.003	0.001	*	−0.004	0.003	
Unemployment	−0.015	0.005	**	−0.024	0.009	**
Trust in gov.	−0.211	0.121		−0.027	0.231	
Pseudo-R^2	−0.27			0.15		
No. obs.	3564			3564		

The units of analysis are country-months.
Levels of significance: $^{*}p \leq 0.05$; $^{**}p \leq 0.01$; $^{***}p \leq 0.001$.

Table 9.3b. *Influence of cross-border diffusion on different forms of protest in East-Central Europe: Results from fixed effects spatial panel regressions on the number of protests*

Central-eastern Europe	Demonstrations			Strikes		
	Est.	Std. err.	Pr(>|t|)	Est.	Std. err.	Pr(>|t|)
Spatial coefficient	0.421	0.081	***	0.346	0.094	***
Spatial error	−0.314	0.092	***	−0.346	0.099	***
Dep. var. (t−1)	0.029	0.033		−0.043	0.035	
Elections	0.034	0.299		−0.114	0.110	
Gov. ideology	0.055	0.056		0.040	0.021	
IMF lending	−0.712	0.399		0.195	0.147	
Union density	−0.023	0.010	*	−0.005	0.003	
Unemployment	−0.007	0.036		−0.025	0.013	
Trust in gov.	−0.458	0.869		−0.146	0.318	
Pseudo-R^2	0.25			−0.01		
No. obs.	660			660		

Central-eastern Europe	Confrontation			Violent		
	Est.	Std. err.	Pr(>|t|)	Est.	Std. err.	Pr(>|t|)
Spatial coefficient	0.046	0.308		0.261	0.127	*
Spatial error	0.011	0.312		−0.273	0.131	*
Dep. var. (t−1)	0.062	0.038		0.077	0.037	*
Elections	0.012	0.054		−0.036	0.092	
Gov. ideology	−0.009	0.010		0.035	0.017	*
IMF lending	−0.085	0.067		0.062	0.121	
Union density	−0.001	0.002		0.001	0.003	
Unemployment	0.008	0.007		0.004	0.011	
Trust in gov.	−0.361	0.156	*	0.152	0.265	
Pseudo-R^2	0.08			0.04		
No. obs.	660			660		

The units of analysis are country-months. IMF, International Monetary Fund.
Levels of significance: *$p \leq 0.05$; **$p \leq 0.01$; ***$p \leq 0.001$.

all protests (see Table 9.1a, right panel).[5] It indicates that cross-border diffusion plays an even bigger role for specific protest forms than for the protest level in general. Concretely, this means for example that an increase in the number of demonstrations in a country mainly brings about a rise in the number of demonstrations in adjacent countries but less so a higher number of strikes, confrontational or violent protests. Thus, it is not only the occurrence of protests inspiring social movements in geographically proximate countries to become active but it is also the protest form which is diffused. This finding is plausible as different protest forms can be expected to be used by different actors who might primarily pay attention to events in other countries that are staged with the same action repertoire.

As for the other protest forms, we would expect strong cross-border diffusion also for strikes. Although its standing in European politics is still built on sand if compared to political parties and business interests (Wüest 2017), the labour movement should be better organized at the European level than most other movements (Gajewska 2008). Hence, cross-border coordination and information dissemination on strikes should comparatively easily lead to the diffusion of this form of protest. While the result in Table 9.3a points to a different result, we argue that the negative spatial coefficient for strikes might be misleading. As was the case with the shock period, this result is driven by Greece. Nearly one-sixth of all strike activity in our sample takes place in Greece, with its number clearly exceeding strike levels in any other country. Dropping Greece from the analysis in this case reverses the spatial lag coefficient.[6] If we ignore Greece as an outlier, strike activity in Europe is thus diffused as much as the other protest forms. However, the level of strike-related diffusion still is not above average.

A clearer differentiation concerning the importance of diffusion for different protest forms emerges in CEE (see Table 9.3b). In this most diffusion-intensive region, spillovers occur most frequently concerning strikes and demonstrations. In contrast, the spatial coefficient for violent protest events is relatively small in size and significant by a narrow margin only. For confrontational protests, in the East we find no indication for cross-border diffusion taking place. These differences in effect size between different protest forms resonate with the general finding that especially violence might discourage rather than encourage protest participation (della Porta and Tarrow 1986).

[5] Because the sample and all controls are exactly identical in all these models such a comparison is meaningful.

[6] Estimate of 0.626 with a standard error of 0.023 at a significance level of 0.001.

9.7 Conclusion

Our analysis has shown that diffusion processes, at least the ones related to shared-border proximity, are an integral part of the movement landscape in Europe. Spin-off movements across the continent learn from or emulate initiator movements in many instances. This confirms established findings from the literature that different instances of political mobilization often are interdependent (Koopmans 2004; McAdam 1995). However, the evidence provided in this chapter also bears important qualifications for the importance of diffusion. We did not find sustained protest waves that capture all – or at least the majority – of European countries. The European and regional layer of diffusion is not substantially changing the likelihood for protest in the single countries, and cross-border diffusion is also relevant only for some regions and during some time periods but not universally. The grievance and opportunity structures in the European countries seem to differ too much for the development of widespread and long-ranging networks of protest diffusion. The at least two decades old promise of the Europeanization of protests therefore, if at all, still is a promise for the future (Tarrow 1995).

Our results, of course, are also a consequence of our empirical strategy to focus on all forms of protests and almost all European countries. If we restricted the study to the major events during the Great Recession, we probably would have drawn a completely different conclusion. From our perspective on the protest landscape in Europe as a whole, this, however, would not be feasible. Our analysis therefore has a very different focus than previous research on the Indignados and Occupy movements (e.g. della Porta and Mattoni 2014a; Mason 2012). We tried to identify general patterns of interdependence between protests in single countries or within specific regions. Hence, we look at all demonstrations, strikes, and other protests, and so the Indignados and Occupy movements are but a small share of all events that happened in the aftermath of the financial and economic crisis.

Further results indicate that protest diffusion is contingent on the region, time period, and to a certain degree form of protest. First, our findings further substantiate the evidence gained in other chapters that the European protest landscape looks decisively different in the three regions. The more recently democratized countries of CEE thereby show the highest interdependence of political protests. Political mobilizations in this region are therefore comparatively well interconnected, not only during the 'colour revolution' but also more in general (see Beissinger 2007). The egregious economic hardship endured in the

Great Recession and the exceptionally high levels of protest mobilization in the SE countries, in contrast, did not lead to strong diffusion neither between geographical neighbours nor in the region as a whole. As there is a higher level of protests in many SE countries, and as the other chapters in the book consistently find indicators at the national level to be important in explaining protests, it seems that high levels of protests more likely lead to national differentiation of the protest landscape.

Second, we also found a pronounced structuring of protest diffusion by time period. Whereas the period from 2005 until about 2010 sees only spurious spillovers of political mobilization, diffusion is significant during the time of the Euro crisis. However, because the spatial correlation is strong only for shared border proximity, the results do not allow us to speak of an emerging European-wide network of political mobilization either. On the one hand, this nicely matches the argument in the previous literature that the dawn of the Great Recession brought about protests that were organized in the individual capitals and aimed to shape national politics (della Porta and Mattoni 2014a). On the other hand, our results show that protest mobilization expanded beyond the national spheres of protest only after it became clear that the economic hardship induced by the crisis is not going away in the hard-hit countries.

Third, diffusion processes are stronger for some forms of protest, while they are weaker for others. The information networks between social movements engaging in demonstrations and strikes in general seem to enable a high degree of cross-border diffusion. This confirms notions of the comparatively high organizational capacity and persistence of organizers of these protest forms, as well as the mostly substantial coverage in the media that helps these movements to make their claims heard (Smith et al. 2001; Van Laer 2010). For confrontational and violent protests, we report strong diffusion for the entire Europe but non-diffusion in CEE. In this region, such protests thus seem to suppress spin-off movements, be it because of the episodic and negative media coverage or because of the discouragement of potential fellow campaigners (della Porta and Tarrow 1986).

Part IV

Interaction Between Convention and Contention

10 Electoral Punishment and Protest Politics in Times of Crisis

Björn Bremer, Swen Hutter, and Hanspeter Kriesi

10.1 Introduction

This chapter links the political consequences of the Great Recession in the electoral arena and the protest arena. Integrated research on the two types of responses is important because, in democratic regimes, the citizens' response to the crisis might, first of all, be an electoral one. However, contentious reactions in the protest arena are another, often closely related way for the people to express their discontent especially in periods of economic and political crises. Unfortunately, electoral research tends to ignore the connections between the dynamics of opposition in the two arenas of mass politics (e.g., Hutter 2014b; McAdam and Tarrow 2010, 2013). This is unfortunate because these connections may trigger profound changes in the dynamics and structure of political conflict – as exemplified by the recent waves of protest and the rise of so-called movement parties in southern Europe (e.g., Altiparmakis and Lorenzini 2018; della Porta et al. 2017).

The chapter presents yet another step to further advance our understanding of the link between protest and electoral politics. It focuses on aggregate shifts in voting behaviour and protest politics across the thirty countries covered by this volume. More specifically, we examine the relationship between the two arenas in two steps. First, we ask whether electoral and protest politics are driven by the same kind of economic and political factors. Then, we ask whether protest mobilization influences the extent of the economic vote.

To derive our expectations, we combine the literature on economic voting with social movement research. As shown in previous chapters, the link between economic factors and protest politics varies depending on the type of economic grievances and features of the political context. In this chapter, we draw on economic voting literature to discuss electoral punishment in times of crisis, and on the social movement literature to highlight that even if there are no opportunities for immediate electoral punishment, the electoral cycle is embedded in an ongoing process of political mobilization that interacts with elections in complex ways. More precisely, we emphasize the role of protests in politicizing economic grievances: We argue that protests act as a 'signalling mechanism' by attributing blame to decision-makers and by highlighting the political dimension of deteriorating economic conditions. Ultimately, massive protest mobilization should, therefore, amplify the impact of economic hardship on electoral punishment.

For the empirical analysis, we combine our protest event data with data on electoral outcomes in the thirty European countries covered by the study. The electoral dataset builds on the one used by Hernández and Kriesi (2016) in their study on the electoral consequences of the Great Recession. We updated this dataset so that it includes all national parliamentary elections in the thirty countries from January 2000 to December 2015. Overall, the data cover 118 elections. The first election included in the dataset is the Romanian election in November 2000; the last election included in the dataset is the Spanish election in December 2015. A key ambition of the chapter is to make the results for electoral and protest politics as comparable as possible. Therefore, we aim to standardize the units of analysis and measures across the two arenas.[1]

10.2 Economic Crisis, Political Context, and Citizens' Responses in Electoral and Protest Politics

In contrast to the literature on economic voting, social movement studies have neglected the role of economic conditions as an explanatory factor for increasing or declining protest levels for several decades. This changed with the onset of the Great Recession which brought questions of economic strains, deprivation, and capitalism back to the study of social movements (e.g. Beissinger and Sasse 2014; della Porta 2015; Galais and Lorenzini 2017; Grasso and Giugni 2016; Klandermans and van Stekelenburg 2016; Muñoz et al. 2014; Quaranta 2016; Vráblíková 2017). Following this line of research, the previous chapters of this volume have also reconsidered the effects of economic grievances and their interactions with political factors on protest mobilization

[1] The chapter is based on a revised and shortened version of our article Dynamics of Protest and Electoral Politics in the Great Recession published by the European Journal of Political Research, doi: https://doi.org/10.1111/1475-6765.12375. In this chapter, we rely on an alternative measure for the dynamics of protest mobilization which emphasizes within-country variations. Interested readers should consult the journal article and its online appendix because they offer additional robustness checks and descriptive information.

(in particular, Chapters 7–9). In what follows we scan the economic voting literature to highlight its very similar expectations with regard to the effects of economic trends on electoral politics.

Like the explanatory model introduced in Chapter 1 of this volume, the economic voting literature starts with the *economic context*. That is, it assumes instrumentally rational voters, who reward or punish the incumbents with their vote depending on the economic conditions. It thus adopts a simple reward–punishment mechanism (e.g. Duch and Stevenson 2008; Lewis-Beck and Stegmaier 2007). Empirical research based on the idea shows that economic voting is pervasive both in 'normal' and 'crisis' periods. Increasing work also documents how strongly incumbents were punished in the Great Recession and that the punishment varies in line with the predictions of the economic voting literature, i.e. according to how hard the economic crisis hit individual countries (e.g. Bartels 2014; Hernández and Kriesi 2016; Kriesi 2014; Talving 2017, 2018).

The pervasiveness of the effects in times of crisis is far from obvious given that the economic voting literature has also highlighted that the extent of electoral punishment is conditioned by the *political context*. Since Powell and Whitten's (1993) landmark study, the concept 'clarity of political responsibility' has been used to describe the finding that the voters' assessment of the government's economic performance plays a stronger role, if the institutional context allows the voters to clearly attribute the responsibility for the economic performance to the government (see also Duch and Stevenson 2008). In times of increasing economic globalization and authority shifts to supra- and international institutions, scholars have documented that voters are less likely to punish national governments in bad economic periods because they perceive the constraints of national governments' influence on economic developments (e.g., Duch and Stevenson 2008; Hellwig 2010; Hellwig and Samuels 2007; Soroka and Wlezien 2010).

As the current economic crisis brought to the fore the strong economic and political interdependencies in Europe, the previous arguments would let us expect that the impact of economic conditions on the punishment of incumbents should be weaker – or at least not stronger – in the Great Recession. This is also what some empirical studies show (e.g. Magalhães 2014; Talving 2017). However, other scholars in the economic voting field suggest that we should be cautious here. For example, Lobo and Lewis-Beck (2017: 616f.) emphasize that some of the negative findings might simply be methodological artefacts. That is, studies based on individual-level cross-sectional data are not able to grasp the effects of the economic vote because of restricted variance. In a context of a profound economic crisis, a large part of society – regardless of partisan attachments – acknowledges the economic problems.[2]

Following Hernández and Kriesi (2016), there is yet another reason for why scholars might have found differing results of the crisis on the economic vote, namely *timing*. The current economic crisis in Europe unfolded in stages that unleashed dramatic political dynamics in some of the hardest-hit countries. However, it is important to keep in mind that while the initial economic shock affected almost all European countries, the economic prospects of most, but not all, improved fairly quickly thereafter (see Chapter 1). Thus, the voters in the countries where the economy continued to stagnate or even experienced a pronounced double-dip recession are likely to have perceived the incumbents' failure as particularly serious, not only compared to their pre-2008 situation, but also compared to other countries (on the role of benchmarking, see Kayser and Peress 2012).

Moreover, the diverging economic trends have become most pronounced within the eurozone and the political processes to cope with the situation involved above all the EU's intergovernmental channel (e.g. Laffan 2016). Ultimately, countries that needed assistance to bail out their financial and public institutions had to accept strong conditions by their international creditors. While this might again have diffused political responsibility, it may also have strengthened the role of national governments in the public debate and their perceived (in-)ability to successfully negotiate internationally (Hutter et al. 2016). As Marsh and Mikhaylov's (2012) study on the Irish case convincingly illustrates, the national governments' decisions on how to cope with the crisis and mounting pressures from international institutions and financial markets has been decisive for their electoral punishment rather than the sheer size of the economic decline.

Overall, the arguments on the conditional effects of the economic context on electoral losses of incumbents resemble the effects on protest mobilization that we have uncovered in the previous chapters. In other words, both electoral losses and protest mobilization seem to be

[2] Thus, one needs to rely on other types of research designs: Focus either on aggregate electoral outcomes in a large-N setting (e.g. Dassonneville and Lewis-Beck 2014; Hernández and Kriesi 2016) or on a pooled design of several surveys (e.g. Fraile and Lewis-Beck 2014), or structural equation modelling with individual-level panel data (e.g. Chzhen et al. 2014). Such designs indicate that the economic vote is stronger in a crisis situation.

driven by poor economic performance, especially in later stages of the crisis and under conditions of external political constraints. In the present chapter we shall document the parallel effects of the economic crisis on protest and electoral politics in a more systematic way.

10.3 The Signalling Function of Protest Politics

Establishing whether the same economic and political forces drive the ups and downs in electoral losses and protest mobilization can only be a first step, however. Given that the electoral arena is embedded in an ongoing process of political mobilization, the present chapter also seeks to analyse whether and how protests might have aggravated electoral losses of incumbents in the Great Recession. More specifically, we emphasize the role of protest as a 'signalling mechanism' that attributes blame to decision-makers and highlights the *political* dimension of deteriorating economic conditions.

Regarding the dynamics of electoral and protest politics, we start by observing, as we have already done in Chapter 8, that, in democratic societies, citizens have the right to vote and they have the opportunity to express their grievances as voters. In democracies, grievances are first expressed in the voting booth simply because, as Piven and Cloward (1977: 15) have pointed out, 'whether defiant or not, people have been socialized within a political culture that defines voting as the mechanism through which political change can and should properly occur'. Accordingly, one of the first signs of popular discontent are sharp shifts in the voting patterns. However, the movement literature emphasizes also that, in the absence of immediately available options in the institutionalized arenas, discontented groups of citizens are likely to resort to the protest arena, and try to force political concessions from political elites by directly appealing to the general public. This is Schattschneider's (1960) idea of the 'expansion of conflict'. Such a view of political conflict is most prominent in the agenda-setting literature, and recent contributions from that tradition emphasize the power of protest to signal discontent and raise the salience of certain issues and concerns in more institutionalized arenas (e.g. Vliegenthart et al. 2016).

The pressure from below tends to strengthen the opposition and other allies of the protesting groups in the political system, which may be the main reason why opposition parties support or even create such protest in the first place. The controversial public debates that result from the expansion of conflict by protest mobilization increase the legitimacy of speakers and allies of protest movements with journalists and decision-makers, who tend to closely follow the public debates (Gamson and Meyer 1996: 288). Wolfsfeld's (1997: 47) 'principle of political resonance' formulates this relationship in a concise way: Challengers who succeed in producing events which resonate with the professional and political culture of important news media can compete with much more powerful adversaries. As the literature on movement outcomes highlights, the stronger the pressure exerted from below, the more likely it is that the government will be forced to make some concessions (for a recent overview, see Bosi et al. 2016).

For our argument, it is important that such protest actions may set in motion contentious episodes involving a sequence of interactions between the government and its challengers (see McAdam et al. 2001). In these sequences, the protest mobilization puts pressure on the governing elites to make some concessions and, most importantly, it attributes responsibility to these elites for deteriorating economic conditions. Thus, protest serves as a signal that points to the political dimension of the problem at stake. The protest campaigns that have emerged in the context of the Great Recession and that opposed austerity and called for democratic renewal are telling examples of these dynamics. As the previous chapters in this volume have shown, the public's response in the protest arena had a clear message – a message that emphasized the responsibility of both national and European elites for mismanaging the economic crisis and for exacerbating problems of democratic representation (see also Altiparmakis and Lorenzini 2018; della Porta 2015).

To accommodate the pressure from the streets, incumbent parties have above all resorted to procedural concessions: changes in leadership, reshuffles of the cabinet composition, calls for early elections or ceding responsibility to a care-taker government composed of technocrats (which will manage the consequences of the crisis until the regularly scheduled elections). In the Great Recession, these were all reoccurring strategies used by incumbents. The most important case is clearly Greece, where all these elements occurred in an exceptionally short period (e.g. Verney 2014). Procedural concessions were more likely than substantive ones, given the general predicament of European governments today. As a result of the financial and economic crisis, the governments all over Europe found themselves between the proverbial rock (international pressure) and a hard place (domestic expectations) (Mair 2013). The situation of governments in the countries that were hardest hit by the crisis proved to be particularly uncomfortable in this respect. Not only were they likely to be exposed to domestic pressure in the streets, but they also faced international pressure by a series of international stakeholders, who expected them to act responsibly, i.e. to execute the measures deemed necessary by the 'market'.

Against the background of these observations, the interaction between protest and electoral punishment likely played out in scenario like this: At the first possible occasion, the voters punish the incumbents as predicted by the economic voter approach. In countries most severely hit by the crisis, the discontented groups mobilize against austerity measures even before the first elections, in an active attempt to signal their discontent to the incumbents, or to bring them down (in the next national elections). In response to the protest mobilizations, the incumbents make some procedural concessions, but they do not succeed in satisfying the discontented voters, who severely punish them in the first national elections after the beginning of the crisis. In these elections, voters will vote into office the established opposition parties. Once in charge of the government, the former opposition however, is hardly able to adopt any other policy than the previous government, given the economic constraints imposed by the legacy of the former government, the conditions imposed by the rescuers (International Monetary Fund [IMF] and EU), and by the 'markets'. Such a situation is likely to further boost protest in the streets, which emphasizes the responsibility of the government for the economic situation and therefore increases electoral punishment in follow-up crisis elections. Partly as a result of the protests, the voters are bound to notice that the new government is forced to take just the same measures as its predecessors, whom they had voted out of office, and they may resort to punishing the mainstream parties as a whole in the following elections – by turning to new challengers or by exiting from the established electoral channel altogether. Thus, the result may be an even more profound destabilization of party systems (see Hernández and Kriesi 2016; Roberts 2014, 2017).

While the punishment of mainstream parties might concern parties from all ideological camps, there are at least two reasons why the mainstream left might be in a particularly uncomfortable situation. On the one hand, the left's traditional policy programs are even more at odds with the recommended austerity policies and structural reforms that governments in most countries implemented after 2010. Therefore, as illustrated by the Latin American experience (Lupu 2014; Roberts 2014, 2017), the mainstream left in power risks an even stronger brand dilution and alienation of its support base than the mainstream right when it adopts and implements austerity. On the other hand, the traditionally close alliances between political parties from the left and social movements (Kriesi 1995; Maguire 1995) might further erode in the context of the current crisis and backfire in terms of electoral support. That is, the challengers in the streets might be particularly adversarial towards their former allies while voters of mainstream left parties might be particularly receptive to the signalling mechanism of protests.

In this chapter, we do not study the proposed sequences in detail, but we develop several important expectations about the impact of protest mobilization on electoral punishment in the Great Recession. First, we expect that deteriorating economic conditions lead to electoral punishment and protest mobilization, especially in later periods of the crisis and under conditions of external political constraints. Second, we expect that protests play an important role in attributing responsibility for the economic decline and the growing cross-national disparities to the national and European elites. Thus, massive protests should amplify the connections between economic misery and the punishment of governments in national elections. We suggest calling this the 'signalling mechanism' of protest and, empirically, we expect to find that economic voting is stronger in contexts of high protest mobilization. Third, protest mobilization should intensify the feeling among voters that there is a more fundamental 'crisis of representation' as a change in government may not result in a change of policy. Thus, we expect that protest mobilization may act as an important trigger of the destabilization of European party systems by highlighting that mainstream parties (both in opposition and in government) no longer fulfil their representative functions. Finally, the effect of protest on the punishment of incumbents might be particularly severe for the mainstream left.

To sum up, we formulate the following hypotheses:

H1: The same economic and political factors influence the electoral losses of incumbents and the strength of protest mobilization (*equivalence hypothesis*).

H2: The impact of economic misery on electoral losses of the incumbent should be amplified by protest mobilization (*signalling hypothesis*).

H3: The positive effect of protest on electoral losses holds for all mainstream parties in both government and opposition (*party system destabilization hypothesis*).

H4: The positive effect of protest on electoral losses of the incumbents is stronger when the political left is in power (*left-wing punishment hypothesis*).

10.4 Measuring Shifts in Electoral and Protest Politics

To make the measures for the aggregate shifts in protest and electoral politics as comparable as possible, we focus on electoral changes and protests in a given legislative period. For this purpose, we calculate two key variables from our electoral dataset. First, we calculate the electoral loss of the prime minister's party in a given country as the change in the vote share of that party between a given election at time t and $t-1$. Second, we calculate the electoral losses for individual parties as the change in the vote share for each party between a given election at time t and $t-1$. The two variables allow us to focus on the electoral support of the chief executive (the key indicator of most economic voting studies) and of all types of parties. From our protest dataset we calculate one key variable. Specifically, we focus on public economic protests and compute the relative number of protest events per legislative period in every country. This number is calculated by comparing the number of events in a given legislative period in a given country to the average (or normal) level of protest in that country. Specifically, it is calculated in the following way:

$$\text{Relative Number of Protest Events} = \frac{\sum PP_{LP}}{M_{LP}} - \overline{\sum PP_{m,c}}$$

where $\sum PP_{LP}$ is the sum of all protest events in a given legislative period, M_{LP} is the number of months in a given legislative period, and $\overline{\sum PP_{m,c}}$ is the average number of protest events per month in a given country.[3] The measure indicates up- or downward deviations from the 'normal' flow of protest in a given country. Moreover, the focus on the legislative periods reflects the practice in the economic voting literature and takes into account more sustained upward trends over a longer period of time. We combine the information about the relative number of protest

[3] For this analysis, we follow the other chapters and weigh protest participation by the sampling probability (applied on the document level), the log of population size, and the agency weight. Please see Bremer et al. (2020) for an analysis with a simpler dependent variable and extensive robustness checks.

events with the first dataset on electoral outcomes and, finally, we standardize all our dependent and continuous independent variables in order to make them more easily comparable.

10.5 Economic Misery, Timing, and Bailouts as Drivers of Electoral and Protest Politics

Following the literature on economic voting, we start our analysis by assessing the importance of the economic context on both electoral losses and protest mobilization. In contrast to the previous chapters, we study changes in protest over longer units of time, i.e. legislative periods. Therefore, we can rely on three different economic indicators to measure the change in economic conditions in a given country at a given time: (1) change in the unemployment rate between the election at time $t-1$ and t; (2) change in the gross domestic product (GDP) between the election at time $t-1$ and t; (3) and change in the level of government debt (as a percentage of GDP) between the election at time $t-1$ and t. We combine these three indicators to create a summary measure of a country's 'economic misery' because we expect that citizens should respond more strongly to general economic trends than evolution of specific macroeconomic indicators, such as unemployment. An exploratory factor analysis indicates that all three indicators load strongly on a single dimension and thus we estimate a misery index based on the factor scores. This index increases as economic conditions worsen.

In the first step of our analysis we compare the factors that drive punishment in electoral and protest politics. To that end, we use simple ordinary least square (OLS) regression analysis with the electoral loss of the prime minister's party and the relative number of protest events in a given legislative period as two dependent variables in separate analyses. Table 10.1 presents the results for both electoral and protest politics. As predicted, a higher level of economic misery is related to higher electoral losses in the bivariate model shown in the first column of the table: A one standard deviation increase in misery will lead to a 0.34 standard deviation increase in electoral loss of the incumbent. Turning to protest, we find a similar pattern and confirm the results of previous chapters: A higher level of economic misery is related to a higher level of protest mobilization. This effect is a little bit smaller than the one for electoral politics, but still significant: A one standard deviation increase in misery will lead to a 0.31 standard deviation increase in the number of protests. Disaggregating the economic misery index in its individual components shows that all components are correlated with electoral and protest punishment (results not shown). However, in a

Table 10.1. *Electoral loss and protest*

	(1) Elect.	(2) Protest	(3) Elect.	(4) Protest	(5) Elect.	(6) Protest
Misery	0.34***	0.31***	0.00	−0.01	0.06	−0.01
	(3.86)	(3.78)	(0.02)	(−0.07)	(0.35)	(−0.04)
1st Crisis Elect.			0.30	0.17	0.18	0.16
			(1.26)	(0.84)	(0.77)	(0.79)
Later-Crisis Elect.			0.17	−0.17	−0.05	−0.18
			(0.72)	(−0.85)	(−0.22)	(−0.86)
1st Crisis Elect. # Misery			0.32	0.13	0.22	0.13
			(1.44)	(0.72)	(1.01)	(0.68)
Later-Crisis Elect. # Misery			0.70*	1.41***	0.49+	1.39***
			(2.47)	(5.97)	(1.74)	(5.70)
Bailout = 1					0.73**	0.04
					(2.87)	(0.19)
Constant	0.00	0.04	−0.23	−0.11	−0.23	−0.11
	(0.00)	(0.44)	(−1.56)	(−0.87)	(−1.60)	(−0.86)
Observations	118	118	118	118	118	118
R^2	0.11	0.11	0.17	0.35	0.22	0.35

t statistics in parentheses.
$^+p < 0.1$; $^*p < 0.05$; $^{**}p < 0.01$; $^{***}p < 0.001$.

joint model, only unemployment has a statistically significant effect on electoral punishment, whereas both rising unemployment and public debt significantly affect protest mobilization.

To test whether timing plays a role for both protest and electoral politics, we created a variable that indicates whether an election was a pre-crisis election, a first-crisis election, or a later-crisis election. For elections that have occurred after the collapse of Lehman Brothers in September 2008, we distinguish between 'first' and 'later-crisis elections': In each country, the first election that took place after October 2008 is coded as 'first-crisis election', while all later elections are coded as 'later-crisis elections'.[4]

Our expectation is also supported by the results presented in Table 10.1. Models 3 and 4 indicate that both the electoral punishment of the incumbent and protests were greater during the Great Recession

[4] Overall, the analysis covers fifty-nine pre-crisis elections, thirty first-crisis elections, and twenty-nine later-crisis elections. Austria had an election in September 2008 two weeks after the collapse of Lehman Brothers. We consider this crisis still as a pre-crisis election as it was not really fought in the shadow of the financial crisis.

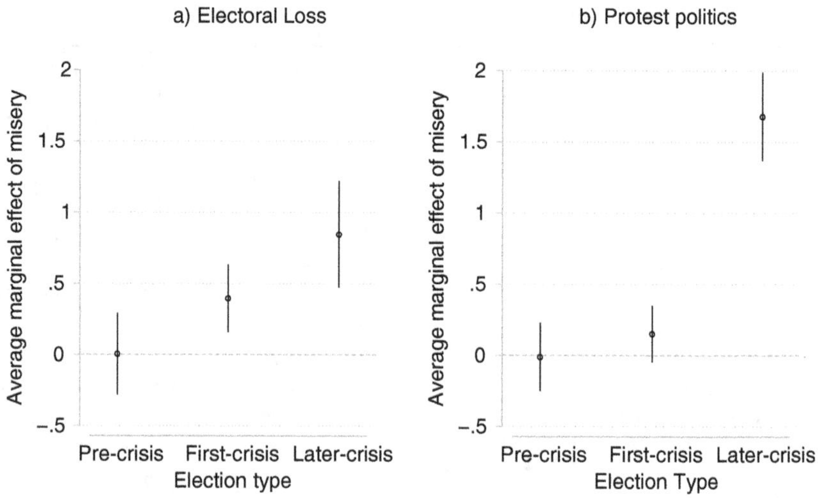

Figure 10.1 Average marginal effect of misery on electoral loss and protest – the importance of the crisis. (a) Electoral loss and (b) protest politics.
Note: Figures based on models 3 and 4 of Table 10.1, respectively.

than prior to it, but the results are not statistically significant. However, to test the timing argument, we need to consider the interaction effect of economic misery and our timing variable. As shown in models 3 and 4, the interaction between economic misery and both electoral losses and protests is positive and statistically significant in later-crisis elections. That is, in later-crisis elections, economic misery increases electoral losses and protests more than it did in previous elections. These interactions are also shown in Figure 10.1, which plots the average marginal effect of economic misery by election type. Figure 10.1a suggests that citizens perceived the worsening economic conditions as a greater failure of the incumbent party during later-crisis elections than in first-crisis elections. As the crisis progressed, governments that failed to address the economic situations of their countries were more severely punished than parties that were in office at the beginning of the crisis. Figure 10.1b shows the same pattern for protest. It indicates that in the immediate aftermath of the collapse of Lehman Brothers, citizens did not increasingly voice their discontent in the streets as the economic conditions worsened. However, there is a strong positive effect of economic misery on the level of protest during later stages of the economic crisis.

Finally, we look at the associations between bailouts and citizens' responses in the two arenas. Here, we rely on a variable that indicates whether a country was bailed out by the IMF or the European Stability Mechanism, implying external political constraints (see Chapter 9). According to the results of models 5 and 6 in Table 10.1, bailouts are associated only with higher electoral punishment but not protest punishment. Although the coefficient in model 6 is also positive, it is not statistically significant. It indicates that international bailouts did not systematically increase the number of people that protested during our period of study, at least not when we use legislative periods as the unit of analysis (for a more fine-grained analysis of this question, see Chapter 9).

Overall, we interpret these results as supporting our *equivalence hypothesis* (H1). We find very similar effects of economic misery on the electoral support of incumbents and on the level of economic protests. Moreover, these effects tend to become stronger in 'later-crisis elections' when the economic situation in Europe diverged ever more and voters already had a chance to punish their governments at the ballot box. However, when focusing on legislative periods, we cannot detect a statistically significant and positive effect of bailouts on the level of protest mobilization, whereas we observe such an effect for the electoral performance of the ruling party.

10.6 Protest, the Economic Vote, and the Signalling Mechanism

However, as suggested earlier, it is misleading to treat the two arenas of mass politics as independent. Instead, both are interwoven with national and international political dynamics and there is reason to believe that protest politics and electoral politics are closely related. Consequently, we move beyond the existing economic voting model and test the importance of protest mobilization as an explanatory variable for electoral punishment. To that end, we test the influence of protest on electoral punishment. Using OLS regression analysis, we repeat the analysis from the first step with electoral punishment as the dependent variable, but we now include protest mobilization in the legislative period before the election as an independent variable. To test our signalling hypothesis, we include an interaction between protest mobilization and the economic misery indicator. Otherwise this analysis mirrors the analysis in the first step.

Table 10.2 presents the results from this exercise. The first column indicates that the bivariate relationship between protest and electoral

Table 10.2. *Electoral loss: Protest as an independent variable*

	(1)	(2)	(3)	(4)	(5)	(6)
	All countries			Western Europe		
	Elect.	Elect.	Elect.	Elect.	Elect.	Elect.
Protest	0.32**	0.22*	0.14	0.28***	0.14*	0.02
	(3.36)	(2.29)	(1.10)	(4.05)	(2.23)	(0.27)
Misery		0.27**	0.26**		0.42***	0.39***
		(2.95)	(2.77)		(5.48)	(5.08)
Protest # Misery			0.05			0.08*
			(0.87)			(2.04)
Constant	−0.01	−0.01	−0.02	−0.21**	−0.27***	−0.29***
	(−0.13)	(−0.09)	(−0.25)	(−2.69)	(−3.94)	(−4.33)
Observations	118	118	118	77	77	77
R^2	0.09	0.15	0.16	0.18	0.42	0.45

t statistics in parentheses.
$^+p < 0.1$; $^*p < 0.05$; $^{**}p < 0.01$; $^{***}p < 0.001$.

punishment is positive and statistically significant: A 1 standard deviation increase in protest is associated with a 0.32 standard deviation increase in economic voting. However, when controlling for misery (model 2), this effect becomes smaller. Moreover, contrary to our expectations, there seems to be no interaction effect between economic misery and protest (model 3): Instead the bivariate relationship between electoral and protest punishment is mostly driven by a third factor, namely economic misery. However, when repeating the same analysis for western Europe only (models 4–6), the results change. Importantly, there is now a positive and statistically significant interaction effect of protest and economic misery in model 6, which indicates that in western Europe the impact of economic misery on electoral punishment can be amplified by protest punishment (which supports the *signalling hypothesis H2*). This effect is also shown in Figure 10.2, which plots the average marginal effect of misery on the electoral loss of the incumbent across different levels of protest for western Europe. It shows that in western Europe this effect is substantial: When there is little protest, economic misery is not associated with electoral losses for incumbents; only when there are large protests, the effect of misery becomes important.

The regional differences in this analysis confirm findings from the previous chapters and existing research. For eastern Europe, where party systems are less institutionalised, Hernández and Kriesi (2016)

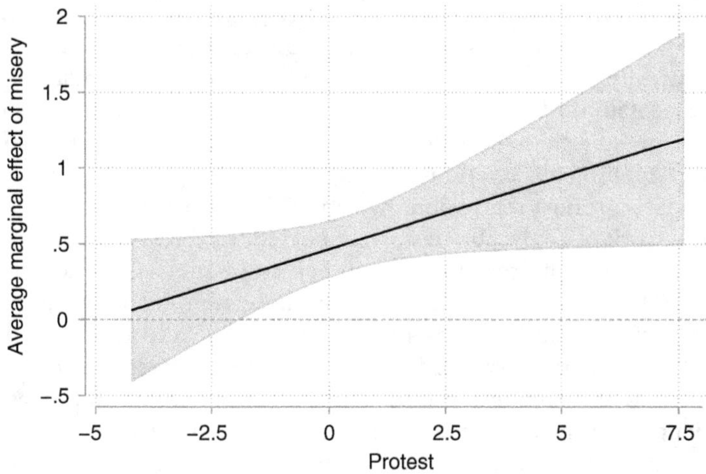

Figure 10.2 Average marginal effect of misery on electoral loss at different levels of protest.
Note: Figure based on model 6 of Table 10.2.

already showed that voters punish governments less for worsening economic conditions than in western Europe.[5] Hence, it is not surprising that we do not find a signalling effect of protest on electoral punishment for eastern Europe, either. Moreover, as Chapter 4 emphasized, protest during the Great Recession was to a large extent a phenomenon in the southern Europe. Since we cannot test our models for southern Europe only because of the small number of observations, we aimed to detect the effect of influential cases on our regressions. More specifically, we calculated the Cook's distance for each observation used in model 6 in Table 10.2 to allow us to identify influential observations. The analysis indicates that there are three observations with a relatively large Cook's distance in our western European sample: Ireland 2002 and 2011 and Greece 2012. Only one of these observations stems from southern Europe, indicating that the Greek election in May 2012 is an influential case in our analysis. Prior to this election, there were especially large and numerous protests that were followed by an electoral realignment related to the breakthrough of the challenger party Syriza and the almost-collapse of the former ruling party Pasok. However, the

[5] Instead, incumbents are more punished for increasing corruption, which we do not expect to be related to *economic* protest that we analyse in this paper.

other observations from Greece and, more generally, southern Europe are not influential observations, which indicates that our results are not systematically driven by the experience of southern Europe during the Great Recession. Moreover, no observation in our sample has a Cook's distance greater than 1, which is a common cut-off used to identify highly influential observations.[6] Hence, the results do not change when we estimate a robust regression instead of a OLS regression.

In the spirit of a 'placebo' test, we repeated the foregoing analysis but used the number of protest events on cultural issues as our key dependent variable (results not shown). For these non-economic protests, economic misery and the crisis did not systematically affect the number of protests. In other words, only economic protests are positively correlated with economic misery and the crisis, which increases our confidence that the relationship between misery and economic protests that we identified is, indeed, meaningful.

10.7 Protest, the Economic Vote, and the Decline of Mainstream Parties

We now turn to a more careful analysis of whether certain types of parties systematically suffered or benefited from the instability that the Great Recession brought about. First, we classify parties as mainstream versus non-mainstream parties according to their party family, as indicated by the Chapel Hill Expert Survey (Bakker et al. 2015): Parties from the conservative, Christian democratic, social democratic, and liberal party families are classified as mainstream, whereas parties from all other party families are classified as non-mainstream. Second, we classify parties as left-wing parties as opposed to all other political parties.

Given our results so far, we restrict our analysis to western Europe only.[7] To assess the gains and losses of the different types of parties, we first analyse the impact of the economic crisis on the change in the vote share from election at time t and $t - 1$. In the first step, we are interested in testing whether the crisis has accelerated the pre-existing long-term

[6] There are different cut-off values for spotting influential cases. Some suggest the simple guideline of $D > 1$; others suggest going for $4/N$ (=number of observations), which in our case is 0.05. The three cases in our analysis resulted in the following values (listed in descending order): Ireland 2011 with a Cook's Distance of 0.25, Greece 2012 with 0.25, Ireland 2002 with 0.11.

[7] The countries included in this part of the analysis are the following: Austria, Belgium, Cyprus, Denmark, Finland, France, Germany, Greece, Iceland, Ireland, Italy, Luxembourg, Malta, Norway, Netherlands, Portugal, Spain, Sweden, Switzerland, and the United Kingdom.

decline of mainstream parties and how this decline is related to political contestation in the arena of protest politics. Therefore, we again resort to a simple OLS regression using the electoral punishment of individual parties as our dependent variable. We use the same independent variables as in the previous steps of the analysis. Following the literature on economic voting we also include two dummy variables that capture whether a party was in government and whether the prime minister was from that party during the legislative period between election at time t and $t - 1$. Moreover, in the baseline model we include a dummy for mainstream parties and we then test the differential effect of economic misery and protest punishment on mainstream versus non-mainstream parties by including interaction effects with this dummy. Similarly, in a second step, we repeat the analysis and evaluate the differential effect of economic misery and protest punishment on left-wing parties in separate models.[8]

The results of this analysis are shown in Table 10.3. The results confirm our earlier finding that governing is costly for parties in electoral terms. Parties that are in government are punished more consistently at elections than other parties and parties that are leading the government (i.e. the prime minister's party) are punished even more. In general, there is no negative effect for mainstream parties, though. These parties are not punished more consistently during our period of study, shedding some doubt on the general thesis of the long-term decline of mainstream parties. Yet, model 1 suggests that the electoral fortune of mainstream parties is related to the relative level of protest in a given legislative period. The interaction effect between mainstream parties and protest is positive and statistically significant, indicating that the electoral losses of mainstream parties increase as protest increases. To interpret this interaction effect, it is useful to plot the average marginal effects of protest on electoral loss by party type. The results shown in Figure 10.3 are clear: On average, mainstream parties lose from protest over economic issues, while non-mainstream parties benefit from heightened levels of protest (i.e. they 'lose less'). This reinforces the long-term decline of established mainstream parties and supports our *party system destabilization hypothesis (H3)*.

Model 2 in Table 10.2 investigates whether the signalling effect of protest also holds at the level of individual parties and contributes to

[8] In total our dataset includes 548 observations, including observation for 276 mainstream parties and 272 observations for non-mainstream parties. Similarly, our dataset includes 296 observations for left-wing parties and 252 observations for parties that are not left-wing.

Table 10.3. *Electoral loss of mainstream and left parties in western Europe*

	(1)	(2)	(3)	(4)
	Mainstream		Left-wing	
	Elect.	Elect.	Elect.	Elect.
PM = 1	0.23*	0.23*	0.22*	0.20*
	(2.28)	(2.26)	(2.15)	(1.99)
Government = 1	0.48***	0.49***	0.48***	0.49***
	(6.47)	(6.56)	(6.58)	(6.62)
Protest	−0.08**	−0.02	−0.03	−0.02
	(−2.84)	(−0.41)	(−0.79)	(−0.33)
Mainstream party	−0.04	−0.10		
	(−0.71)	(−1.61)		
Mainstream party # Protest	0.23***	0.04		
	(4.86)	(0.61)		
Misery	−0.00	−0.10*	−0.00	0.05
	(−0.06)	(−2.02)	(−0.11)	(1.09)
Protest # Misery		−0.02		−0.01
		(−0.95)		(−0.57)
Mainstream party # Misery		0.16*		
		(2.48)		
Mainstream party # Protest # Misery		0.08*		
		(2.38)		
Left party			0.02	0.02
			(0.27)	(0.27)
Left party # Protest			0.05	0.02
			(1.10)	(0.28)
Left party # Misery				−0.13+
				(−1.89)
Left party # Protest # Misery				0.04
				(1.26)
Constant	−0.15***	−0.12**	−0.18***	−0.18***
	(−3.71)	(−2.95)	(−4.30)	(−4.24)
Observations	548	548	548	548
R^2	0.18	0.21	0.15	0.16

t statistics in parentheses.
$^{+}p < 0.1$; $^{*}p < 0.05$; $^{**}p < 0.01$; $^{***}p < 0.001$.

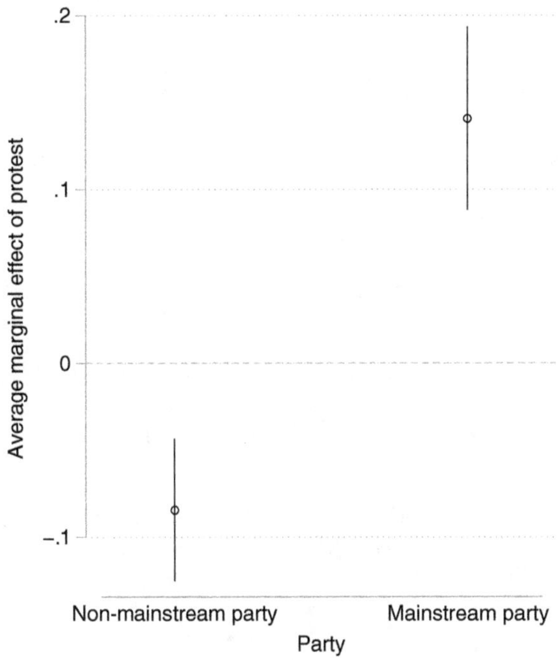

Figure 10.3 Average marginal effect of protest on electoral loss of mainstream versus challenger parties.
Note: Figure based on model 1 from Table 10.3.

the restructuring of the party system in western Europe. It includes a three-way interaction between party type, protest punishment, and economic misery in order to test whether the impact of economic misery on the electoral support for mainstream parties is amplified by protest. This three-way interaction term is positive and statistically significant, which indicates that political protest indeed strengthens the effect of economic misery on the punishment of mainstream parties. This is also shown in Figure 10.4, which shows the marginal effect of misery on the electoral performance of mainstream parties across different levels of protest. It suggests that the average marginal effect of misery increases with protest for mainstream parties, while it decreases for non-mainstream parties. This suggests that the relationship between protest and the electoral losses of mainstream parties is not direct. Instead, citizens are more likely to defect from mainstream parties when the economic conditions worsen and this effect becomes

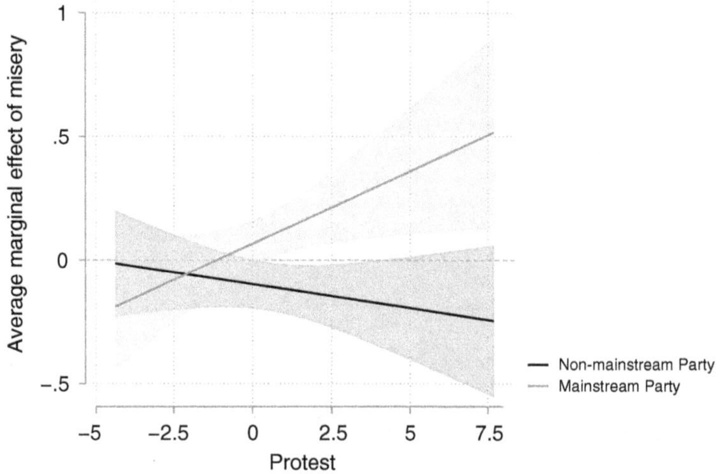

Figure 10.4 Average marginal effect of economic misery on electoral loss of mainstream versus challenger parties at different levels of protest.
Note: Figure based on model 2 from Table 10.3.

stronger when there is a relatively large amount of economic protest. This effect still exists even when we control for possible crisis-effects (results not shown). Therefore, the signalling effect of protest does not seem only to be a phenomenon of the Great Recession. Instead, protest increases the likelihood that mainstream parties are attributed responsibility for declining economic performance throughout our period of investigation.

Going one step further, we repeat the analysis but now we distinguish between left-wing and other parties. The results are shown in models 3 and 4 in Table 10.3. They indicate that there are no significant effects between protest politics and the electoral fortunes of left-wing parties, which does not support the more general idea that there is a close alliances between social movements and parties from the left in Europe (see Kriesi 1995; Maguire 1995).[9] Consequently, the destabilization of the party system during the Great Recession and the effect of protest on its restructuration did not swing in one direction or the other in terms of the traditional left–right spectrum. Although the Great Recession and the resulting economic misery led to heightened contestation in the protest

[9] We do not find that protests have an effect on the electoral fortune of far-left parties only (results not shown), either.

Table 10.4. *Electoral loss of left parties in western Europe by government status*

	(1) Elect.	(2) Elect.
PM = 1	0.22*	0.24*
	(2.12)	(2.46)
Government = 1	0.43***	0.41***
	(4.97)	(4.90)
Left party	−0.03	−0.04
	(−0.47)	(−0.54)
Protest	−0.00	−0.10**
	(−0.09)	(−2.69)
Misery	−0.00	−0.00
	(−0.08)	(−0.12)
Government = 1 # Left party	0.16	0.17
	(1.27)	(1.42)
Government = 1 # Protest		0.23***
		(3.65)
Left party # Protest		0.03
		(0.51)
Government = 1 # Left party # Protest		0.20*
		(1.99)
Constant	−0.16***	−0.16***
	(−3.62)	(−3.71)
Observations	548	548
R^2	0.15	0.22

t statistics in parentheses.
$^{+}p < 0.1$; $^{*}p < 0.05$; $^{**}p < 0.01$; $^{***}p < 0.001$.

and the electoral arena, this contestation has not (yet) been resolved in a systematic way across western Europe. This reflects the earlier analysis by Bartels (2014), who could not find clear-cut ideological shifts to the left or right in the electoral arena during the Great Recession.

Interestingly, while we cannot detect a general swing to the left or the right under conditions of protest mobilization in the previous analysis, our more detailed results on the role of government participation do support the claim that the mainstream left in power has more to lose when it is targeted by mobilization in the streets (supporting our *left-wing punishment hypothesis H4*). Table 10.4 shows the importance of government status and protest for left-wing parties. According to

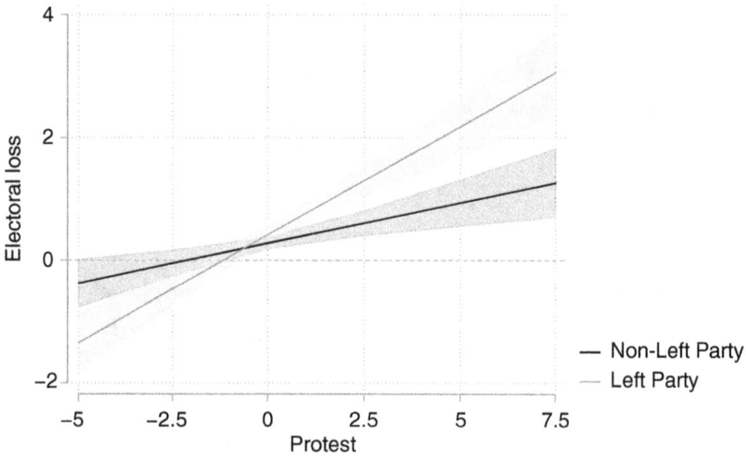

Figure 10.5 Marginal effect of protest on electoral loss of left parties vs. non-left parties in government.
Note: Figure based on model 2 from Table 10.4.

model 1, there is no statistically significant effect of being in government for left-wing parties. In other words, all parties independent of partisan colour are, on average, punished for being in government in our sample. However, model 2 shows the three-way interaction between being in government, left-wing parties, and protest. The results of this effect are again best interpreted with the help of a marginal effect plots, shown in Figure 10.5.[10] They indicate that all parties in government tend to lose more under conditions of high protest. However, this effect is especially pronounced for left-wing parties. Thus, the traditional allies of social movements seem to suffer most if economic protests target their activities in government.

10.8 Conclusions

In the Great Recession, incumbents were heavily punished in the electoral arena. However, this punishment has not been limited to the electoral arena and, instead, citizens have also opposed governments by voicing their grievances in the street. By and large our

[10] The figure shows the effect of protest on the punishment of left-wing parties versus all other parties for parties that were in government prior to a given election only. The marginal effects for opposition parties are not shown.

analyses show electoral punishment and protests are both driven by poor economic performance of a given country, confirming the economic voting model. This relationship between economic conditions and economic voting as well as protests, respectively, is particularly strong in later stages of the crisis, as the economic fate of countries in Europe diverged and citizens mobilized against governments in countries that continued to be stuck in the economic recession. Moreover, electoral punishment was higher in countries that relied on international bailouts, which further increased the perception that national governments failed to steer their countries out of the crisis. However, surprisingly based on analysing legislative periods, we do not find similar effects for protest politics (see Chapter 9 for a more detailed analysis).

Still, it is misleading to treat punishment in the electoral arena and protests as independent from each other. In Europe, the citizens' response to the economic crisis was first of all an electoral one, but people also expressed their discontent through protest as shown in previous chapters of this volume. The analyses in this chapter show that these protests were coupled with electoral punishment in the sense that larger protests were also associated with stronger electoral punishment of incumbents. We present evidence that protests can amplify the importance of economic conditions for electoral punishment: By attributing responsibility, mobilizing citizens, and channelling their grievances into the electoral arena, protests increase the importance of economic conditions for the next general election. The 'placebo test' with cultural protests underlines that this is driven by economic protests that target public policies and institutions.

In addition, our findings show that the signalling effect of protest is not only limited to the punishment of incumbent, but it extends to all mainstream parties: As economic conditions worsen, citizens are more likely to defect from mainstream parties when there is a relatively large amount of protests. The beneficiaries of this destabilization of the party existing system are non-mainstream parties in general. They feed off the discontent that citizens voice in protest politics and following large protest, irrespective of the economic conditions, they are likely to win more votes in the next general election. In sum, our analyses point to a destabilizing effect of the Great Recession on political competition in Europe but this destabilization has not been resolved in one way or another: The political system across Europe has not systematically swung in one direction or the other, as different parties have benefited in different regions. Importantly, we do not observe a close connection between the electoral fortunes of the political left and economic protests in general, although it is the political left that gets punished most heavily when in government under conditions of high protest mobilization.

The next chapter will again take up the question of how electoral and protest politics are connected to each other in times of crisis, but it will zoom in on political parties' activities in the streets of Europe. The result from this chapter suggests that especially parties in opposition might have a lot to gain from realigning with actors in the streets.

11 Are Political Parties Recapturing the Streets of Europe?

A Cross-regional Study of Party Protests in the Great Recession

Endre Borbáth and Swen Hutter

11.1 Introduction

The chapter focuses on political parties' activities in the streets. That is, it takes the main collective actors engaged in electoral competition but looks at their involvement in a major form of non-electoral mobilization. More specifically, the chapter concentrates on the level and type of protests that are sponsored by political parties. Sponsorship is broadly defined and means that parties (co-)organize, take part in, and/or call for the participation in a protest event (Rucht 1998: 41). We refer to our research object as party-sponsored protests or, in short, party protests. Our main questions are as follows: To what extent do political parties sponsor protests in Europe? How does the level and type of party protests differ across the European macro regions? And, most importantly for this volume, have the recent economic and political crises in Europe significantly changed parties' activities in the streets?

By studying party protests, we complement other research on how parties have responded to the economic upheaval and mounting distrust towards representative institutions and political parties in the countries hardest hit by the Great Recession and the subsequent Euro crisis (see Chapter 1). Against the background of parties' withdrawal from civil society (Mair 2013; Schmitter 2001) – as well-documented by declining party membership or party identification (e.g. Dalton and Wattenberg 2002; Poguntke et al. 2016; van Biezen et al. 2012) – the economic crisis might potentially constitute a critical juncture for the relationship between parties and civil society.

Apart from adapting their programmatic stances (e.g. Conti et al. 2017; Traber et al. 2017), established and new political parties might try to realign with the social forces in the streets to show their responsiveness to increasing public pressure. Following the scenario outlined in the previous chapter (Chapter 10), opposition parties should be particularly keen on 'riding the wave of political contention' to profit from the close links between protest mobilization and electoral punishment of incumbents. Most telling examples for the closely coupled dynamics of opposition in protest and electoral politics are the rise of so-called 'movement parties' in southern Europe (SE) (della Porta et al. 2017). Regarding party protests, we should thus expect that parties are more likely to sponsor protests and to join forces with other challengers of the dominant austerity policies.

However, as we show in this chapter, political parties have not been very successful in recapturing the streets, i.e. in increasing their standing in the protest arena (see also Borbáth and Hutter 2020). By contrast, we observe differentiated political arenas and a sort of 'crowding-out' of parties from the streets in SE in the shadow of the Great Recession. The latter finding mirrors the interdependence of the economic and political crisis dynamics in the region which led to the discrediting of established political elites and parties. The finding also confirms the conclusions of previous chapters on the character and key actors driving the protest wave in SE (see Chapters 4 and 5). Thus, our findings put the emerging links between social movements and new challenger parties in perspective. As important these linkages might have been at some moment in the development of these parties, the large-N approach we adopt here qualifies the general role political parties played in mobilizing protestors in response to the Great Recession.

The structure of the chapter reflects the general ambition of the volume as we expect cross-regional differences not only because of the varying extent of the crisis but also because of the long-term trends in the structure and dynamics of political conflict. As the literature has not yet addressed cross-regional variations in how parties have traditionally crossed the boundaries of the electoral arena and mobilized in the streets, the first two sections provide the theoretical framework of our analysis. In Section 11.2, we rely on Kitschelt's (2003) differentiation thesis to get to our baseline assumptions about the intensity and type of party protests. More precisely, we expect that party protests are rather rare and show a distinct profile, i.e. they center on cultural issues. Next in Section 11.3, we highlight that Kitschelt's prediction very much reflects the evolution of conflict and interest intermediation in north-western Europe (NWE). By contrast, we expect different varieties of party protests in SE and especially in eastern Europe (EE). In EE, political parties are often organized in a top-down fashion and aim to control existing means of mobilization in order to consolidate their power. It is also the region where democratization happened most recently and there is a comparatively weak 'non-partisan' civil society to counterbalance the mobilization efforts of parties. Once we have established our baseline assumption and its regional variations, in Section 11.4 we sketch the potential impact of the Great Recession as a critical juncture for the way political parties approach protest politics before we empirically test our expectations in Section 11.5.

The data used in this volume allow us to draw the big picture of party protests in a large set of thirty European countries. This has not yet been done, reflecting the bifurcation of research on elections and political parties, on the one hand, and research on protest and social movements, on the other (McAdam and Tarrow 2010, 2013; see also Chapter 10 of this volume). Moreover, such analyses have been hampered by a lack of appropriate datasets (the few large-N protest event datasets usually contain no detailed information on organizational sponsors). In our opinion, drawing the big picture is an important first cut at an interesting research topic and complements recent case studies (see Cisar and Navrátil 2017; Dolezal 2017; Heaney and Rojas 2015; Hutter 2013).

11.2 Party Protests in Europe: Relatively Rare and Distinct

We rely on Herbert Kitschelt's work (2003) to establish our baseline argument about the level and types of party protests in Europe. According to Kitschelt, we have witnessed an increasing differentiation in the patterns of interest mobilization since the end of the 'Golden Age' of Western capitalism. According to his argument, the post-war period was characterized by fused patterns of political mobilization, while the various arenas have become increasingly differentiated since the 1970s.

> The progressive differentiation of modes of collective interest mobilization and growing separation of political entrepreneurs in movements, interest groups, and parties from each other is the big story of the last third of the twentieth century in European democracies. (Kitschelt 2003: 89)

In a theoretical tour de force, Kitschelt explains this development by learning processes of political entrepreneurs and their followers which were fueled by economic, social, and political-institutional changes. Two challenges faced by political entrepreneurs are of central importance for the argument: problems of collective action and social choice. In contrast to social movements and interest groups, political parties are portrayed as the actors that have invested the most in solving both types of problems. Political parties frame their stakes as long-term, durable, and encompassing programs. To realize such programs, political entrepreneurs need to invest in an infrastructure that allows communicating with potential adherents and disbursing selective incentives for solving collective action problems (Olson 1965). Furthermore, parties need to invest in techniques of collective preference alignment (e.g. formal rules for aggregating individual preferences into organizational purposes). Such techniques help to overcome social choice problems, 'namely, the instability and paralysis of a collectivity with many activists that results from the heterogeneity of individual preferences' (Kitschelt 2003: 85). In the long run, political actors that have invested differently in solving problems of collective action and social choice are more or less adapted to compete in the different arenas. Importantly for party protests, Kitschelt (2003: 97) argues, 'Parties focus increasingly on electoral competition, at the expense of interest group representation or social movement protest actions.... Social movements, finally, concentrate on public actions outside institutionalized arenas of bargaining to affect public opinion and political elites through the media."

Regarding the catalysts of the breakdown of traditionally 'fused' patterns of interest intermediation, Kitschelt (2003: 90ff) considers such diverse developments as the revolution of information technology, the up-skilling of the labour force, the increasing openness of national economies, the intensifying physical and social mobility as well as the internal politics of the welfare state. These processes have fundamentally transformed European societies and ultimately undermined the social bases of mass parties and party-centred networks which characterized European democracies in the Golden age of capitalism in the 1950s and 1960s.

Arguably, these processes have transformed the party systems in two waves: a first wave driven by the mobilization of new social movements and left-libertarian parties in the 1970s and early 1980s, and a second wave driven by the mobilization of the populist radical right since the 1990s. Both driving forces are seen as breaking with the past and challenging the political order of their time. Most importantly, the challenge arose from new issues and demands that these actors brought into the political process. The challengers from the left advocated individual autonomy, the free choice of lifestyles, and other universalistic values. The challengers from the right, by contrast, focused on immigration and European integration as threats to the homogenous nation-state. Both waves concerned above all cultural issues. That is, they primarily transformed the meaning of the cultural dimension of the two-dimensional political spaces. Interpreting the impact of the new left, Kitschelt (1994) re-baptized the cultural dimension as 'libertarian-authoritarian' dimension, while Kriesi et al. (2008, 2012) focusing on the impact of the populist radical right labelled it as 'integration-demarcation.' What is common to both accounts is the emphasis on the new divides which weaken traditional patterns of interest intermediation and the role of mainstream parties.

In his analysis of protest politics in six NWE countries from 1975 to 2005, Hutter (2014b) has shown that the new integration-demarcation cleavage has restructured protest politics as well. Most importantly, issues centring on cultural liberalism and – since the 1990s – immigration have dominated the protest landscapes. However, the impact of the populist-right has been less important than the left-libertarian turn given that the protest arenas has been mainly used by the political left. The challengers from the right, in contrast, tend to follow a different logic in the way they use protest and electoral politics to mobilize their adherents. Given ideological and strategic considerations, the political right tends to refrain from street protests, the more successful it gets in electoral politics. Overall, this is also reflected in a lower overall share of protests sponsored by parties from the right (around 40 per cent) compared to parties from the left (around 60 per cent) in the six countries under scrutiny (Hutter 2014: 125).

Based on Kitschelt's differentiation thesis and the observed changes in the structure of political conflict, we expect rather disconnected arenas of mobilization in contemporary European democracies in terms of the main actors involved in electoral and protest politics. Thus, our baseline assumption is that political parties are no longer dominant actors in European protest politics (*differentiation hypothesis*). Rather, we expect that party-sponsored protest events make up a small share of all coded events. The protest arena should be the site where less institutionalized social movement organizations and other civil society actors mobilize their constituencies. Moreover, the baseline assumption of differentiated political arenas leads us to expect that, if at all, protests are sponsored by parties with an 'outsider' status (*outsider hypothesis*). We refer here to both parties' ideological radicalism and their formal power, as indicated by parliamentary representation and opposition status. In addition, the dominant challenges to the established order let us expect that if parties still use the streets, they do so to push forward their demands related to new cultural issues associated with green and radical right parties and not traditional economic concerns.

11.3 Varieties of Party Protests in Europe

Do the arguments about the limited extent of party protests and their specific shape hold across the European continent? Or should we rather expect different regional varieties? To answer these questions, we would like to emphasize two important scope conditions of the differentiation argument, namely, the far-reaching restructuration of political conflict and the rise of a strong independent civil society. Both conditions seem crucial for the establishment of functionally differentiated arenas that are populated by specialized political actors.

Regarding the first scope condition, it seems important to note that the sketched two-fold transformation of political conflict seems mainly a story of NWE. Political conflict in SE and EE has been far less transformed by the two waves. In bold strokes, the party systems in SE have until recently remained essentially bipolar with cultural and economic issues amalgamated in one single left–right dimension (e.g., Hutter et al. 2018; Polk and Rovny 2016) and parties weakly rooted in the cleavage structure (Gunther 2005). In particular, the rise of the populist radical right has been comparatively weak in most SE countries. In turn, the lack of a strong new left and populist radical right has contributed to keeping the new cultural issues rather off the agenda of electoral politics. Also, economic issues have been more important in structuring protest politics in the south of Europe as are alliances between actors from the old and the new left (e.g. della Porta 2007; Koopmans 1996; see also Chapter 6, this volume).

The development of political conflict in EE differs from the general story in yet another way. First, eastern Europe party systems still appear to be much less institutionalized than party systems in western Europe (e.g. Casal Bértoa and Enyedi 2016). The very high level of volatility in these systems since the democratic transition is the most important empirical evidence for their lack of institutionalization (e.g., Powell and Tucker 2014). Second, many of the parties on the left in EE trace back their organizational origin to former communist parties and struggle to dissociate themselves from the former regimes (Tavits and Letki 2009). Lacking strong parties of the 'new left' to challenge the post-communist successors, anti-system mobilization is often left to the right in both the electoral and the protest arenas (Borbáth and Gessler 2020). Finally, the emerging new conflicts in EE usually centre on cultural issues but of a different kind (Coman 2010; Rovny 2014). As Kriesi (2016: 38) aptly put it, '[t]he common denominator of the cultural issues mobilizing the traditionalist side of the CEE electorates seems to be a 'defensive nationalism' asserting itself against internal enemies (such as ethnic minorities: Russians, Roma, and Jews) and external ones (such as foreign corporations colonizing the national economy)'.

The second important condition of the differentiation story seems the development of a strong and independent civil society. Even if we expect that the traditionally dominant mass parties might withdraw from certain sites of mobilization, there need to be other collective political organizations with the capacity to fill the 'void'. In fact, there is a nearly universal consensus in the literature on post-communist civil society about the weaknesses of these organizations in EE. The weak civil society is often considered to be the result of the lack of trust in these societies, originating from the totalitarian past, as well as of the non-transparent and elite-driven transition processes (Bernhard 1996; Howard 2003). In addition, the organizations that have emerged are often financially dependent on state resources, private sponsors, and/or transnational networks, and these resources are often linked to a specific political agenda. As a result, many organizations stay away from politics altogether or turn into vehicles of realizing the political goals of their sponsors (e.g. Lomax 1997).

Taking these scope conditions into account, we expect that the differentiation hypothesis holds mainly for NWE, and we expect different types and levels of party protests in SE and, in particular, in EE (*regional varieties hypothesis*). More precisely, we expect that political parties are more likely to sponsor protests in EE than in NWE; SE should be an intermediate case. In addition, we expect that the type of sponsored events reflects the dominant conflicts in the different regions. That is, party protests in NWE and EE should centre more on cultural issues compared to SE where economic issues should be more salient.

11.4 The Great Recession as a Critical Juncture?

In the period covered by our research, Europe experienced the worst economic crisis since the Great Depression in the 1930s. Regarding its influence on party-sponsored protest events, we want to emphasize here again that the crisis developed in stages and, in many countries, the economic crisis has developed alongside a political crisis (see Chapter 1). In general, we expect that the economic crisis and an aggravated political crisis remain not without consequences for how political parties get involved in protests.

In addition to programmatic changes (e.g. Conti et al. 2017; Traber et al. 2017), political parties (in opposition) should have strong incentives to realign with the social forces in the streets to show their responsiveness to mounting public pressure. In turn parties are expected to be more likely to co-sponsor protest events in times of crisis. As highlighted in the previous chapter of this volume (Chapter 10), protests did reinforce the electoral punishment of incumbents under conditions of economic hardship. Thus, opposition parties could profit in electoral terms if they are associated with the challenges against the governments in the streets. The most telling examples for this association are the transformed or newly emerging challenger parties in SE. While their classification as 'movement parties' is contested, the new challengers, such as Syriza in Greece, Movimento Cinque Stelle in Italy, or Podemos in Spain, clearly appropriated claims and frames from the anti-austerity protests and, in part, they were closely related to the activists' networks involved in staging the protests (see della Porta et al. 2017).

However, given the strong interdependence between economic and political crises dynamics, we do not expect that political parties have been very successful in recapturing the street, i.e. in increasing their relative standing in the protest arena. By contrast, we expect that the crisis leads to a sort of 'crowding-out effect'. Thus, the period after 2008 should be characterized by even lower levels of party-sponsored events than the pre-crisis period (*crowding-out hypothesis*). This effect should be strongest in the countries of SE. These countries have been very hard hit by the economic crisis and trust in political parties, as modes of interest articulation, has dropped most dramatically in recent years (see Chapter 1). These dynamics should not only result in the most pronounced protest waves (see Chapter 4), but also in bottom-up mobilization by new actors which does (at least initially) not reinforce the relative presence of parties in the streets but rather breaks existing relations between parties and social movements. Thus, as important as the emerging link between protests and the new challenger parties might be, we do not expect that they trigger a more general rise of political parties as mobilizing agents in the protest arena in the countries hardest hit by the crisis.

By contrast, it seems more likely that the crisis should be associated with a change in the type of party protests because political parties are expected to align with the major challengers in protest politics regarding the issues they emphasize. Therefore, we expect that, even if relatively less prominent, party protests should reflect the rise in economic and political grievances. Overall, we should thus find increasing party protests related to economic and political issues (*'riding the wave hypothesis'*). Therefore, considering the development of the major issues in the protest arena in the different regions (see Chapter 6), we expect the rise of party protests on economic issues in NWE and EE in the shock period, while these types of party protests should become relatively more important in SE in the subsequent Euro-crisis period. Finally, if parties are trying to ride the wave, we should also see a pronounced increase of party protests related to culturally conservative claims in EE in all crisis periods.

11.5 Empirical Findings

For the empirical analysis, we focus on the subset of protest events in the dataset for which we have coded at least one political party as an actor involved in protest events. Moreover, to avoid problems of missing data for our key variable of interest (i.e. share of party protests), we decided to restrict the sample to those events for which at least one organizational sponsor was reported in the news. The decision to exclude protests which do not have any organizational sponsor was guided by an empirical rationale. Our sources are international newswires, and these tend to often report on protest events in a brief, schematic style without listing any sponsoring organizations (see Chapter 3). To minimize the impact of this description bias and its variation across news agencies and countries, we focus on the subset of the dataset with the least amount of missing data. In addition, restricting the sample to events with at least one organizational sponsor considers the potential underreporting of parties in international news wires as compared to national newspapers.[1]

While it is difficult to directly test our baseline assumption, the overall share of around 14 per cent party-sponsored events indicates that such events are a relatively rare phenomenon in the European protest landscape. In line with the differentiation argument, political parties' primary interest seems to lie in the electoral arena. It is also important to repeat that the value compares events that are co-sponsored

[1] Note that the tests reported in Chapter 3 highlight some underreporting for four of the six countries. Importantly, the bias seems stronger if we compare our English-language news agencies to national newspapers than to national news agencies (the latter were used in the comparison for the two Eastern European countries in the sample, i.e. Hungary and Poland). We further checked the impact of these bias on our results by omitting the selected countries from our analysis and by running regressions that consider the various sources of bias introduced in Chapter 3. Overall, these tests show that the substantive results in this chapter are robust.

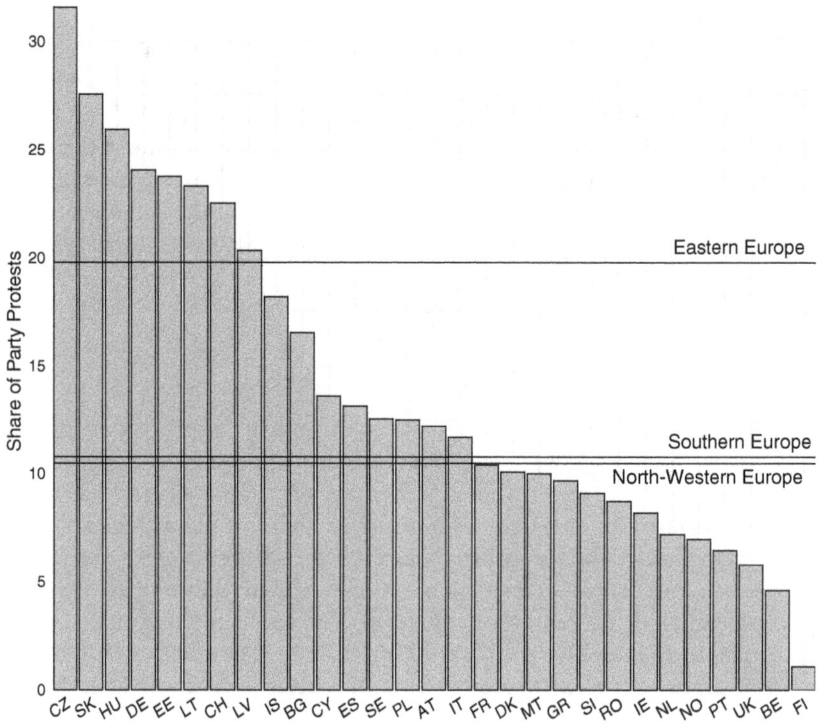

Figure 11.1 Average share of party protests in thirty European countries.
Note: The figure shows the share of party-sponsored protests relative to the events with at least one organizational sponsor.

by parties with events for which we coded at least one organizational sponsor. Thus, the share is even smaller if we consider all coded protests including those without any reported organizational sponsor (7.5 per cent).

Nevertheless, the 14 per cent highlights that parties occasionally sponsor protests and, in line with our expectations, their relative presence in the protest arena varies across countries and over time. To show the large cross-national differences, Figure 11.1 presents the share of party-sponsored protests in each of the thirty countries during the sixteen years under scrutiny. According to our data, the Czech Republic experienced the highest share of party-sponsored protests with a share of 31 per cent, whereas such events make up only 1 per cent in the case of Finland. Broadly speaking, most of the countries that saw the highest shares of party protests are in EE. As Figure 11.1 shows, seven of

Table 11.1. *Average share of party protests by region*

Region	Overall	Normal times	Shock period	Euro crisis	Refugee crisis
North-western Europe	10.5 (18.4)	9.5 (21.9)	9.6 (13.9)	12.8 (13.6)	18.9 (5.6)
Southern Europe	10.8 (21.8)	13.3 (30.3)	5.0 (7.6)	8.7 (8.8)	11.8 (11.0)
Eastern Europe	22.4 (30.8)	21.0 (28.6)	20.2 (25.2)	24.7 (36.1)	43.2 (27.5)
All regions	13.7 (22.2)	13.7 (26.4)	11.7 (14.3)	13.8 (16.5)	25.3 (11.3)

Note: The table shows the relative share of party-sponsored protests in per cent of all protests with at least one coded organizational sponsor. The values in parentheses show the relative share of participants involved in these events.

the top-ten countries in terms of party-sponsored events are from that region: the Czech Republic, Slovakia, Hungary, Estonia, Lithuania, Latvia, and Bulgaria. In contrast, the countries from NWE and SE are remarkably similar and show lower levels of party protests. As Table 11.1 shows, the average share of party-sponsored protests is around 22.4 per cent in EE compared to around 10.5 per cent in NWE and 10.8 per cent in SE. Overall, this supports our expectations about regional variety in the level of party protests.

In terms of event-level characteristics, parties tend to sponsor relatively large protests. In SE and NWE, party sponsored protests account for about one fifth of protest turnout, almost twice as high as their share of events indicates. In EE, almost one third of protest participation happens in party sponsored protests. Unsurprisingly, parties primarily sponsor demonstrations (about 70 per cent) or petitions (about 10 per cent in NWE and SE and about 20 per cent in EE), while they are much less likely to be involved in industrial actions (3 per cent) or violent confrontations (11 per cent).

Figure 11.2 shows the type of issues parties contest in the protest arena by region. Overall, parties are most likely to sponsor events centred on cultural issues. Comparing the share of cultural issues (i.e. the total of what we label as cultural liberalism and conservatism; see also Chapter 6) with the share of political issues, we see that the former tends to dominate in NWE and EE but not in SE. The differences regarding cultural issues are associated with the fact that, in SE, there is hardly any party-sponsored counter mobilization against the claims of the new social movements. Moreover, in relative terms, economic protests are most important in SE. In contrast, in EE, demands against immigration and for cultural conservatism are more salient in the

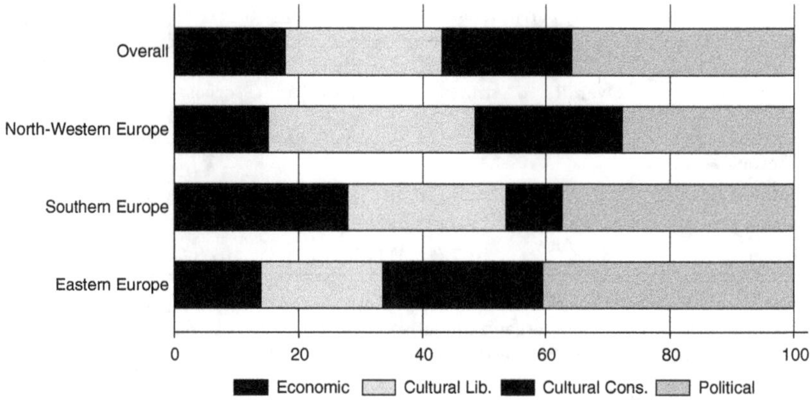

Figure 11.2 Share of issue categories of party protests by region. *Note:* The figure shows the share of an issue category in per cent of all events sponsored by parties, centred on any of the four categories in each region. Other issues have been excluded from the calculation (see Table 11.2).

protest scene. Finally, NWE parties sponsor protests organized around claims on both sides of the 'cultural' divide. This is indicated by the relatively similar share of the categories 'cultural liberalism' and 'cultural conservatism'. Overall, the issue claims of party protests resemble the issue claims in the protest arena at large (see Chapter 6), which suggest that parties organize protests with a similar focus to other organizations in the protest arena (see later).

Figure 11.3 presents the type of parties which are likely to sponsor protests. First, our dataset allows to differentiate between 'left' and 'right' parties. Second, we followed the approach in Chapter 10 and coded parties as either mainstream or non-mainstream based on the classification into party families. The conservative, Christian democratic, social democratic, and liberal party families are classified as mainstream, whereas parties from all other party families are classified as non-mainstream. Finally, we checked whether the parties in the streets were in opposition or in government and whether they were represented in the national parliament or not.

The results on the ideology of the parties in the streets of Europe underline what we have already seen when looking at the issue composition (again, see Figure 11.2): While in NWE and especially in SE party protests are associated with the political left, the political right is taking the conflicts to the streets in EE. The other three features (mainstream vs. non-mainstream, opposition status, and parliamentary

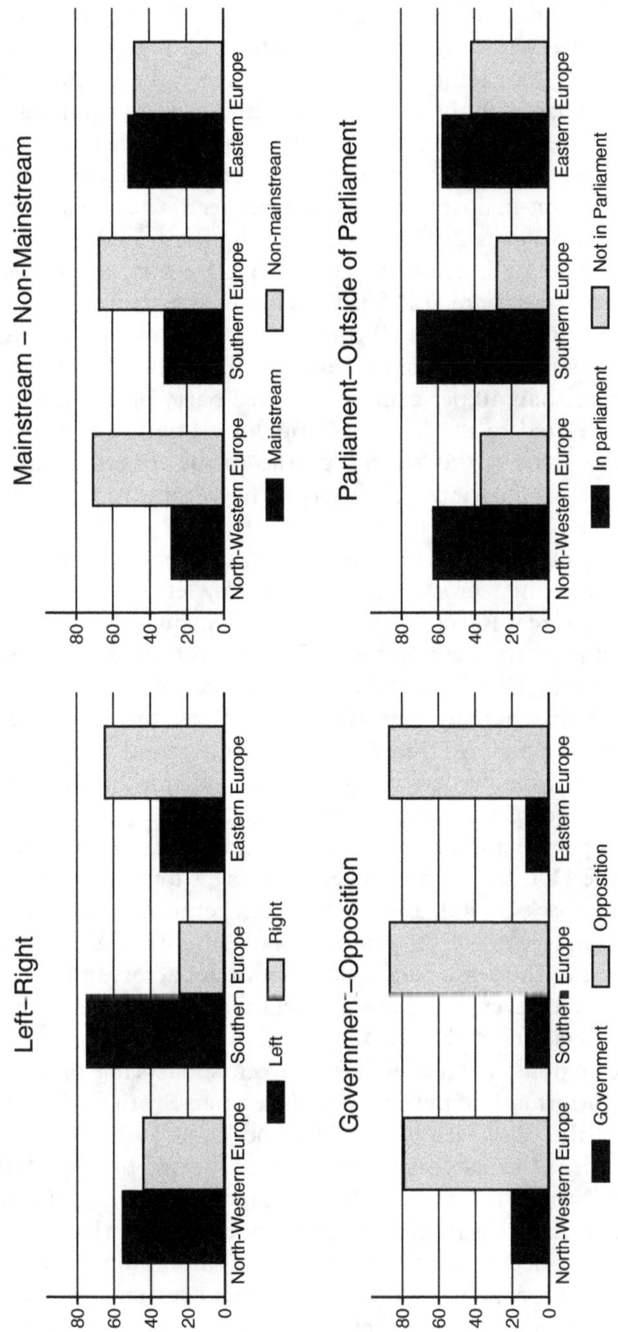

Figure 11.3 Types of parties in party protests.
Note: The figure shows the relative share of a certain category in per cent of all coded party-sponsored protests by region.

representation) support our 'outsider hypothesis' but again point to regional differences. Although party protests in all regions are almost exclusively used by opposition parties, we observe the dominance of non-mainstream parties only in NWE and SE. The less prominent role of challenger parties in the streets of EE reflects (1) the weakness of the radical left in the region and (2) the rather blurred distinction between mainstream and non-mainstream actors in terms of their mobilization strategies (e.g. Greskovits 2017). Finally, taking their weak position in the political systems into account, parties that are not represented in the national parliament are still fairly visible in the streets of Europe (with more than 20 per cent in all three regions). However, this time, we observe the strongest 'outsider' bias for EE, where such parties account for more than 40 per cent of all coded party protests. In part, this finding is related to the less institutionalized nature of the party systems because some of the 'strong' parties in the streets might gain parliamentary representation only after we have captured their presence in the protest arena.

Having tested our baseline assumptions on the general relevance of party protests and their cross-regional varieties, let us now focus on the effects of the Great Recession and the subsequent crises. To begin, Figure 11.4 presents the development of party protests by year. More specifically, it shows the trends in the relative shares of party-sponsored protests and the absolute numbers across Europe as well as for the different European regions. All figures include a horizontal reference line for the mean and three vertical reference lines: one for 2008, the start of the shock period of the financial crisis, one for 2010, the start of the Euro-crisis period and one for 2014, the start of the refugee crisis. Moreover, Table 11.1 indicates the overall averages for the four periods (normal times, shock period, Euro crisis, and refugee crisis) for each European region separately. In general, the results indicate that parties have in none of the years become the dominant actors in European protest politics. However, there are important short-term fluctuation, reflecting the dynamics of the crisis.

In all three regions, parties withdraw from sponsoring protests in the immediate aftermath of the collapse of Lehman Brothers, i.e. in the shock period of the crisis (see Figure 11.4 and Table 11.1). During the Euro crisis, parties returned to sponsor protests, first in north-west, then in the east, and last in the south. The developments during the shock period and the Euro crisis in SE tend to support the idea that when an economic crisis co-occurs with a crisis of representation, political parties become less important for organizing street protests. In contrast, they are rather crowded out by other types of organizational networks.

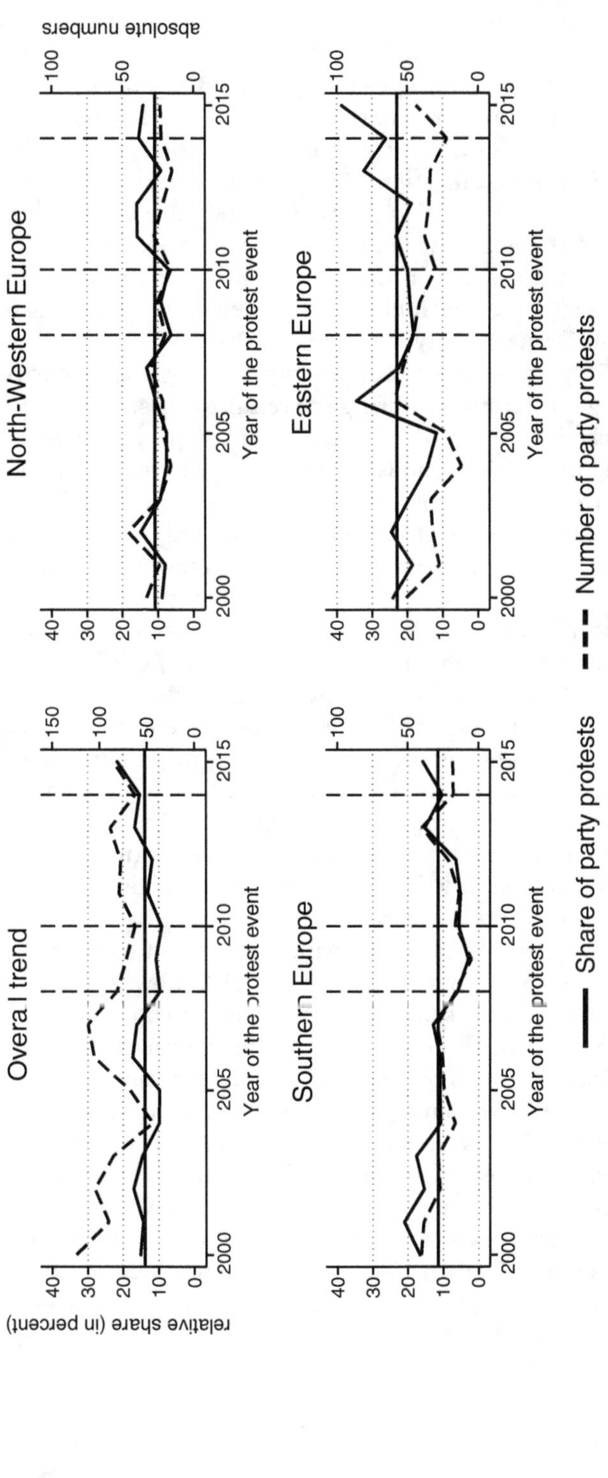

Figure 11.4 The development of party protests by region and year.

Note: The figure shows the share of party-sponsored protests in per cent of all protests with at least one organizational sponsor being reported by region and year (solid line). Moreover, it shows the absolute number of such party-sponsored protests by year (dashed line). For the latter, we take the number of events weighted by sampling probability, log country population, as well as an agency bias (see Chapter 2).

Note that this effect is visible not only when looking at relative shares but also when looking at the absolute number of party protests. Most importantly, we see a short-lived peak only in 2013 regarding both the share and the absolute number of party protests in SE. Thus, the lower shares of party protests in SE during the shock period and the Euro crisis do not hide a remobilization of parties in absolute terms. The 'crowding out' hypothesis is also supported by the share of participants in party protests: Whereas these tend to be very large events in the pre-crisis period, in the crisis period the turnout in these events declines relative to their frequency (see Table 11.1). However, the 'crowding out' dynamic is not inherent in all types of crisis. Although our coverage is very short, the EE pattern in particular shows a strong presence of parties in mobilizing on the streets during the refugee crisis.

We also checked potential differences in the type of parties that sponsor protests during the various time periods. There are few clear-cut trends, and the results by period tend to support the 'outsider status' of sponsors and the cross-national differences highlighted before (again, see Figure 11.3). However, there is one noteworthy exception as the share of non-mainstream compared to mainstream parties in SE has increased from around 50 per cent of all party protests in the so-called 'normal times' to 66.8 per cent in the shock period and more than 78 per cent during the Euro crisis.[2] The finding further qualifies the observation that political parties did not recapture the streets in SE during the economic crisis. As it turns out, non-mainstream or challenger parties increased their standing in the protest arena, but mainstream parties disappeared almost completely. This mirrors the negative effects of economic protests on the electoral fortunes of mainstream parties (regardless of whether they are in opposition or government) which we uncovered in Chapter 10.

In the crisis, we observe not only changing levels of party protests but also changing types of party protests. Table 11.2 shows the distribution of issues in party protests before the crisis, in the shock period and during the Euro crisis. Contrary to our 'riding the wave' hypothesis, the share of political issues in party protests decline (although they still stay at a relatively high level) and there is no universal increase of party protests on economic issues. But note that the share of party protests on economic issues almost triples in SE during the Euro crisis, and there is a small increase although on a lower level in NWE in the shock period as well. However, except for the south in the Euro crisis, political parties are the least likely to protest on economic relative to other

[2] Detailed results available from the authors.

Table 11.2. *The development of issues in party protests by region and period*

	Normal times				Shock period				Euro crisis			
	Econ.	Cult-lib.	Cult-cons.	Pol.	Econ.	Cult-lib.	Cult-cons.	Pol.	Econ.	Cult-lib.	Cult-cons.	Pol.
North-western Europe	11	29	18	29	**23**	35	19	23	14	27	**29**	*20*
Southern Europe	12	20	5	27	13	**33**	*0*	35	**37**	15	**11**	25
Eastern Europe	16	15	15	40	*0*	18	**41**	*27*	*11*	20	**31**	*27*

Note: The table shows the relative share on an issue category in per cent of all protests in a given region and period. They do not add up to a 100 per cent, as 'other' issues are included in the calculation but not shown in the table. We do not show the values for the refugee crisis given the very short coverage in our dataset. We highlight strong upward changes as compared to the reference period in bold and strong downward changes in italics; $\ln(x\_crisis/x\_normal\ times) > 0.4$ or > -0.4.

issues in all regions and periods. In EE, the share of economic issues in party protests has even declined since the onset of the Great Recession. In contrast, there is a relative increase in party protests on cultural issues. In NWE and EE, the increase is driven by culturally conservative mobilization. In SE the increase is mostly driven by mobilization in favour of cultural liberalism in the shock period, although we also observe a strong increase of culturally conservative claims as compared to the so-called 'normal times'.

If we look at the ideological stances of the party sponsors, we observe that the shift towards economic issues in NWE during the shock period and in SE during the Euro crisis is driven mainly by the political left. Left-wing parties in the two regions are more likely to sponsor protests over economic issues than their competitors on the right throughout the research period, but the differences become most pronounced in those two periods. Around 41 per cent of all events sponsored by the left in NWE during the shock period centre on economic issues as compared to 8 per cent of the events sponsored by the right; the respective values for the south during the Euro crisis are 46 per cent (left) versus 6 per cent (right).[3] However, it is important to note that both in the north-west and in the south left-wing parties are more likely to sponsor protests over non-economic issues in all other periods. Interestingly, we observe no such differences in the salience of economic issues between the political left and right in EE during any period. There, non-economic issues are key for the protest mobilization of both left and right throughout the research period.

In the final step of the analysis, we explore the descriptive findings in a regression framework to test their robustness when we simultaneously control for contextual and event level characteristics. In addition, we use the regression setup to map the extent to which the various types of parties differ from each other. In terms of statistical models, our analysis relies on logit models with standard errors clustered according to country*year. We use our models to predict party sponsored protests in general and protests sponsored by left/right or mainstream/non-mainstream parties. The independent variables refer to the European macro regions, the phases of the crisis, the issues of the event, the number of participants, and the presence of unions or other organizations. Instead of the logit coefficients we report average marginal effects to ease interpretation and provide comparable estimates. Table 11.3 presents the results.

[3] Detailed results available from the authors.

First, we checked the baseline assumption that parties are more important actors in the protest arena in eastern Europe than in western Europe. The simple models (which do not control for any event-level characteristics) once again support this claim, although the predictive power of the models is rather small. Note that it is higher if we predict sponsorship by right-wing and moderate parties, respectively. This mirrors our previous findings on the different types of parties sponsoring protest in the different regions. In addition, the models once again highlight that there is no cross-regional 'crisis effect' in terms of party-sponsorship. By contrast, the marginal effects plot shown in Figure 11.5 indicates the very region-specific effects of the different 'period dummies'.[4] Most importantly, the results highlight that, in relative terms, parties in SE have been crowded out by other types of protest actors in the immediate shock period and in the Euro crisis. In contrast, in NWE and EE the share of parties seems to be increasing during the Euro crisis. In all three regions parties are the most present in the refugee crisis. However, one should note the high uncertainty of these estimates due to the relatively short coverage of the refugee crisis in our dataset.

Finally, the models with event level characteristics in Table 11.3 show (1) that our expectations and the descriptive findings on issues, alliances, and participants do hold in the regression context and (2) that the predictive power of the models substantially increases if we take the composition of events into account. Parties are not likely to sponsor events with unions or other organizations. Although it is somewhat counterintuitive, the presence of unions or other organizations has the smallest predictive power for the presence of parties on the left. That is because left parties are the most present in party protests (Figure 11.3), therefore these parties hardly rely on co-sponsorship to make themselves seen in the 'streets'. As the small coefficients for issues show, the events that parties sponsor are similar to the supply of events in the protest arena at large, with some notable differences. Parties on the left are the only ones more likely to sponsor protests on economic issues. Parties in general, and particularly on the right, are less likely to sponsor events on economic issues and more likely to sponsor events on cultural issues. Unsurprisingly, the right has a slight tendency to sponsor events advocating cultural conservatism and xenophobia, while the mainstream parties avoid sponsoring protests on cultural issues. The findings for the number of participants confirm that party protests tend to be larger than other protests.

[4] Detailed results available from the authors.

Table 11.3. *Average marginal effects from logit models of general party sponsorship and sponsorship by specific party types*

	Parties		Left		Right		Non-mainstream		Mainstream	
Southern Europe (ref:	−0.00	0.00	0.01	0.01	−0.00	0.00	−0.01	0.00	0.01**	0.01***
north-western Europe)	(0.01)	(0.01)	(0.01)	(0.01)	(0.01)	(0.00)	(0.01)	(0.01)	(0.00)	(0.00)
Eastern Europe	0.11***	0.01	0.02***	−0.01	0.07***	0.03***	0.03***	−0.01	0.06***	0.03***
	(0.02)	(0.01)	(0.01)	(0.00)	(0.01)	(0.00)	(0.01)	(0.01)	(0.01)	(0.00)
Shock period	−0.02	−0.01	−0.00	0.01	−0.01	−0.01	0.01	0.01	−0.02***	−0.01
(ref: normal times)	(0.02)	(0.01)	(0.01)	(0.01)	(0.01)	(0.01)	(0.01)	(0.01)	(0.01)	(0.01)
Euro crisis	0.01	−0.00	0.00	0.00	−0.01	−0.01***	0.01	0.00	−0.01**	−0.01**
	(0.01)	(0.00)	(0.01)	(0.00)	(0.01)	(0.00)	(0.01)	(0.01)	(0.01)	(0.00)
Refugee crisis	0.09*	0.01	−0.01*	−0.02**	0.03	−0.01	0.03	−0.01	−0.01	−0.01
	(0.05)	(0.01)	(0.01)	(0.01)	(0.02)	(0.01)	(0.02)	(0.01)	(0.01)	(0.01)
Economic issue		−0.02**		0.01*		−0.01		−0.00		0.00
(dichotomous)		(0.01)		(0.01)		(0.01)		(0.01)		(0.01)
Cultural liberalism		0.04***		0.03***		−0.01		0.04***		−0.00
(dichotomous)		(0.01)		(0.01)		(0.00)		(0.01)		(0.00)
Cultural conservatism		0.05***		−0.03***		0.03***		0.04***		−0.02***
(dichotomous)		(0.01)		(0.00)		(0.01)		(0.01)		(0.00)
Political issue		0.06***		0.02***		0.01**		0.02***		0.01***
(dichotomous)		(0.01)		(0.01)		(0.00)		(0.01)		(0.00)
No. of participants		0.00***		0.00		0.00***		−0.00		0.00***
(continuous)		(0.00)		(0.00)		(0.00)		(0.00)		(0.00)
Unions (dichotomous)		−0.56***		−0.18***		−0.13***		−0.16***		−0.14***
		(0.03)		(0.02)		(0.02)		(0.02)		(0.02)
Other organizations		−0.40***		−0.12***		−0.12***		−0.14***		−0.09***
(dichotomous)		(0.01)		(0.01)		(0.01)		(0.01)		(0.01)
Pseudo-R^2	0.03	0.60	0.01	0.30	0.06	0.45	0.01	0.37	0.06	0.37
No. of observations	16,921	16,921	16,921	16,921	16,921	16,921	16,921	16,921	16,921	16,921

Note: Standard errors are clustered by country*years. Standard errors in parentheses.
***$p < 0.01$; **$p < 0.05$; *$p < 0.1$.

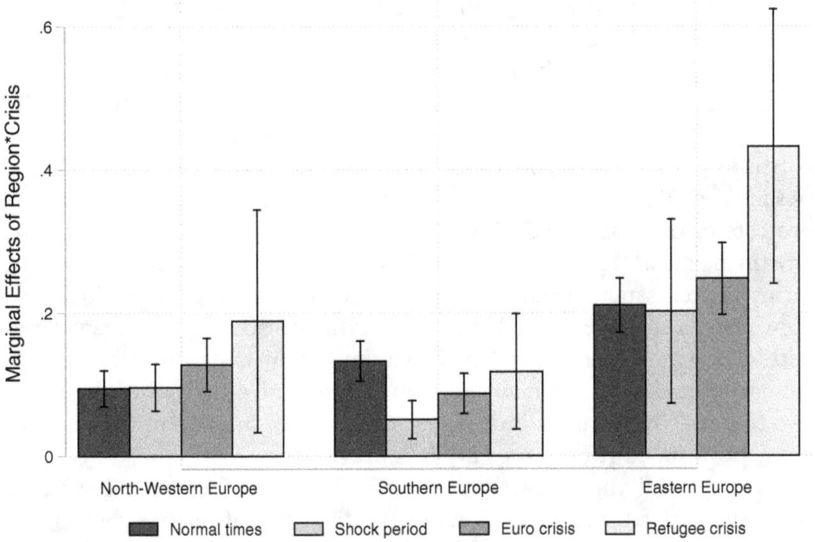

Figure 11.5 Marginal effects of two-way interactions between region and crisis period.
Note: The marginal effects are estimated from the interaction between the region and crisis categorical variables. The model does not control for event-level characteristics.

11.6 Conclusions

We started the chapter with the aim to describe and explain the 'big picture' of party protests across the three European macro regions. Most importantly, we were interested in whether political parties could 'recapture' the streets in Europe in times of crisis. Building on the work of Kitschelt (2003), we expected differentiation between the two arenas of protest and electoral politics, with parties primarily located in the latter. Nevertheless, we argued, there are important regional differences both in how parties responded to the crisis – as observed through the lens of party protests – and in the extent to which the two arenas are differentiated.

Our analysis built on new grounds to the extent to which the boundaries of the two arenas have hardly been empirically shown. The results confirm our expectations: Party protests are a relatively rare phenomenon and overwhelmingly used by the opposition. Nevertheless, parties occasionally decide to mobilize on the 'streets', and there are important regional differences to explain their presence. Most importantly, our results highlight that in EE – where parties are seen as the main political actor, often the 'only game in town' – we observe the highest level of party protests. In addition, we uncovered regional differences in the type of party protests, i.e. in terms of the type of parties and issues. Whereas in NWE and SE, we observe a strong presence of radical parties and parties from the left, in EE, we find a different dynamic. Party protests in the East are driven by parties from the right and by mainstream parties. Nevertheless, the East is rather like the north-west in terms of the issues of party protests, with a focus on cultural claims. However, as we have argued these are cultural issues of a different type, with a strong dominance of mobilization against the cultural liberalism associated with the new social movements. Compared to the other two regions, in SE, economic issues play a more important role, and in party protests cultural issues are less prevalent.

We expected the Great Recession to influence both the level and the type of party protests. Concerning the level of party protests, we expected that parties become less important in the countries hardest hit by the crisis. Our results confirm our expectation: We observe a 'crowding-out' of parties from the streets in SE in the shadow of the Great Recession. The latter finding mirrors the discrediting of established political elites and parties in that region and confirms the analysis in previous chapters on the character and driving forces of protest waves (Chapters 5 and 6). The mainstream parties almost completely disappeared from the streets in SE during the Great Recession. This is in line with the finding from Chapter 10 as protests reinforced the negative effects of economic misery on electoral support of mainstream parties in general. Although left-wing parties were more likely to sponsor protests on economic issues during certain periods in NWE and SE, the Great Recession has not brought about a drastic change in the type of parties and issues involved in party protests.

Overall, political parties were not very successful in 'recapturing' the streets, i.e. in increasing their standing in the protest arena. Thus, our bird's eye view on parties in the protest arena qualifies the emerging links between social movements and challenger parties. These links left important marks on the development of the new or transformed parties and, in some cases, on the entire party systems (see della Porta et al. 2017). However, they did not lead to ever more party protests and, based on this indicator, the two arenas remain much more differentiated in SE and NWE than in EE. In this regard, the crisis has reinforced existing patterns rather than transformed the dynamics of party protests.

12 Conclusion

Hanspeter Kriesi and Bruno Wüest

During the Great Recession, citizens took to the streets in opposition to the political and economic crises across Europe, albeit to very different extents and in different ways. The first key finding of this study is that the Great Recession was not answered by one big wave of political mobilization in the European protest arena after 2008. European protest largely remained regionally and nationally confined. In reaction to the unequal effects of the financial market shock and Euro crisis on the European economies, the extent, intensity, and content of contentious mobilization in the national protest arenas have been remarkably different. The chapters in this book have shown that these differences can be explained mainly by the interaction between economic and political grievances and the national political contexts. Most importantly, we have shown large *regional* differences in the way protest was mobilized during the Great Recession. North-western Europe (NWE), southern Europe (SE), and central and eastern Europe (CEE), indeed, constitute very different contexts for the mobilization of protest and it is crucial for the understanding of political protest in Europe not to lose sight of these differences. Moreover, within each region, there are also national differences which proved to be very important.

In spite of the absence of a generalized wave of protest mobilization during this period of crisis, in SE, there was indeed a wave of protest in reaction to the Euro crisis. This wave was driven by economic grievances and reinforced by failures in the public management of the economic crisis, which led to a massive decline in political satisfaction and trust. During the Euro crisis, SE in general, and Greece above all, experienced a critical juncture that was characterized by a unique intensity of protest and of political consequences of protest. This is the second key finding.

At the outset of this book, we also asked whether the Great Recession triggered a general resurgence of sustained economic protest. The answer we find is negative. While economic protest indeed resurfaced in several contexts (especially when reinforced by a political crisis), we do not find generalizable evidence that the economic crisis has brought economic protest back to the forefront of protest mobilization. It also did not generally transform the action repertoire of the protestors, nor did it lead to a de-differentiation of the electoral arena and the protest arena. Apart from some very important exceptions, the Great Recession provoked protest as usual, in terms of its issues, action repertoire, radicalness, and actor involvement, and it did not prove to be the critical juncture that many observers made it out to be. This is the third key finding of our study. Rather, the Great Recession did lead to a resurgence of more short-term, spontaneous, and situational grievances-driven protest, as we have known it from the 'movement of crisis' that respond to great economic and political hardship (Kerbo 1982). But this protest proved to be relatively short lived and unsustainable, with limited political consequences in most of the countries both in terms of policies and in terms of revaluing the protest arena as a locus of democratic contention.

Our findings regarding the heterogeneity in protest reactions to the crisis across countries and regions and over time, as well as our qualifications regarding the innovativeness and sustainability of the crisis-related protests highlight the importance of the broad, comparative empirical approach we have adopted in this study. More precisely, our decision to establish a quantitative comparative dataset that includes countries from all regions of Europe and encompasses virtually all forms and issues of protest has paid off analytically, as it enabled us to draw generalizable conclusions about contentious mobilization in Europe in the new millennium. The construction of this massive dataset was made possible by innovations we introduced in the automated preprocessing and filtering of news wire reports, which were subsequently manually coded in a classical manual Protest Event Analysis. Although our data is not perfect, we could show that it meets rigorous standards and enables us to portray the development of contentious mobilization in all three regions of Europe before and during the Great Recession. This is all the more important because most of the previous studies of protest in the Great Recession have focused on major events that attracted disproportionally high media and public attention such as the protests staged by the Indignados and Occupy movements (e.g. della Porta and Mattoni 2014) and that have been characteristic of some countries but not of others. Our systematic approach has allowed us to put these exceptional events into context, which renders the emerging picture less dazzling but certainly more accurate.

In the following, we will summarize the main findings of our study and put them into the broader context of the future of democratic politics in Europe.

12.1 European Protest in Times of Crisis

Despite the drastic consequences for many European economies, the Great Recession did not generally lead to a long-lasting uproar in the European protest arena. Accordingly, neither the financial market shock nor the Euro crisis led to Europe-wide waves of protest. There has of course been a lot of contentious mobilization in Europe throughout the period from 2000 to 2015, but it has not been sustained and encompassing enough to shake up large parts of the continent for a longer period of time. The unusually high levels and the specific forms of contention that we actually observe in reaction to the crisis are geographically and temporally concentrated. Our results cannot confirm previous notions of sustained European-wide protest waves (Castells 2015). Hence, what can be learnt from the study of specific social movements such as the Indignados and Occupy movements cannot be translated to the full range of movements engaged in contentious mobilization in Europe.

In general, protest waves remain the exception. Two reasons account for this. On the one hand, taking the aggregate point of view, in Europe's movement societies, there always is a certain stock of protests, which results from the accumulation of locally, nationally, and regionally specific reactions to a diverse set of issues and problems (Dodson 2011; Meyer and Tarrow 1998). In the north-west of Europe, the crisis was not severe enough to add in a decisive fashion to this permanent stock of protest. In CEE, this stock of protest was originally much lower. While it had increased already before the economic crisis hit this part of Europe, the economic crisis did not really reinforce it either, although it was severe and even combined with a political crisis in some cases. It is only in the south of Europe that the economic crisis really made a difference and led to the development of a wave of protest during the Euro crisis.

On the other hand, from the point of view of individual protest campaigns, protests typically flare up locally and are rather short lived. Protests are difficult to sustain, given the motivational and resource constraints of the participants. This is true in normal times, but it applies even more so in times of crisis. In the crisis periods we covered, protest has been driven by economic and political grievances, and it proved to be rather *short-lived*, except in SE. Movements of crisis which express themselves spontaneously and lack an adequate organization base find it difficult to sustain the mobilization of protest over time. Moreover, protest *diffusion* in spatial terms has been of a rather limited nature during the Great Recession (see Chapter 9). We found indications of cross-border diffusion only between neighbouring countries, while diffusion across regions, not to say across Europe, was exceedingly scarce. Also, diffusion varied across regions, time periods and action forms. It was concentrated mainly in CEE in the Euro-crisis period and it occurred above all for the most widespread action forms – demonstrations, and to some extent also for strikes. The exceptionally strong mobilization in the SE countries and during the shock period did not lead to strong diffusion. It seems that high levels of protests more likely lead to national differentiation of the European protest landscape.

While we did find some systematic increase of protest across Europe at the beginning of the crisis, this wave proved to be rather short lived and only partially related to the onset of the Great Recession (see Chapters 4 and 7). Numerous protest activities during the Great Recession responded to country-specific conditions which were entirely unrelated to the crisis. A good example is the case of Hungary, where protest during the crisis was much preoccupied with events independent of the economic crisis, such as the adoption of the new constitution proposed by the Fidesz government in 2011. On the whole, political and cultural issues with only a tenuous or no relation to the crisis were just as important triggers for protest as economic and political issues related to the crisis during the period covered. Viewed from the perspective of Europe as a whole, the great economic crisis did not make much of a difference in terms of protest. If anything, counter-intuitively, it contributed to the pacification of protest in the long run. As the Great Recession tapered out, the level of protest across Europe was lower than at any time before since the turn of the century.

12.2 Business as Usual in the Protest Arena

What is most notable about the action repertoire of protest during the crisis is the return to traditional forms of contentious mobilization. The rather old-fashioned protest form of *demonstrations* dominates when it comes to the mobilization of opposition to the political and economic crisis (Chapter 5). In spite of everything that has been written about the growing importance of the digital revolution, i.e. the increasing role of the Internet in general and social media in particular, for the goals, strategies, and resources of contentious mobilization, we did not find an upsurge in new unconventional forms of protests (e.g. Bakker and De Vreese 2011; de Zúñiga et al. 2012; Van Laer and Van Aelst 2010). Of course, we do not have data on the role of digital communication for the organization of the traditional forms of mobilization, but, overall, crisis protest seems to have been expressed in 'good old' protest politics. Moreover, to the extent that we have information on the organizations involved in the protest events, it is striking that old protest actors such as the *unions* have been the organizations by far the most responsible for protest in the streets during the Great Recession: In all three regions, they (co-)organized roughly a third of the events where organizations were involved.

Many observers of protest against austerity during the Great Recession have been impressed by the *innovations* of the action repertoire that have been picked up by the Indignados and the Occupy movement in the aftermath of the Arab Spring (e.g. the contributions in Ancelovici et al. 2016): the use of protest camps and assemblies in the main squares of large cities. Innovations of the action repertoire are typical for early phases of protest waves. In line with this notion, we have indeed found an increasing share of confrontations, of which the occupations are a part, in SE during the shock period, i.e. in the early phases of the wave of protest that swept across this region. However, the other two regions did not experience a comparable rise of confrontations, and even in SE, this innovation did not have a lasting effect and disappeared as rapidly as it had been flaring up. What earlier observers who were most impressed by the encompassing movements that mobilized in Greece and Spain (and Israel, the US and other countries for that matter) tended to overlook is that the bulk of protest that took place across Europe during the crisis period was not influenced by innovative ways to do protest, but stuck to the well-worn repertoire that had been introduced more than two centuries ago. The prominence of the unions in organizing protests that we found points in a similar direction. As an institutionalized actor, unions, of course, are more likely to turn to conventional forms of protest.

Moreover, European protests mainly remain *domestic* protests. Contentious mobilization very much depends on country-specific conditions such as the level, distribution, and interplay of grievances; the performance of governments; and other opportunities such as the timing of elections. Thus, we could provide evidence that the promise of the Europeanization of protests, announced two decades ago, still is a promise for the future (della Porta and Caiani 2011; Tarrow 1995). Although, with our data, we are not able to study more fundamental aspects of Europeanization such as polarization and the importance of supranational addressees of protests, we cannot find enough cross-national linkages between the protest events in order to sustain such a claim. Our interpretation of these findings is that the protest arena has not become the key locus of democratic innovation in Europe during the turbulent times of crisis – neither at the domestic nor at the European level.

We have learned from the end of the heydays of the new social movements in Western Europe that protest waves either end in institutionalization or radicalization (Koopmans 2004). Remarkably, in the case of the Great Recession, the crisis did not lead to any *radicalization* over the course of the years. If anything, violence peaked early on in the shock period, especially in SE and here above all in Greece. Although violence has been the second most frequent action form after demonstrations, violence was confined to some very specific moments (often unrelated to the economic crisis) in selected countries, most notably Northern Ireland ('the troubles'), Spain (ETA violence) and, indeed, Greece during the Great Recession. It is highly significant that the overwhelming majority of political protests remained peaceful. At no time and in no place, not even in Greece, was there any sign of a revolutionary situation. We also found few signs of the expansion of conflict to new, unorganized groups. Only in SE did we encounter indications of the expansion of conflict to such groups during the shock period, when students became an important driver of protest to the detriment of the unions. During the Euro crisis, however, the students lost most of their importance in the south, while the unions recovered their dominant position as drivers of protest.

In terms of *institutionalization* of protest waves, our study shows the complex pattern of interaction between the electoral arena and the protest arena. On the one hand, we found that, with the exception of CEE, the two arenas have become increasingly differentiated in terms of the actors involved. Thus, party sponsorship of protests is generally rare, and parties were actually crowded out of the protest realm in the Great Recession, especially in SE (Chapter 11). Only in CEE, where the civil society is notoriously weak, in a compensatory fashion parties have come to play a more important role for the mobilization of protest. Moreover, contrary to the other two regions, where parties from the left and challenger parties more generally predominated in the protest arena (to the extent that there were parties mobilizing in this arena at all), in CEE, it was parties from the right which were dominant in this arena and mainstream parties (in the opposition) were just as much involved in protest as challenger parties.

On the other hand, the two arenas are intimately linked in terms of *outcomes*. First, we have been able to show that both elections and protests are similarly affected by economic grievances. Such grievances increase both the mobilization in the protest arena and the punishment of incumbents in the electoral arena. Most importantly, however, we have also been able to show that, in western, although not in eastern Europe, economic protest has served as a signal for the electoral punishment of incumbents in particular and of mainstream parties in general. Thus, the electoral losses of mainstream parties increase as protest increased, while non-mainstream parties benefited from increases in protest during the crisis. We could even show that, in western Europe, economic grievances have had an impact on electoral outcomes if and only if the elections were preceded by an intensification of economic protest. In this way, economic protest has contributed to the destabilization of the party system in the countries hard hit by the crisis of SE in particular. The analysis of Chapter 10 finally also showed that the mainstream left in power is particularly vulnerable to protest mobilization: When targeted by protest, it stands more to lose than incumbents from the mainstream right. This interaction between protest and electoral outcomes in the Great Recession is a crucial result of our study that points beyond business as usual in the protest arena.

The large-scale demobilization in the protest arena that took place at the end of the period covered by our study points to yet another important interaction between the protest arena and the electoral arena that may also go beyond business as usual. It concerns the increasing success of new challenger parties in the electoral arena in NWE and SE and, to a lesser extent in CEE (where the electoral volatility had been very high already before the crisis and where it rather tended to decrease during the crisis). In NWE, during the crisis new challenger parties from the radical new right have arisen in countries where they had not yet been established previously – UKIP in the United Kingdom, AfD in Germany, the Finns in Finland, or the Swedish Democrats in Sweden. In SE, it was above all new challenger parties from the radical new left that rose even more forcefully in reaction to the crisis – Podemos in Spain, Syriza in Greece (see Hutter et al. 2017). The Italian new challenger, M5S, arguably was not necessarily a party from the new left, but 'neither left, nor right'. The rise of these parties can be interpreted as a form of institutionalization of the protest. Alternatively, they might, however, also be interpreted as a shift of the mobilization of protest from the protest arena to the electoral arena. While Goldstone (2003: 9) had suggested, that protest politics might be 'both an alternative and a valuable supplement' to electoral politics, we would like to suggest that electoral politics may increasingly serve as an alternative to protest politics. In line with this alternative interpretation, McAdam and Kloos (2014) have shown how social movements have contributed to the radicalization of party stances in the United States and to the polarization of American institutional politics more generally. Thus, in the United States social movements from the left and the right – i.e., from the civil rights movement in the 1950 and 1960s to the Tea Party movement in more recent years – have pushed both major US parties (the Republicans and Democrats) toward the fringes of the political spectrum. In Europe, the new 'movement parties' (Kitschelt 2006) have in part at least – above all in Greece and Spain (Altiparmakis 2019; Spourdalakis 2014: 358; Martín 2015; Vidal 2019), but also in other countries – grown out of/developed in the context of the mobilization in the protest arena during the Great Recession, and are equally contributing to the radicalization/polarization of electoral politics, to the fragmentation of the national party systems and to the concomitant complication of the process of governmental coalition formation. In short, the institutionalization of new challenger parties from the left and the right has gone hand in hand with a secular decline of the mobilization in the protest arena across Western Europe.

12.3 The Return of the Economy and the Emphasis on Grievances as Drivers of Protest

One would have expected a general *return of economic protest* in times of crisis. This, however, is not what we find. The return of economic protest is confined to public economic protest and it is regionally specific (see Chapter 6). Public economic protest is targeting the economic crisis management of the governments, while private economic protest targets private actors, above all business corporations. In NWE and in CEE, public economic protest increased in the shock period, but given the rapid recovery in both regions, it subsided subsequently during the Euro crisis. It is only in SE that public economic protest increased massively during the Euro-crisis period. At the same time, the increase in public economic protest crowded out private economic protest in all three regions during the crisis and it also crowded out non-economic protest in SE.

This return of economic protests is by no means a natural consequence of the Great Recession, as we could as well have expected a cultural conservative backlash in terms of an intensification of anti-immigration and nationalist mobilization. There is some evidence for such a backlash, but it is restricted to CEE and weakens rather quickly. In NWE, we also observe a rise of cultural conservative protest, but this rise was linked to the refugee crisis, i.e. it is at best an indirect consequence of the economic crisis.

The articulation of public economic protest has been driven by the *economic grievances* of the populations in the countries hardest hit by the crisis. While part of the earlier literature argued that economic grievances have a demobilizing effect, we show, in line with literature on the

Great Recession (e.g. Grasso and Giugni 2016; Kern et al. 2015; Rüdig and Karyotis 2014), that protest is, indeed, reacting to economic hardship: the higher the increase of unemployment in a given country, the higher the level of (public) economic protest. This result is driven by SE, where unemployment rates have not only increased the most during the crisis, but where they also have the greatest effect on protest. As a matter of fact, in NWE, economic grievances as measured by unemployment rates do not have any effect on economic protest at all, and in CEE their effect is much smaller than in SE.

Given its focus on public economic crisis management, it is not surprising that the economic protest is closely linked to political crises and related *political grievances*.

Different chapters in this book have studied the interaction of economic grievances with indicators of systemic political crisis (lack of government capacity and responsiveness, international constraints on government actions) and attitudinal political crisis (satisfaction with democracy). The interplay between economic grievances and these political grievances is not homogeneous. In Chapter 7, we found a strong link between political grievances and public economic protest, again most clearly in the European south. The most important results of that chapter, however, concern the interaction of economic and political grievances in determining public economic protest. First of all, we could show that economic grievances had a strong impact on political grievances during the crisis, especially in SE. The fact that the SE countries not only were hard hit by the economic crisis, but also experienced a relative decline with regard to the other parts of Europe enhanced the impact of economic on political grievances in the south. Second, and even more importantly, we could show that economic protest in general and public economic protest in particular strongly increased, when the two types of grievances rose together. This joint effect again proved to be strongest in SE, where it manifested itself especially during the Euro crisis. In other words, in SE, the sharp increases in economic grievances during the Euro crisis not only contributed to the rise of political grievances, but they also enhanced the effect of political grievances on (public) economic protest. The double economic and political crisis was the key determinant of the protest waves in SE.

As a third aspect of political crisis and political grievances, we indeed focused on supra- and international constraints of domestic politics (Chapter 8). We analysed the impact of bailouts and austerity measures in a selected set of countries. This third type of analysis, which enters more into the details of the political measures that caused the grievances and the resulting protest, shows again the variation of the effects across the regions. Thus, bailout agreements had a direct effect on protest in Ireland and SE (Cyprus, Greece, and Portugal), but not in eastern Europe (in Hungary and Romania, with Latvia being an exception). Austerity measures, in turn, had an effect on protest only in SE, and only when they were conditional on the bailout agreement. This suggests that citizens are particularly dissatisfied with austerity when it is imposed by supranational interventions – be it in the form of bailout agreements or of austerity measures adopted in compliance with these agreements. Zooming in on *Greece*, the results suggest that the sequence of bailouts and the harsh conditions imposed by them on the Greek population are the key to understanding the extraordinary protest wave that swept across this country after 2010. Hence, this third analytical view on the interaction between economic and political crises again reinforces evidence for an interactive effect of the economic crisis and the systemic political crisis on protest mobilization.

Finally, as we have already pointed out, we found that grievances-driven protests, whether resulting from economic or political grievances, withers away relatively quickly. If such contention is not sustained by favourable resources and opportunities, protest fatigue – political apathy – sets in rapidly after the first mobilization. The Greek case is again exemplary in this regard. The first massive mobilizations were propelled by sharply increasing grievances and a lack of responsiveness on the side of the Greek government and the Troika. But once protesters realized that even the like-minded government under Tsipras could not change the course of events decisively, they resigned from further contention. As for resources of political mobilization, it is striking that political parties in general hardly engage in the protest arena (see Chapter 11). This not only points to the strong differentiation between protest and party politics. The relative absence of such important political actors in the protest arena might also contribute to the absence of large and sustained waves of protest across Europe.

12.4 The Triad of Regional Protest Reactions to the Crisis

The results provided by our analyses point to consistently diverging patterns of protest mobilization across *three European regions* which were characterized by different context conditions – SE, CEE, and NWE. Southern Europeans had – and still have – to weather the combination of a grave economic and political crisis. In SE, the Great Recession gave rise to sustained protest waves during the Euro-crisis period, and to a profound transformation of the electoral arena. In CEE, by contrast, economic and political conditions had already been poor before the Great Recession hit, and the great economic crisis did have much less of an impact. In NWE, the Great Recession did register, but the countries in this region recovered rather rapidly from the crisis and it did not have far-reaching political consequences.

In *NWE*, protest seems to have developed largely independently of the economic crisis. The partial exception is the United Kingdom, were we found a similarly sustained wave of protest as in southern or eastern European countries for some time periods. Due to automatic stabilizers and governments capable to quickly and decisively implement Keynesian rescue packages, political-economic regimes in the north-west showed strong resilience against the crisis. This, in turn, kept political and economic grievances relatively low. As a result, we observed hardly any major protest mobilization in reaction to the economic crisis in this region, and crisis-related action forms of protest such as confrontational protests or strikes did not increase after 2008. As a consequence, the traditionally dominant new social movements that primarily mobilize on cultural liberal issues were able to recapture the protest arena quickly after the financial market shock, leading to a crowding out of attempts to mobilize against the economic crisis. Only in the refugee crisis did protest in NWE rise again, especially in Germany, where it was driven by the radical right.

In *CEE*, the economic crisis only contributed to peaks of already ongoing waves of protest. We have found some country-specific waves, but these waves had either already accelerated before the intervention of the Great Recession, which only contributed to their peaks (Latvia, Lithuania), or delayed their decline (Czech Republic, Hungary), or they were actually unrelated to the Great Recession (Bulgaria, Estonia). The origins of these major protest waves mostly lie in domestic political events such as rigged elections, high-profile corruption cases or national recessions setting in already before the global economic downturn. The low level of political and administrative performance and the corresponding high level of corruption have contributed to widespread dissatisfaction with the way democracy works in these countries, which provided a general breeding ground for challenges in the electoral (Pop-Eleches 2010: 232) and in the protest arena. In times of economic crisis, however, the tolerance for corruption that previously benefited from the good economic performance diminished considerably in these countries. This mechanism has been illustrated by the Klasnja and Tucker (2013) experiments in the case of Moldavia. Our results confirm their findings at the macro level: In the crisis, contentious mobilization in CEE was driven by economic *and* political grievances, but both of these drivers were much weaker than in SE.

In addition, we also found protests to be especially short-lived in this region. Economic and political grievances led to outbursts of protest in CEE, which then were followed by fatigue and resignation. Moreover, cultural conservative issues – i.e. anti-immigration and nationalist mobilization – have been more important for the mobilization of protest in this region than in the other two. However, the surge of cultural conservative protest in CEE is not directly linked to the economic crisis. The political disenchantment and the various domestic political crises contributed to the appeal of national-populist demands in this part of Europe already before the crisis. As noted in Chapter 6, the share of cultural liberal protest is also high in this region, which suggests that cultural conservative protest triggered the counter-mobilization by an emerging new left in these countries.

There are several reasons which may explain why contentious mobilization was not as fierce in this region as in the European south. First of all, the largest country in the region, Poland, got rather well through the crisis and it had already solved its political crisis before the Great Recession hit (Salek and Sztajdel 2017), which served to limit the growth of both economic and political grievances during the largest part of the period covered. Second, the emigration of workers mainly towards Western Europe took away some pressure from the labour markets (OECD 2013). In these countries, instead of raising their voice, many, especially young people, voted with their feat. Third, some governments, such as the governments of the Baltic states, were capable of responding swiftly and effectively to the economic shocks. While the bailout agreement and the first conditional austerity measures in December 2008 did trigger massive protest in Latvia, this protest quickly died down when the government fell and was replaced by a 'grand coalition' government including all the major parties representing the Latvian speakers in spring 2009. Subsequently, from March 2009 to December 2013, Latvia had the same Prime Minister during the largest part of the economic crisis, in spite of the harsh austerity measures implemented by the succession of governments he presided over. The case of Latvia illustrates the difficulty in assessing the impact of economic grievances (and of 'pain tolerance') in CEE. The question of whether the Latvian recovery was a success story is hotly debated among economists. In their detailed assessment of the case, Blanchard et al. (2013: 328) come to the conclusion that, in some ways, it clearly was a success. To be sure, part of the adjustment happened through emigration. But part of it is also due to increases in productivity and exports, with limited reductions in private wages. In other words: The economic pain was focused on public sector employees.

In the private sector it was felt much less or it was eschewed by emigration. In addition, the ethnic conflict between Latvian and Russian speakers served to dampen the political fallout of the crisis in this particular case (Eihmanis 2019). In Hungary, to mention just this other case of a country that was forced to implement an International Monetary Fund (IMF) bailout in late 2008, the bailout did not trigger a particularly strong protest at all, mainly because the bailout came late in a series of protest mobilization against the socialist government that had already been unleashed in the aftermath of the 2006 elections. These cases illustrate the importance of country-specific factors for the understanding of the development of protest. In sum, for different reasons, the CEE economies were much better able to resist the financial market shock as well as the Euro crisis, leading to comparatively less contention in the streets.

SE certainly was different this time. It may be too early to conclude as much with full certainty, but the Great Recession possibly marks a critical juncture for SE. The countries of this region had to suffer the consequences of a double crisis that combines the economic and political factors we identified as strong contributors to protest mobilization. All SE countries experienced a sharp relative decline in economic performance, insufficient government responsiveness, a surge in economic grievances and a downright collapse of satisfaction with democracy. The crisis quickly disclosed the inability of the political elites to implement effective countermeasures against growing economic grievances (Beramendi et al. 2015: 13), fueling a political crisis that erupted in massive protest waves.

As a result, SE experienced significant waves of protest. The paradigmatic case is clearly Greece, where the crisis gave rise to a sustained wave of protest that covered both the shock- and the Euro-crisis period. In the case of Greece, the wave was not originally triggered by the Great Recession but had already been under way once the economic crisis hit the country. The SE waves are clear reactions to the deteriorating economic and political situation. These waves were focused on public economic issues, i.e. the crisis management by the national governments, to an extent that crowded-out most cultural contention. Importantly, the protest against this crisis management was particularly massive, when these measures were imposed by supranational actors. Thus, the bailouts by the Troika and the austerity measures implemented by the governments under the bailout conditionality were the focal events that triggered many of the protests.

It is in SE waves, and especially in Greece, that we saw some of the patterns that we expected to find in the development of the protest waves: an initial set of innovations in the action repertoire (such as the occupation of public spaces by the Indignados) and some radical forms of protest. However, even in SE, large-scale mobilizations in the form of demonstrations remained the predominant action form throughout the crisis, with the number of strikes (general strikes and strikes of public employees) also increasing during the Euro crisis in particular. Nor has the Great Recession brought about an increasing involvement of parties in protest in SE. On the contrary, parties have been crowded out of the protest arena during the massive protest waves. However, as we have shown in Chapter 10, protest in SE served as signalling device for the electoral behaviour of voters: The very large turnouts in the demonstrations are most likely to have influenced the perceptions and expectations of voters with respect to the chances of incumbents and challengers (Lohmann 1994). Moreover, they also contributed to the mobilization of new challenger parties and to their eventual success. In sum, the protest waves in SE decisively contributed to the transformation of the party systems in all the major countries of the region (see Hutter and Kriesi 2019).

12.5 Conclusion

Protest and its consequences have been different in SE, but overall continuity has prevailed in the protest arena during the Great Recession. Neither during the shock period nor during the period of the Euro crisis has this deep economic crisis led to a general return of economic protest across Europe, nor has it led to a transformation of the action repertoire of the protestors in the streets. SE has been different, because it experienced a double crisis – economic and political, which expressed itself in a tremendous wave of protest above all in Greece, but also in Spain and to a lesser extent in Portugal. In Italy, we saw more of the business as usual that characterized the protest arena in the rest of Europe. The main effect of the protest wave that swept through SE has been the transformation of the party systems in the respective countries. New challenger parties rose up, party systems fragmented, and coalition formation became difficult.

Let us conclude by noting that our focus on protest in the streets is limited in two respects. It does not take into account two transformations of the action repertoire of protesting Europeans that are currently taking place. On the one hand, as we have already hinted at in our summary of the results, with the rise of new challenger parties from the left and the right, protest politics are shifting into the electoral arena, which may reflect an increasing awareness on the part of the protestors that, at the end of the day, this is where political decisions are actually made in a democracy. Protest may serve as a signalling device for decision-makers, as we have already argued. But protest is a very indirect means to influence public policies, given that it relies on allies within the electoral arena. Thus, the labour movement has developed not only unions for the articulation of its challenges in industrial relations, but also political parties for the mobilization of its adherents in the electoral arena. Similarly, Green parties have been mobilizing the former supporters of the new social movements in the electoral arena in NWE since the 1980s. Also, in this part of Europe, populist parties from the radical right have been mobilizing the demands of the globalization losers without ever having relied on the protest arena. They have directly mobilized their supporters in the electoral arena since the early 1980s. In NWE, the Great Recession served as a catalyst for the rise of the challengers of the populist radical right in the countries, where they had not yet been present before and it stabilized them in the countries where they were already established. In SE, by contrast, the Great Recession served as a catalyst for the rise of potent new challengers from the new left (Podemos and Syriza) and from an as yet undefined place in the political space (M5S). Electoral politics therefore appears to have outstripped protest politics also in terms of the mobilization against the financial and economic crises.

On the other hand, protest politics may be increasingly influenced by the new opportunity structure provided by the information communication technologies (ICT). A considerable amount of work has pointed out the important role of online communication for offline protests in the street in the course of large scale mobilizations during the Arab Spring, by the Indignados or by Occupy (e.g. Anduiza et al. 2014; Theocharis et al. 2015). Current activism often blends offline and online elements which suggests that protest is becoming a hybrid form of activity relying on a combination of the two arenas (Bennett and Segerberg 2013). Eventually the key question, however, is whether mobilization online will increasingly replace mobilization in the streets. There are indications that such a shift is taking place. Thus, many social movement organizations mobilize online (e.g. MoveOn) and, as Earl and Kimport (2011) have demonstrated, a great deal of organizing today happens online without social movement organizations. Moreover, there are many different ways to participate online, from less confrontational protest forms such as signing electronic petitions to more antagonistic and confrontational forms such as politically motivated hacking. Online forms of participation tend to draw on what Earl (2016) calls ‘flash activism’, i.e. on the very rapid but massive mobilization that is possible online. This kind of activism may seem ephemeral, but, as Earl also argues, it can be quite effective.

For the time being, these trends have not yet put an end to protest mobilization in the streets. The sequence of crises that followed on the Great Recession in Europe – the refugee crisis, the terrorist attacks and the public security crisis, the Brexit crisis, the 'values crisis' triggered by the populist governments in Hungary and Poland – successively unleashed a series of protest mobilizations in the countries most concerned. Although it is for future research to cover these mobilizations, we do not expect them to have fundamentally altered the general picture we have drawn of the protest arena in this volume: In Europe's movement societies, contentious politics in the streets as we described them are here to stay, even if they will increasingly be integrated with forms of online protest and with conventional politics in the electoral arena.

References

Accornero, Guya and Pedro Ramos Pinto. 2015. 'Mild Mannered Protest'? Protest and Mobilization in Portugal under Austerity, 2010–2013. *West European Politics* 38, 3, 491–515.

ACE. 2005. ACE (Automatic Content Extraction) English Annotation Guidelines. www.ldc.upenn.edu/sites/www.ldc.upenn.edu/files/english-relations-guidelines-v6.2.pdf

Afonso, Alexandre and Line Rennwald. 2018. The Changing Welfare State Agenda of Radical Right Parties in Europe. In Philip Manow, Bruno Palier, and Hanna Schwander, eds., *Welfare Democracies and Party Politics: Explaining Electoral Dynamics in Times of Changing Welfare Capitalism*. Oxford: Oxford University Press, pp. 171–96.

Afonso, Alexandre, Sotirios Zartaloudis, and Ioannis Papadopoulos. 2015. How Party Linkages Shape Austerity Politics: Clientelism and Fiscal Adjustment in Greece and Portugal during the Eurozone Crisis. *Journal of European Public Policy* 22, 3, 315–34.

Ahn, David. 2006. The Stages of Event Extraction. In *Proceedings of the Workshop on Annotating and Reasoning about Time and Events*, pp. 1–8.

Alonso, Sonia. 2014. You Can Vote but You Cannot Choose: Democracy and the Sovereign Debt Crisis in the Eurozone. Estudio Working Paper. Instituto Mixto Universidad Carlos III de Madrid: Fundación Juan March de Ciencias Sociales.

Alonso, Sonia and Cristóbal Rovira Kaltwasser. 2015. Spain: No Country for the Populist Radical Right? *South European Society and Politics* 20, 1, 21–45.

Altiparmakis, Argyrios. 2019a. The Age of the Bailout: Contention, Party-System Collapse and Reconstruction in Greece, 2009–2015. PhD thesis, European University Institute, Florence.

Altiparmakis, Argyrios. 2019b. Greece – Punctuated Equilibrium: The Restructuring of Greek Politics. In Swen Hutter and Hanspeter Kriesi, eds., *European Party Politics in Times of Crises*. Cambridge: Cambridge University Press, pp. 95–117.

Altiparmakis, Argyrios and Jasmine Lorenzini. 2018. Disclaiming National Representatives: Protest Waves in Southern Europe during the Crisis. *Party Politics* 24, 1, 78–89.

Amenta, Edwin, Neal Caren, Sheera J. Olasky, and James E. Stobaugh. 2009. All the Movements Fit to Print: Who, What, When, Where, and Why SMO Families Appeared in the *New York Times* in the Twentieth Century. *American Sociological Review* 74, 4, 636–56.

Ancelovici, Marcos, Pascale Dufour, and Héloïse Nez (eds.). 2016. *Street Politics in the Age of Austerity*. Amsterdam: Amsterdam University Press.

Andrews, Kenneth T. and Michael Biggs. 2006. The Dynamics of Protest Diffusion: Movement Organizations, Social Networks, and News Media in the 1960 Sit-Ins. *American Sociological Review* 71, 5, 752–77.

Andrews, Kenneth T. and Neal Caren. 2010. Making the News. *American Sociological Review* 75, 6, 841–66.

Andronikidou, Aikaterini and Iosif Kovras. 2012. Cultures of Rioting and Anti-Systemic Politics in Southern Europe. *West European Politics* 35, 4, 707–25.

Anduiza, Eva, Camilo Cristancho, and José M. Sabucedo. 2014. Mobilization through Online Social Networks: The Political Protest of the Indignados in Spain. *Information, Communication and Society* 17, 6, 750–64.

Arceneaux, Kevin. 2003. The Conditional Impact of Blame Attribution on the Relationship between Economic Adversity and Turnout. *Political Research Quarterly* 56, 1, 67–75.

Arellano, Manuel and Stephen Bond. 1991. Some Tests of Specification for Panel Data: Monte Carlo Evidence and an Application to Employment Equations. *The Review of Economic Studies* 58, 2, 277–97.

Armingeon, Klaus and Besir Ceka. 2014. The Loss of Trust in the European Union during the Great Recession since 2007: The Role of Heuristics from the National Political System. *European Union Politics* 15, 1, 82–107.

Armingeon, Klaus and Kai Guthmann. 2014. Democracy in Crisis? The Declining Support for National Democracy in European Countries, 2007–2011. *European Journal of Political Research* 53, 3, 423–42.

Aslanidis, Paris and Nikos Marantzidis. 2016. The Impact of the Greek Indignados on Greek Politics. *Southeastern Europe* 40, 2, 125–57.

Auvinen, Juha Y. 1996. IMF Intervention and Political Protest in the Third World: A Conventional Wisdom Refined. *Third World Quarterly* 17, 3, 377–400.

Baccaro, Lucio and Jonas Pontusson. 2016. Rethinking Comparative Political Economy: The Growth Model Perspective. *Politics & Society* 44, 2, 175–207.

Bakker, Ryan, Caterhin de Vries, Erica Edwards, et al. 2015. Measuring Party Positions in Europe: The Chapel Hill Expert Survey Trend File, 1999–2010. *Party Politics* 21, 1, 143–52.

Bakker, Tom and Claes De Vreese. 2011. Good News for the Future? Young People, Internet Use, and Political Participation. *Communication Research* 38, 4, 451–70.

Barnes, Samuel H. and Max Kaase. 1979. *Political Action: Mass Participation in Five Western Democracies*. Beverly Hills, CA: SAGE.

Bartels, Larry M. 2014. Ideology and Retrospection in Electoral Responses to the Great Recession. In Nancy Bermeo and Larry Bartels, eds., *Mass Politics in Tough Times: Opinions, Votes, and Protest in the Great Recession*. Oxford: Oxford University Press, pp. 185–223.

Beck, Nathaniel, Kristian S. Gleditsch, and Kyle Beardsley. 2006. Space Is More Than Geography: Using Spatial Econometrics in the Study of Political Economy. *International Studies Quarterly* 50, 1, 27–44.

Beck, Nathaniel and Jonathan N. Katz. 2011. Modeling Dynamics in Time-Series–Cross-Section Political Economy Data,. *Annual Review of Political Science* 14, 331–52.

Beck, Nathaniel, Jonathan N. Katz, and Umberto G. Mignozzetti. 2014. Of Nickell Bias and Its Cures: Comment on Gaibulloev, Sandler, and Sul. *Political Analysis* 22, 2, 274–78.

Becker, Regina and Swen Hutter. 2017. Europäisierte Protestlandschaft: Ausmaß und Formen europäisierter Proteste mit deutscher Beteiligung von Maastricht bis zur Eurokrise, *Leviathan*, 45. Jg, Sonderheft 33/2017, 37–62.

Beieler, John. 2016. Generating Politically-Relevant Event Data. arXiv preprint arXiv:1609.06239.

Beissinger, Mark R. 2007. Structure and Example in Modular Political Phenomena: The Diffusion of Bulldozer/Rose/Orange/Tulip Revolutions. *Perspectives on Politics* 5, 2, 259–76.

Beissinger, Mark R. and Gwendolyn Sasse. 2014. An End to 'Patience'? The Great Recession and Economic Protest in Eastern Europe. In Nancy Bermeo and Larry M. Bartels, eds., *Mass Politics in Tough Times*. Oxford: Oxford University Press, pp. 334–70.

Bennett, W. Lance and Alexandra Segerberg. 2013. *The Logic of Connective Action: Digital Media and the Personalization of Contentious Politics*. Cambridge: Cambridge University Press.

Beramendi, Pablo, Silja Häusermann, Herbert Kitschelt, and Hanspeter Kriesi. 2015a. Introduction. In Pablo Beramendi, Silja Häusermann, Herbert Kitschelt, and Hanspeter Kriesi, eds., *The Politics of Advanced Capitalism*. Cambridge: Cambridge University Press, pp. 1–64.

Beramendi, Pablo, Silja Häusermann, Herbert Kitschelt, and Hanspeter Kriesi (eds.). 2015b. *The Politics of Advanced Capitalism*. New York: Cambridge University Press.

Bermeo, Nancy and Larry M. Bartels. 2014a. Mass Politics in Tough Times. In Nancy Bermeo and Larry M. Bartels, eds., *Mass Politics in Tough Times: Opinions, Votes and Protest in the Great Recession*. Oxford: Oxford University Press, pp. 1–39.

Bermeo, Nancy and Larry M. Bartels. 2014b. *Mass Politics in Tough Times: Opinions, Votes and Protest in the Great Recession*. Oxford: Oxford University Press.

Bernburg, Jon G. 2015. Economic Crisis and Popular Protest in Iceland, January 2009: The Role of Perceived Economic Loss and Political Attitudes in Protest Participation and Support. *Mobilization* 20, 2, 231–52.

Bernhard, Michael. 1996. Civil Society after the First Transition: Dilemmas of Postcommunist Democratization in Poland and Beyond. *Communist and Post-Communist Studies* 29, 3, 309–30.

Bernhard, Michael and Ekrem Karakoç. 2007. Civil Society and the Legacies of Dictatorship. *World Politics* 59, 4, 539–67.

Biggs, Michael. 2003. Positive Feedback in Collective Mobilization: The American Strike Wave of 1886. *Theory and Society* 32, 2, 217–54.

Blanchard, Olivier J., Mark Griffiths, and Bertrand Gruss. 2013. Boom, Bust, Recovery: Forensics of the Latvian Crisis. *Brookings Papers on Economic Activity* 2013, 2, 325–71.

Bohle, Dorothee. 2016. European Integration, Capitalist Diversity and Crises Trajectories on Europe's Eastern Periphery. *New Political Economy* 23, 2, 239–53.

Boix, Carles. 2015. Prosperity and the Evolving Structure of Advanced Economics. In Pablo Beramendi, Silja Hausermann, Herbert Kitschelt, and Hanspeter Kriesi, eds., *The Politics of Advanced Capitalism*. Cambridge: Cambridge University Press, pp. 67–88.

Borbáth, Endre and Theresa Gessler. 2020. Different Worlds of Contention? Protest in Northwestern, Southern and Eastern Europe. *European Journal of Political Research*. Online first.

Borbáth, Endre and Swen Hutter. 2020. Protesting Parties in Europe: A Comparative Analysis. *Party Politics*. Online first.

Bornschier, Simon. 2010. The New Cultural Divide and the Two-Dimensional Political Space in Western Europe. *West European Politics* 33, 3, 419–44.

Boschee, Elizabeth, Jennifer Lautenschlager, Sean O' Brien, Steve Shellman, James Starz, and Michael Ward. 2015. ICEWS Coded Event Data. *Harvard Dataverse*. https://dataverse.harvard.edu/dataverse/icews.

Boschee, Elizabeth, Premkumar Natarajan, and Ralph Weischedel. 2013. Automatic Extraction of Events from Open Source Text for Predictive Forecasting. In V. S. Subrahmanian, ed., *Handbook of Computational Approaches to Counterterrorism*. New York: Springer, pp. 51–67.

Bosi, Lorenzo, Marco Giugni, and Kathrin Uba. 2016. *The Consequences of Social Movements*. Cambridge: Cambridge University Press.

Brancati, Dawn. 2014. Pocketbook Protests: Explaining the Emergence of Pro-Democracy Protests Worldwide. *Comparative Political Studies* 47, 11, 1503–30.

Brand, Jennie E. 2015. The Far-reaching Impact of Job Loss and Unemployment. *Annual Review of Sociology* 41, 359–57.

Braun, Robert and Ruud Koopmans. 2010. The Diffusion of Ethnic Violence in Germany: The Role of Social Similarity. *European Sociological Review* 26, 1, 111–23.

Bremer, Björn, Swen Hutter, and Hanspeter Kriesi. 2020. Dynamics of protest and electoral politics in the Great Recession. *European Journal of Political Research*. Online first, https://doi.org/10.1111/1475-6765.12375

Buechler, Steven M. 2007. The Strange Career of Strain and Breakdown Theories of Collective Action. In David A. Snow, Sarah A. Soule, and Hanspeter Kriesi, eds., *The Blackwell Companion to Social Movements*. Oxford: Blackwell, pp. 47–66.

Burden, Barry C. and Amber Wichowsky. 2014. Economic Discontent as a Mobilizer: Unemployment and Voter Turnout. *Journal of Politics* 76, 4, 887–98.

Casal Bértoa, Fernando. 2014. Party Systems and Cleavage Structures Revisited: A Sociological Explanation of Party System Institutionalization in East Central Europe. *Party Politics* 20, 1, 16–36.

Casal Bértoa, Fernando and Zsolt Enyedi. 2016. Party System Closure and Openness: Conceptualization, Operationalization and Validation. *Party Politics* 22, 3, 265–77.

Castells, Manuel. 2015. *Networks of Outrage and Hope: Social Movements in the Internet Age*. Cambridge: Polity Press.

Charles, Kerwin K. and Melvin Stephens. 2013. Employment, Wages, and Voter Turnout. *American Economic Journal: Applied Economics* 5, 4, 111–43.

Chzhen, Kat, Geoffrey Evans, and Mark Pickup. 2014. When Do Economic Perceptions Matter for Party Approval? Examining the Endogeneity of Economic Perceptions Before and During the Economic Downturn. *Political Behavior* 36, 2, 291–313.

Cisar, Ondrej and Jiri Navratil. 2015. At the Ballot Boxes or in the Streets and Factories: Economic Contention in the Visegrad Group. In Marco G. Giugni and Maria T. Grasso, eds., *Austerity and Protest: Popular Contention in Times of Economic Crisis*. Farnham: Ashgate, pp. 35–53.

Coffey, Eva. 2013. Pain Tolerance. Economic Voting in the Czech Republic. *Electoral Studies* 32, 3, 432–37.

Coman, Emanuel. 2017. Dimensions of Political Conflict in West and East: An Application of Vote Scaling to 22 European Parliaments. *Party Politics* 23, 3, 248–61.

Conti, Nicolò, Swen Hutter, and Kyriaki Nanou. 2017. Party Competition and Political Representation in Crisis: An Introductory Note. *Party Politics* 24, 1, 3–9.

Copelovitch, Mark, Jeffrey Frieden, and Stefanie Walter. 2016. The Political Economy of the Euro Crisis. *Comparative Political Studies* 49, 7, 811–40.

Cordero, Guillermo and Pablo Simón. 2016. Economic Crisis and Support for Democracy in Europe. *West European Politics* 39, 2, 305–25.

Croicu, Mihai and Nils B. Weidmann. 2015. Improving the Selection of News Reports for Event Coding Using Ensemble Classification. *Research & Politics* 2, 3, 1–8.

Crowley, Stephen. 2004. Explaining Labor Weakness in Post-Communist Europe: Historical Legacies and Comparative Perspective. *East European Politics and Societies* 18, 3, 394–429.

Dahlberg, Stefan and Sören Holmberg. 2014. Democracy and Bureaucracy: How Their Quality Matters for Popular Satisfaction. *West European Politics* 37, 3, 515–37.

Dalton, Russell. 2008. The Quantity and the Quality of Party Systems: Party System Polarization, Its Measurement, and Its Consequences. *Comparative Political Studies* 41, 7, 899–920.

Dalton, Russel J. and Martin P. Wattenberg (eds.). 2002. *Parties Without Partisans: Political Change in Advanced Industrial Democracies: Political Change in Advanced Industrial Democracies*. Oxford: Oxford University Press.

Dancygier, Rafaela and Michael Donnelly. 2014. Attitudes Toward Immigration in Good Times and Bad. In Larry Bartels and Nancy Bermeo, eds., *Mass Politics in Tough Times*. Oxford: Oxford University Press, pp. 148–84.

Darmofal, David. 2006. *Spatial Econometrics and Political Science*. Paper presented at the Annual Meeting of the Southern Political Science Association, Atlanta, GA, January 5–7.

Dassonneville, Ruth and Michael S. Lewis-Beck. 2014. Macroeconomics, Economic Crisis and Electoral Outcomes: A National European Pool. *Acta Politica* 49, 4, 372–94.

Davies, James C. 1962. Toward a Theory of Revolution. *American Sociological Review* 27, 1, 5–19.

Decker, Oliver, Johannes Kiess, and Elmar Brähler. 2015. *Die Stabilisierte Mitte. Rechtsextreme Einstellung in Deutschland 2014*. Leipzig: Die "Mitte"-Studien der Universität Leipzig.

della Porta, Donatella (ed.). 2007. *The Global Justice Movement: Cross-national and Transnational Perspective*. Boulder, CO: Paradigm Publishers.

della Porta, Donatella. 2015. *Social Movements in Times of Austerity: Bringing Capitalism Back into Protest Analysis*. Cambridge, MA: Polity Press.

della Porta, Donatella. 2017. Riding the Wave: Protest Cascades, and What We Can Learn from Them. In Donatella della Porta, ed., *Global Diffusion of Protest: Riding the Protest Wave in the Neoliberal Crisis*. Amsterdam: Amsterdam University Press, pp. 9–30.

della Porta, Donatella, Massimiliano Andretta, Tiago Fernandes, Francis O'Connor, Eduardo Romanos, and Markos Vogiatzoglou. 2017. *Late Neoliberalism and Its Discontents in the Economic Crisis: Comparing Social Movements in the European Periphery*. Cham: Springer.

della Porta, Donatella and Manuela Caiani. 2011. *Social Movements and Europeanization*. Oxford: Oxford University Press.

della Porta, Donatella, Joseba Fernández, Hara Kouki, and Lorenzo Mosca. 2017. *Movement Parties Against Austerity*. Cambridge: Polity Press.

della Porta, Donatella, Hanspeter Kriesi, and Dieter Rucht (eds.). 2009. *Social Movements in a Globalizing World*. Basingstoke: Palgrave Macmillan.

della Porta, Donatella and Alice Mattoni. 2014a. Patterns of Diffusion and the Transnational Dimension of Protest in the Movements of the Crisis: An Introduction. In Donatella della Porta and Alice Mattoni, eds., *Spreading Protest: Social Movements in Times of Crisis*. Colchester: ECPR Press, pp. 2–18.

della Porta, Donatella and Alice Mattoni. 2014b. *Spreading Protest: Social Movements in Times of Crisis*. Essex: ECPR Press.

della Porta, Donatella and Dieter Rucht. 1991. Left-Libertarian Movements in Context: A Comparison of Italy and West Germany, 1965–1990. Discussion Paper FSIII 91-102. Berlin: WZB.

della Porta, Donatella and Sidney Tarrow. 1986. Unwanted Children: Political Violence and the Cycle of Protest in Italy, 1966–1973. *European Journal of Political Research* 14, 5–6, 607–32.

Deuze, Mark. 2008. The Changing Context of News Work: Liquid Journalism for a Monitorial Citizenry. *International Journal of Communication* 2, 848–65.

de Zúñiga, Homero Gil, Nakwon Jung, and Sebastiàn Valenzuela. 2012. Social Media Use for News and Individuals' Social Capital, Civic Engagement and Political Participation. *Journal of Computer-Mediated Communication* 17, 3, 319–36.

Diani, Mario and Maria Kousis. 2014. The Duality of Claims and Events: The Greek Campaign Against the Troika's Memoranda and Austerity, 2010–2012. *Mobilization: An International Quarterly* 19, 4, 387–404.

Dodson, Kyle. 2011. The Movement Society in Comparative Perspective. *Mobilization* 16, 4, 475–94.

Doherty, Brian and Graeme Hayes. 2018. Tactics and Strategic Action. In David A. Snow, Sarah A. Soule, Hanspeter Kriesi, and Holly J. McCammon, eds., *The Wiley Blackwell Companion to Social Movements*. Oxford: Wiley Blackwell, pp. 269–88.

Duch, Raymond M. and Randolph T. Stevenson. 2008. *The Economic Vote: How Political and Economic Institutions Condition Election Results*. New York: Cambridge University Press.

Earl, Jennifer. 2016. Protest Online: Theorizing the Consequences of Online Engagement. In Lorenzo Bosi, Marco Giugni, and Katrin Uba, eds., *The Consequences of Social Movements*. Cambridge: Cambridge University Press, pp. 363–400.

Earl, Jennifer and Katrina Kimport. 2011. *Digitally Enabled Social Change: Activism in the Internet Age*. Cambridge, MA: MIT Press.

Earl, Jennifer, Andrew Martin, John D. McCarthy, and Sarah A. Soule. 2004. The Use of Newspaper Data in the Study of Collective Action. *Annual Review of Sociology* 30, 65–80.

Eihmanis, Edgars. 2019. Latvia – An Ever-Wider Gap: The Ethnic Divide in Latvian Party Politics, in European Politics in Times of Crises. In Swen Hutter and Hanspeter Kriesi, eds., *European Politics in Times of Crisis*. Cambridge: Cambridge University Press, pp. 236–58.

Ferrin, Monica. 2016. An Empirical Assessment of Satisfaction with Democracy. In Monica Ferrin and Hanspeter Kriesi, eds., *How Europeans View and Evaluate Democracy*. Oxford: Oxford University Press, pp. 283–306.

Fillieule, Olivier. 2010. *Penser les mouvements sociaux*. Paris: La Découverte.

Flesher-Fominaya, Cristina. 2017. European Anti-austerity and Pro-democracy Protests in the Wake of the Global Financial Crisis. *Social Movement Studies* 16, 1, 1–20.

Fourcade, Marion, Philippe Steiner, Wolfgang Streeck, and Cornelia Woll. 2013. Moral Categories in the Financial Crisis. *Socio-Economic Review* 11, 3, 601–27.

Fraile, Marta and Michael S. Lewis-Beck. 2014. Economic Vote Instability: Endogeneity or Restricted Variance? Spanish Panel Evidence from 2008 and 2011. *European Journal of Political Research* 53, 1, 160–79.

Francisco, Ronald A. 1996. Coercion and Protest: An Empirical Test in Two Democratic States. *American Journal of Political Science* 40, 4, 1179–204.

Franzese, Robert J. and Jude C. Hays. 2007. Spatial Econometric Models of Cross-sectional Interdependence in Political Science Panel and Time-Series-Cross-Section Data. *Political Analysis* 15, 2, 140–64.

Gajewska, Katarzyna. 2008. The Emergence of a European Labour Protest Movement? *European Journal of Industrial Relations* 14, 1, 104–21.

Galais, Carol and Jasmine Lorenzini. 2017. Half a Loaf Is (Not) Better Than None: How Austerity-Related Grievances and Emotions Triggered Protests in Spain. *Mobilization* 22, 1, 77–95.

Gall, Gregor. 2013. Quiescence Continued? Recent Strike Activity in Nine Western European Economies. *Economic and Industrial Democracy* 34, 4, 667–91.

Gamson, William A. and David S. Meyer. 1996. Framing Political Opportunity. In Dough McAdam, John D. McCarthy, and Mayer N. Zald, eds., *Comparative Perspectives on Social Movements: Political Opportunities, Mobilizing Structures, and Cultural Framings*. Cambridge: Cambridge University Press, pp. 275–90.

Genovese, Federica, Gerald Schneider, and Pia Wassmann. 2016. The Eurotower Strikes Back: Crises, Adjustments and Europe's Austerity Protests. *Comparative Political Studies* 49, 7, 939–67.

Gentile, Antonina and Sidney Tarrow. 2009. Charles Tilly, Globalization, and Labor's Citizen Rights. *European Political Science Review* 1, 3, 465–93.

Gerbaudo, Paolo. 2013. Protest Diffusion and Cultural Resonance in the 2011 Protest Wave. *The International Spectator* 48, 4, 86–101. DOI: 10.1080/03932729.2013.847689

Gerner, Deborah J., Philip Schrodt, Ronald A. Francisco, and Judith L. Weddle. 1994. Machine Coding of Event Data Using Regional and International Sources. *International Studies Quarterly* 38, 1, 91–119.

Gerner, Deborah J., Philip A. Schrodt, Omür Yilmaz, et al. 2002. Conflict and Mediation Event Observations (CAMEO): A New Event Data Framework for the Analysis of Foreign Policy Interactions. International Studies Association, New Orleans.

Geschwender, James A. 1968. Explorations in the Theory of Social Movements and Revolution. *Social Forces* 47, 2, 119–27.

Gilardi, Fabrizio. 2012. Transnational Diffusion: Norms, Ideas, and Policies. In Walter Carlsnaes, Thomas Risse, and Beth A. Simmons, eds., *Handbook of International Relations*. Thousand Oaks, CA: SAGE, pp. 453–77.

Gingrich, Jane and Silja Häusermann. 2015. The Decline of the Working-Class Vote, the Reconfiguration of the Welfare Support Coalition and Consequences for the Welfare State. *Journal of European Social Policy* 25, 1, 50–75.

Giugni, Marco and Maria T. Grasso. 2015. *Austerity and Protest: Popular Contention in Times of Economic Crisis*. Burlington, VT: Ashgate.

Givan, Rebecca K., Kenneth M. Roberts, and Sarah A. Soule. 2010. *Diffusion of Social Movements: Actors, Mechanisms, and Political Effects*. Cambridge, MA: Cambridge University Press.

Goldstone, Jack A. 2003. Introduction: Bridging Institutionalized and Noninstitutionalized Politics. In Jack A. Goldstone, ed., *States, Parties, and Social Movements*. Cambridge: Cambridge University Press, pp. 1–24.

Grant, Taylor and Matthew J. Lebo. 2016. Error Correction Methods with Political Time Series. *Political Analysis* 24, 1, 3–30.

Grasso, Maria T. and Marco Giugni. 2016. Protest Participation and Economic Crisis: The Conditioning Role of Political Opportunities. *European Journal of Political Research* 55, 4, 663–80.

Greskovits, Béla. 1998. *The Political Economy of Protest and Patience*. Budapest: Central European University Press.

Greskovits, Béla. 2015. Ten Years of Enlargement and the Forces of Labour in Central and Eastern Europe. *Transfer: European Review of Labour and Research* 21, 3, 269–84.

Greskovits, Béla. 2017. Rebuilding the Hungarian Right through Civil Organization and Contention: The Civic Circles Movement. Working Paper. http://cadmus.eui.eu//handle/1814/47245.

Grimmer, Justin and Brandon M. Stewart. 2013. Text as Data: The Promise and Pitfalls of Automatic Content Analysis Methods for Political Texts. *Political Analysis* 21, 3, 267–97.

Gunitsky, Sewa. 2013. *From the Spring of Nations to the Arab Spring: Building Better Typologies of Democratic Diffusion*. Paper presented at the American Political Science Association Annual Meeting, Chicago, IL, August 29–September 1.

Gunther, Richard. 2005. Parties and Electoral Behavior in Southern Europe. *Comparative Politics* 37, 3, 253–75.

Gurney, Joan Neff and Kathleen J. Tierney. 1982. Relative Deprivation and Social Movements: A Critical Look at Twenty Years of Theory and Research. *The Sociological Quarterly* 23, 1, 33–47.

Gurr, Ted R. 1970. *Why Men Rebel*. Princeton, NJ: Princeton University Press.

Gwet, Kilem L. 2014. *Handbook of Inter-Rater Reliability*. Gaithersburg, MD: Advanced Analytics.

Hall, Peter. 2013. The Political Origins of Our Economic Discontents: Contemporary Adjustment Problems in Historical Perspective. In Miles Kahler and David A. Lake, eds., *Politics in the New Hard Times: The Great Recession in Comparative Perspective*. Ithaca, NY: Cornell University Press, pp. 129–49.

Hall, Peter A. and David Soskice. 2001. *Varieties of Capitalism: The Institutional Foundations of Comparative Advantage*. Oxford: Oxford University Press.

Hamann, Kerstin, Alison Johnston, and John Kelly. 2013. Unions Against Governments: Explaining General Strikes in Western Europe, 1980–2006. *Comparative Political Studies* 46, 9, 1030–57.

Hanna, Alex. 2017. MPEDS: Automating the Generation of Protest Event Data. SocArXiv.

Hardarson, Ólafur Th. and Gunnar Helgi Kristinsson. 2010. Iceland. *European Journal of Political Research* 49, 7–8, 1009–16.

Hassel, Anke. 2014. Adjustments in the Eurozone: Varieties of Capitalism and the Crisis in Southern Europe. LEQS Paper.

Haughton, Tim and Kevin Deegan-Krause. 2015. Hurricane Season: System of Instability in Central and East European Party Politics. *East European Politics and Societies* 29, 1, 61–80.

Häusermann, Silja. 2015. *Electoral Realignment and Social Policy Positions of Social Democratic Parties*. Revised Draft for the Project 'Party Competition and Voter Alignments in Times of Welfare State Transformation'. EUI Florence, June 18–19.

Heaney, Michael T. and Fabio Rojas. 2015. *Party in the Street: The Antiwar Movement and the Democratic Party after 9/11*. Cambridge: Cambridge University Press.

Hellwig, Timothy. 2010. Elections and the Economy. In Lawrence LeDuc, Richard G. Niemi, and Pippa Norris, eds., *Comparing Democracies 3: Elections and Voting in the 21st Century*. London: SAGE, pp. 184–201.

Hellwig, Timothy and David Samuels. 2007. Voting in Open Economies: The Electoral Consequences of Globalization. *Comparative Political Studies* 40, 3, 283–306.

Hernández, Enrique and Hanspeter Kriesi. 2016. The Electoral Consequences of the Financial and Economic Crisis in Europe. *European Journal of Political Research* 55, 2, 203–24.

Hirschman, Albert O. 1970. *Exit, Voice and Loyalty: Responses to Decline in Firms, Organizations, and States*. Cambridge, MA: Harvard University Press.

Howard, Marc. 2003. *The Weakness of Civil Society in Post-Communist Europe*. Cambridge: Cambridge University Press.

Hutter, Swen. 2013. Political Parties in the Streets: The Development and Timing of Party-Sponsored Protests in Western Europe. In Peter Esaiasson and Hanne Marthe Narud, eds., *Between-Election Democracy: The Representative Relationship after Election Day*. Colchester: ECPR Press, pp. 127–50.

Hutter, Swen. 2014a. Protest Event Analysis and Its Offspring. In Donatella della Porta, ed., *Methodological Practices in Social Movement Research*. Oxford: Oxford University Press, pp. 335–67.

Hutter, Swen. 2014b. *Protesting Culture and Economics in Western Europe. New Cleavages in Left and Right Politics*. Minneapolis, MN: University of Minnesota Press.

Hutter, Swen, Edgar Grande, and Hanspeter Kriesi. 2016. *Politicising Europe: Integration and Mass Politics*. Cambridge: Cambridge University Press.

Hutter, Swen and Hanspeter Kriesi. 2013. Movements of the Left, Movements of the Right Reconsidered. In Jacquelien van Stekelenburg, Conny Roggeband, and Bert Klandermans, eds., *The Future of Social Movement Research: Dynamics, Mechanisms, and Processes*. Minneapolis, MN: University of Minnesota Press, pp. 281–98.

Hutter, Swen and Hanspeter Kriesi (eds.). 2019. *European Politics in Times of Crisis*. Cambridge: Cambridge University Press.

Hutter, Swen, Hanspeter Kriesi, and Jasmine Lorenzini. 2017. Social Movements in Interaction with Political Parties. In David A. Snow, Sarah A. Soule, Hanspeter Kriesi, and Holly J. McCammon, eds., *The Wiley Blackwell Companion to Social Movements*, new and expanded ed. New York: Wiley, pp. 322–37.

Hutter, Swen, Hanspeter Kriesi, and Guillem Vidal. 2018. Old versus New Politics: The Political Spaces in Southern Europe in Times of Crises. *Party Politics* 24, 1, 10–22.

Ignazi, Piero. 2003. *Extreme Right Parties in Western Europe*. Oxford: Oxford University Press.

Imig, Doug and Sidney Tarrow. 2001. Mapping the Europeanization of Contention: Evidence from a Quantitative Data Analysis. In Doug Imig and Sidney Tarrow, eds., *Contentious Europeans: Protest and Politics in an Emerging Polity*. Lanham, MD: Rowman & Littlefield, pp. 27–49.

Incantalupo, Matthew B. 2011. The Effects of Unemployment on Voter Turnout in US National Elections. http://scholar.princeton.edu/sites/default/files/mincanta/files/incantalupo_turnout_0.pdf.

Inglehart, Ron and Pippa Norris. 2016. Trump, Brexit and the Rise of Populism: Economic Have-Nots and Cultural Backlash. Research Working Paper 16-026, Harvard Kennedy School.

Jackman, Robert and Karin Volpert. 1996. Conditions Favouring Parties of the Extreme Right in Western Europe. *British Journal of Political Science* 2, 4, 501–21.

Jahoda, Marie. 1982. *Employment and Unemployment: A Social-psychological Analysis*. Cambridge: Cambridge University Press.

Jenkins, J. Craig and Thomas V. Maher. 2016. What Should We Do about Source Selection in Event Data? Challenges, Progress, and Possible Solutions. *International Journal of Sociology* 46, 1, 42–57.

Jenkins, J. Craig, Charles Lewis Taylor, Marianne Abbott, Thomas V. Maher, and Lindsey Peterson. 2012. *The World Handbook of Political Indicators IV*. Columbus, OH: Mershon Center for International Security Studies, The Ohio State University.

Jurafsky, Daniel and James H. Martin. 2009. *Speech and Language Processing: An Introduction to Natural Language Processing, Computational Linguistics, and Speech Recognition*, 2nd ed. Upper Saddle River, NJ: Prentice-Hall.

Kahler, Miles and David A. Lake. 2013. Introduction: Anatomy of Crisis: The Great Recession and Political Change. In Miles Kahler and David A. Lake, eds., *Politics in the New Hard Times: The Great Recession in Comparative Perspective*. Ithaca, NY: Cornell University Press, pp. 1–24.

Kanellopoulos, Kostas, Konstantinos Kostopoulos, Dimitris Papanikolopoulos, and Vasileios Rongas. 2017. Competing Modes of Coordination in the Greek Anti-Austerity Campaign, 2010–2012. *Social Movement Studies* 16, 1, 101–18.

Karyotis, Georgios and Wolfgang Rüdig. 2018. The Three Waves of Anti-Austerity Protest in Greece, 2010–2015. *Political Studies Review* 16, 2, 158–69.

Kattel, Rainer and Ringa Raudla. 2013. The Baltic Republics and the Crisis of 2008–2011. *Europe-Asia Studies* 65, 3, 426–49.

Kayser, M. A. and M. Peress. 2012. Benchmarking Across Borders: Electoral Accountability and the Necessity of Comparison. *American Political Science Review* 106, 3, 661–84.

Kerbo, Harold R. 1982. Movements of 'Crisis' and Movements of 'Affluence'. *Journal of Conflict Resolution* 26, 4, 645–63.

Kern, Anna, Sofie Marien, and Marc Hooghe. 2015. Economic Crisis and Levels of Political Participation in Europe (2002–2010): The Role of Resources and Grievances. *West European Politics* 38, 3, 465–90.

Kitschelt, Herbert. 1986. Political Opportunity Structures and Political Protest: Anti-Nuclear Movements in Four Democracies. *British Journal of Political Science* 16, 1, 57–85.

Kitschelt, Herbert. 1989. *The Logics of Party Formation: Ecological Politics in Belgium and West Germany*. Ithaca, NY: Cornell University Press.

Kitschelt, Herbert. 1994. *The Transformation of European Social Democracy*. Cambridge: Cambridge University Press.

Kitschelt, Herbert. 2003. Landscapes of Political Interest Intermediation: Social Movements, Interest Groups, and Parties in the Early Twenty-First Century. In Pedro Ibarra, ed., *Social Movements and Democracy*. New York: Palgrave Macmillan, pp. 81–103.

Kitschelt, Herbert. 2006. Movement Parties. In Richard S. Katz and William Crotty, eds., *Handbook of Party Politics*. London: SAGE, pp. 278–90.

Klandermans, Bert, Jojanneke van der Toorn, and Jacquelien van Stekelenburg. 2008. Embeddedness and Identity: How Immigrants Turn Grievances into Action. *American Sociological Review* 73, 6, 992–1012.

Klandermans, Bert and Jacquelien van Stekelenburg. 2016. Taking Austerity to the Streets: Fighting Austerity Measures or Austerity States. *Mobilization* 21, 4, 431–48.

Klašnja, Marko and Joshua A. Tucker. 2013. The Economy, Corruption, and the Vote: Evidence from Experiments in Sweden and Moldova. *Electoral Studies* 32, 3, 536–43.

Klašnja, Marko, Joshua A. Tucker, and Kevin Deegan-Krause. 2014. Pocketbook vs. Sociotropic Corruption Voting. *British Journal of Political Science* 46, 1, 67–94.

Koopmans, Ruud. 1993. The Dynamics of Protest Wave: West Germany, 1965 to 1989. *American Sociological Review* 58, 5, 637–58.

Koopmans, Ruud. 1995. *Democracy from Below: New Social Movements and the Political System in West Germany*. Boulder, CO: Westview Press.

Koopmans, Ruud. 1996. New Social Movements and Changes in Political Participation. *West European Politics* 19, 1, 28–50.

Koopmans, Ruud. 2004. Protest in Time and Space: The Evolution of Waves of Contention. In David A. Snow, Sarah A. Soule, and Hanspeter Kriesi, eds., *The Blackwell Companion to Social Movements*. Oxford: Blackwell, pp. 19–46.

Koopmans, Ruud and Dieter Rucht. 2002. Protest Event Analysis. *Methods of Social Movement Research* 16, 231–59.

Kousis, Maria and Maria Paschou. 2017. Alternative Forms of Resilience: A Typology of Approaches for the Study of Citizen Collective Responses in Hard Economic Times. *Partecipazione e Conflitto* 10, 1, 136–68.

Kriesi, Hanspeter. 1995. Alliance Structures. In Hanspeter Kriesi, Ruud Koopmans, Jan Willem Duyvendak, and Marco Giugni, eds., *New Social Movements in Western Europe: A Comparative Analysis*. Minneapolis, MN: University of Minnesota Press, pp. 53–81.

Kriesi, Hanspeter. 2004. Political Context and Opportunity. In David A. Snow, Sarah A. Soule, and Hanspeter Kriesi, eds., *The Blackwell Companion to Social Movements*. Oxford: Blackwell, pp. 67–90.

Kriesi, Hanspeter. 2014. The Political Consequences of the Economic Crisis in Europe: Electoral Punishment and Popular Protest. In Nancy Bermeo and Larry Bartels, eds., *Mass Politics in Tough Times: Opinions, Votes, and Protest in the Great Recession*. Oxford: Oxford University Press, pp. 297–333.

Kriesi, Hanspeter. 2015. Political Mobilization in Times of Crises: The Relationship between Economic and Political Crises. In Marco Giugni and Maria T. Grasso, eds., *Austerity and Protest: Popular Contention in Times of Economic Crisis*. Farnham: Ashgate, pp. 19–34.

Kriesi, Hanspeter. 2016. The Politicization of European Integration. In Nathaniel Copsey and Tim Haughton, eds., *JCMS Annual Review of the European Union in 2015*. Oxford: Blackwell, pp. 32–48.

Kriesi, Hanspeter. 2017. The Implications of the Euro Crisis for Democracy. *Journal of European Public Policy*. DOI: 10.1080/13501763.2017.1310277.

Kriesi, Hanspeter and Edgar Grande. 2016. The Euro Crisis: A Boost to the Politicisation of European Integration? In Swen Hutter, Edgar Grande, and Hanspeter Kriesi, eds., *Politicising Europe: Integration and Mass Politics*. Cambridge: Cambridge University Press, pp. 240–76.

Kriesi, Hanspeter, Edgar Grande, Martin Dolezal, Marc Helbling, Dominic Hoeglinger, Swen Hutter, and Bruno Wüest. 2012. *Political Conflict in Western Europe*. Cambridge: Cambridge University Press.

Kriesi, Hanspeter, Edgar Grande, Romain Lachat, Martin Dolezal, Simon Bornschier, and Timotheos Frey. 2008. *West European Politics in the Age of Globalization*. Cambridge: Cambridge University Press.

Kriesi, Hanspeter, Ruud Koopmans, Jan W. Duyvendak, and Marco G. Giugni. 1995. *New Social Movements in Western Europe: A Comparative Analysis*. Minneapolis, MN: University of Minnesota Press.

Kriesi, Hanspeter, Willem E. Saris, and Anchrit Wille. 1993. Mobilization Potential for Environmental Protest. *European Sociological Review* 9, 2, 155–72.

Kübler, Daniel and Hanspeter Kriesi. 2017. How Globalisation and Mediatisation Challenge our Democracies. *Swiss Political Science Review* 23, 3, 231–45.

Kuran, Timur. 1991. Now Out of Never: The Element of Surprise in the East European Revolution of 1989. *World Politics* 44, 1, 7–48.

Kurer, Thomas, Silja Häusermann, Bruno Wüest, and Matthias Enggist. 2018. Economic Grievances and Political Protest. *European Journal of Political Research*. DOI: 10.1111/1475-6765.12311.

Laffan, Brigit. 2016. Europe's Union in Crisis: Tested and Contested. *West European Politics* 39, 5, 915–32.

Lancaster, Tony. 2002. Orthogonal Parameters and Panel Data. *The Review of Economic Studies* 69, 3, 647–66.

Langman, Lauren. 2013. Occupy: A New New Social Movement. *Current Sociology* 61, 4, 510–24.

Lewis-Beck, Michael S. and Mary Stegmaier. 2007. Economic Models of Voting. In Russell J. Dalton and Hans-Dieter Klingemann, eds., *The Oxford Handbook of Political Behaviour*. Oxford: Oxford University Press, pp. 519–37.

Lim, Chaeyoon and Thomas Sander. 2013. Does Misery Love Company? Civic Engagement in Economic Hard Times. *Social Science Research* 42, 1, 14–30.

Linde, Jonas. 2012. Why Feed the Hand that Bites You? Perceptions of Procedural Fairness and System Support in Post-communist Democracies. *European Journal of Political Research* 51, 3, 410–34.

Lindvall, Johannes. 2013. Union Density and Political Strikes. *World Politics* 65, 3, 539–69.

Lobo, Marina Costa and Michael S. Lewis-Beck. 2017. Economic Voting in Ordinary and Extraordinary Times. In Kai Arzheimer, Jocelyn Evans, and Michael S. Lewis-Beck, eds., *Sage Handbook of Electoral Behaviour.* London: SAGE, pp. 660ff.

Lohmann, Susanne. 1994. The Dynamics of Informational Cascades: The Monday Demonstrations in Leipzig, East Germany, 1989–91. *World Politics* 47, 1, 42–101.

Lomax, Bill. 1997. The Strange Death of 'Civil Society' in Post-communist Hungary. *Journal of Communist Studies and Transition Politics* 13, 1, 41–63.

Lupu, Noam. 2014. Brand Dilution and the Breakdown of Political Parties in Latin America. *World Politics* 66, 4, 561–602.

Maeckelbergh, Marianne. 2012. Horizontal Democracy Now: From Alterglobalization to Occupation. *Interface* 4, 1, 207–34.

Magalhães, Pedro C. 2014. Government Effectiveness and Support for Democracy. *European Journal of Political Research* 53, 1, 77–97.

Maguire, Diarmuid. 1995. Opposition Movements and Opposition Parties: Equal Partners or Dependent Relations in the Struggle for Power and Reform? In J. Craig Jenkins and Bert Klandermans, eds., *The Politics of Social Protest: Comparative Perspectives on States and Social Movements.* Minneapolis, MN: University of Minnesota Press, pp. 99–112.

Mainwaring, Scott, Ana Marìa Bejarano, and Eduardo Pizarro Lengómez. 2006. The Crisis of Democratic Representation in the Andes: An Overview. In Scott Mainwaring, Ana Marìa Bejarano, and Eduardo Pizarro Lengómez, eds., *The Crisis of Democratic Representation in the Andes.* Stanford, CA: Stanford University Press, pp. 1–44.

Mair, Peter. 2006. Ruling the Void: The Hollowing of Western Democracy. *New Left Review* 42, 25–51.

Mair, Peter. 2013a. *Ruling the Void: The Hollowing of Western Democracy.* London: Verso.

Mair, Peter. 2013b. Smaghi versus the Parties: Representative Government and Institutional Constraints. In Armin Schäfer and Wolfgang Streeck, eds., *Politics in the Age of Austerity.* Cambridge: Polity, pp. 143–68.

Manning, Christopher D., Prabhakar Raghavan, and Hinrich Schütze. 2008. *Introduction to Information Retrieval,* Vol. 1. Cambridge: Cambridge University Press.

Marsh, Alan and Slava Mikhaylov. 2012. Economic Voting in a Crisis: The Irish Election of 2011. *Electoral Studies* 31, 3, 478–84.

Martín, Irene. 2015. Podemos and Other Party-Movement Models. *Revista Española de Sociologia* 24, 1, 107–14.

Marx, Paul and Christoph Nguyen. 2016. Are the Unemployed Less Politically Involved? A Comparative Study of Internal Political Efficacy. *European Sociological Review* 32, 5, 634–48.

Mason, Paul. 2012. *Why It's Kicking Off Everywhere: The New Global Revolutions.* London: Verso.

McAdam, Doug. 1982. *Political Process and the Development of Black Insurgency, 1930–1970.* Chicago, IL: University of Chicago Press.

McAdam, Doug. 1995. 'Initiator' and 'Spin-Off' Movements: Diffusion Processes in Protest Cycles. In Mark Traugott, ed., *Repertoires and Cycles of Collective Action*. Durham, NC: Duke University Press, pp. 217–39.

McAdam, Doug and Karina Kloos. 2014. *Deeply Divided: Racial Politics and Social Movements in Postwar America*. Oxford: Oxford University Press.

McAdam, Doug and Dieter Rucht. 1993. Citizens, Protest, and Democracy. *The Annals of the American Academy of Political and Social Science* 528, 1, 56–74.

McAdam, Doug and Sidney Tarrow. 2010. Ballots and Barricades: On the Reciprocal Relationship between Elections and Social Movements. *Perspectives on Politics* 8, 2, 529–42.

McAdam, Doug and Sidney Tarrow. 2013. Social Movements and Elections: Toward a Broader Understanding of the Political Context of Contention. In Jacquelien Van Stekelenburg, Conny Roggeband, and Bert Klandermans, eds., *The Future of Social Movement Research: Dynamics, Mechanisms, and Processes*. Minneapolis, MN: University of Minnesota Press, pp. 326–46.

McAdam, Doug, Sidney G. Tarrow, and Charles Tilly. 1996. To Map Contentious Politics. *Mobilization* 1, 1, 17–34.

McAdam, Doug, Sidney G. Tarrow, and Charles Tilly. 2001. *Dynamics of Contention*. Cambridge and New York: Cambridge University Press.

McCarthy, John D., Clark McPhail, and Jackie Smith. 1996. Images of Protest: Dimensions of Selection Bias in Media Coverage of Washington Demonstrations, 1982 and 1991. *American Sociological Review* 61, 3, 478–99.

McCarthy, John D., Larissa Titarenko, Clark McPhail, Patrick S. Rafail, and Boguslaw Augustyn. 2008. Assessing Stability in the Patterns of Selection Bias in Newspaper Coverage of Protest during the Transition from Communism in Belarus. *Mobilization* 13, 2, 127–46.

McCarthy, John D. and Mayer N. Zald. 1977. Resource Mobilization and Social Movements: A Partial Theory. *The American Journal of Sociology* 82, 6, 1212–41.

Meyer, David S. and Sidney Tarrow. 1998a. A Movement Society: Contentious Politics for the New Century. In David S. Meyer and Sidney Tarrow, eds., *The Social Movement Society*. Lanham, MD: Rowman & Littlefield, pp. 1–28.

Meyer, David S. and Sidney Tarrow (eds.). 1998b. *The Social Movement Society: Contentious Politics for a New Century*. Boulder, CO: Rowman & Littlefield.

Millo, Giovanni and Gianfranco Piras. 2012. Splm: Spatial Panel Data Models in R. *Journal of Statistical Software* 47, 1, 1–38.

Muñoz, Jordi, Eva Anduiza, and Guillem Rico. 2014. Empowering Cuts? Austerity Policies and Political Involvement in Spain. In: Staffan Kumlin and Isabelle Stadelmann-Steffen, eds., *How Welfare States Shape the Democratic Public: Policy Feedback, Participation, Voting and Attitudes*. Cheltenham: Edward Elgar Publishing, pp. 19–40.

Muro, Diego and Guillem Vidal. 2016. Political Mistrust in Southern Europe since the Great Recession. *Mediterranean Politics*. DOI: 10.1080/13629395.2016.1168962.

Myers, Daniel J. 2010. Violent Protests and Heterogeneous Diffusion Processes: The Spread of U.S. Racial Rioting from 1964 to 1971. *Mobilization* 15, 3, 289–321.

Nam, Taehyun. 2006. What You Use Matters: Coding Protest Data. *PS: Political Science & Politics* 39, 2, 281–87.

Nam, Taehyun. 2007. Rough Days in Democracies: Comparing Protests in Democracies. *European Journal of Political Research* 46, 1, 97–120.

Nardulli, Peter F., Scott L. Althaus, and Matthew Hayes. 2015. A Progressive Supervised-Learning Approach to Generating Rich Civil Strife Data. *Sociological Methodology* 45, 1, 148–83.

Navrátil, Jiri and Ondrej Cisar. 2014. Chapter Ten: Towards a 'Non-global Justice Movement'? Two Paths to Re-scaling the Left Contention in the Czech Republic. In Donatella della Porta and Alice Mattoni, eds., *Spreading Protest: Social Movements in Times of Crisis*. Colchester: ECPR Press, pp. 227–52.

Nickell, Stephen. 1981. Biases in Dynamic Models with Fixed Effects. *Econometrica* 49, 6, 1417–26.

Nulman, Eugene and Raphael Schlembach. 2018. Advances in Social Movement Theory since the Global Financial Crisis. *European Journal of Social Theory* 21, 3, 376–90.

OECD. 2013. *Coping with Emigration in Baltic and East European Countries*. www.oecd-ilibrary.org/social-issues-migration-health/coping-with-emigration-in-baltic-and-east-european-countries_9789264204928-en.

Oesch, Daniel. 2008. Explaining Workers' Support for Right-Wing Populist Parties in Western Europe: Evidence from Austria, Belgium, France, Norway and Switzerland. *International Political Science Review* 29, 3, 349–73.

Oesch, Daniel. 2013. The Class Basis of the Cleavage between the New Left and the Radical Right: An Analysis for Austria, Denmark, Norway and Switzerland. In Jens Rydgren, ed., *Class Politics and the Radical Right*. London: Routledge, pp. 31–51.

Oesch, Daniel and Oliver Lipps. 2013. Does Unemployment Hurt Less If There Is More of It Around? A Panel Analysis of Life Satisfaction in Germany and Switzerland. *European Sociological Review* 29, 5, 955–67.

Offe, Claus. 2013. Participatory Inequality in the Austerity State: A Supply-Side Approach. In Wolfgang Streeck and Armin Schäfer, eds., *Politics in the Age of Austerity*. Cambridge: Polity, pp. 196–218.

Oliver, Pamela E. 1989. Bringing the Crowd Back: In the Nonorganizational Elements of Social Movements. *Research in Social Movements, Conflicts and Change* 11, 1–30.

Oliver, Pamela E. and Gregory M. Maney. 2000. Political Processes and Local Newspaper Coverage of Protest Events: From Selection Bias to Triadic Interactions. *American Journal of Sociology* 106, 2, 463–505.

Oliver, Pamela E. and Daniel J. Myers. 2002. The Coevolution of Social Movements. *Mobilization* 8, 1, 1–24.

Olson, Mancur. 1965. *The Logic of Collective Action: Public Goods and the Theory of Groups*. Cambridge, MA: Harvard University Press.

Opp, Karl-Dieter. 1988. Grievances and Participation in Social Movements. *American Sociological Review* 53, 6, 853–64.

Ortiz, David, Daniel Myers, Eugene Walls, and Maria-Elena Diaz. 2005. Where Do We Stand with Newspaper Data? *Mobilization* 10, 3, 397–419.

Pallinger, Zoltán Tibor. 2012. Citizens' Initiative in Hungary: An Additional Opportunity for Power-Sharing in an Extremely Majoritarian System. In Theo Schiller and Maija Setälä, eds., *Citizens' Initiative in Europe: Procedures and Consequences of Agenda-Setting by the People*. Basingstoke: Palgrave Macmillan, pp. 113–30.

Pappas, Takis and Eoin O'Malley. 2014. Civil Compliance and 'Political Luddism': Explaining Variance in Social Unrest during the Crisis in Ireland and Greece. *American Behavioral Scientist* 58, 12, 1592–613.

Pedregosa, Fabian, Gaël Varoquaux, Alexandre Gramfort, et al. 2011. Scikit-Learn: Machine Learning in Python. *Journal of Machine Learning Research* 12, October, 2825–830.

Peterson, Abby, Mattias Walström, and Magnus Wennerhag. 2015. Beyond 'Old' and 'New' Social Movements. *Acta Sociologica* 58, 4, 293–310.

Petropoulos, P. Nicholas. 2014. A Sociopolitical Profile and the Political Impact of the Greek Indignados: An Exploratory Study. In P. Nicholas Petropoulos and O. George Tsobanoglou, eds., *The Debt Crisis in the Eurozone: Social Impacts*. Newcastle upon Tyne: Cambridge Scholars Publishing, pp. 342–94.

Philips, Andrew Q. 2018. Have Your Cake and Eat It Too? Cointegration and Dynamic Inference from Autoregressive Distributed Lag Model. *American Journal of Political Science* 62, 1, 230–44.

Pierson, Paul. 2001. Coping with Permanent Austerity: Welfare State Restructuring in Affluent Democracies. In Paul Pierson, ed., *The New Politics of the Welfare State*. Oxford: Oxford University Press, pp. 410–56.

Pierson, Paul and Miriam Smith. 1993. Bourgeois Revolutions? The Policy Consequences of Resurgent Conservatism. *Comparative Political Studies*, 25, 4, 487–520.

Piven, Frances Fox and Richard A. Cloward. 1977. *Poor People's Movements: Why They Succeed, How They Fail*. New York: Pantheon Books.

Plümper, Thomas and Eric Neumayer. 2010. Model Specification in the Analysis of Spatial Dependence. *European Journal of Political Research* 49, 3, 418–42.

Poguntke, Thomas, Susan E. Scarrow, Paul D. Webb, and Elin Haugsgjerd Allern. 2016. Party Rules, Party Resources and the Politics of Parliamentary Democracies: How Parties Organize in the 21st Century. *Party Politics*. DOI:10.1177/1354068816662493.

Polavieja, Javier. 2013. Economic Crisis, Political Legitimacy and Social Cohesion. In Duncan Gallie, ed., *Economic Crisis, Quality of Work and Social Integration: The European Experience*. Oxford: Oxford University Press, pp. 256–78.

Polk, Jonathan and Jan Rovny. 2018. Worlds of Welfare and Multidimensional Party. In Philip Manow, Bruno Palier, and Hanna Schwander, eds., *Welfare Democracies and Party Politics: Explaining Electoral Dynamics in Times of Changing Welfare Capitalism*. Oxford: Oxford University Press, pp. 29–60.

Polletta, Francesca. 2014. Participatory Democracy's Moment. *Journal of International Affairs* 68, 1, 79.

Pontusson, Jonas and Damian Raess. 2012. How (and Why) Is This Time Different? The Politics of Economic Crisis in Western Europe and the United States. *Annual Review of Political Science* 15, 13–33.

Pop-Eleches, Grigore. 2010. Throwing out the Bums: Protest Voting and Unorthodox Parties after Communism. *World Politics* 62, 2, 221–60.

Pop-Eleches, Grigore and Joshua Tucker. 2013. Associated with the Past? Communist Legacies and Civic Participation in Post-Communist Countries. *East European Politics and Societies* 27, 1, 45–68.

Portos-Garcia, Martin. 2016. *Voicing Outrage, Contending with Austerity: Mobilization in Spain under the Great Recession*. Unpublished PhD thesis, Florence: European University Institute.

Powell, Eleanor and Joshua A. Tucker. 2014. Revisiting Electoral Volatility in Post-Communist Countries: New Data, New Results and New Approaches. *British Journal of Political Science* 44, 1, 123–47.

Powell, G. Bigham and Guy D. Whitten. 1993. A Cross-national Analysis of Economic Voting: Taking Account of the Political Context. *American Journal of Political Science* 37, 2, 391–414.

Quaranta, Mario. 2016. Protesting in 'Hard Times': Evidence from a Comparative Analysis of Europe, 2000–2014. *Current Sociology* 64, 5, 736–56.

Quaranta, Mario and Sergio Martini. 2016. Does the Economy Really Matter for Satisfaction with Democracy? Longitudinal and Cross-country Evidence from the European Union. *Electoral Studies* 42, June, 164–74.

Reising, Uwe K. H. 1998. Domestic and Supranational Political Opportunities: European Protest in Selected Countries 1980–1995. *European Integration Online Papers (EIoP)* 2, 5.

Reising, Uwe K. H. 1999. United in Opposition? A Cross-National Time-Series Analysis of European Protest in Three Selected Countries, 1980–1995. *The Journal of Conflict Resolution* 43, 3, 317–42.

Roberts, Andrew. 2008a. Hyperaccountability: Economic Voting in Central and Eastern Europe. *Electoral Studies* 27, 3, 533–46.

Roberts, Kenneth M. 2008b. The Mobilization of Opposition to Economic Liberalization. *Annual Review of Political Science* 11, 1, 327–49.

Roberts, Kenneth M. 2014. *Changing Course in Latin America: Party Systems in the Neoliberal Era*. Cambridge: Cambridge University Press.

Roberts, Kenneth M. 2017. Party Politics in Hard Times: Comparative Perspectives on the European and Latin American Economic Crises. *European Journal of Political Research* 56, 218–33.

Rochon, Thomas R. 1990. The West European Peace Movement and the Theory of New Social Movements. In Russell J. Dalton and Manfred Kuechler, eds., *Challenging the Political Order*. Cambridge: Polity Press, pp. 105–21.

Rosenstone, Steven J. 1982. Economic Adversity and Voter Turnout. *American Journal of Political Science* 26, 1, 25–46.

Rovny, Jan. 2014. Communism, Federalism, and Ethnic Minorities: Explaining Party Competition Patterns in Eastern Europe. *World Politics* 66, 4, 669–708.

Rovny, Jan. 2015. Party Competition Structure in Eastern Europe: Aggregate Uniformity versus Idiosyncratic Diversity? *East European Politics and Societies* 29, 1, 40–60.

Royo, Sebastián. 2014. Institutional Degeneration and the Economic Crisis in Spain. *American Behavioural Scientist* 58, 2, 1568–91.

Rucht, Dieter. 1998. The Structure and Culture of Collective Protest in Germany since 1950. In David S. Meyer and Sidney Tarrow, eds., *The Social Movement Society: Contentious Politics for a New Century*. Lanham, MD: Rowman & Littlefield, pp. 29–57.

Rüdig, Wolfgang and Georgios Karyotis. 2014. Who Protests in Greece? Mass Opposition to Austerity. *British Journal of Political Science* 44, 3, 487–513.

Ruggeri, Andrea, Theodora-Ismene Gizelis, and Han Dorussen. 2011. Events Data as Bismarck's Sausages? Intercoder Reliability, Coders' Selection, and Data Quality. *International Interactions* 37, 3, 340–61.

Sabucedo, José-Manuel, Cristina Gomez-Roman, Monica Alzate, Jacquelien van Stekelenburg, and Bert Klandermans. 2017. Comparing Protests and Demonstrators in Times of Austerity: Regular and Occasional Protesters in Universalistic and Particularistic Mobilizations. *Social Movement Studies* 16, 6, 704–20.

Salek, Paulina and Agnieszka Sztajdel. 2017. 'Modern' versus 'Normal': The Increasing Importance of the Cultural Divide. In Swen Hutter and Hanspeter Kriesi, eds., *European Politics in Times of Crises*. New York: Cambridge University Press, pp. 189–213.

Samuels, David and Timothy Hellwig. 2010. Elections and Accountability for the Economy: A Conceptual and Empirical Reassessment. *Journal of Elections, Public Opinion & Parties* 20, 4, 393–419.

Sanchez-Cuenca, Ignacio. 2017. From a Deficit of Democracy to a Technocratic Order: The Postcrisis Debate on Europe. *Annual Review of Political Science* 20, 1, 351–69.

Schattschneider, Elmer E. 1960[1975]. *The Semi-Sovereign People: A Realist's View of Democracy in America*. New York: Holt, Rinehart and Winston.

Schlozman, Kay L. and Sidney Verba. 1979. *Injury to Insult: Unemployment, Class, and Political Response*. Cambridge, MA: Harvard University Press.

Schmitter, Philippe C. 2001. Parties Are Not What They Once Were. In Larry J. Diamond and Richard Gunther, eds., *Political Parties and Democracy*. Baltimore, MD: Johns Hopkins University Press, pp. 67–89.

Schrodt, Philip A. 2012. Precedents, Progress, and Prospects in Political Event Data. *International Interactions* 38, 4, 546–69.

Schrodt, Philip A. and Deborah J. Gerner. 1994. Validity Assessment of a Machine-Coded Event Data Set for the Middle East, 1982–92. *American Journal of Political Science* 38, 3, 825–54.

Scott, James C. 2012. *Two Cheers for Anarchism*. Princeton, NJ: Princeton University Press.

Sebastiani, Fabrizio. 2002. Machine Learning in Automated Text Categorization. *ACM Computing Surveys (CSUR)* 34, 1, 1–47.

Smith, Jackie, John D. McCarthy, Clark McPhail, and Boguslaw Augustyn. 2001. From Protest to Agenda Building: Description Bias in Media Coverage of Protest Events in Washington, D.C. *Social Forces* 79, 4, 1397–423.

Snow, David A., Daniel M. Cress, Liam Downey, and Andrew W. Jones. 1998. Disrupting the "Quotidian": Reconceptualizing the Relationship between Breakdown and the Emergence of Collective Action. *Mobilization* 3, 1, 1–22.

Solt, Frederick. 2008. Economic Inequality and Democratic Political Engagement. *American Journal of Political Science* 52, 1, 48–60.

Solt, Frederick. 2015a. Economic Inequality and Non-violent Protest. *Social Science Quarterly* 96, 5, 1314–327.

Solt, Frederick. 2015b. On the Assessment and Use of Cross-National Income Inequality Datasets. *Journal of Economic Inequality* 63, 683–91.

Soroka, Stuart N. and Christopher Wlezien. 2010. *Degrees of Democracy: Politics, Public Opinion, and Policy.* Cambridge: Cambridge University Press.

Soule, Sarah A. 2004. Diffusion Processes within and across Movements. In David A. Snow, Sarah A. Soule, and Hanspeter Kriesi, eds., *The Blackwell Companion to Social Movements.* Malden, MA: Blackwell's, pp. 294–309.

Spourdalakis, Michalis. 2014. The Miraculous Rise of the 'Phenomenon SYRIZA'. *International Critical Thought* 4, 3, 354–66.

Strawn, Kelley. 2008. Validity and Media-Derived Protest Event Data: Examining Relative Coverage Tendencies in Mexican News Media. *Mobilization* 13, 2, 147–64.

Streeck, Wolfgang and Armin Schäfer (eds.). 2013. *Politics in the Age of Austerity.* Cambridge: Polity.

Talving, Lisa. 2017. The Electoral Consequences of Austerity: Economic Policy Voting in Europe in Times of Crisis. *West European Politics* 40, 3, 560–83.

Talving, Lisa. 2018. Economic Voting in Europe: Did the Crisis Matter? *Comparative European Politics* 16, 4, 695–723.

Tarrow, Sidney. 1988. National Politics and Collective Action: Recent Theory and Research in Western Europe and the United States. *Annual Review of Sociology* 14, 1, 421–40.

Tarrow, Sidney. 1989. *Democracy and Disorder: Social Conflict, Political Protest and Democracy in Italy, 1965–1975.* New York: Oxford University Press.

Tarrow, Sidney. 1993. Cycles of Collective Action: Between Moments of Madness and the Repertoire of Contention. *Social Science History* 17, 2, 281–307.

Tarrow, Sidney. 1995. The Europeanisation of Conflict: Reflections from a Social Movement Perspective. *West European Politics* 18, 2, 223–51.

Tarrow, Sidney. 1998. *Power in Movement: Social Movements and Contentious Politics.* Cambridge: Cambridge University Press.

Tarrow, Sidney. 2005. *The New Transnational Activism.* Cambridge: Cambridge University Press.

Tarrow, Sidney. 2011 [1994]. *Power in Movement: Social Movements and Contentious Politics.* Cambridge: Cambridge University Press.

Tavits, Margit and Natalia Letki. 2009. When Left Is Right: Party Ideology and Policy in Post-communist Europe. *American Political Science Review* 103, 4, 555–69.

Taylor, Verta and Nella van Dyke. 2004. 'Get Up, Stand Up': Tactical Repertoires of Social Movements. In David A. Snow, Sarah A. Soule, and Hanspeter Kriesi, eds., *The Blackwell Companion to Social Movements.* Oxford: Blackwell, pp. 262–93.

Tejerina, Benjamin, Ignacia Perugorria, Tova Benski, and Lauren Langman. 2013. From Indignation to Occupation: A New Wave of Global Mobilization. *Current Sociology* 61, 4, 377–92.

Theobald, Martin, Jonathan Siddharth, and Andreas Paepcke. 2008. Spotsigs: Robust and Efficient Near Duplicate Detection in Large Web Collections. In *31st Annual International ACM SIGIR Conference on Research and Development in Information Retrieval.* Association for Computing Machinery.

Theocharis, Yannis, Will Lowe, Jan W. van Deth, and Gema Garcia-Albacete. 2015. Using Twitter to Mobilize Protest Action: Online Mobilization Patterns and Action Repertoires in the Occupy Wall Street, Indignados, and Aganaktismenoi Movements. *Information, Communication and Society* 18, 2, 202–20.

Theocharis, Yannis and Jan van Deth. 2016. The Continuous Expansion of Citizen Participation: A New Taxonomy. *European Political Science Review* 10, 2, 139–63.

Tilly, Charles. 1978. *From Mobilization to Revolution.* Reading, MA: Addison-Wesley.

Tilly, Charles. 2008. *Contentious Performances.* New York: Cambridge University Press.

Tooze, Adam. 2018. *Crashed: How a Decade of Financial Crises Changed the World.* London: Allen Lane.

Torcal, Mariano. 2014. The Decline of Political Trust in Spain and Portugal: Economic Performance or Political Responsiveness. *American Behavioral Scientist.* DOI: 10.1177/0002764214534662.

Traber, Denise, Nathalie Giger, and Silja Häusermann. 2017. How Economic Crises Affect Political Representation: Declining Party-Voter Congruence in Times of Constrained Government. *West European Politics* 41, 5, 1100–24.

Van Aelst, Peter and Stefaan Walgrave. 2001. Who Is That (Wo)man in the Street? From the Normalisation of Protest to the Normalisation of the Protester. *European Journal of Political Research* 39, 4, 461–86.

Van Biezen, Ingrid, Peter Mair, and Thomas Poguntke. 2012. Going, Going, ... Gone? The Decline of Party Membership in Contemporary Europe. *European Journal of Political Research* 51, 1, 24–56.

van Dyke, Nella and Sarah A. Soule. 2002. Structural Social Change and the Mobilizing Effect of Threat. Explaining Levels of Patriot and Militia Organizing the United States. *Social Problems* 49, 4, 497–520.

Van Laer, Jeroen. 2010. Activists Online and Offline: The Internet as an Information Channel for Protest Demonstrations. *Mobilization* 15, 3, 347–66.

Van Laer, Jeroen and Peter Van Aelst. 2010. Internet and Social Movement Action Repertoires. *Information, Communication & Society* 13, 8, 1146–71.

Vandaele, Kurt. 2016. Interpreting Strike Activity in Western Europe in the Past 20 Years: The Labour Repertoire under Pressure. *Transfer: European Review of Labour and Research* 22, 3, 277–94.

Varga, Mihai. 2015. Trade Unions and Austerity in Central and Eastern Europe. *Transfer: European Review of Labour and Research* 21, 3, 313–26.

Verney, Susannah. 2014. 'Broken and Can't be Fixed': The Impact of the Economic Crisis ion the Greek Party System. *The International Spectator* 49, 1, 18–35.

Vidal, Guillem. 2019. *The Political Consequences of the Great Recession in Southern Europe: Crisis and Representation in Spain*. PhD thesis, Florence: European University Institute.

Visser, Jelle. 2013. Database on Institutional Characteristics of Trade Unions, Wage Setting, State Intervention and Social Pacts in 34 Countries between 1960 and 2012. www.uva-aias.net/207.

Vliegenhart, Rens, Stefaan Walgrave, Ruud Wouters, et al. 2016. The Media as a Dual Mediator of the Political Agenda–Setting Effect of Protest. *Social Forces* 95, 2, 837–59.

Walsh, Edward J. 1981. Resource Mobilization and Citizen Protest in Communities around Three Mile Island. *Social Problems* 29, 1, 1–21.

Walter, Stefanie. 2016. Crisis Politics in Europe: Why Austerity Is Easier to Implement in Some Countries Than in Others. *Comparative Political Studies* 49, 7, 841–73.

Walton, John. 1987. Urban Protest and the Global Political Economy: The IMF Riots. In Michael Peter Smith and John R. Feagin, eds., *The Capitalist City*. Oxford: Basil Blackwell, pp. 354–86.

Walton, John and Charles Ragin. 1990. Global and National Sources of Political Protest: Third World Responses to the Debt Crisis. *American Sociological Review* 55, 6, 876–90.

Wasserfallen, Fabio. 2016. Policy Diffusion and European Public Policy Research. In Edoardo Ongaro and Sandra van Thiel, eds., *The Palgrave Handbook of Public Administration and Management in Europe*. Basingstoke: Palgrave Macmillan, pp. 621–33.

Weidmann, Nils B. 2016. A Closer Look at Reporting Bias in Conflict Event Data. *American Journal of Political Science* 60, 1, 206–18.

Wolfsfeld, Gadi. 1997. *Media and Political Conflict: News from the Middle East*. Cambridge: Cambridge University Press.

Wooldridge, Jeffrey M. 2002. *Econometric Analysis of Cross-Section and Panel Data*. Cambridge, MA: MIT Press.

Wu, Denis. 2000. Systemic Determinants of International News Coverage: A Comparison of 38 Countries. *Journal of Communication* 50, 2, 110–30.

Wueest, Bruno. 2017. *The Politics of Economic Liberalization*. Basingstoke: Palgrave Macmillan.

Zamponi, Lorenzo. 2012. 'Why Don't Italians Occupy?' Hypotheses on a Failed Mobilization. *Social Movement Studies* 11, 3–4, 416–26.

Zou, Hui and Trevor Hastie. 2005. Regularization and Variable Selection via the Elastic Net. *Journal of the Royal Statistical Society B: Statistical Methodology* 67, 2, 301–20.

Index

Note: Page numbers in italic and bold refer to figures and tables, respectively.